second edition

CORNERSTONES
FOR
PROFESSIONALISM

Robert M. Sherfield
Professor, College of Southern Nevada

Patricia G. Moody
Professor and Dean Emerita, University of South Carolina

Boston • Columbus • Indianapolis • New York • San Francisco • Upper Saddle River
Amsterdam • Cape Town • Dubai • London • Madrid • Milan • Munich • Paris • Montreal • Toronto
Delhi • Mexico City • São Paulo • Sydney • Hong Kong • Seoul • Singapore • Taipei • Tokyo

Editor-in-Chief: Jodi McPherson
Acquisition Editor: Katie Mahan
Managing Editor: Shannon Steed
Development Editor: Claire Hunter
Editorial Assistant: Clara Ciminelli
Executive Marketing Manager: Amy Judd
Production Editor: Janet Domingo
Editorial Production Service: Electronic Publishing Services Inc.
Manufacturing Buyer: Megan Cochran
Electronic Composition: Jouve
Interior Design: Electronic Publishing Services Inc.
Photo Researcher: Annie Fuller
Cover Designer: Diane Lorenzo

Library of Congress Cataloging-in-Publication Data

Sherfield, Robert M.
  Cornerstones for professionalism / Robert M. Sherfield, Patricia G. Moody.—2nd ed.
    p.   cm.
  ISBN-13: 978-0-13-278934-9 (pbk.)
  ISBN-10: 0-13-278934-5 (pbk.)
  1. Success—Psychological aspects. 2. Self-actualization (Psychology) I. Moody, Patricia G. II. Title.

BF637.S8S4688 2013
650.1—dc23

                                                                    2011044811

10 9 8 7 6 5 4 3 2 1

www.pearsonhighered.com

ISBN 10: 0-13-278934-5
ISBN 13: 978-0-13-278934-9

ROBERT M. SHERFIELD, PH.D.

Robert Sherfield has been teaching public speaking, theater, and student success, as well as working with first-year orientation programs for over 25 years. Currently, he is a professor at the College of Southern Nevada, teaching student success, professional communication, public speaking, and drama.

An award-winning educator, Sherfield was named Educator of the Year at the College of Southern Nevada. He twice received the Distinguished Teacher of the Year Award from the University of South Carolina at Union and has received numerous other awards and nominations for outstanding classroom instruction and advisement.

He has extensive experience with the design and implementation of student success programs, including one that was presented at the International Conference on the First-Year Experience in Newcastle upon Tyne, England. He has conducted faculty development keynotes and workshops at over 350 institutions of higher education across the United States. He has spoken in 46 states and several foreign countries.

In addition to his coauthorship of *Cornerstones for Professionalism* (Pearson, 2013), he has coauthored *Cornerstones for Community College Success* (Pearson, 2012), *Solving the Professional Development Puzzle: 101 Solutions for Career and Life Planning* (Prentice Hall, 2009), *Cornerstone: Creating Success Through Positive Change* (Pearson, 2011), *Roadways to Success* (Prentice Hall, 2001), the trade book *365 Things I Learned in College* (Allyn & Bacon, 1996), *Capstone: Succeeding Beyond College* (Prentice Hall, 2001), *Case Studies for the First Year: An Odyssey into Critical Thinking and Problem Solving* (Prentice Hall, 2004), *The Everything Self-Esteem Book* (Adams Media, 2004), and *Cornerstones for Career College Success* (Pearson, 2013).

Sherfield's interest in student success began with his own first year in college. Low SAT scores and a dismal high school ranking denied him entrance into college. With the help of a success program, Sherfield was granted entrance into college and went on to earn five college degrees, including a doctorate. He has always been interested in the social, academic, and cultural development of students and sees this book as his way to help students enter the world of work and establish lasting, rewarding careers. Visit www .robertsherfield.com.

PATRICIA G. MOODY, PH.D.

Patricia G. Moody is dean emerita of the College of Hospitality, Retail, and Sport Management at the University of South Carolina, where she has served on the faculty and in administration for over 30 years. An award-winning educator, Moody was honored as Distinguished Educator of the Year at her college and as Collegiate Teacher of the Year by the National Business Education Association. She was also a top-five finalist for the Amoco Teaching Award at the University of South Carolina. She received the prestigious John Robert Gregg Award, the highest honor in her field of over 100,000 educators.

Moody has coauthored many texts and simulations, including *Solving the Professional Development Puzzle: 101 Solutions for Career and Life Planning; Cornerstone: Creating Success Through Positive Change; Cornerstones for Career College Success; 365 Things I Learned in College; Capstone: Succeeding Beyond College; Case Studies for the First Year: An Odyssey into Critical Thinking and Problem Solving;* and *Cornerstones for Community College Success.*

A nationally known motivational speaker, consultant, and author, Moody has spoken in most states, has been invited to speak in several foreign countries, and frequently keynotes national and regional conventions. She has presented her signature motivational keynote address, "Fly Like an Eagle," to tens of thousands of people, from Olympic athletes to corporate executives to high school students.

As the dean of her college, Moody led international trips to build relationships and establish joint research projects in hospitality. Under her direction, faculty members in her college began a landmark study of Chinese tourists. She now travels the country delivering workshops, keynotes, and presentations on topics such as Managing Change, Working in the New Global Community, the Future of the Future, Student Motivation, and Emotional Intelligence. Moody also serves as a personal coach for business executives.

DEDICATION

FROM PAT:

To my husband, Wally, who has always supported me in all my endeavors. Because of his love and dedication, I have been able to achieve much more than I ever would have done without him. I admire and respect him for being a dedicated husband, father, and grandfather and for putting family above everything else.

FROM ROBB:

To my mother, who has always been there for me and believed in me more than I believed in myself. I am grateful to her for all her hard work and dedication to family that allowed me to grow and become who I am today.

The second edition of *Cornerstones for Professionalism* is written specifically for college students who are preparing to go into the workforce. It prepares students for finding their career path, maintaining success in their workplace, and continuing their upward mobility once on the job. Significantly expanded and updated to cover every aspect of success in today's workplace, this new edition focuses on a full gamut of preparation skills designed to assist students in getting the right job and maximizing their performance. It is filled with timely information, including ethics development, personal financial management, goal setting strategies, priority and stress management, navigation of the human resource maze, delivering excellent customer service techniques, working effectively with multigenerational colleagues, functioning on a global virtual team, using technology to work more productively, managing conflict and difficult people, finding the right career and driving productivity, and learning to navigate change while in a career. Unique features include Digital Briefcase and Professionals from the Field. New chapters such as "Prosper: Understanding Financial Intelligence" and "Communicate: Effective Communication for the Social Media Generation" are sure to benefit students.

NEW TO THIS EDITION

New   Although this is a second edition, the **new topics** make it a completely new book. This edition prepares students to get the job, learn skills to be successful in the workplace, and then excel once they are employed. Many topics not covered in other books include

- Global virtual teams
- The use of social media professionally and socially
- Advice from real professionals who are in the workplace
- Personal finance

See new coverage focusing on personal finance (Chapter 3), global teams (Chapter 11), and technology (Chapter 13). Be sure to see the Digital Briefcase exercise related to each chapter.

New   **NEW CHAPTERS** focus on the needs of new employees and are designed to help them plan and navigate their careers. The most prominent new coverage is found in the following chapters:

- Chapter 3, "Prosper: Understanding Financial Intelligence"
- Chapter 7, "Manage: Navigating the Human Resource Maze"
- Chapter 8, "Serve: Maximizing Customer Service and Productivity in the Workplace"
- Chapter 9, "Communicate: Effective Communication for the Social Media Generation"
- Chapter 10, "Relate: Relationships, Diversity, and Multigenerational Differences"

In addition, see Chapters 14 and 15 for revised and new coverage of resumé writing, cover letter development, interviewing, and electronic resumés.

New   A major new asset to this book, the **Digital Briefcase** is a unique feature for professionalism books. The Digital Briefcase incorporates a technology exercise at the end of each chapter designed to complement chapter coverage. Using social media such as Poll Everywhere and Facebook, the Digital Briefcase offers students many new experiences, such as developing themselves as a brand. This feature is designed to engage students in using the most cutting-edge technologies and social media. See examples at the end of each chapter.

New A **new chapter on technology** entitled "Connect" helps students understand the basics of computer software programs they will be expected to know when they go to work, understand today's social media and how to use them professionally and socially, and monitor their online behaviors using "netiquette." See this new coverage in Chapter 13.

New In the feature **Professionals from the Field,** the voice of experience is shared in the form of real professionals who are in the workplace. These professionals range from physical therapists to executive assistants to financial planners. Excellent advice related to each chapter's topic is provided so students have the benefit of learning from experienced professionals. Read these real stories at the beginning of each chapter.

New A **new chapter on navigating the human resources maze,** "Manage," teaches students the names and definitions of the major benefits available in companies today, discusses the dress code for different types of jobs, and shows them how to ace performance evaluations.

Revised **GRADUATE QUOTES** have been updated. Readers hear from recent graduates who are in the workplace and who offer valuable tips and advice. These real voices are found in every chapter.

Revised The feature **Biggest Interview Blunders** showcases classic mistakes that interviewers make that cause them not to be hired. These vignettes are designed to make students stop and think as they prepare for interviews. See this feature in every chapter.

Revised The feature **Positive Habits at Work** points out ways students can get ahead and get noticed at work for conducting themselves in an outstanding manner. See this feature in every chapter.

New Figure 12.8, **"Types of Difficult People,"** is a practical guide to help students as employees and managers to understand and manage difficult relationships.

PROFESSIONAL ACKNOWLEDGMENTS AND GRATITUDE

We would like to thank the following individuals at **The College of Southern Nevada** for their support:

Dr. Michael Richards, *President*
Dr. Darren Divine, *Vice President for Academic Affairs*
Dr. Hyla Winters, *Associate Vice President for Academic Affairs*
Dr. Wendy Weiner, *Dean–The School of Arts and Letters*
Dr. John Ziebell, *Department Chair–English*
Professor Levia Hayes, *Assistant Chair–English*
Professor Linda Gannon, *Lead Faculty, Academic and Life Strategies*

We would also like to thank individuals at **The University of South Carolina** and administration and faculty members in the Department of Hospitality, Retail, and Sport Management.

Our sincere and grateful appreciation to the following contributors to this publication for "Professionals from the Field" and "Graduate Quotes."

Professionals from the Field:

Dawn Daniel Thompson	Leo G. Borges
Sonya Lane	Bert Pooser
Kevin Fringer	Mike Collins
C. Steven Spearman	Cathy Lanier
F. Javier Ortiz B.	Mark Jones
Lee Templeton	Brian Epps
Tina Petrie	James Metts
Hade Robinson	

Graduates:

Nancy Kirkess	Eric Despinis
Catherine Schleigh	Sakeenah Pendergrass
Kerrie Dee	Zzavvalynn Orleanski
Mary Harris	Jennifer Rosa
Christian Garcia	Lawrence Cain
Jonathan T. Ellis	Derwin Wallace
William Paddock	Brayton Williams
Erica R. Harrison	Zack Karper

We offer our sincere thanks to the members of our **Cornerstones Advisory Council** who have provided valuable ideas and guidance throughout the development and revision of this new edition:

Emily Battaglia, *UEI Colleges*
Glenn F. Corillo, *Ph.D., ECPI University*

Patricia Davis, *Houston Community College/Southwest*
Steve Forshier, *M.Ed.,R.T.(R), Pima Medical Institute*
Michelle Kloss, *South University*
Zachary Lesak, *Miller-Motte Technical College, North Charleston, SC*
Ashley Hailston McMillion, *Daymar Colleges Group*
Adam Oldach, *Western Governors University*
Anthony Siciliano, *Western Governors University*
Zachary Stahmer, *Anthem Education Group*
LaToya L. Trowers, *MBA, CMAA, CPM, COM, Mildred Elley College–NYC Metro Campus*
Lori Ebert, *Brown Mackie College*

Reviewers for previous editions of *Cornerstones* whom we recognize with deep appreciation and gratitude:

Elvira Johnson, Central Piedmont Community College; Ryan Messatzzia, Wor-Wic Community College; Sarah K. Shutt, J. Sergeant Reynolds Community College; Kristina Leonard, Daytona Beach College; Kim Long, Valencia Community College; Taunya Paul, York Technical College; Charlie L. Dy, Northern Virginia Community College; Gary H. Wanamamker, Houston Community College; Jo Ann Jenkins, Moraine Valley Community College; Judith Lynch, Kansas State University; Timothy J. Quezada, El Paso Community College; Cathy Hall, Indiana University NW; Beverly J. Slaughter, Brevard Community College; Peg Adams, Northern Kentucky University; Sheryl Duquette, Erie Community College; Melanie Deffendall, Delgado Community College; Arthur Webb, Oklahoma State University; Stephanie Young, Butler Community College; Tara Wertz, MTI College; Diana Clennan, College of Southern Nevada; Jennifer Huss-Basquiat, College of Southern Nevada; Wayne A. Jones, Virginia State University; Barbara Auris, Montgomery County Community College, Betty Fortune, Houston Community College; Joel V. McGee, Texas A & M University; Jan Norton, University of Wisconsin–Osh Kosh; Todd Phillips, East Central College; Christian M. Blum, Bryan and Stratton College; James Briski, Katherine Gibbs School; Pela Selene Terry, Art Institute of NYC; Christina Donnelly, York Technical College; Connie Egelman, Nassau Community College; Amy Hickman, Collins College; Beth Humes, Pennsylvania Culinary Institute; Kim Joyce, Art Institute of Philadelphia; Lawrence Ludwig, Sanford-Brown College; Bethany Marcus, ECPI College of Technology; Kate Sawyer, Pittsburgh Technical Institute; Patricia Sell, National College of Business and Technology; Janis Stiewing,

PIMA Medical Institute; June Sullivan, Florida Metropolitan University; Fred Amador, Phoenix College; Kathy Bryan, Daytona Beach Community College; Dorothy Chase, Community College of Southern Nevada; JoAnn Credle, Northern Virginia Community College; Betty Fortune, Houston Community College; Doroteo Franco Jr., El Paso Community College; Cynthia Garrard, Massasoit Community College; Joel Jessen, Eastfield College; Peter Johnston, Massasoit Community College; Steve Konowalow, Community College of Southern Nevada; Janet Lindner, Midlands Technical College; Carmen McNeil, Solano College; Joan O'Connor, New York Institute of Technology; Mary Pepe, Valencia Community College; Bennie Perdue, Miami-Dade Community College; Ginny Peterson-Tennant, Miami-Dade Community College; Anna E. Ward, Miami-Dade Community College; Wistar M. Withers, Northern Virginia Community College; Marie Zander, New York Institute of Technology; Joanne Bassett, Shelby State Community College; Sandra M. Bovain-Lowe, Cumberland Community College; Carol Brooks, GMI Engineering and Management Institute; Elaine H. Byrd, Utah Valley State College; Janet Cutshall, Sussex County Community College; Deborah Daiek, Wayne State University; David DeFrain, Central Missouri State University; Leslie L. Duckworth, Florida Community College at Jacksonville; Marnell Hayes, Lake City Community College; Elzora Holland, University of Michigan, Ann Arbor; Earlyn G. Jordan, Fayetteville State University; John Lowry-King, Eastern New Mexico University; Charlene Latimer; Michael Laven, University of Southwestern Louisiana; Judith Lynch, Kansas State University; Susan Magun-Jackson, The University of Memphis; Charles William Martin, California State University, San Bernardino; Jeffrey A. Miller; Ronald W. Johnsrud, Lake City Community College; Joseph R. Krzyzanowski, Albuquerque TVI; Ellen Oppenberg, Glendale Community College; Lee Pelton, Charles S. Mott Community College; Robert Rozzelle, Wichita State University; Penny Schempp, Western Iowa Community College; Betty Smith, University of Nebraska at Kearney; James Stepp, University of Maine at Presque Isle; Charles Washington, Indiana University–Purdue University; Katherine A. Wenen-Nesbit, Chippewa Valley Technical College; Kristina Leonard, Daytona Beach College; Kim Long, Valencia Community College; Taunya Paul, York Technical College; Charlie L. Dy, Northern Virginia Community College; Gary H. Wanamamker, Ph. D., Houston Community College; Jo Ann Jenkins, Moraine Valley Community College; Judith Lynch, Kansas State University; Timothy J. Quezada, El Paso Community College; Cathy Hall, Indiana University NW; Beverly J. Slaughter, Brevard Community College; Peg Adams, Northern Kentucky University; Sheryl Duquette, Erie Community College; Melanie Deffendall, Delgado Community College; Arthur Webb, Oklahoma State University; Stephanie Young, Butler Community College; Tara Wertz, MTI College; Diana Clennan, College of Southern Nevada; Jennifer Huss-Basquiat, College of Southern Nevada; and Wayne A. Jones, Virginia State University.

Without the support and encouragement of **our creative and supportive team at Pearson,** this book would not be possible. Our sincere thanks to Jodi McPherson, Margaret Waples, Amy Judd, Shannon Steed, Janet Domingo, Clara Ciminelli, Claire Hunter, Antionette Payne, Walt Kirby, Debbie Ogilvie, Alan Hensley, Pam Jeffries, Barbara Donlon, Cathy Bennett, Matt Mesaros, Wendy DiLeonardo, Deborah Wilson, Eric Weiss, Julie Morel, Julie Hilderbrand, and Richard Rowe.

Your constant belief in us has been a most cherished gift. We are lucky to know you and are better people because of you. Thank you!

Supplemental Resources

INSTRUCTOR SUPPORT –
Resources to simplify your life and support your students.

Book Specific

Online Instructor's Manual – This manual is intended to give professors a framework or blueprint of ideas and suggestions that may assist them in providing their students with activities, journal writing, thought-provoking situations, and group activities. This supplement is available for download from the Instructor's Resource Center at www.pearsonhighered.com/irc

Online PowerPoint Presentation – A comprehensive set of PowerPoint slides that can be used by instructors for class presentations or by students for lecture preview or review. These slides highlight the important points of each chapter to help students understand the concepts within each chapter. Instructors may download these PowerPoint presentations from the Instructor's Resource Center at www.pearsonhighered.com/irc

MyStudentSuccessLab – Are you teaching online, in a hybrid setting, or looking to infuse technology into your classroom for the first time? MyStudentSuccessLab is an online solution designed to help students build the skills they need to succeed for ongoing personal and professional development. Visit www.mystudentsuccesslab.com for more information and to access activities, videos, and test items for your course.

Other Resources

"Easy access to online, book-specific teaching support is now just a click away!"
Instructor Resource Center – Register. Redeem. Login. Three easy steps that open the door to a variety of print and media resources in downloadable, digital format, available to instructors exclusively through the Pearson 'IRC'. www.pearsonhighered.com/irc

"Provide information highlights on the most critical topics for student success!"
Success Tips is a 6-panel laminate with topics that include MyStudentSuccessLab, Time Management, Resources All Around You, Now You're Thinking, Maintaining Your Financial Sanity, and Building Your Professional Image. Other choices are available upon request. This essential supplement can be packaged with any student success text to add value with 'just in time' information for students.

Supplemental Resources

Other Resources

"Infuse student success into any program with our 'IDentity' Series booklets!" - Written by national subject matter experts, the material contains strategies and activities for immediate application. Choices include:

- Financial Literacy (Farnoosh Torabi)
- Financial Responsibility (Clearpoint Financial)
- Now You're Thinking about College Success (Judy Chartrand et.al.)
- Now You're Thinking about Career Success (Judy Chartrand et.al.)
- Ownership (Megan Stone)
- Identity (Stedman Graham).

"Through partnership opportunities, we offer a variety of assessment options!"
LASSI – The LASSI is a 10-scale, 80-item assessment of students' awareness about and use of learning and study strategies. Addressing skill, will and self-regulation, the focus is on both covert and overt thoughts, behaviors, attitudes and beliefs that relate to successful learning and that can be altered through educational interventions. Available in two formats: Paper ISBN: 0131723154 or Online ISBN: 0131723162 (access card).

Robbins Self Assessment Library – This compilation teaches students to create a portfolio of skills. S.A.L. is a self-contained, interactive, library of 49 behavioral questionnaires that help students discover new ideas about themselves, their attitudes, and their personal strengths and weaknesses. Available in Paper, CD-Rom, and Online (Access Card) formats.

"For a truly tailored solution that fosters campus connections and increases retention, talk with us about custom publishing."
Pearson Custom Publishing – We are the largest custom provider for print and media shaped to your course's needs. Please visit us at www.pearsoncustom.com to learn more.

STUDENT SUPPORT –
Tools to help make the grade now, and excel in school later.

"Now there's a Smart way for students to save money."
CourseSmart is an exciting new choice for students looking to save money. As an alternative to purchasing the printed textbook, students can purchase an electronic version of the same content. With a CourseSmart eTextbook, students can search the text, make notes online, print out reading assignments that incorporate lecture notes, and bookmark important passages for later review. For more information, or to purchase access to the CourseSmart eTextbook, visit www.coursesmart.com

"Today's students are more inclined than ever to use technology to enhance their learning."
MyStudentSuccessLab will engage students through relevant YouTube videos with 'how to' videos selected 'by students, for students' and help build the skills they need to succeed for ongoing personal and professional development. www.mystudentsuccesslab.com

"Time management is the #1 challenge students face."
Premier Annual Planner - This specially designed, annual 4-color collegiate planner includes an academic planning/ resources section, monthly planning section (2 pages/month), weekly planning section (48 weeks; July start date), which facilitate short-term as well as long term planning. Spiral bound, 6x9.

"Journaling activities promote self-discovery and self-awareness."
Student Reflection Journal - Through this vehicle, students are encouraged to track their progress and share their insights, thoughts, and concerns. 8 1/2 x 11. 90 pages.

MyStudentSuccessLab

Start Strong. Finish Stronger.
www.MyStudentSuccessLab.com

MyStudentSuccessLab is an online solution designed to help students acquire the skills they need to succeed for ongoing personal and professional development. They will have access to peer-led video interviews and develop core skills through interactive practice exercises and activities that provide academic, life, and professionalism skills that will transfer to ANY course.

It can accompany any Student Success text or used as a stand-alone course offering.

How will MyStudentSuccessLab make a difference?

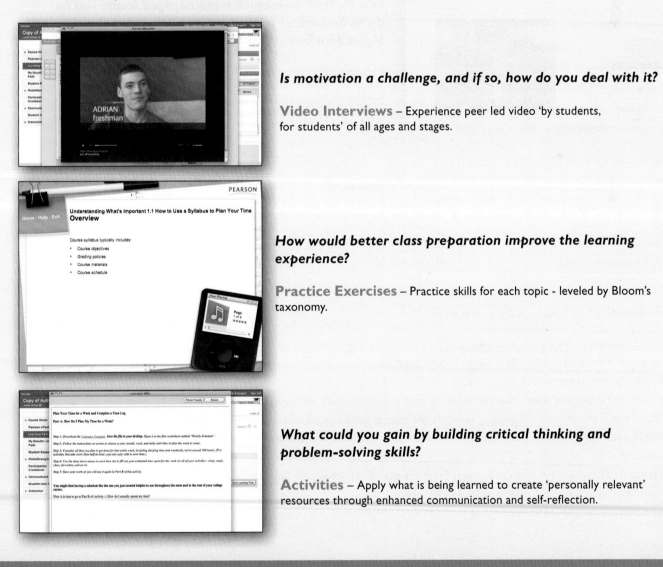

Is motivation a challenge, and if so, how do you deal with it?

Video Interviews – Experience peer led video 'by students, for students' of all ages and stages.

How would better class preparation improve the learning experience?

Practice Exercises – Practice skills for each topic - leveled by Bloom's taxonomy.

What could you gain by building critical thinking and problem-solving skills?

Activities – Apply what is being learned to create 'personally relevant' resources through enhanced communication and self-reflection.

PEARSON

MyStudentSuccessLab

Start Strong. Finish Stronger.
www.MyStudentSuccessLab.com

As an instructor, how much easier would it be to assign and assess on MyStudentSuccessLab if you had a Learning Path Diagnostic that reported to the grade book?

Learning Path Diagnostic

- For the **course**, 65 Pre-Course questions (Levels I & II Bloom's) and 65 Post-Course questions (Levels III & IV Bloom's) that link to key learning objectives in each topic.

- For each **topic**, 20 Pre-Test questions (Levels I & II Bloom's) and 20 Post-Test questions (Levels III & IV Bloom's) that link to all learning objectives in the topic.

As a student, how much more engaged would you be if you had access to relevant YouTube videos within MyStudentSuccessLab?

Student Resources

A wealth of resources like our FinishStrong247 YouTube channel with 'just in time' videos selected 'by students, for students'.

MyStudentSuccessLab Topic List -

1. A First Step: Goal Setting
2. Communication
3. Critical Thinking
4. Financial Literacy
5. Information Literacy

6. Learning Preferences
7. Listening and Taking Notes in Class
8. Majors and Careers
9. Memory and Studying
10. Problem Solving

11. Professionalism
12. Reading and Annotating
13. Stress Management
14. Test Taking Skills
15. Time Management

MyStudentSuccessLab Feature set:

Learning Path Diagnostic: 65 Pre-Course (Levels I & II Bloom's) and 65 Post-Course (Levels III & IV Bloom's) / Pre-Test (Levels I & II Bloom's) and Post-Test (Levels III & IV Bloom's).

Topic Overview: Module objectives.

Video Interviews: Real video interviews 'by students, for students' on key issues.

Practice Exercises: Skill-building exercises per topic provide interactive experience and practice.

Activities: Apply what is being learned to create 'personally relevant' resources through enhanced communication and self-reflection.

Student Resources: Pearson Students Facebook page, FinishStrong247 YouTube channel, MySearchLab, Online Dictionary, Plagiarism Guide, Student Planner, and Student Reflection Journal.

Implementation Guide: Grading rubric to support instruction with Overview, Time on Task, Suggested grading, etc.

ALWAYS LEARNING

PEARSON

Pearson Success Tips, 1/e

ISBN-10: 0132788071 • ISBN-13: 9780132788076

Success Tips is a **6-panel laminate** that provides students with information highlights on the most critical topics for student success. These topics include MyStudentSuccessLab, Time Management, Resources All Around You, Now You're Thinking, Maintaining Your Financial Sanity, and Building Your Professional Image. Other choices are available upon request via our www.pearsoncustomlibrary.com program, as well as traditional custom publishing. This essential supplement can packaged with any student success text to add value with 'just in time' information for students.

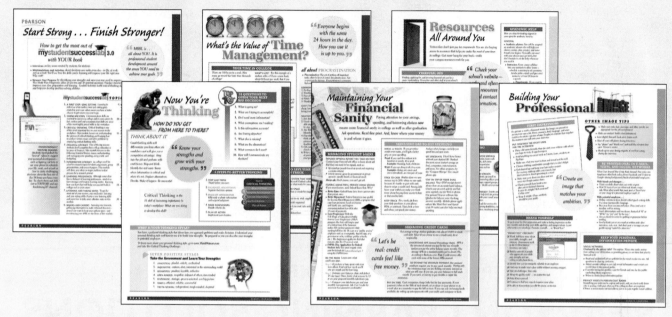

Features

- **MyStudentSuccessLab** — Helps students 'Start strong, Finish stronger' by getting the most out of this technology with their book.

- **Time Management** — Everyone begins with the same 24 hours in the day, but how well students use their time varies.

- **Resources All Around You** — Builds awareness for the types of resources available on campus for students to take advantage of.

- **Now You're Thinking** — Learning to think critically is imperative to student success.

- **Maintaining Your Financial Sanity** — Paying attention to savings, spending, and borrowing choices is more important than ever.

- **Building Your Professional Image** — Students are motivated by preparing for their future careers through online and in person professionalism tips, self-branding, and image tips.

- **Additional Topics** — Topics above are 'default.' These topics include MyStudentSuccessLab, Time Management, Resources All Around You, Now You're Thinking, Maintaining Your Financial Sanity, and Building Your Professional Image. Other choices are available upon request via our www.pearsoncustomlibrary.com program, as well as traditional custom publishing. This essential supplement can be packaged with any student success text to add value with 'just in time' information for students.

Topic List

- MyStudentSuccessLab*
- Time Management*
- Resources All Around You*
- Now You're Thinking*
- Maintaining Your Financial Sanity*
- Building Your Professional Image*
- Get Ready for Workplace Success
- Civility Paves the Way Toward Success

- Succeeding in Your Diverse World
- Information Literacy is Essential to Success
- Protect Your Personal Data
- Create Your Personal Brand
- Service Learning
- Stay Well and Manage Stress
- Get Things Done with Virtual Teams
- Welcome to Blackboard!

- Welcome to Moodle!
- Welcome to eCollege!
- Set and Achieve Your Goals
- Prepare for Test Success
- Good Notes Are Your Best Study Tool
- Veterans/Military Returning Students

NOTE: those with asterisks are 'default' options; topic selection can be made through Pearson Custom Library at www.pearsoncustomlibrary.com, as well as traditional custom publishing.

Introducing CourseSmart, the world's largest online marketplace for digital texts and course materials.

A Smarter Way for Instructors

▶ **CourseSmart saves time.** Instructors can review and compare textbooks and course materials from multiple publishers at one easy-to-navigate, secure website.

▶ **CourseSmart is environmentally sound.** When instructors use CourseSmart, they help reduce the time, cost, and environmental impact of mailing print exam copies.

▶ **CourseSmart reduces student costs.** Instructors can offer students a lower-cost alternative to traditional print textbooks.

▶ **"Add this overview to your syllabus today!"**
REQUIRED COURSE MATERIALS - ALTERNATE VERSION AVAILABLE:

CourseSmart is an exciting new choice for students looking to save money. As an alternative to purchasing the printed textbook, students can purchase an electronic version of the same content. With a CourseSmart eTextbook, students can search the text, make notes online, print out reading assignments that incorporate lecture notes, and bookmark important passages for later review.

A Smarter Way for Students

▶ **CourseSmart is convenient.** Students have instant access to exactly the materials their instructor assigns.

▶ **CourseSmart offers choice.** With CourseSmart, students have a high-quality alternative to the print textbook.

▶ **CourseSmart saves money.** CourseSmart digital solutions can be purchased for up to 50% less than traditional print textbooks.

▶ **CourseSmart offers education value.** Students receive the same content offered in the print textbook enhanced by the search, note-taking, and printing tools of a web application.

CourseSmart is the Smarter Way
To learn for yourself, visit www.coursesmart.com

BRIEF CONTENTS

CONTENTS

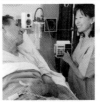

chapter four
GROW
BUILDING A LIFE PLAN THROUGH
GOAL SETTING 71

PART TWO: MANAGING YOUR LIFE

chapter five
PRIORITIZE
STRATEGIES FOR MANAGING
PRIORITIES AND STRESS 89

chapter six
SOCIALIZE
AVOID WORKPLACE LAND MINES
AND PERFECT YOUR PERSONAL
IMAGE 117

chapter seven
MANAGE
NAVIGATING THE HUMAN
RESOURCE MAZE 137

chapter eight

SERVE

MAXIMIZING CUSTOMER SERVICE
AND PRODUCTIVITY IN THE
WORKPLACE 153

PART THREE: MANAGING RELATIONSHIPS

chapter nine

COMMUNICATE

EFFECTIVE COMMUNICATION
FOR THE SOCIAL MEDIA
GENERATION 165

chapter ten

RELATE

RELATIONSHIPS, DIVERSITY,
AND MULTIGENERATIONAL
DISTINCTIONS 189

chapter eleven

LEAD

TEAMWORK—HOW TO LEAD
AND HOW TO FOLLOW 209

chapter sixteen
CHANGE

BEGIN

THE GOAL OF *CORNERSTONES FOR PROFESSIONALISM* AND OUR COMMITMENT TO YOU

Talent alone won't make you a success. Neither will being in the right place at the right time, unless you are ready. The most important question is: "Are you ready?"—Johnny Carson

THE WORKPLACE OF 2020 AND THE FORCES THAT ARE SHAPING IT

You are entering the workforce at a challenging time, a time when many changes are taking place globally and domestically. We live in a world that is connected by technologies that become more amazing every day and are changing even as we speak. Our country's economy is intertwined with others all over the world, making decisions more complicated. "And these changes will only continue to accelerate as we move toward 2020 because the Millennial Generation, which refers to the 88 million people born between the years 1977 to 1997, will make up nearly half of the workforce by 2014" (Meister and Willyerd, 2010). Your workplace will be very different from that of your grandparents and parents, and your responsibilities for shaping your own destiny will be significant. Some of the differences include the following:

- The workplace is now made up of several generations, each of which brings its own set of beliefs, values, and work styles.
- Employees today are often working in virtual teams with colleagues located all over the world.
- Requirements for use of technology far surpass those of the past.
- A great deal of U.S. manufacturing has been outsourced and shipped overseas, leaving the great middle class floundering and searching for new jobs.
- The new jobs are likely to come in the form of new sources of energy, green jobs, health care, and technological innovations.
- Social media have become a force in how we form our personal communities but also in how companies identify new employees, engage their customers, and market their services and products.
- Employees entering the workforce today may change jobs as many as seven times in their lifetimes.
- You are in the driver's seat and therefore must take a greater role in shaping your destiny.

The employees who come out on top in this new world order will be those who develop sought-after skills, those who can create and promote their own personal brands, and those who have goals and know where they are going. Our hope is that this book will serve as a guide for you as you begin your career.

HOW TO PREPARE TO BE SUCCESSFUL TODAY AND TOMORROW

Navigating the world of work today is more difficult than it once was. Perhaps your grandfather went to work at one company and stayed there all his life. He was loyal to the company, and the company was loyal to him. He retired with a pension for his commitment to the company. Those days are gone—and it's more than a little frightening. Many people, however, will navigate these turbulent waters well and be just as successful—or even more so—than those who came before. This book is filled with tips and advice on how to work successfully in today's changing workplace. Some of the major tips follow:

- Build an ethical and dependable reputation by giving a good day's work for a good day's pay.

- Be a person of your word. If you say you are going to do something, do it.

- Come early to work and stay late if necessary. While you are at work, work hard. More importantly, work smart! Stay focused on your job, but keep an eye on the future. What opportunities are available for you? What do you need to do to be prepared for these opportunities?

- Think about the big picture—what are your company's values, what are the strategic goals of your company, how is the company organized, and how is your company faring with the competition in its class?

- Plan your long-term and short-term goals carefully, and work toward them every day. Design a personal mission statement with goals and objectives.

- Learn all the new technology you can. Be sure you learn how to use social media in ways that complement your work—not just for socializing.

- Keep learning! Much of the knowledge you leave college with will be obsolete very quickly. Take advantage of opportunities to go back to school for advanced degrees, attend in-house seminars and training, and read, read, read—everything related to your job and to the future of work.

- Be open to working collaboratively, whether it be on a local team or a virtual team located all around the country or the world. Those who can adapt to new working strategies are the ones who will thrive.

- Be willing to work with all kinds of people—all ages, ethnic backgrounds, religious beliefs, geographic differences, sexual orientations. Learn to judge people as individuals, not as a group or a class or a race. Most people want what you want. They want to be treated fairly; they want to be respected; they want to be somebody; and they want to be successful.

- Hone your listening skills and stay alert to what is happening around you. Most people don't listen very well, so this will give you an advantage. Listen to what is being said—and what is not being said. Pay attention to body language and politics. What is coming down the grapevine?

- Learn a new language and look for ways to work internationally. The global workplace will offer many opportunities to those who are prepared.

- Get involved in community activities that are sanctioned by your company. There has never been a time when companies are feeling as much pressure to be socially oriented.

- Be prepared to change. Plan your personal changes carefully. Adjust to and assist your managers in making change happen.

- Plan your own retirement package. No one is looking after you but you, so this is one of the most important things you can do for yourself. Start planning for your personal future and that of your family immediately.

Shutterstock

chapter one

DISCOVER

DISCOVERING WHO YOU ARE

PART ONE: MANAGING YOU

Believe you can and you are halfway there.
—Theodore Roosevelt

Why
read this chapter?

Because you'll learn...

- The traits and characteristics that make you special
- The importance of establishing an excellent value system
- The power of optimism and positive self-esteem

Because you'll be able to...

- Complete a Personality Assessment Profile and identify your personality type
- Develop your own brand and know what qualities you need to market yourself to future employers

PROFESSIONALS
from the
Field

Name:	Dawn Daniel Thompson
Business:	Executive Assistant to the President, CEO, and Chairman of the Board, Haverty's

When you go to work in a new job, you are still trying to find out who you really are as a person, who you want to become, and what is expected of you. My advice to a person entering the workforce today is to learn everything you can about the company as quickly as you can. Learn all the technology you can; learn to read and interpret financial statements and balance sheets; pay attention to company reports. Work hard to become a good communicator and a team player. Work smart and use time-saving devices and strategies to produce more effectively. One of the most important things I can share with you is to be available and willing to work after hours if necessary to get the job done.

MyStudentSuccessLab

MyStudentSuccessLab (www.mystudentsuccesslab.com) is an online solution designed to help you "Start strong, Finish stronger" by building skills for ongoing personal and professional development.

PROFESSIONALISM DEFINED

How Do I Become a Professional?

Professionalism is defined by a number of characteristics and traits: your character, which is who you are; your knowledge which is what you know and what experiences you can draw on; and your image which is how you project yourself and how others perceive you. A true professional cares deeply about what the job is and how well it is done, and, at the same time, cares about the company for which he or she works and the colleagues with whom they work. Professionals are willing to go above and beyond to be sure that customers and colleagues are taken care of in an exemplary manner.

SETTING YOURSELF APART AND FINDING YOUR DIRECTION

How Do You Separate Yourself from the Pack?

How do you distinguish yourself from the countless job seekers out there? What are you going to do that sets you apart from your competition? What do you have to offer that no one else can possibly offer to an employer? What unique skills do you have to help you thrive and survive in a rapidly changing world where outsourcing is commonplace and technology is constantly evolving? Answering these questions is the primary focus of this chapter, and indeed, this book and the course in which you are presently enrolled.

> You laugh at me because I am different. I laugh at you because you are all the same.
>
> —Unknown

In his book *The 2010 Meltdown,* Edward Gordon (2008) writes, "Simply stated, today in America, there are just too many people trained for the wrong jobs. Many jobs have become unnecessary, technically obsolete . . . or worse yet, the job/career aspirations of too many current and future workers are at serious odds with the changing needs of the U.S. labor market." An example of this disconnect between the workforce and the market place can be found in this fact: **Eight million U.S. workers speak English so poorly that they cannot hold high-paying jobs** (Center for Law and Social Policy). Conversely, people who are highly skilled, possess superb oral and written communication skills, know how to solve problems, have excellent technology skills, and can work well with others should be in great demand for many years to come.

Careers in the following areas are projected for high growth in the coming decade: **health sciences** (dental assistants, home health aids, physician assistants, medical assistants, occupational therapy, physical therapist, cardiovascular technologists, etc.), **aviation** (airplane mechanics and air traffic controllers), **skilled trades** (plumbers, electricians, mechanics, etc.); **teaching** (K–12 and college); **technology** (aerospace and GPS engineers, water and sanitation engineers, transportation services, systems analyst, programmers, interactive media designers, software engineers, desktop publishing, database administrators, etc.), and **management, marketing, and public relations** (business managers, human resource directors, advertising and public relations, accounting, etc.).

This chapter will help you discover your unique qualities and characteristics that can give you the competitive edge in today's workplace. Several solutions to help you kick-start your career and your personal development will be introduced here.

KNOW WHO YOU ARE AND WHERE YOU ARE GOING

Who Are You and What Do You Want to Do with Your One Lifetime?

When asked, "Who are you?" so many people answer with "I'm a student" or "I'm a mom" or "I'm a teacher." Often, we answer this question with *what* we are and not *who* we are. There is a huge difference between the two. What you are is your work, your position, and your family standing. Who you are is much deeper. Who you are involves your work and relationships, but it is also the basis for your core—your foundation. Who you are involves much more than your title as a brother, a mother, a nurse, a mechanic, or a friend. Who you are involves your morality, your intellect, your spirituality, your emotions, your beliefs, your values, your culture, your choices, and your dreams.

By understanding the difference between *what* you are and *who* you are, you can truly begin to understand yourself on a higher level. Few people are willing to take this journey. Fear, time pressures, or lack of motivation may cause people to avoid finding the answer, but finding out who you are can be one of the most rewarding opportunities in your life—and it can give you the competitive edge that you need to survive and thrive in today's world of work.

> The Constitution only gives people the right to pursue happiness. You have to catch it yourself.
> —Benjamin Franklin

In their book *The Dragonfly Effect*, Aaker and Smith (2010) state that "human beings have three basic needs in terms of their self-worth: competence (feeling that we are effective and able), autonomy (feeling that we are able to dictate our own behavior), and relatedness (feeling that we are connected to others)." As you go through this journey of discovering who you are and what you want to become, remember those thoughts.

Consider the "me puzzle" in Figure 1.1 As you can see, it involves nine different pieces. Understanding how each piece affects your actions, goals, relationships, work ethic, and motivation can mean the difference between success and failure in work . . . and in life. As you study the puzzle, consider your strengths and challenges in each area. How does each piece drive your choices and how does each piece help you understand more about who you are? Are there pieces of the puzzle that you have never considered? If so, how has this affected your life in the past? Has something been missing in your life because you did not address a certain piece of the overall puzzle? At this time and place in your life, which piece is the most or least important? Which pieces can you use to gain a competitive edge and which parts of your life need improvement?

As you look at each piece of the "me puzzle," think about **one strength** for each puzzle piece that you have to offer in the workplace and how it will help you in the future. Then, think about **one challenge** you will have to overcome for each piece of the "me puzzle" and how you plan to do so.

Example:

Moral Me

Strength: I am very grounded in my work ethic. I consider myself to be a loyal and dedicated employee and will do my best every day.

The Future: This strength will help me gain the trust of my superiors and peers. They will know that I am a person to whom they can turn in times of stress. They will know that I can make ethical and honest decisions.

Figure 1.1   Solving the "Me Puzzle"

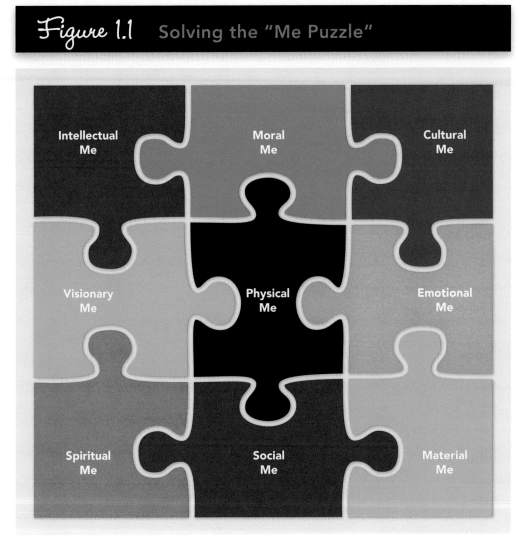

Source: Based on the work of psychologist William James (1842–1910).

Challenge: I sometimes judge others too harshly when they do not have the same work ethic that I possess. This can become a problem when I move up the ladder and begin supervising people.

Overcome: I plan to begin listening more and to try to understand others' backgrounds and problems before making judgments.

Intellectual Me

Strength: _____

_____

The Future: _____

_____

Challenge: _____

_____

Overcome: _____

_____

Moral Me

Strength: _____

_____

The Future: _____

_____

Challenge: _____

_____

Overcome: _____

_____

Cultural Me

Strength: _____

_____

The Future: _____

_____

Challenge: _____

_____

Overcome: _____

_____

Visionary Me

Strength: _____

_____

The Future: _____

_____

Challenge: _____

_____

Overcome: _____

_____

Physical Me

Strength: _____

_____

The Future: _____

_____

Challenge: _____

_____

Overcome: _____

_____

Emotional Me

Strength: _____

_____

The Future: _____

_____

Challenge: _____

_____

Overcome: _____

_____

Spiritual Me

Strength: _____

_____

The Future: _____

_____

Challenge: _____

_____

Overcome: _____

_____

Social Me

Strength: _____

_____

The Future: _____

_____

Challenge: _____

_____

Overcome: _____

_____

Material Me

Strength: _____

_____

The Future: _____

_____

Challenge: _____

_____

Overcome: _____

_____

Spiritual Me	**Social Me**	**Material Me**
What I believe	My relationships	What I have
My religion	My activities	What I want
Wisdom gained	My associations	What I need to survive
Meditation	My social involvement	Economic background
Altruistic notions		
My "grounding"		
Intellectual Me	**Moral Me**	**Cultural Me**
What I know	Character	How I interact with others
Common sense	Ethics/Values	Knowledge of my own culture, norms, heritage, environment, race, etc.
Skills I possess	Choices and decisions	
Critical thinking	Reactions	
Reasoning	Principles	
Problem solving		
Visionary Me	**Physical Me**	**Emotional Me**
Where I am going	My health	What I feel
My goals and dreams for the future	My appearance and grooming	How am I guided by emotions
What skills I need to be successful	My body	My heart vs. my head
	My habits	How I manage conflicts and challenges

CAPITALIZING ON YOUR STRENGTHS

What Do You Have Going for You?

Study the following statements carefully:

"I am super organized."

"I am extremely good at my profession."

"I know I can solve that problem."

"I can't find a thing on this desk."

"I feel so stupid at work."

"I don't even know where to begin."

Do you capitalize on all your strengths at work?

Shutterstock

Notice the difference between these perspectives? One person seems optimistic and appears to know his or her abilities and strengths, and the other is unsure, timid, and pessimistic. Who would you hire? Who would you like working on your team? Knowing what you're good at and owning those strengths can be an enormously positive attribute and can give you another competitive asset to highlight on your resumé. Basically, the question that must be answered is, "What do I have going for me?" If you don't know your strengths, it will be impossible to convey them to an employer. It is also impossible to use the strengths that you don't even know you have.

Perhaps you've never thought of yourself as a problem solver, but think again. Don't you do this on a daily basis with your personal budget? Your children? Your studies? Juggling schedules with work and classes? Making your iPad or smartphone work properly? You solve problems every day, and acknowledging these skills can only make it stronger.

You probably have strengths that you have never thoroughly identified. Take your time and consider the following list of traits and abilities. Circle your strengths and add any that are not listed. Be honest with yourself because you will return to this list later.

Accountable	Budget-minded	Organized
Positive attitude	Intuitive	Stable
Punctual	Inquisitive	Rational
Ethical	Reliable	Tolerant
Resourceful	Humorous	Compassionate
Hopeful	Self-reliant	Decisive
Courageous	Competent	Grateful
Loyal	Sincere	Open-minded
Stylish	Helpful	Friendly
Optimistic	Respectful	Trusting
Well-groomed	Neat	Prepared
Supportive	Honest	Strong
Reserved	Logical	Spiritual
Warm	Versatile	Motivated
Grounded	Trustworthy	Creative
Modest	Imaginative	Fair
Flexible	Persuasive	Analytical
Loving	Yielding	Fun-loving
Forgiving	Articulate	Giving

IDENTIFY YOUR PERSONALITY TYPE AND USE IT TO BEST ADVANTAGE

Understanding your personality type enables you to use your best assets to your advantage. Having the knowledge of different personality types also helps you better understand others. In Figure 1.2 you will be able to take the PAP, a personality profile assessment that is designed to help you understand your personality type.

Figure 1.2   Take the PAP

The Personality Assessment Profile

Directions: Read each statement carefully and thoroughly. After reading the statement, rate your response using the scale below. There are no right or wrong answers. This is not a timed survey. The PAP is based, in part, on the Myers-Briggs Type Indicator (MBTI) by Katharine Briggs and Isabel Briggs-Myers.

3 = Often Applies   2 = Sometimes Applies   1 = Never or Almost Never Applies

_____ 1a. I am a very talkative person.

_____ 1b. I am a more reflective person than a verbal person.

_____ 2a. I am a very factual and literal person.

_____ 2b. I look to the future and I can see possibilities.

_____ 3a. I value truth and justice over tact and emotion.

_____ 3b. I find it easy to empathize with other people.

_____ 4a. I am very ordered and efficient.

_____ 4b. I enjoy having freedom from control.

_____ 5a. I am a very friendly and social person.

_____ 5b. I enjoy listening to others more than talking.

_____ 6a. I enjoy being around and working with people who have a great deal of common sense.

_____ 6b. I enjoy being around and working with people who are dreamers and have a great deal of imagination.

_____ 7a. One of my motivating forces is to do a job very well.

_____ 7b. I like to be recognized for, and I am motivated by, my accomplishments and awards.

_____ 8a. I like to plan out my day before I go to bed.

_____ 8b. When I get up on a non-school or non-work day, I just like to let the day "plan itself."

_____ 9a. I like to express my feelings and thoughts.

_____ 9b. I enjoy a great deal of tranquility and quiet time to myself.

_____ 10a. I am a very pragmatic and realistic person.

_____ 10b. I like to create new ideas, methods, or ways of doing things.

_____ 11a. I make decisions with my brain.

_____ 11b. I make decisions with my heart.

_____ 12a. I am a very disciplined and orderly person.

_____ 12b. I don't make a lot of plans.

_____ 13a. I like to work with a group of people.

_____ 13b. I would rather work independently.

_____ 14a. I learn best if I can see it, touch it, smell it, taste it, or hear it.

_____ 14b. I learn best by relying on my gut feelings or intuition.

_____ 15a. I am quick to criticize others.

_____ 15b. I compliment others very easily and quickly.

_____ 16a. My life is systematic and organized.

_____ 16b. I don't really pay attention to deadlines.

_____ 17a. I can be myself when I am around others.

_____ 17b. I can be myself when I am alone.

_____ 18a. I live in the here and now, in the present.

_____ 18b. I live in the future, planning and dreaming.

_____ 19a. I think that if someone breaks the rules, the person should be punished.

_____ 19b. I think that if someone breaks the rules, we should look at the person who broke the rules, examine the rules, and look at the situation at hand before a decision is made.

_____ 20a. I do my work, then I play.

_____ 20b I play, then do my work.

Refer to your score on each individual question. Place that score beside the appropriate question number below. Then, tally each line at the side.

Score					Total Across	Code
1a _____	5a _____	9a _____	13a _____	17a _____	_____	E Extrovert
1b _____	5b _____	9b _____	13b _____	17b _____	_____	I Introvert
2a _____	6a _____	10a _____	14a _____	18a _____	_____	S Sensing
2b _____	6b _____	10b _____	14b _____	18b _____	_____	N Intuition
3a _____	7a _____	11a _____	15a _____	19a _____	_____	T Thinking
3b _____	7b _____	11b _____	15b _____	19b _____	_____	F Feeling
4a _____	8a _____	12a _____	16a _____	20a _____	_____	J Judging
4b _____	8b _____	12b _____	16b _____	20b _____	_____	P Perceiving

PAP Scores
Personality Indicator

Look at the scores on your PAP. Is your score higher in the E or I line? Is your score higher in the S or N line? Is your score higher in the T or F line? Is your score higher in the J or P line? Write the code to the side of each section below.

Is your higher score	**E or I**	Code _____
Is your higher score	**S or N**	Code _____
Is your higher score	**T or F**	Code _____
Is your higher score	**J or P**	Code _____

Source: © Robert M. Sherfield, Ph.D.

UNDERSTANDING PERSONALITY TYPING (TYPOLOGY)

What Do These Letters Mean to Me?

The questions on the PAP helped you discover whether you are extroverted or introverted (E or I), sensing or intuitive (S or N), thinking or feeling (T or F), and judging or perceiving (J or P). These questions were based, in part, on work done by Carl Jung, Katharine Briggs, and Isabel Briggs-Myers.

In 1921, Swiss psychologist Carl Jung (1875–1961) published his work *Psychological Types.* In this book, Jung suggested that human behavior is not random. He felt that behavior follows patterns, and these patterns are caused by differences in the way people use their minds. In 1942, Isabel Briggs-Myers and her mother, Katharine Briggs, began to put Jung's theory into practice. They developed the Myers-Briggs Type Indicator, which after more than 50 years of research and refinement has become the most widely used instrument for identifying and studying personality.

Please keep in mind that no part of this assessment measures your worth, your success factors, how smart you are, or your value as a human being. The questions on the PAP assisted you in identifying your type, but we do not want you to assume that one personality type is better or worse, more or less valuable, or more or less likely to be successful. What personality typing can do is to "help us discover what best motivates and energizes each of us as individuals" (Tieger & Barron-Tieger, 2001).

WHY PERSONALITY MATTERS

What Does My Personality Type Say about Me?

When all of the combinations of E/I, S/N, T/F, and J/P are combined, there are 16 personality types. Everyone will fit into one of the following categories:

ISTJ	ISFJ	INFJ	INTJ
ISTP	ISFP	INFP	INTP
ESTP	ESFP	ENFP	ENTP
ESTJ	ESFJ	ENFJ	ENTJ

Let's take a look at the four major categories of typing. Notice that the higher your score in one area, the stronger your personality type is for that area. For instance, if you scored 15 on the E (extroversion) questions, this means that you are a strong extrovert. If you scored 15 on the I (introversion) questions, this means that you are a strong introvert. However, if you scored 7 on the E questions and 8 on the I questions, your score indicates that you possess almost the same amount of extroverted and introverted qualities. The same is true for every category on the PAP.

E Versus I (Extroversion/Introversion)

This category deals with the way we interact with others and the world around us.

Extroverts prefer to live in the outside world, drawing their strength from other people. They are outgoing and love interaction. They usually make decisions with others in mind. They enjoy being the center of attention. There are usually few secrets about extroverts.

Introverts draw their strength from the inner world. They need to spend time alone to think and ponder. They are usually quiet and reflective. They usually make decisions by themselves. They do not like being the center of attention. They are private.

S Versus N (Sensing/Intuition)

This category deals with the way we learn and deal with information.

Sensing types gather information through their five senses. They have a hard time believing something if it cannot be seen, touched, smelled, tasted, or heard. They like concrete facts and details. They do not rely on intuition or gut feelings. They usually have a great deal of common sense.

Intuitive types are not very detail-oriented. They can see possibilities, and they rely on their gut feelings. Usually, they are very innovative people. They tend to live in the future and often get bored once they have mastered a task.

T Versus F (Thinking/Feeling)

This category deals with the way we make decisions.

Thinkers are very logical people. They do not make decisions based on feelings or emotion. They are analytical and sometimes do not take others' values into consideration when making decisions. They can easily identify the flaws of others. They can be seen as insensitive and lacking compassion.

Feelers make decisions based on what they feel is right and just. They like to have harmony, and they value others' opinions and feelings. They are usually very tactful people who like to please others. They are very warm people.

J Versus P (Judging/Perceiving)

This category deals with the way we live.

Judgers are very orderly people. They must have a great deal of structure in their lives. They are good at setting goals and sticking to their goals. They are the type of people who would seldom, if ever, play before their work was completed.

Perceivers are just the opposite. They are less structured and more spontaneous. They do not like timelines. Unlike the judger, they will play before their work is done. They will take every chance to delay a decision or judgment. Sometimes, they can become involved in too many things at one time.

HOW PERSONALITY AFFECTS CAREER CHOICE

What Do I Want to Be When I Grow Up?

Taking personality and career tests and using them to help you decide which career you want to pursue is somewhat like playing the childhood game of "What Do I Want to Be When I Grow Up?" When taking career and personality tests, you need to remember that the results are indicators that will help you narrow the choices related to your personality, skills, and abilities; tests won't provide you with a specific career choice. Tests cannot pinpoint exactly what career you should pursue, but they can provide additional information to help you find your way. There are many free personality/career tests online and others you can access for a fee. To locate sites that will provide additional information related to personality types and career choices, use your Internet browser and type in keywords such as "careers for different personality types." Figure 1.3 provides suggestions of the types of careers that are best for specific personality types.

Figure 1.3 A Closer Look at Your Personality Type

Type	Attributes	Possible Careers
ISTJ—The Dutiful (7–10% of Americans)	Have great power of concentration; very serious; dependable; logical and realistic; take responsibility for their own actions; not easily distracted.	Accountant, purchasing agent, real estate, IRS agent, corrections officer, investment counselor, law researcher, technical writer, judge, mechanic
ISTP—The Mechanic (4–7% of Americans)	Very reserved; good at making things clear to others; interested in how and why things work; like to work with their hands; can sometimes be misunderstood as idle.	Police officer, intelligence officer, firefighter, athletic coach, engineer, technical trainer, logistic manager, EMT, surgical technician, banker, office manager, carpenter, landscape architect
ISFJ —The Nurturer (7–10% of Americans)	Hard workers; detail-oriented; considerate of others' feelings; friendly and warm to others; very conscientious; down-to-earth and like to be around the same.	Dentist, physician, biologist, surgical technician, teacher, speech pathologist, historian, clerical, bookkeeper, electrician, retail owner, counselor
ISFP—The Artist (5–7% of Americans)	Very sensitive and modest; adapt easily to change; they are respectful of others' feelings and values; take criticism personally; don't enjoy leadership roles.	Artist, chef, musician, nurse, medical assistant, surgeon, botanist, zoologist, science teacher, travel agent, game warden, coach, bookkeeper, clerical, insurance examiner
INFJ—The Protector (2–3% of Americans)	Enjoy an atmosphere where all get along; do what is needed of them; have strong beliefs and principles; enjoy helping others achieve their goals.	Career counselor, psychologist, teacher, social worker, clergy, artist, novelist, filmmaker, health care provider, human resource manager, agent, coach, crisis manager, mediator

(continued)

Figure 1.3 A Closer Look at Your Personality Type (*continued*)

Type	Attributes	Possible Careers
INFP—The Idealist (3–4% of Americans)	Work well alone; must know others well to interact; faithful to others and their jobs; excellent at communication; open-minded; dreamers; tend to do too much.	Entertainer, artist, editor, musician, professor, researcher, counselor, consultant, clergy, dietitian, massage therapist, human resources manager, events manager, corporate leader
INTJ—The Scientist (2–3% of Americans)	Very independent; enjoy challenges; inventors; can be skeptical; perfectionists; believe in their own work, sometimes to a fault.	Economist, financial planner, banker, budget analyst, scientist, astronomer, network specialist, computer programmer, engineer, curriculum designer, coroner, pathologist, attorney, manager
INTP—The Thinker (3–4% of Americans)	Extremely logical; very analytical; good at planning; love to learn; excellent problem solvers; don't enjoy needless conversation; hard to understand at times.	Software designer, programmer, systems analyst, network administrator, surgeon, veterinarian, lawyer, economist, architect, physicist, mathematician, college professor, writer, agent, producer
ESTP—The Doer (6–8% of Americans)	Usually very happy; don't let trivial things upset them; have very good memories; very good at working with things and taking them apart.	Police officer, firefighter, detective, military, investigator, paramedic, banker, investor, promoter, carpenter, chef, real estate broker, retail sales, insurance claims
ESTJ—The Guardian (12–15% of Americans)	"Take charge" people; like to get things done; focus on results; very good at organizing; good at seeing what will not work; responsible; realists.	Insurance agent, military, security, coach, credit analyst, project manager, auditor, general contractor, paralegal, stockbroker, executive, information officer, lawyer, controller, accounts manager
ESFP—The Performer (8–10% of Americans)	Very good at sports and active exercises; good common sense; easygoing; good at communication; can be impulsive; do not enjoy working alone; have fun and enjoy living and life.	Nurse, social worker, physician assistant, nutritionist, therapist, photographer, musician, film producer, social events coordinator, news anchor, fund raiser, host, retail sales
ESFJ—The Caregiver (11–14% of Americans)	Enjoy many friendly relationships; popular; love to help others; do not take criticism very well; need praise; need to work with people; organized; talkative; active.	Medical assistant, physician, nurse, teacher, coach, principal, social worker, counselor, clergy, court reporter, office manager, loan officer, public relations, customer service, caterer, office manager
ENFP—The Inspirer (6–7% of Americans)	Creative and industrious; can easily find success in activities and projects that interest them; good at motivating others; organized; do not like routine.	Journalist, writer, actor, newscaster, artist, director, public relations, teacher, clergy, psychologist, guidance counselor, trainer, project manager, human resources manager
ENFJ—The Giver (3–5% of Americans)	Very concerned about others' feelings; respect others; good leaders; usually popular; good at public speaking; can make decisions too quickly; trust easily.	Journalist, entertainer, TV producer, politician, counselor, clergy, psychologist, teacher, social worker, health care provider, customer service manager
ENTP—The Visionary (4–6% of Americans)	Great problem solvers; love to argue either side; can do almost anything; good at speaking/motivating; love challenges; very creative; do not like routine; overconfident.	Entrepreneur, manager, agent, journalist, attorney, urban planner, analyst, creative director, public relations, marketing, broadcaster, network solutions, politician, detective
ENTJ—The Executive (3–5% of Americans)	Excellent leaders; speak very well; hardworking; may be workaholics; may not give enough praise; like to learn; great planners; enjoy helping others reach their goals.	Executive, senior manager, administrator, consultant, editor, producer, financial planner, stockbroker, program designer, attorney, psychologist, engineer, network administrator

As I was investigating and applying for employment during this stage in my life, I found that my criteria for the perfect job had changed from when I was younger.

I realized that an environment of mutual respect, where value and a sense of dignity were given to coworkers as well as clients, had risen to the top of my list.

KNOW WHAT YOU WANT FROM LIFE AND WORK

Are You Prepared to Go Get What You Want?

Some of the strongest, most dedicated people in the world struggle in their work and personal lives. Why? Because they have never really thought about what they want out of life or from their careers. They have never done the work required to answer this question—and it is work. What is it that you really want and need to be happy, fulfilled, and successful? What is the main thing that you really need to focus on? You may have never thought about the questions below, but consider them as you try to formulate an answer to the question, "What do I want from my life and my work?"

- Is my success tied to the amount of money I make?
- Are my friends and family more important than my career?
- What would I be willing to do to get ahead?
- What can I contribute to the world through my career?
- What really makes me happy? Will my career choice give this to me?
- Does my career choice suit my genuine interests?
- Does my current career choice really motivate me?
- Am I working toward this career for convenience or passion?
- Would I rather work inside or outside?
- Am I more of a leader or a follower?
- Do I want to travel with my work?
- Am I truly grounded in my ethics?
- Am I focused on the things that are life changing?

There is an old quote that says, "If you don't know where you're going, it doesn't matter which path you take." Many people have found this to be true in their personal and professional lives. Knowing what you want and need from your career and your life will be ultimately important to your happiness and success.

In the space below, jot down a few things that you think you want and need from your career. Remember, the two categories are different.

I need . . .	I want . . .
_____	_____
_____	_____
_____	_____

IDENTIFY AND EMULATE YOUR ROLE MODELS

Whom Do You Admire Most?

Whom do you admire most in your life right now? Is it a parent or grandparent who struggled to raise you and offer you things he or she never had? Is it your current supervisor who treats people well and with respect? Is it a famous person, such as Oprah Winfrey, who overcame adversity to help make life better for others?

We all have role models in our lives for a reason. They help us see what is possible. They help us see a better future. Think about a person that you greatly admire. Who is that person?

_____

What personal and professional qualities do they possess that you would like to someday have?

Personal Qualities	Professional Qualities
_____	_____
_____	_____
_____	_____

Choose one of the qualities from the list you created above. How will this quality help you become successful and advance in your chosen career? Be specific in your answer.

_____

_____

_____

_____

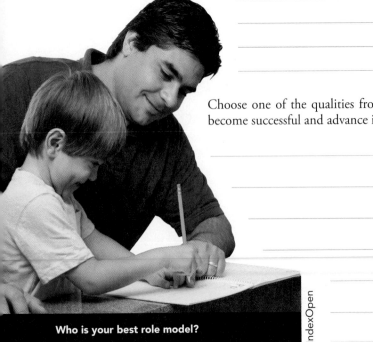

Who is your best role model?

IndexOpen

DETERMINE WHAT YOU VALUE

What Really Matters to You?

Values are unique to each individual. What you value and consider important to your life and success may be at the bottom of the list for someone else. A value is simply a principle or quality that you think is worthwhile and regard highly. You may value honesty or love or friendship in your life. Others may put primary importance on money or possessions. Others' values might include family, children, or career.

So, why are values important to us? They usually drive our decisions, determine how we treat others, guide us in reacting to certain situations, and help direct our moral behavior. When we act in a way that goes against what we value, our conscience begins to gnaw at us. That little voice inside our head begins to let us know that what we have done, or what we are about to do goes against our moral code—our values. When we make decisions or act in a way that goes against the values established by society or our workplace, we begin to suffer in different ways, such as being terminated or reprimanded. Therefore, knowing what you value *and* what society and your workplace value will be exceedingly important to your success and mobility.

Our personal value system also serves as a motivational force in our lives. What we value, we work to keep, protect, enrich, and get more of. We are motivated by what brings us joy and peace, and unless we hold a firm picture of our value system in our hearts and minds, we may be working for the wrong things.

Take a moment and circle the words in the following list that best indicate what you value. If one or more of your personal values is not on the list, add them to the bottom.

Service to others	Privacy	Interaction
A healthy love relationship	Money	Honesty
Fairness	Challenges	Respect
The environment	Family	Friends
Justice	Success	Education
Leisure time	Faith	Money
Leadership abilities	Fun activities	Beauty
A nice home	Fine car	Stylish clothes
Safety	Health	Comfort
Fame/popularity	Independence	Control
Reputation	Physical activity	Pets
Decision making	Speaking	Writing

_____   _____   _____

_____   _____   _____

Now for the hard part—if you could only have one thing in your life that you valued and this value had to sustain you in your personal and professional life, which value above would you choose? _____

Why? _____

_____

How will this one value help you be successful in your career? _____

_____

_____

THE POWER OF YOUR VALUES AND BELIEFS

What Do You Believe In and Hold in High Esteem?

It has been said, "If you think you can't, you can't. If you think you can, you can." Countless studies have been conducted on the power of personal beliefs and positive thinking. A belief is what we consider to be true or false. A belief is a conviction that we hold so dearly that it literally causes us to act in one way or another. If you believe that you are going to fail your math test, you probably will. If you believe that you have nothing to offer to the world, you probably do not. Our beliefs are powerful and central to our self-esteem and personal motivation. Consider the following examples:

Courtesy of the Library of Congress

Abraham Lincoln lost eight elections, went bankrupt twice, lost two children, and had a complete nervous and mental breakdown all before he became president of the United States. He believed that he could govern this country . . . and he did. He helped change the world.

Everett Collection/Alamy

Walt Disney was fired from his first job because his boss thought he did not have any creativity or good ideas and considered him to be a poor sketch artist. Disney believed that he was much more talented than his boss gave him credit for.

Daily Mirror/MirrorPix/Newscom

Tina Turner, raped and beaten by her own husband, Ike, had to sue in a court of law to keep her identity—her name. Ike believed that she would never be successful without him. She believed otherwise. After their divorce and business partnership ended, she recorded many songs, won several Grammys, and has sold over 300 million albums. Her beliefs paid off.

Allstar Picture Library/Alamy

Ray Romano was fired from the TV show *NewsRadio* while it was still in rehearsal. He believed that he had talent as a comedian and went on to develop, produce, and write the Emmy-winning series *Everybody Loves Raymond*.

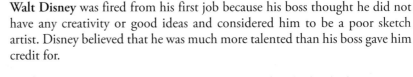
Judy Eddy/Wenn Photos/Newscom

Maya Angelou has won three Grammys for the spoken word and has been nominated twice for Broadway's prestigious Tony Award. However, as a young girl, she was raped by her mother's boyfriend and did not speak again for four years. By the time she was in her twenties, she had been a cook, streetcar conductor, cocktail waitress, dancer, madam, high school dropout, and unwed mother. However, she believed that she had talent as a writer and poet. Her beliefs paid off, too. She became only the second poet in U.S. history to write and deliver an original poem at a presidential inauguration (for Bill Clinton).

Some examples of beliefs are:

- I believe that honesty is always the best policy.
- I believe that it is important to save 10 percent of my paycheck each month.
- I believe that hard work will always pay off in the end.
- I believe that people are basically good, not evil.
- I believe in God.

I am somebody. I am me. I like being me. And I need nobody to make me somebody.
—Louis L'Amour

Our beliefs can guide us through many troubled times. They can help us when everything seems to be going against our hopes and dreams. They influence our attitudes and behaviors. However, even though they are very powerful, beliefs alone will not get you an Emmy or the presidency of the United States. Beliefs must be followed by hard work, active goals, and many sacrifices.

Think about a belief that you hold dear. What is that belief? _____

_____

_____

_____

_____

How can this belief help guide you in your career or job-making decisions? _____

_____

_____

_____

_____

CREATING YOUR OWN PERSONAL BRAND—ME, INC.

Who Do You Want to Become?

Brands are everywhere. The Nike swoosh, the Starbucks cup, Levi rivets, the AT&T globe—the list goes on and on. Big companies understand the importance of establishing a distinctive brand. You need to take a lesson from big companies and establish a brand for yourself. You are literally the CEO of your own company: Me, Inc. As you prepare to interview for a job, you need to be preparing to market yourself. You should be striving to "develop the micro equivalent of the Nike Swoosh" (Peters, 1997). You need to develop your brand!

You have an opportunity to stand out and to develop your own brand, to become exactly what you want to be. You have to figure out how to create a distinctive role for yourself, a message that conveys who you are. As you work through this book, you may want to change parts of your brand, but the main thing for you to focus on right now is getting started.

> The remarkable thing we have is a choice every day regarding the attitude we will embrace for that day. We cannot change our past . . . We cannot change the fact that people will act in a certain way. We cannot change the inevitable. The only thing we can do is play on the one string we have, and that is our attitude.
>
> —Charles R. Swindoll

THE POWER OF OPTIMISM AND THE RIGHT ATTITUDE

What Do You Need to Improve?

You've heard it all your life: "You have a great attitude." Or maybe "You have a bad attitude." Or "You need to improve your attitude." Perhaps you have heard it said this way: "Attitude is not important—attitude is everything." Parents, teachers, coaches, and bosses all talk constantly about attitude. Why are attitude and optimism so important? Perhaps it is because what you think and how you feel about yourself has so much to do with how your perform at school and later at work. Attitude is important in all aspects of your life: school, work, relationships. A recent national survey asked the question, "What counts more: Employee aptitude; hard skills and technical competencies; employee attitude; or relational skills, motivation and positive outlook? Nearly 60% of corporations said attitude was the no. 1 concern" (Teamwork Newsletter, 2008).

Exactly what is attitude? Attitude is the manner in which you act or your views toward whatever is happening. For example, you may care about your schoolwork, or you may not be interested. You might treat people with respect, or you may be disrespectful toward some people. You either come to school on time and listen, or you get there late and slouch in your desk and look disgusted. You have a willing attitude at work or you have a "let somebody else do it" disposition. All of this has to do with your personal attitude.

Your attitude affects your performance at school and at work; it also affects others' performance because one person with a bad attitude can have a negative effect on everyone around him

Figure 1.4   Working on Yourself

- **Smile** even when you really just want to sit down and cry or when being grouchy and hurtful is easier than being nice. Greet everyone with a smile and good thoughts and feelings.

- **Push yourself** to be outgoing and friendly even when you feel shy and want to withdraw. Remember that most people feel shy and insecure at times. By being friendly, you will be helping others who are struggling.

- **Try to avoid worrying** about things that *might* happen. Deal with the here and now—that will usually be more than enough to keep you busy. It has been said that only 8 percent of our worries actually come true and they are usually small worries when they happen. Instead of worrying, focus your energy on doing great work at school or on your job.

- **Give people sincere compliments.** Tell them how nice they look or specifically what a great job they did. Look right at the person and brag on him or her. Being nice to someone else takes nothing away from you, and it wins friends and influences people if you are sincere.

- **Avoid getting caught up in the gossip mill.** Volunteer nice remarks about people when they are not present, especially if someone else is running them down. Stand up for people who are being mistreated when you can.

- **Try to be helpful to others**, especially someone who is having a really bad day or a difficult time in their

Only 8 percent of our worries are actually over legitimate troubles. 40 percent of our worries never happen. 30 percent of our worries concern the past. 12 percent are needless worries about health. 10 percent are insignificant.
—Dr. Walter Cavert

lives. Offer to pick up something for them or buy them lunch or just listen. Kindness is never forgotten, and everyone needs it.

- **Get up early and exercise for a few minutes** to get your adrenaline working. Meditate and concentrate on all the good things in your life. Count your blessings instead of your problems.

- **Rid yourself of negative baggage** that you have been carrying around with you—bad things that happened, and you keep bringing them up in your mind. Forgive yourself and others for things that happened in the past that hurt you. It is very important for you to forgive yourself! In your mind, put all the negative things you are still holding onto in a big suitcase. Take this suitcase into the forest and leave it there with all the negativity that you have been carrying around way too long. Now, pretend that you are walking out of the forest into the sunshine.

- **Be aware that everyone you meet is carrying some kind of burden or dealing with a problem.** A negative reaction from someone may be a reflection of a difficult problem they are struggling with rather than the fact they are simply not nice people. Try to listen to people's words but also their body language. Look at people around you. What can you do to help them? You will find that if you help others, you will feel better about yourself, and they will help you when you need it.

or her. Not only must you work on your personal attitude, you also have to learn not to let others make you feel bad about yourself or to put a damper on your day. So how do you get this magical attitude that makes things so much better for you and everyone with whom you come in contact? Consider the tips in Figure 1.4.

GETTING RID OF NEGATIVISM AND AVOIDING NEGATIVE PEOPLE

Who Drags You Down and Makes You Feel Small?

One thing you need to know is that you can't change anyone unless he or she wants to change—that includes people with negative attitudes. You can only change yourself and how you allow other people's negative attitudes to affect you. As you deal with certain people who make you feel small or put you down, consider your feelings after you have interacted with them. What was the result of your being in contact with that person? Did you feel worse or distressed or depressed? Did talking to a certain person make you begin to doubt your ability to do something that you really wanted to do? This is what attitude is all about—you simply can't let those people control you and your emotions. So what do you do to rid yourself of this negativism and negative people's attitudes? Study the tips in Figure 1.5.

Shutterstock

Do you allow people with negative attitudes to rub off on you?

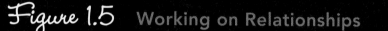

Figure 1.5 Working on Relationships

- Make up your mind that you are in control of yourself and that you will not let anyone else steal your joy and optimism. This may take time. The person who makes you feel bad could be your mother or your significant other or a good friend. Is there a person or people who make you feel bad almost every time you interact with them? Sometimes you simply have to distance yourself from these people so you can get healthy yourself—even if it is someone whom you love very much.

- Try to be helpful to negative people. Point out the positive. Try to offer them constructive solutions, but don't let them become destructive to you.

- Be aware of how you feel after you have been in contact with certain people. Who lifts you up? Makes you laugh? Encourages you? Increase your time with these people, and decrease your time with those who bring you down.

- When faced with challenges that are very difficult, think about all the good things and the good people you have in your life. Spend time with a person who really cares about you. Remember to listen to them as well as talk about your own problems.

- Remember that you have to get along with negative people, especially at work. You might put this advice under the category "social diplomacy." "Employees who have good professional skills but do not relationally get along with co-workers, clients or management are now considered incompetent" (Teamworks Fall Newsletter, 2008). More people are terminated because of attitude-related problems than lack of job skills. Social diplomacy can take you a long way at work and in life.

> *The optimist sees opportunity in every danger; the pessimist sees danger in every opportunity.*
> —Winston Churchill

Do you use the power of positive people to improve your own attitude?

Shutterstock

CHOOSE OPTIMISM AND SURROUND YOURSELF WITH OPTIMISTIC PEOPLE

What Can I Gain by Surrounding Myself with Positive People?

Your attitude is yours. It belongs to you. You own it. Good or bad, happy or sad, optimistic or pessimistic, it is yours and you are responsible for it. However, your attitude is greatly influenced by situations in your life and by the people with whom you associate. Developing a winning, optimistic attitude can be hard, yet extremely rewarding work. Motivated and successful people have learned that one's attitude is the mirror to one's soul.

Optimism has many benefits beyond helping you develop a winning attitude. Researchers have found that people who are optimistic live longer, are more motivated, survive cancer treatment at a greater rate, have longer and more satisfying relationships, and are mentally healthier than pessimists. This would suggest that developing and maintaining a winning, optimistic attitude can help you have a longer and more satisfying quality of life.

Listen to yourself for a few days. Are you more of an optimist or a pessimist? Do you hear yourself whining, complaining, griping, and finding fault with everything and everybody around you? Do you blame others for things that are wrong in your life? Do you blame your bad grades on your professors? Is someone else responsible for your unhappiness? If these thoughts or comments are in your head, you are suffering from ***"I CAN'T" Syndrome*** (**I**rritated, **C**ontaminated, **A**ngry, **N**egative **T**houghts). This pessimistic condition can negatively influence every aspect of your life, from your self-esteem and your motivation level to your academic performance, your relationships, and your career success.

If you want to eliminate "***I CAN'T***" from your life, consider the following tips:

- Work every day to find the good in people, places, and things.
- Discover what is holding you back and what you need to push you forward.
- Visualize your success—visualize yourself actually being who and what you want to be.
- Locate and observe positive, optimistic people and things in your life.
- Make a list of who helps you, supports you, and helps you feel positive; then make a point to be around them more.
- Take responsibility for your own actions and their consequences.
- Force yourself to find five positive things a day for which to be thankful.

POSITIVE HABITS at Work

When you hear someone gossiping and spreading rumors, do not participate in the conversation. It can only lead to resentment and trouble. If you feel it is appropriate, say something positive about the person who is being maligned.

You've seen the difference between an optimist and a pessimist. Both are everywhere—at work, at school, and probably in your own family. Positive, upbeat, and motivated people are easy to spot. You can basically see their attitude in the way they walk, the way they carry themselves, the way they approach people, and the way they treat others. Negative people are also easy to spot—they are grouchy, late, and depressing.

Learn from both as you move through the days and months ahead. Choose your friends carefully. Seek out people who have ambition, good work habits, positive attitudes, and high ethical standards. Look for those who study hard, enjoy learning, are goal oriented, and don't mind taking a stand when they believe strongly about something. Befriend people who have interests and hobbies that are new to you. Step outside your comfort zone and add people to your circle of friends who are from a different culture, are of a different religion, or who have lived in a different geographic region. You'll be happily surprised at how much enrichment they can bring to your life and how much you grow personally and professionally in the process.

Be wary, however, of *the others*. Whiners. Degraders. Attackers. Manipulators. Pessimists. Backstabbers. Abusers. Cowards. Two-faced racists, sexists, ageists, homophobes, ethnocentrists. These people carry around an aura so negative that it can almost be seen as a dark cloud above them. They degrade others because they do not like themselves. They find fault with everything because their own lives are unrewarding. Many of these people will do nothing to use their potential but will attack you for being motivated and trying to improve your life. We call them contaminated people.

Examine the two lists that follow. As you read through the lists, consider the people with whom you associate. Are the majority of your friends, family, peers, and work associates positive or contaminated?

Positive People:	Contaminated People:
■ Bring out the best in you	■ Bring out the worst in you
■ Find the good in bad situations	■ Find the bad in every situation
■ Are gracious and understanding	■ Are rude and uncaring
■ Build people up	■ Sabotage people, even loved ones
■ Support your dreams	■ Criticize your hopes and plans
■ Make you feel comfortable and happy	■ Make you feel uneasy, nervous, and irritable
■ Tell you the truth and offer constructive criticism	■ Are two-faced and use harsh language to "put you in your place"
■ Are open-minded and fair	■ Are narrow and ethnocentric
■ Are patient	■ Are quick to anger
■ Are giving	■ Are jealous and smothering
■ Love to learn from others	■ Think they know everything

As you think about the list above and the people in your life, ask yourself, "Do I surround myself with more positive or contaminated people?" As you consider your friends, family, classmates, and work associates, use the space below to compare and contrast one *positive person* with one *contaminated person* in your life.

Positive Person _____

His/Her Attributes _____

_____

_____

Contaminated Person _____

His/Her Attributes _____

_____

_____

Compare and Contrast _____

_____

_____

UNDERSTAND YOUR EMOTIONAL RESPONSES

Who Pushes Your Buttons?

Should evolution be taught in the public school system? Should the drinking age be lowered to 18? Should 16-year-olds be allowed to drive? Should hate crime laws be abolished? Should same-sex couples be allowed to marry and adopt children? What emotions are you feeling right now? Did you immediately formulate answers to these questions in your mind? Do your emotions drive the way you think or act?

Your mentality shapes your reality.
—Bert Goldman

Emotions play a vital role in our lives. They help us feel compassion, offer assistance to others, reach out in times of need, and relate with compassion and empathy. On the other hand, our emotions can cause problems in our thinking process. They can cloud issues and distort facts. They can make us act in inappropriate ways when normally, we would not—and this can affect our performance and attitude in the workplace. Emotions are not bad—as a matter of fact, they are good and help us be human. However, it is of paramount importance that you know how to identify when your emotions are calling the shots and how to control them. You do not have to eliminate emotions from your thoughts or actions, but it is crucial that you know when your emotions are clouding an issue.

ARTICULATE YOUR HOPES AND GOALS

Where Are You Going with Your One Lifetime?

BIGGEST INTERVIEW *Blunders*

Rosalynn had done a very good job with her resumé and cover letter and had secured an interview with her dream company. Things got off to a good start at the interview, but Rosalynn knew she had blown it when the interviewer asked her to tell her what she knew about the company. Rosalynn realized too late that she should have made the effort to learn a great deal about the company before going to an interview!

LESSON: Always research the company and be prepared to talk about the positive things you know about it and to ask thoughtful questions. If the interviewer doesn't ask you about the company, try to find ways to weave some of your knowledge related to the company's policies into the conversation.

"Go tell it on the mountain, over the hills and everywhere . . . " "Why would I want to do that?" you might ask. "If I tell everyone my hopes and dreams and goals, they'll know if I don't make it." Yes, but they will also know when you do—and they can help you make it.

If others know what you want from your life or your career, they can help you bring it to fruition. When you share what type of position you want or where you would like to work, others can be on the lookout for you, and you can do the same for your peers.

Consider this: You have a secret desire to become an animation artist for Pixar Animation Studios. Yes, it is a major film company producing such hits as *Finding Nemo, Cars,* and *Toy Story.* "How stupid to think that someone from Newell, Iowa (population 887) could ever go to work for one of Disney's major studios," you might think. Wrong. Wrong. Wrong. Everyday people get fabulous dream jobs. Someone became the veterinarian for Lady Gaga's pets, someone became Oprah's personal trainer, and someone became an animator for an upcoming Disney/Pixar film. Others became the head mechanic for Delta Airlines and a chef at MGM Grand in Las Vegas, a nurse at Mercy Hospital, a firefighter for New York City, and a fashion design intern for Versace. Why? Because they had talent, they worked hard, they had a belief that they could do it, and they let others know of their hopes and dreams.

Consider this. You told your classmate that you really want to become a physical therapist. Your peer takes his mother to physical therapy one day and overhears a conversation between two staff members about an opening. She mentions this to you. You stop by the therapy center to inquire, and they are very impressed that you knew about the position and took the initiative to stop by. You fill out an application, leave your resumé, and two days later, you're called in for an interview to become an intern.

> *You are fast becoming what you are going to be.*
> —Patricia G. Moody

Reflections: PUTTING IT ALL TOGETHER

A great deal of your success in the workplace depends on the characteristics and qualities you bring with you. Your attitude, optimism, and personality type will all affect your performance at work. It is important that you find good role models to emulate, that you build a strong set of values and beliefs, and that you rid yourself of negativity about yourself and others. Knowing what you want, staying focused on your goals, and working hard will be valuable assets in the workplace.

DIGITAL BRIEFCASE

PERSONAL BRANDING

Review the information on personal branding on page 19. Answer the following questions as you think about creating your own brand: Me, Inc.

- What is unique about you? (Do you have special talents? Are you loyal and dedicated to your company and coworkers? Do you have unique technology talents?)
- What is a feature benefit about you? (Are you always on time? Do you deliver high-quality work? Do you get along well with team members? Are you great at problem solving?)
- What have you done that you are most proud of? (Were you on the debate team? Did you lead a team? Did you succeed at a part-time job? Did you volunteer for a charitable activity?)
- How do you sell the "sizzle" about yourself? (What can you do to be noticed and appreciated? Can you take on a project for an organization? Can you volunteer for tasks at work? Are you careful what you send out via technology that can easily be passed on to anybody else? (How about your personal advertisements when you text, e-mail, or post something to your Facebook wall? Do you stop and think before engaging in popular pastimes like "sexting?" Are you thinking when you post pictures on Facebook that might come back to haunt you later?)
- Do you volunteer or participate in things that give you power? If your meetings are disorganized, can you volunteer to write an agenda that keeps your group on track? Can you put together an informal user's group that can give you honest feedback on how your brand is doing? Ask them to give you an honest assessment of how you are perceived and what they think you need to do differently.)
- How do you measure up against four important benchmarks?
  - Are you a great team member and supportive colleague?
  - What are you a real expert at that adds value to your personal brand?

- What are you doing that adds to your ability to apply vision to everything you do?
- Are the things you are trying to accomplish practical and doable?

If you are smart, you will figure out the answer to all these questions and create a brand for which you are known, a brand that sells the best features of who you are and what you have to offer. It takes time, and it's not easy, but it is absolutely essential to your success. Know who you are! Know what you want! Build the brand that takes you there!

By thinking about who you really are, what you want, what you need, and what you have to offer an employer, you can better determine the type of position you will need in order to be happy, successful, and continue growing. If you focus on matching your vocation together with your passion, you will never face a day of "work" in your life. Work hard on developing your personal brand (Peters, 1997).

So, let's get to work on creating your personal brand.

Complete the following questions about yourself as you begin to work on developing your special brand—Me, Inc.

1. Write at least three things that you think are unique about you.

_____

_____

2. Name at least one major benefit about you.

_____

_____

3. What special talent can you add to a company's everyday function that will make you stand out? When answering this question, consider the list you developed on page 9.

_____

_____

4. Name something you have done that you are very proud of.

_____

_____

5. What can you do to get noticed in a subtle, positive way without appearing that you are bragging?

_____

_____

6. Do the personal messages you send reflect positively on you? Which things do you need to start doing or stop doing?

_____

_____

7. What can you volunteer to do at work or school that will give you positive visibility?

_____

_____

8. Name at least three people who can serve as your "user's group" and who will tell you honestly what you need to know and what you need to do differently.

_____

_____

9. Measure yourself against the four benchmarks mentioned on pages 25–26. How are you doing? For each one, give yourself a grade from A to F.

1. _____   3. _____

2. _____   4. _____

You should now be ready to focus on developing your brand, an important step in discovering who you are and what you have to offer.

REFERENCES

Aaker, J., & Smith, A. (2010). *The dragonfly effect.* San Francisco: Jossey-Bass.

Center for Law and Social Policy. (2003). *The language of opportunity: Expanding employment for adults with limited English skills.* Washington, DC: Author

Gordon, E. (2008). *The 2010 meltdown: Solving the impending job crisis.* Lanham, MD: Rowman & Littlefield Education.

Peters, T. (August 31, 1997). "The Brand Called You." *Fast Company.*

Teamworks Newsletter. (2008). Retrieved on March 3, 2011, from www.iwolff.com/files /teamworks/Newsletter-attitudeIsEverythingInTheWorkplace.pdf.

Tieger, P., & Barron-Tieger, B. (2001). *Do what you are: Discover the perfect career for you through the secrets of personality type* (3rd ed.). Boston: Little, Brown.

chapter two

BUILD

BUILDING A STRONG CHARACTER WITH IMPECCABLE ETHICS

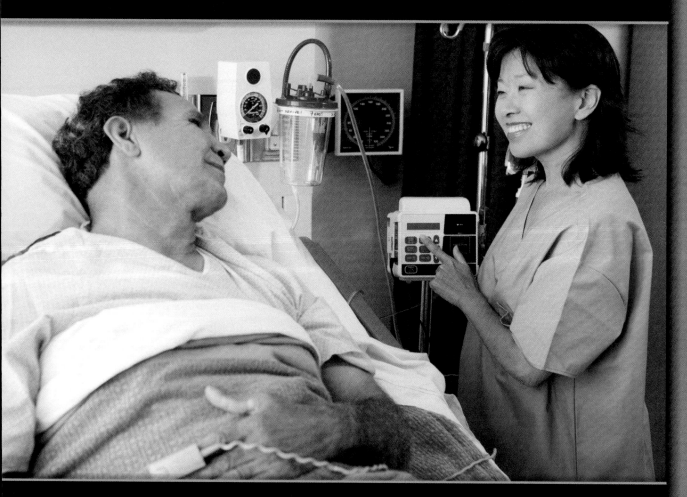

Ethics is knowing the difference between what you have a right to do and what is right to do.
—Potter Stewart

Why read this chapter?

Because you'll learn...

- How to develop your personal character and ethics
- The value of trustworthiness
- The importance of honoring commitments

Because you'll be able to...

- Discuss the six levels of ethical decision making
- Build a good name and reputation

PROFESSIONALS from the Field

Name: Sonya Lane

Business: Physical Therapist, In Shape Physical Therapy

You only have one reputation, and it's therefore very important to build one that you are proud of, one that will earn respect from your peers and coworkers, and one that is built on solid, ethical principles. Regardless of your position, you need to have a good ethical and moral character in order to earn people's trust in who you are and what you do. If you make a commitment to someone, you should honor that promise regardless of the circumstances, because someone is counting on you to keep your word. You need to respect and believe in yourself in order to develop a strong moral character and reputation. Build your personal character in such a way that you can look in the mirror every day, knowing that you are a good, decent person who has treated everyone fairly and in the way that you would want to be treated.

MyStudentSuccessLab

MyStudentSuccessLab (www.mystudentsuccesslab.com) is an online solution designed to help you "Start strong, Finish stronger" by building skills for ongoing personal and professional development.

CULTIVATING YOUR CHARACTER AND ETHICS

How Do I Know How to Do the Right Thing?

Exactly what does *ethics* mean? Ethics is a set of moral principles that guide our decisions and behavior and help us make the appropriate decisions when faced with choices. Quite simply, ethics is how we choose to live our lives and how we treat other people. These decisions build our character. In the workplace, as in your social environment, you will be known by your character and ethics—or your lack of both. You only have one reputation, so it is very important to build a quality one, to be respected for the way you conduct your life day in and day out and for the way you treat others.

At a very early age, we begin to learn right from wrong, and we begin shaping our basic character and ethics. We learn not to hit our playmates, to share our possessions, to clean up after ourselves, and to not take things that don't belong to us; these are kindergarten mantras. Translated into workplace ethics, they might be stated this way: Treat your coworkers with respect, assist them when they need help with a project, keep your work area clean and organized, and don't take credit for someone else's work. While these statements are only a small part of the ethics puzzle, they are important to the process of getting along with others at work and making the right decisions.

Who Are You When No One Else Is Looking?

What if there were no rules or laws to govern your behavior? What if there were no consequences or ramifications for any of your actions? Let's pretend for a moment that you could never go to jail or face fines or be shunned for your actions or behaviors. If these statements came to pass, what would your life—or the lives of those you love—look like? This is one of the best ways to offer a practical definition of ethics. Basically, ethics is the accepted moral code or standard within a society by which we all live. Codes of ethics vary from culture to culture, country to country, and group to group, but each carries with it certain rules that members of that culture, country, or group are expected to follow.

Ethics, however, is about much, much more than following the law, adhering to your society's accepted code, or following your religion's teachings. Each will usually contain ethical standards, but as argued in the article "What Is Ethics?" (Velasquez, Andre, Shanks, & Meyer, 1987), following a corrupt society's "moral" standard can have dire consequences. Nazi Germany is a perfect example of this situation. Consider also slavery laws in the United States prior to the Civil War. Few people would now suggest those laws were "ethical." And think about the Crusades, in which hundreds of thousands of people were murdered in the name of religion. Was that ethical?

Think back in history for a moment (and you won't have to think back too far) and consider some national and international leaders, entertainers, sports figures, or even local professionals in your community who made monumental ethical mistakes that cost them dearly. Richard Nixon. Michael Vick. Barry Bonds. Bill Clinton. Martha Stewart. Prince Harry. Jerry Sandusky. O. J. Simpson. Each of these people, to varying degrees, failed to maintain the accepted moral code of his or her community and the consequences were grave. From jail sentences to public shame, each suffered a demoralizing defeat and a tarnished public image due

> *Ethical errors end careers more quickly and more definitively than any other mistakes in judgment or accounting.*
>
> —*Unknown*

to his or her ethical error. All of these people failed to follow their moral compasses. You, too, have a moral compass—it is simply your gut feeling of what is right or wrong. If you have a nagging feeling that you should not be doing something, chances are very good that your moral compass is pointing you in a different direction.

The word *ethics* is derived from the ancient Greek *ethos* (which loosely translates to "habit," "custom," or "character"). The study of ethics has also been called "moral philosophy." There are many factors that influence our ethics, from our family and friends to our teachers and relatives. TV, music, media, religion, and politics also play a tremendous role in how our ethical footprint is developed. We are constantly bombarded with conflicting messages about what is right and wrong or good and bad. Thus, more and more people slip into the gray twilight where it is hard to determine what the "right" thing to do really is. To prove this point, consider the following facts:

- 25 San Diego State University students failed a business ethics class because they were caught cheating.
- 75 percent of college students admit cheating at some point.
- According to a poll of Who's Who among American High School Students, 80 percent admitted to cheating to get to the top of his or her class.
- 61 percent of surveyed adults have gone against personal ethics for money.

As you enter the professional world, your moral conduct will become increasingly important to you, your managers, and your colleagues. The following are included to help you learn more about ethics, morality, and character to better enable you to make informed, logical, and smart decisions.

UNDERSTAND THE DYNAMICS OF ETHICS, INTEGRITY, AND CHARACTER

Do You Conduct Yourself in an Honorable Manner?

Ethics, integrity, and character can be hard to pin down because in today's discussions, they are all mixed up together. Basically, they all have to do with how you behave. Your actions are usually guided by a combination of your own personal ethical code, integrity, and character. As discussed earlier, ethics is a habit or a custom for behavior. Integrity, from the Latin *integri* (which means wholeness—as in wholeness of action and wholeness of thoughts), deals with fairness, courage, respect, temperance, and sound judgment. It is about choosing *right* over *easy* and *fairness* over *personal gain*.

Character, from the Greek *charakter* (which means "to stamp," "to scratch or mark," or "to engrave"), refers to the attributes that make up or distinguish you as an individual. In essence, your character is how your soul is "marked" or "engraved," and this is directly related to your ethical and moral behavior.

Making ethical choices usually involves three factors or levels: the law, fairness, and your conscience (Anderson & Bolt, 2008). You might also consider adding three other levels: time, pride, and publicity. When you are faced with

If given the opportunity to cheat in order to make a good grade, what would you do?

Shutterstock

a challenging professional or personal decision, ask yourself these vitally important questions: "Is it legal, is it fair, can I live with my decision, is this decision in my long-term best interest, could I tell my mama about it, and how would I feel if this showed up on the front page of the newspaper?" These questions will keep you on the right path if you just listen to your inner voice.

If you can answer yes to all six questions, this decision would most likely be in your best interest and the best interest of those around you. Ethics always includes the best interest of other people—not just yourself!

BE PROUD OF YOUR NAME AND REPUTATION

How Do You Build a Fine Reputation?

What's in a name? Smith. Johnson. Alexander. Ortiz. Aharonian. Brannon. "Nothing, really," you might say. "It's just a name. It was given to me when I was born." Few statements could be further from the truth. The pride that you have in your name and how protective you are of your name (your reputation) will drive many of your decisions. If you don't care what others think about your name or if your name has no value to you, then your decisions and actions will reflect this. If you are fiercely protective of your name's standing and meaning, your decisions and actions will reflect this. Having pride in your name and your reputation is paramount in considering ethics, integrity, and character.

Consider the play *The Crucible,* by Arthur Miller. It was written in 1953 and set in Salem, Massachusetts, during the 1692 witch trials. However, the play is really Miller's statement on McCarthyism in the United States (Congressman Joseph McCarthy's Committee on Un-American Activities intended to sniff out any Communists in the United States, and, in the process, ruined the lives and livelihoods of many innocent people.)

John Proctor, a main character in the play, is a husband, father, and farmer and one of the people accused of being a witch. Later in the play, he is convicted of witchcraft and sentenced to hang. During the last act of the play, another character from the play, Reverend Hale, begs those accused to confess to witchcraft so that they can be cleansed and not put to death. Hale sends John's wife, Elizabeth to try to convince him to confess so that he can save his life for the sake of his family. Reluctantly, he agrees to confess to the false charge and admits to witchcraft. Later, when he learns that the judges in the matter confession to the church door for all of Salem to see, he recants and refuses to confess.

> Your character is determined by how you treat people who can do you no good and how you treat people who can't fight back.
>
> —Abigail Van Buren

When the judges hear of this, they are angry and frustrated. They cannot understand why he won't simply sign the paper and choose life. They confront him again. Again, he refuses. In an angry confrontation, one judge, trying again to make him sign the paper, says, "I must have good and legal proof . . . explain to me, Mr. Proctor, why you will not let . . ."

To this, Proctor interrupts in a passionate, soul-wrenching scream, "Because it is my name! Because I cannot have another in my life . . . How am I to live without my name? I have given you my soul; leave me my name."

When you care this passionately about your reputation and character, your life is governed by protecting your name. Your actions, beliefs, and decisions are all tied to the belief, "My name and my reputation matter and I will do nothing to bring shame or embarrassment to them."

To protect your name and reputation, when in doubt about what to do, reflect on the Six Levels of Ethical Decision Making (Figure 2.1). You might also consider the following tips:

- Define what is right *before* you are faced with an ethical decision.
- Have faith in what you know to be right and just.
- Trust your heart and your conscience and that nagging little feeling in the pit of your stomach.

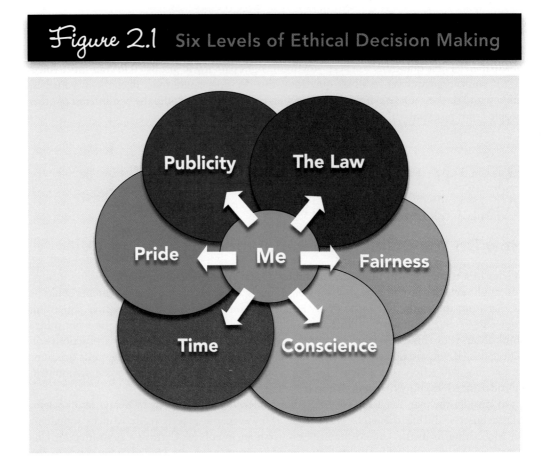

Figure 2.1 Six Levels of Ethical Decision Making

- Don't let your desires for bigger, better, faster, prettier, and greener cloud your judgment.
- Never let competition or the "need to win" overtake your knowledge of what you know is right.

DEVELOPING A STRONG MORAL CHARACTER

Why Is Character Important in the Workplace?

The word *morality* is associated with many terms such as ethics, principles, decency, honesty, integrity, honor, virtue, and goodness. So, what does it mean to have a strong moral character? As mentioned earlier, the word *character* comes from the Greek *charakter*, which means "to stamp or engrave." Therefore, in today's terms, your character is defined by the "markings or stamping" of honesty, virtue, decency, and goodness.

You might be asking yourself, "Why does character matter in the workplace?" Character matters because it is important that your employer be able to trust you, to know that you will keep your word and that you will honor the company's confidentiality policy. Character also matters because many professions require that records and information be kept private. If your character is suspect and you can't be trusted, most likely you will not remain employed very long.

Every time you make a choice, you choose your character.

—Unknown

Figure 2.2 Six Pillars of Character

Trustworthiness

Be honest • Don't deceive, cheat, or steal • Be reliable—do what you say you'll do • Have the courage to do the right thing • Build a good reputation • Be loyal—stand by your family, friends, and country

Respect

Treat others with respect • Be tolerant of differences • Use good manners, not bad language • Be considerate of the feelings of others • Don't threaten, hit, or hurt anyone • Deal peacefully with anger, insults, and disagreements

Responsibility

Do what you are supposed to do • Persevere: keep on trying! • Always do your best • Use self-control • Be self-disciplined • Think before you act—consider the consequences • Be accountable for your choices

Fairness

Play by the rules • Take turns and share • Be open-minded; listen to others • Don't take advantage of others • Don't blame others carelessly

Caring

Be kind • Be compassionate and show you care • Express gratitude • Forgive others • Help people in need

Citizenship

Do your share to make your school and community better • Cooperate • Get involved in community affairs • Stay informed; vote • Be a good neighbor • Obey laws and rules • Respect authority • Protect the environment

> *Always do right—this will gratify some people and astonish the rest.*
>
> —Mark Twain

Source: © 2011 CHARACTER COUNTS! The definitions of the Six Pillars of Character are reprinted with permission. Los Angeles: Josephson Institute of Ethics. www.charactercounts.org.

The CHARACTER COUNTS! Coalition, a project of the Josephson Institute of Ethics, suggests that there are Six Pillars of Character, as shown in Figure 2.2. By employing these Six Pillars of Character, you can begin to develop a strong moral character that will carry you far in the world of work and in your personal life as well.

Develop an Excellent Work Ethic

If you are in the right job, you will love your work and look forward to going to your workplace, and you will most likely demonstrate an excellent work ethic. Your work ethic is how you perform at work without a job description and without being told to do so. Your work ethic is not tied to what you do for a raise, what you do to impress others, or what you do to be promoted. Your work ethic is what you do at work because you know it is the right and just thing to do. Pride, ownership, and honor all play a role in one's work ethic.

Your work ethic can also be defined by how you approach the day. Do you only do what is required of you and the things that are laid out in your formal job description, or are you willing

Catherine Schleigh
Graduate!
The Katherine Gibbs School, Norristown, PA
Career: Customer Service Coordinator,
FedEx/Kinkos, Inc.

The most important thing I learned when interviewing was to truly assess my capabilities, my talents, and my skills. I learned that a resumé was not about big fancy words, but rather about being truthful and making your skills, training, and education stand out. I learned that you have to sell yourself as a product in this world.

to go "beyond" based on your own initiative and values? Do you bring a sense of energy and optimism to the workplace on a daily basis? Do you enjoy your colleagues and do all that you can to assist them without thinking of the rewards? Do you feel like what you do for a vocation is contributing to the good and whole of humanity? All of these questions get at the heart of the matter with regards to work ethic.

A work ethic is a set of values based on the ideals of hard work and discipline. Building a reliable work ethic means training yourself to follow these values. Training yourself so that work becomes automatic instead of a struggle. According to Lifehack (2007), work ethic is based on four habits:

- Persistence
- Focus
- Do it now
- Do it right

What strategies do you need to use to build positive relationships at work?

Stockbyte/Jupiter Images

With **persistence**, you are building a habit of working until the job is completed. Some days you may have to work 12 hours, whereas other days you may only have to work for seven hours. Persistence involves doing whatever it takes to get the job done.

Focus involves having clarity (and persistence) while working on a task. Focusing for one hour is better than working in a cloud for eight hours. Focus means that you have taken every precaution to eliminate distractions, interruptions, and needless wandering. An important part of focus is being sure you have chosen the right task to focus on.

The habit of **do it now** involves eliminating procrastination in your work and personal life. Yes, we advocate taking time for relaxation and joy, but those two things should come only when your work is done. If you procrastinate without completing a task *and* try to have time for joy, your spare time will be filled with stress and worry over not getting the work done.

Finally, **do it right** means that you are going to bring your very best to the table every time you do a task. It means that you have considered that your name is going to be attached to this project and it has to be the very best that it can be. Consider this: If your supervisor told you that your work would be posted or displayed for everyone to see and that your name would be displayed with your work, "do it right" takes on an entirely new meaning. There is only one way to perform a task: the right way!

Dale Dauten (2007) suggests that what is needed now is a "contribution ethic." By this, he suggests that those who make a valued contribution to their place of work are the "rare people who drive the economy and the world conversation." His contribution ethic includes the following:

- Just help. Make yourself useful. You aren't just there, waiting. There's no waiting. Just help.
- Your half is 60 percent.
- Innovation is a subversive activity. You can't expect management and/or coworkers to drool with excitement over your "I have an idea!" After all, most ideas and most suggestions are complaints. On the other hand, if an idea is truly original, then expect resistance; indeed, welcome it as a measure of originality.
- Giving time without attention is a gift-wrapped empty box.
- Being right is overrated. If your goal is usefulness, then what matters is progress.
- Being wrong is underrated. Admitting you were wrong is wisdom gained.
- Always bring something to read that is related to improving your job performance and yourself as a person.
- Think like a hero; work like an artist. When kindly attention meets curiosity, you move gracefully through the world. (Copyright © Dale Dauten, dauten.com)

POSITIVE HABITS *at Work*

Work hard to be a person who always gives more than is expected, works harder than is required, contributes more than you are obliged to do, and complains less than everyone else. Be the person who does the right thing just because it's right. "Just do it" is a very good motto.

THE IMPORTANCE OF RESPECT

How Do I Earn Respect?

The world is full of powerful people who have no respect. Conversely, the world is filled with people who have an abundance of respect, but no power and little money. Why? Because most people confuse the two or have no idea what either means. Few people understand that true respect can only be earned. Yes, there are people who think they are respected, but unless it was earned, they are only fooling themselves if they believe their respect is real or meaningful.

Respect can be earned many ways, including the following:

- Giving respect to others
- Being fair
- Being honest, even in difficult times
- Doing the right thing
- Listening
- Asking for opinions and suggestions and creating ownership
- Empowering others
- Standing up for those you see mistreated
- Helping others reach their dreams and goals
- Practicing open communication
- Being knowledgeable and constantly learning more
- Owning your mistakes and admitting when you are wrong
- Maintaining your principles, even when things are turbulent
- Treating people who are in positions lower than yours respectfully and honorably

Each of these acts shows that you care about not only other people, but that you care about yourself as well. If you think about your actions and what they mean to another person and your place of employment, you

Change occurs, progress is made, and difficulties resolved if people merely do the right thing. And rarely do people not know what is the right thing to do.
—Father Hessburg, Notre Dame University

will begin earning the respect of those around you. Respect is not an immediate gift to you from others. Respect comes with time, proven trust, open communication, and living a life above reproach. Respect is always earned.

AVOIDING MORAL BANKRUPTCY

Is The Price Worth the Prize?

You know who they are—the people you've met in your personal and professional life who will do anything, say anything, avoid anything, betray anyone, and change like a chameleon to get what they want. Seldom do we have positive or endearing things to say about these people because we see them as morally bankrupt. They have no scruples, no values, no guiding belief system, and no loyalty.

But worst of all, they have no continuity. You can't depend on them for anything because while you may have witnessed them being loyal or displaying values one day, you also saw them toss their loyalty and values aside for the sake of personal gain. They change from day to day, trying to carve out a power base, a leadership position, a promotion, or even to maintain their own status quo. Morally bankrupt people are impossible to befriend, depend on, or trust because you never know who they are from day to day.

Seldom do morally bankrupt people see themselves as "broken." They say to themselves, "I have done nothing to break the law or disobey the rules of our company." This may be completely true, but morality and integrity involve much more than following the written law or adhering to company policy. While those two factors are important, you need to understand that they are not the only two factors that make you moral and give you integrity.

There are many indicators to identify behaviors and traits of a morally bankrupt person, but the following are the most prominent:

How do you think this young woman will feel when others find out that she has been in jail?

Rhoda Sidney/PH College

- **They have unhealthy self-esteem.** Morally bankrupt people care little about themselves because they do not respect themselves; therefore, they cannot care about you or respect you. They value themselves so little that they can't even see how their actions damage their credibility and reputation.

- **They lack courage.** Morally bankrupt people only have the courage to stand up for what is right for them. They do not stand up for what is simply right. Courage is a quality of strong people, and morally bankrupt people are weak.

- **They use poor judgment.** Just as is the case with courage, morally bankrupt people make judgments and decisions that only affect them in a positive way. They base their judgments more on personal gain and loss than on right and wrong.

- **They are always looking for more (especially money).** Morally bankrupt people never have enough. They cannot be satisfied with abundance; they have to have super-abundance. They are driven by the pursuit of money or power and they will stop at nothing to have more of both.

- **They are untruthful.** "Truth is an expendable commodity to the morally bankrupt person" (Sherfield, 2004). Winning, money, power, and status always trump truth.

- **They are jealous and arrogant.** If morally bankrupt people see that you have more than them—more respect, more power, more money, a nicer car, a bigger home, more friends—they will work with diligence to take this from you, or at best, outdo you. They use what little status or power they have to make you look small so that

The hottest places in hell are reserved for those who, in times of great moral crisis, maintained their neutrality.

—Dante

your accomplishments pale in comparison to what they have. They mistakenly believe that by diminishing you, they improve their own stature.

- **They practice deception and betrayal.** Deception and betrayal are not necessarily loud and obvious. Morally bankrupt people know how to practice quiet deception and hushed betrayal. They will stab anyone in the back to get what they want and to advance as far as they can. They use blame, shame, and lies to quietly turn the tides in their favor. Often these people get other people to do their dirty work so they can keep up their outward appearances.

- **They are unfair.** *Fairness* is an unknown word to morally bankrupt people—unless, of course, the unfair act is directed toward them. They have learned how to convince themselves that any means justify a positive end for themselves—and fairness simply does not fit into the equation.

- **They put self-interest ahead of everything.** Self-interest is not a bad or morally wrong trait. In fact, it can be good and healthy to look out for yourself. However, when your every thought, action, and decision is based on what is good and right for you, this can be dangerous and immoral. When you look out for others and help them along, they will help you along.

We do not mean to suggest that every person with whom you come into contact will be morally bankrupt. In fact, the opposite is probably true. There are countless wonderful, remarkable, talented, truthful, honest people in the world of work and you will meet many of them. It is important, however, that you know the signs of moral bankruptcy so that you can avoid the personal and professional pitfalls of this deadly characteristic.

> 'tain't no law on earth dat can make a man be decent if it ain't in 'em.
> —Zora Neale Hurston, "Sweat"

THE IMPORTANCE OF TRUSTWORTHINESS

How Do I Earn Trust?

Whether choosing a mate or someone to work closely with, trust really matters. University of Florida research finds that of all major character traits, people value trustworthiness the most in others (http://news.ufl.edu/2007/10/03/trustworthiness).

There are two types of people in the world: those who distrust everyone until it is proven they **can be trusted,** and those who trust everyone until it is proven that they **cannot be trusted.** Neither is right nor wrong, but rather a fact of life. Gaining trust and giving trust are both about time. It either happens immediately or is built over time.

Trustworthiness is a quality that most people admire and want in friends, employees, and coworkers. People want to know that you can be trusted to keep your word, that you adhere to moral standards, do what is right, remain ethical under dire pressure, and tell the truth even in times of struggle. If you are perceived as trustworthy, you will most likely be treated with respect and admiration. Trustworthiness earns respect and can be earned by acts as simple as delivering packages when you said you would or as complex as being loyal to your coworkers even when they are in trouble. Consider the following factors that promote trustworthiness.

> Watch your thoughts; they become words. Watch your words; they become actions. Watch your actions; they become habits. Watch your habits; they become character. Watch your character; it becomes your destiny.
> —Frank Outlaw

A Trustworthy Person:

1. Is truthful even in times of personal turmoil
2. Does the right thing even if it's not popular
3. Is courageous and does what they say they will do
4. Listens to his or her conscience

5. Supports and protects family, friends, and community
6. Works hard to build and maintain his or her reputation
7. Seeks advice from others when in doubt about the right thing
8. Is honorable in all actions
9. Does not go against his or her personal beliefs or ethics for gain
10. Constantly tries to improve

HONORING YOUR COMMITMENTS
Why Is It Important to Do What You Say You Will Do?

Commitments are a vital and real part of trust and character. Learning to honor your commitments is perhaps one of the most mature, rational, and loving things that you can do in this world. You should always think deeply and consider all angles before you make a commitment to another person—whether that commitment is picking up your friend from work or marrying a loved one. There are no degrees of commitment. It is black and white. Either you keep your word or you do not. You can't be a little pregnant, you can't be a little dead, and you can't be somewhat committed.

Making a commitment, whether in writing or verbal, means that you pledge to do something mutually agreed on. You can (and should) also have commitments with yourself. A commitment is an obligation. Some people consider the word *obligation* to be negative and restrictive. Yes, it can be, but you should view both commitment and obligation as an anchor. They are the characteristics that ground us—the qualities that make life worth living. When we are committed to others and ourselves, our lives begin to have purpose and meaning. Without commitment, we are kites in the wind with no strings attached. We are not connected to anyone or anything.

Strangely, however, being "anchored down" through a commitment or obligation is one of the most liberating feelings on earth. With commitment, we are still kites, free to fly and float and wander, but we are tethered to the earth and the people we love.

People who honor their commitments enjoy a variety of benefits that both enrich and improve the quality of life. For example, people who make a full and lasting commitment to their personal goals are among some of the most successful and notable in history (Arkoff, 1995).

Lee Foster/Alamy

Vincent Van Gogh, considered one of the world's greatest painters, only sold one of his works during his lifetime. He did not let this deter him from painting. Recently, a Van Gogh painting sold for over 75 million dollars. He was committed to his profession and his talents.

Zuma Press/Newscom

Lucille Ball was dismissed from drama school because her teacher thought she was too shy to ever do any effective stage work. She went on to earn 13 Emmys, was a Kennedy Center Honoree, and was awarded the Presidential Medal of Freedom. She was committed to her profession and her talents.

Photos 12/Alamy

The Beatles were turned down by Decca Recording Studio because the company's executives did not like their sound and felt that the guitar was a thing of the past. The Beatles went on to have over 40 number-one hits, sold over one billion songs worldwide, and are listed as the most successful recording act of all time. They were committed to their profession and their talents.

Michael Jordan was cut from his high school varsity basketball team and went home in tears. He later went on to join the Chicago Bulls, was named as the NBA's Most Valuable Player, holds

Greg Forwreck/Ai Wire Photo/Newscom

the NBA record for highest career regular season scoring average, and is considered by most basketball aficionados as the greatest basketball player of all time. He was committed to his profession and his talents.

Commitment, then, is a powerful and dynamic quality that can sustain you in times of doubt, lift you in times of defeat, inspire you in times of creative stillness, and guide you in times of turbulence. If you work to honor your commitments, the rewards will be powerful.

YOUR PERSONAL GUIDING STATEMENT AND INTEGRITY PLAN

What Philosophy Guides Your Actions?

You're wearing a t-shirt to class. It is not your normal, run-of-the-mill t-shirt, however. You designed this t-shirt for everyone to see and read. It is white with bright red letters. On the front of the t-shirt is written your personal guiding statement—the words by which you live. The words that govern your life. What will your t-shirt read? Perhaps you will use the golden rule, "Do unto others . . ." It might be an adaptation of the Nike slogan, "Just do it," or it might be something more profound such as, "I live my life to serve others and to try to make others' lives better."

Whatever your guiding statement, it must be yours. It can't be your parents', your professor's, or your best friend's statement. It must be based on something you value and it must be strong enough to motivate and carry you in tough times. Your guiding statement must be so powerful that it will literally *guide you* when you are ethically challenged, broke, alone, angry, hurt, sad, or feeling vindictive. It is a statement that will guide you in relationships with family, friends, spouses, partners, or would-be love interests. It is a statement that will earn you respect and rewards in the world of work.

As you've been reading, have you thought of your statement? If you already have a statement, great! However, if you do not, you are not alone. This is a very difficult question and most likely, you've never been asked to develop a guiding statement before. It may take you some time to write your statement, and this section is included to help you. Focus on keywords that are part of your personal makeup and character as you write your guiding statement.

For example, you may have chosen the words *respect, giving,* and *optimistic* as keywords that you value. These words become a basis for your guiding statement and might read something like this:

> "I will live my life as a positive, upbeat, motivated person who respects others and enjoys giving to others on a daily basis."

If you chose the words *integrity, truth,* and *fairness,* your statement may read something like:

> "My integrity is the most important value in my life and I will never act in any way that compromises it. I will be truthful, fair, and honest in all my endeavors."

As you can see, if one of these statements was your guiding statement, and you truly lived your life by that statement, your actions would be in alignment with your values. This is the purpose of a guiding statement—to give you direction and support in difficult, troubling times.

In the space on the next page, write the most important words you can think of that describe your values and strengths. You may want to review the list on page 9.

BIGGEST INTERVIEW *Blunders*

Michael was asked by the interview committee, "Suppose we offered you a position here at Ace Medical Supplies tomorrow with a 12-month contract. Then, in three months, another company offered you more money to move to their company. What would you do?" Michael responded, "Well, I hope you would understand that I have my family to consider and I'd have to seriously consider taking the other position. I know I'm under contract and all, but seriously, my future is important, too." The committee appreciated his honesty, but not his level of commitment.

LESSON: Once you have accepted a position and gone through training, you have an obligation to spend a reasonable amount of time working for that company.

> *I am my choices.*
> —Jean-Paul Sartre

My **dominant strengths include:**   **The most important values are:**

_____   _____

_____   _____

_____   _____

_____   _____

Draft of my guiding statement (Take your time and be sincere. You will need this statement to complete the following section.)

_____

_____

_____

_____

_____

How Will Your Guiding Statement Help:

With your overall job search plan?

_____

_____

_____

If you have a disagreement with your supervisor at work?

_____

_____

_____

If you are asked to do something at work with which you fundamentally disagree?

_____

_____

_____

If you are having a disagreement with someone for whom you care deeply (friend, spouse, partner, parent, work associate, etc.)?

_____

_____

_____

Reflections: PUTTING IT ALL TOGETHER

Reflect on the words of John Proctor: "Because it is my name! Because I cannot have another in my life." If you allow these words to be your guiding mantra, you will begin to see a vast difference in how you approach work, relationships, commitment, fairness, and ethics. Being proud of yourself and your work is a powerfully important aspect of being fulfilled and happy. When you know that your moral compass is pointing in the direction of your dreams, you will have no trouble sleeping at night—or getting up in the morning.

DIGITAL BRIEFCASE

USING SOCIAL MEDIA TO COMBAT ELECTRONIC BULLYING

Some people have a good job, a nice circle of friends, and an interesting lifestyle, but they feel morally bankrupt and empty inside. In other words, they don't have a good inner feeling that makes them believe their life is counting for something other than just taking care of their own personal needs. We hope this chapter will instill in you the importance of giving back to others. As part of your ethics and character development, we want you to experience the wonderful feeling of knowing you have done something good for someone other than yourself. This exercise is designed to have you focus on helping people who may not be able to help themselves.

Assume that you write a personal blog devoted to combating electronic bullying. You want to find a way of creating interactivity among the people who read your blog, and you want to engage them in actively standing up against bullying via Facebook, Twitter, and other electronic media. One way to do this is to tell a compelling story. Using the Internet, identify a story in which someone has been bullied, one in which the bullying has led to a tragic ending. Develop your own blog if you do not have one and retell this story in your blog. Then list steps that you would like to have people take to counteract electronic bullying.

A good source to help you in developing your blog is this website www.dragonflyeffect.com /blog/model/focus-your-goal/. Another good source is the book *The Dragonfly Effect* by Jennifer Aaker and Andy Smith.

REFERENCES

Aaker, J., & Smith, A. (2010). *The dragonfly effect*. San Francisco: Jossey-Bass.

Anderson, L., & Bolt, S. (2008). *Professionalism: Real skills for workplace success*. Upper Saddle River, NJ: Pearson Prentice Hall.

Arkoff, A. (1995). *The illuminated life*. Boston: Allyn and Bacon.

Character Counts! Coalition (2011). *The six pillars of character*. Los Angeles: The Josephson Institute of Ethics. Retrieved from www.charactercounts.org.

Dauten, D. (March 25, 2007). Today's Work Ethic Just No Longer Works. *The Boston Globe*.

Hill, R. (1996). *Historical context of the work ethic*. Retrieved from www.coe.uga.edu/~rhill /workethic/hist.htm.

Lifehack.org. (2007). *How to build a reliable work habit.* Retrieved from www.lifehack.org /articles/management/how-to-build-a-reliable-work-ethic.html.

Miller, A. (1953/2003). *The crucible.* New York: Penguin Press.

Sherfield, R. (2004). *The everything self esteem book.* Avon, MA: Adams Media.

University of Florida. "Trustworthiness." Retrieved October 21, 2011, from http://news.ufl .edu/2007/10/03/trustworthiness.

chapter three

PROSPER

UNDERSTANDING
FINANCIAL INTELLIGENCE

*It's good to have money and the things money can buy,
but it's good, too, to check up once in a while and make
sure you haven't lost the things that money can't buy.*
—George Lorimer

Why read this chapter?

Because you'll learn...

- To take charge of your financial decisions
- To empower yourself through money management by budgeting, saving, and investing
- The importance of your FICO score and how to build a solid credit report

Because you'll be able to...

- Construct and use a budget
- Make wise decisions regarding credit cards, student loans, and financial aid

PROFESSIONALS from the Field

Name: Kevin Fringer

Business: President/Founder, Collegiate Financial Services

Many people go to work and work hard all their lives, only to end up unprepared to retire and unable to pay their bills and take care of themselves. The best advice I can give you is to learn everything you can about personal financial management. Few things will serve you better than learning about IRAs, Roth IRAs, stocks and bonds, 401(k)s, and other financial data.

Companies and organizations rarely offer pensions and retirement plans today, so you have to begin taking care of your own retirement as soon as you go to work. You should not be embarrassed to ask questions because most people know very little about taking care of themselves financially for the long term. Find a financial advisor who can guide you, but the real responsibility is on you to learn to handle your own decisions.

MyStudentSuccessLab

MyStudentSuccessLab (www.mystudentsuccesslab.com) is an online solution designed to help you "Start strong, Finish stronger" by building skills for ongoing personal and professional development.

TAKING CONTROL OF YOUR MONEY

How Can You Manage Your Money Wisely?

Exactly what is personal financial management? Quite simply, it is understanding the process of taking control of your income and expenses and managing them to maximize your assets. Income is the money that you have coming in—it might be from work, loans, parents, or gifts. An expense is anything that you are spending money on—this includes items such as rent, car payment, utilities, bills, eating out, and the like.

Many, if not most, college students have had few lessons in personal financial management when they begin their college careers. In some cases, parents have always just handed over money when students asked for it or needed it. Most students are ill-prepared to make good financial management decisions. Unfortunately, many students get themselves in serious financial trouble simply because they don't know any better. If you want to learn to make wise decisions about how to save, spend, and invest your money, you can do it. Learning to manage money is one of the most valuable lessons you will ever have, and it is certainly one that you will want to take with you as you begin your career!

The importance of managing your personal finances well cannot be overemphasized, regardless of what profession you enter. For the first time, you may become aware of the importance of maintaining a good credit score, the significance of your credit card debt, and how difficult it can be to repay college loans. You will begin to realize how expensive taxes and other deductions are to your take-home pay. The good news is that you can learn to manage your money well and still have many of the things you want and need.

iStockphoto

How many credit cards do you currently have? Do you use them wisely?

Don't tell me where your priorities are. Show me where you spend your money, and I will tell you what they are.
—James W. Frick

EMPOWER YOURSELF THROUGH WISE FINANCIAL DECISIONS—STARTING NOW!

What Goals Do I Need to Set for Financial Success?

Discipline is extremely important to your financial success because it is much easier to spend than to save and much more instantly gratifying to eat out, purchase clothes, or travel now than to struggle to save 10 percent or more of your income. If you can focus on the following, however, it might help you develop more discipline: If you save now and invest wisely, the time will come when you can have almost anything you want! You can retire early and travel; you can educate your children; you can live in a nice home and drive luxury cars; you can spend money without worrying about every dime; you can give generously to your favorite charity. Delayed

> *I've been rich and I've been poor. Rich is better.*
>
> —Sophie Tucker

gratification is the first key. This means that you delay spending money on things that give you instant pleasure and wait until you can afford them. Starting early is the second step to developing financial discipline.

If you earn the typical starting salary and are totally on your own, you will find that you can't buy everything you would like. Before you rush out and buy a new car or a new wardrobe, give yourself time to understand your total financial picture to avoid making huge mistakes that are not easily resolved. You've waited this long; be patient a little longer until you have had time to evaluate your income, debts, and other financial obligations. If you have never had to manage a budget, financial management may be more difficult than you imagined. You need to keep in mind that you have to be able to pay household expenses, taxes, insurance, medical bills—on and on the list goes. And many students must begin repaying student loans soon after graduation.

In the space below, list the things you purchase on a daily basis that are wants rather than needs. (An example might be a grande size latte that you *"must"* have every morning that costs $3.95. Oh, and a muffin to go with it for $3.50 is nice, too.)

_____

_____

_____

TOTAL $ _____

List three strategies that you can use—starting tomorrow—to avoid these spending behaviors.

_____

_____

_____

_____

TAKE TIME TO PLAN A BUDGET AND STICK TO IT

How Will I Ever Pay All These Bills?

> *The only way not to think about money is to have a great deal of it.*
>
> —Edith Wharton

Most people do not budget. Some have a reasonable idea of what they can spend and how much they require to make the house payment, car payment, food, utilities, and the like, but it is just a guess; others just "go with the flow" and spend until they run out of money and then use plastic. Needless to say, people who do not budget their money and plan carefully rarely ever accumulate much. They are the people who are pushing 70 and older and cannot afford to retire. They have never sat down and decided to live within their income and use their money wisely, nor have they really determined exactly where their money is being spent. As a result, they are often strapped for money, late with payments, and have little or no savings and investments. In this section, we want to help you understand how to go about creating a spending/savings budget. Our goal is to help you become financially intelligent, be able to provide for yourself, become wise about spending, saving, and investing money, and be able to retire comfortably. Budgeting is the first step!

Many people do not use their discretionary income wisely. Discretionary income is the money you have left after paying all your expenses. This is the difference in being financially secure and being broke. The information in this chapter is intended to help you make wise decisions about how you spend your money and to instill in you the belief that money management is an everyday process. If you are going to be financially secure, you cannot afford to live day-to-day and hand-to-mouth with no plan for accumulating wealth.

An exercise follows that is designed to help you prepare to manage your money and make wise decisions by using a budget. A budget is an itemized summary of how you plan to spend your financial resources during a specified period of time. By working from a budget, you will be able to pinpoint exactly what your money wasters are and determine how to manage your money more wisely. Money wasters are items on which you spend money that you could have easily done without—for example, a daily grande latte and a muffin that might cost you as much as $8.50 or more.

One very important item on your budget is savings. The best way to save money is to have this money automatically deducted before you ever touch it. You may think you cannot possibly save money, but experts say that you need at least six months' salary in reserve for unexpected emergencies. You will need to discipline yourself to save monthly for items that may come due only once or twice a year, such as car insurance or taxes. In addition, your savings can be used to help you buy a house or replace an old car. If you have children, you will need to save for their education expenses.

Before beginning this exercise, study the following financial tips for new college graduates (Fowles, 2011).

- ■ Pick your job carefully. Select a job you can really enjoy even if it pays less than another one that you might hate.

- ■ Don't live with your parents. You'll receive conflicting advice about this, but you should not move in with your parents if you are going to spend your money on entertainment, new cars, trips, and the like. If you do this, you are not growing or learning to take responsibility for yourself. If, however, you have overwhelming student loans and you will use this opportunity to double up on paying off loans, it's not a bad idea.

- ■ Buy a used car. You can buy a preowned car that looks new but costs a lot less than a new one. The higher your car payments, the more difficulty you may have qualifying for a mortgage loan. Your insurance will also be cheaper.

- ■ Make budgeting a habit. Budgeting can be like dieting. After a few months, it is easy to drift back into bad habits. Construct a carefully planned budget and stick to it!

- ■ Learn about personal finance. There are so many good, easy-to-understand books about personal finance. Read, read, read because you can never know too much about managing your money, saving for big purchases, and planning for retirement. (Fowles, 2011)

Using these tips, along with the following information, answer the questions regarding your personal budget.

In this scenario, we will assume that you live alone, that you make $35,000 a year, and that you are contributing 10 percent to your company's tax-deferred profit-sharing program so you will be taxed on only $31,500. (*Tax deferred* means that you don't pay taxes on income until you withdraw it later in retirement.) Let's also assume that you have company benefits that provide you full coverage for your personal health insurance and 1.5 times your salary in life insurance so you don't have to spend any of your salary on those items. If you are married and have children and cover them under your health insurance, this amount will be deducted from your take-home pay. Providing fewer benefits is the trend in many companies. When you consider a new job, find out about benefits that are provided for you. Benefits include health insurance, life insurance, dental insurance, profit-sharing programs, free parking, child care facilities, exercise facilities, and others. Benefits that are provided by your company are better than money in your pocket in some cases and may offset a lower salary and actually be a better deal for you, especially if the company pays the entire amount.

First, let's differentiate between **fixed** and **variable expenses.** Fixed expenses remain the same and are items such as rent, car payment, and student loan payments. Variable expenses change each month and include utilities, food, medical expenses, and miscellaneous. Budget for variable expenses by making your best estimate.

For purposes of this exercise, let's assume that you are in the 28 percent federal income tax bracket and that you live in a state that has a 7 percent state income tax. This means that 35

POSITIVE HABITS
at Work

Talk to a human resource specialist about any benefits that you do not fully understand before making a decision to enroll in specific options. You should ask questions until you know enough to make wise decisions. The worst thing you can do is to make no decision. Your future depends on your retirement decisions! If your company has a pension plan or a 401(k), learn everything you can about it and enroll as soon as possible.

percent of your salary ($11,025) will be deducted to pay your share of federal and state income taxes before you get your take-home pay. **Take-home pay** is the amount of money in your paycheck after all deductions have been made. In addition to these deductions, **FICA taxes** will also be deducted before you receive your take-home pay. FICA taxes are deductions from your salary to cover Social Security and Medicare. These taxes are 4.2 percent for Social Security ($1323) and 1.45 percent for Medicare ($456.75) of your salary. (This figure is subject to change on a year-to-year basis.)

When you deduct your federal taxes of $8820, your state income taxes of $2205, and your total FICA taxes of $1779.75, your annual take-home pay is now $18,695.25, assuming you have no more deductions taken from your salary for such things as benefits through your company. Dividing this amount by 12 months, you have $1557 a month to budget. This exercise helps you understand why you can't afford a $50,000 car, for example, and why you should be very careful to avoid huge credit card debts. Because costs vary greatly from one part of the country to another, estimating expenses is difficult, but for purposes of this exercise, assume the following monthly expenses, most of which are fixed expenses and may be estimated on the low side for some locations:

- Housing: $400 (this most likely assumes you have a roommate)
- Transportation: $400 (includes car payment, gas, car insurance)
  - Car payment: $250 (this is most likely a small, inexpensive, compact car that is financed for 60 months)
  - Gas: $100 (if you have a long commute, this could be much more)
  - Car insurance: $50 (this varies widely from state to state and is much higher if the driver has had traffic violations or a DUI)
- Utilities (heat, electric, water): $80
- Student loans: $175

You have about $502 left for food, clothes, entertainment, telephone, cable TV, and so on. Right away it becomes apparent that having someone with whom to share expenses is an advantage. Complete the other items of this budget with amounts that you would allocate if this were your personal situation. Most of these items are variable expenses. How would you stretch $502 to cover these expenses?

- Food
- Medical expenses (not covered by insurance)
- Dental expenses (not covered by insurance)
- Car repairs and maintenance
- Internet/cable provider
- Home telephone
- Cell phone
- Entertainment
- Clothing
- Credit cards
- Education (if you are pursuing additional education or specialized training)
- Miscellaneous (shampoo, deodorant, magazines, etc.)
- Savings/investments
- Day care (if you have children)

This exercise can be painful, but is a valuable lesson to learn as early as possible. The good news is that you can increase your income and lessen the pressure on your budget, provided you realize that no matter how much money you make, it is easy to spend it unwisely on frivolous items that are soon forgotten.

Though you are urged to make wise financial decisions, you are encouraged to enjoy life and not be so thrifty that you don't allow yourself to spend money on things and items that bring you pleasure and enjoyment. If you learn early to budget, save, and make wise decisions about your expenditures, you should gain the ability to spend more freely on enjoyment and entertainment items as your salary increases.

Budgeting may seem overwhelming at first, and you may have trouble making ends meet until you learn to manage your money wisely. Here are a few tips that might help:

- Plan your meals carefully each week.
- Take a list to the grocery store and don't buy anything that is not on your list.
- Buy generic instead of brand-name items.
- Buy in bulk from large discount stores.
- Live at home with your parents while you pay your student loans, if you can.
- Live close to your work to save on transportation.
- Use public transportation if you can.
- Take your lunch instead of eating out.
- Eliminate a land line and use only your cell phone.
- Eliminate cable television or certain add-ons if they are too expensive for your budget.
- Avoid expensive drinks, such as lattes, that have no nutritional value.
- Get a part-time job until you have paid off your student loans and credit cards.

Now, access the Digital Briefcase on page 67 and complete the Personal Budget Planner.

WHAT YOU NEED TO KNOW ABOUT STUDENT LOANS

Why Didn't Someone Explain This to Me?

The high cost of college makes tuition out of reach for many families. For many students, if not most, the only way they can attend college is via student loans. If this is the only way you can go to college, borrow the money—but borrow no more than you absolutely must. Unlike other forms of financial aid, education loans must be repaid—with interest. Still, most students use loans to help pay for college. If you're unable to meet all your college costs through other means like scholarships, current family income, part-time jobs, and savings, then saying "yes" to a college loan is a smart move.

Borrowing Tips

Wise borrowers keep these tips about student loans in mind so that they graduate with as little debt as possible:

- Borrow only what you need to cover education expenses. You don't have to borrow the full amount offered in the financial aid award letter.
- Consider working while in school.
- Look for ways to keep living costs down, such having a roommate, using a budget, and packing your lunch.
- Try to finish your college education in the fastest time possible. Every semester means another student loan.

It's also a good idea to keep close track of your loan debt and, when possible, avoid borrowing from multiple programs and lenders (College Board, 2011).

My education made me marketable and employable. I now have skills that I could carry anywhere. My advice to you would be to work hard and don't take anything for granted. Get a support team at home and at school and get it quickly. I would also advise you to follow your heart and your passion. To work in a job you love, you must love what you do.

Repaying Student Loans

According to Torabi (2011), the median student loan debt is at record levels due to rising tuition costs and has now reached an average of $23,000; many students owe much more than this. If you are one of the many students who has borrowed money to go to college, you are probably concerned about your ability to repay the loans while maintaining a good quality of life after you graduate. Before you graduate or transfer, find out everything you need to know about your loan and determine your options. Some of the most pertinent points about student loans are as follows:

- You have a legal obligation to repay your student loans with interest.
- Bankruptcy will not eliminate your obligation to repay any student loans.
- You should get the addresses and phone numbers of lenders before you leave college. Certain circumstances, such as graduate school, allow you to defer your payments. A deferment allows you to postpone your payments, but you will still have to pay these loans with interest.
- Learn all the options you have for repaying your loans. Based on your salary, expenses, and budget, decide which one is best for you. Do this before you leave school!
- If for some reason you cannot make your payment, let the lender know immediately. This is not something that will go away. You do not want to default on your loan, as this will cause you to have a bad credit rating, prohibit you from holding a government job, and prohibit you from getting a tax refund while the loan is repaid.

Following are some do's and don'ts regarding student loans:

Do's

- Get the lender's policies in writing and read them carefully.
- Consolidate your loans if possible and go with the lender that offers you the most benefits, not just the ones required by law.
- Learn what kind of protection you have if you are late with a payment.
- Conduct an Internet search to determine if your FFELP lender is an authorized federal lender.
- Refer to the following website, which includes excellent questions and information to use when identifying a lender for your student loans: www.sfasu.edu/faid/programs/lenderlist.asp.

- If possible, consolidate your loans while you are in your grace period (six months after you graduate) because the interest rate will be lower.

- Complete your consolidation application and send it in before June 30 if possible, because interest rates are most likely to increase on July 1.

Don'ts

- Don't consolidate with anyone but a bona fide lender—not a marketing company.

- Do not use the U.S. Department of Education as a lender with which to consolidate your loans; they offer a very poor benefit package.

- Avoid consolidating with marketing companies, and be aware that many will use terms that sound like government terminology.

- Be careful about being hooked by a lender promising a cash rebate. The odds are favorable that a reduced rate will save you much more money than a rebate.

- Avoid companies that offer free gifts in order to get your consolidation package. This practice is prohibited by federal law. If a company is using this tactic, they are a marketing company and not a bona fide lender.

- If a lender does not state all the terms of benefits in writing, you should not sign up with them.

What Happens If You Default on Student Loans

As mentioned previously, you have a legal obligation to repay student loans, and nothing relieves you from that obligation. Still, people default and suffer the consequences. Some of the actions that can be taken to recover the loan include the following:

- Your federal income tax refund can be intercepted by the government until the debt is paid. The Department of Education collects millions of dollars in delinquent loans every year.

- Up to 15 percent of your paycheck can be garnished each month (meaning the lender can take this amount from your check).

- The government can take part of your Social Security benefits or disability benefits (though it cannot take an amount that would leave you with less than $750 per month).

- The government and private lenders can sue you to recover student loan debts. There are no time limitations on your being sued for delinquent student loan debts.

There are numerous websites that can provide additional information regarding defaulting on student loans and how to handle it if this happens to you. One site is www.nolo.com /legal-encyclopedia/default-student-loan-29859.html.

The best tip we can give you about student loans is this one: When you graduate, pay the loan off as quickly as you can. Consider the examples in Figure 3.1.

Read, Read, Read about Loans

As stated earlier, most students borrow money to attend college. It can also be said that most have no idea what they are getting themselves into, nor do they understand that it could take them 25 years or longer to repay the loan. This is one of the most serious decisions you will ever make, so read everything you can get your hands on about student loans and proceed with caution. Remember: you don't have to take everything that is offered you. Accept only the amount that you absolutely must have to cover your tuition, books, and other necessary expenses.

> To achieve the things you want, you need to understand your relationship with money, your belief system, and why you act the way you do.
> —Farnoosh Torabi

Figure 3.1 Total Interest Paid

Amount of Money Borrowed Paid by You	Your Interest Rate (Average)	Total Years to Repay (20 Years Is the Average)	Your Monthly Payment	Total Interest (Your Cost to Borrow the Money)
$5,000	7%	10	$58.05	$1,966.00
		20	$38.76	$4,302.40
		30	$33.27	$6,977.20
$10,000	7%	10	$116.11	$3,933.20
		20	$77.53	$8,607.20
		30	$66.53	$13,950.80
$15,000	7%	10	$174.16	$5,899.20
		20	$116.29	$12,909.60
		30	$99.80	$20,928.00
$20,000	7%	10	$232.22	$7,866.40
		20	$155.06	$17,214.40
		30	$133.06	$27,901.60
$30,000	7%	10	$348.33	$11,799.60
		20	$232.59	$25,821.60
		30	$199.59	$41,852.40

GOOD VERSUS BAD LOANS

How Do I Make Wise Decisions?

Credit card companies' dream customers are college students. In many cases, college students know very little about credit; they don't have a lot of cash so they frequently get themselves deep in debt. So beware of strangers bearing gifts in the form of credit card applications—they are the "fox in the hen house."

If you already have credit cards, you may want to access www.federalreserve.gov/creditcard and read more about the new government regulations related to credit cards. While credit card debt can still wreak havoc on your financial position, some of the new changes are a great improvement. The new laws include the following:

- Credit card companies cannot change fees, terms, or interest rates without a 45-day notice.

- Payments must come due on the same day every month.

- Credit card companies must provide information that details how long it will take you to pay a debt if you pay only the minimum. (Pay attention to this one!)

- The credit card company cannot change your interest rates during the first year you have the card. For example, if the rate is 13 percent when you open the account, it cannot change for a year unless it is an introductory rate (beware of these) or if you are more than 60 days late in paying your bill.

- Interest rate increases can only be applied to new charges; your old charges will still carry the same rate as before. (Adapted from Farnoosh Torabi's blog, New Credit Card Laws Take Effect, www.farnoosh.tv/financial-basics/debt-management/new-credit-card-laws-take-effect.)

Credit Card Assessment Exercise

Using the form in Figure 3.2 , list each of your credit cards, the interest percentage that you pay, the amount paid each month, the amount owed on each card, and a comment on how you feel about each card. For example, is this the one that you should pay off quickly because it has the lowest balance? Or should you pay another one off quickly because it has the highest interest rate? After you have completed this form, construct a plan for paying off your credit card debts. This means you will have to do something different from what you are doing now. Will you get a part-time job? Will you pack your lunch? Will you put your credit cards in a safe place and stop charging? Do you need to get a roommate or live at home for awhile?

If you are making the minimum payments on $20,000 in credit card debt at 8%, it will take you 23.5 years to pay it off. At 19% (US average), it would take you 46 years.

—Opportunity Debt Management

An example is provided and some of the major credit card companies are listed. Add others that you may have.

Now that you have a picture of what you owe, make decisions about how you are going to get this debt off your back. Motivate yourself by thinking about how great it will feel to not

Figure 3.2 Credit Card Assessment Exercise

Card Company	Percent Interest	Monthly Payment	Amount Owed	Comments
VISA	14.9%	$36 minimum	$478	Lowest amount owed–pay off first
American Express				
Master Card				
Discover				

have this debt hanging over your head. In the space below, describe your plan to pay off your credit card debt.

_____

_____

_____

_____

The ability to borrow money and to use credit can be very positive factors in your life if you learn to use it wisely. If you don't already have a credit card, you should get one credit card—no more than two. Actually, it is easier to get a credit card as a student than it is as an employee. Once you have a credit card, make a purchase of an amount that you are able to pay in full when it comes due. Do this several times, and you are beginning to establish a solid credit rating. One of the smartest ways you can establish good credit is to charge things on your credit card and pay off the entire amount every month, so that you never pay any interest.

If you fall into the credit card trap of making only the minimum payment and you continue to rack up large bills, you will soon find yourself in a deep hole that will be very hard to dig out. If you make a late payment, your credit card company will immediately raise your interest rate. Not only will that specific credit card company raise your interest rate, all the other companies with which you have credit cards might also raise your rates. All they need is a good excuse to start gouging you!

Credit card companies have implemented new strategies to charge you exorbitant rates. In some cases, the payment window has been shortened, making it much easier for you to be late with your payment. If you couldn't pay your bills when your interest rate was 14.9 percent, how are you going to pay it when they raise it to 29.9 percent or higher? Interest rate is the percent of interest you are charged each month on the total amount you owe the credit card company. This amount is added to the principal, which is the amount of money you charged or borrowed.

An even worse scenario is to charge the maximum on several credit cards and to begin making only the minimum payment.

If you continue making partial payments, the interest charges are calculated on the new credit card debt. So you end up paying interest on the last month's interest too. Thus your credit card debt accumulates rapidly and soon you find that what was once a relatively small amount of credit card debt has ballooned into a big amount which you find almost impossible to pay. Moreover, if you don't control your spending habits, your credit card debt rises even faster. This is how the vicious circle of credit card debt works. (Geyer, 2011)

> *Millions of Americans are attempting to pay off $450 billion to credit card companies.*
> —Alexander Daskaloff, *Credit Card Debt*

Another pitfall that affects many people is the ploy used by credit card companies to allow you to skip a month without making a payment because "you are such a good customer." The credit card companies are taking care of themselves—not you. The interest keeps accumulating while you enjoy this so-called "free" month. You are simply getting deeper in debt, not saving.

While addressing pitfalls, you also need to be very much aware that transferring balances to those credit card companies that promise you a low rate of interest for several months or a year may not be the "gift" it appears to be. This is not the same as paying off a debt—it's just moving the misery around. In most cases, this practice simply prolongs the agony. If, for example, you owe money on that card already, the money you send to the credit card company will be applied to the part of the debt you already owe at the higher rate of interest; you could pay for a year and never reduce the debt you transferred if you are not paying attention to the fine print. Plus, you will pay a fee for transferring the money, which increases your debt. Remember: Credit card companies don't want you to know the real truth. Whatever they are offering you is a deal for them, not you!

The only way to get off the credit card merry-go-round is to stop charging, pay more than the minimum, and try to get the credit card company to lower your interest rate. Call the company, ask to speak to a supervisor, and insist on a lower rate. Sometimes this works.

Be wary of **credit counseling services.** These companies offer to help you get out of credit card debt by negotiating on your behalf with your creditors. While some are credible, many are not. If company representatives say the company is a non-profit, this simply means the business shows no profit at the end of the year, but they can still pay themselves big salaries and bonuses. If you contract a debt counseling service, this may show on your credit report and may call your credit worthiness into question. "It is wise to seek credit counseling through a service accredited by the Association of Independent Consumer Credit Counseling Agencies or the National Foundation for Credit Counseling. It is far less likely that an accredited organization will charge excessive fees or try to take advantage of you, than it is for an organization which is not accredited" (Larson, 2011). For more information, access www.expertlaw.com/library/finance/goodcreditcounselor.html.

A positive credit rating can help you make important large purchases; conversely, a poor credit rating can prohibit you from being able to buy a car or a house. Getting this credit card business straight is so important to your future. We highly recommend that you take time to read some of the references listed at the end of this chapter and take steps to reduce credit card debt immediately—starting today! Study Figure 3.3 carefully for more good tips on how to manage credit cards.

Anyone of the opinion money will do everything may well be suspected of doing everything for money.
— Benjamin Franklin

Auto Title Loans, Payday Loans, and Check Cashing Centers—Dangerous Credit Sources

Don't even think about an auto title loan, a payday loan, or a check cashing service! They are worse than credit card debt! This is highway robbery but is legal in most states. Some state legislatures have made these loans and services illegal, but in many states, you are fair game.

Figure 3.3 Check It Out

Before accepting a credit card, check the following items carefully:

- Look for the lowest permanent interest rate.
- Look for credit cards with low or no annual fees. If you will pay your credit card bill off every month, no annual fee is important. Remember that even the best card can be expensive if you don't pay the full amount due each month.
- Don't accept a credit card simply because you can get it or you are offered a high credit limit. Avoid having too many cards. The more cards you own, the more likely you are to get in credit card trouble.
- Read the terms of the credit card offer as well as the disclosure statement that comes with a card. Check for annual fees, late payment fees, over-the-limit fees, account set-up fees, cash advance fees, and the method used to calculate balances.
- Be careful of low introductory rates. These special rates can last for short periods of time and then skyrocket once the introductory period is over if you are late with a payment.
- Call the issuer and make sure they report to a credit agency—you want any positive payment history that you build to be reflected in your credit report.

Comparative credit card rates can be found on the New York State Banking Department's website and are available to consumers for free at www.cardratings.com/surveyhome.html.

Source: Adapted from State of New York Banking Department, 2011.

The Consumer Federation of America (CFA) is warning consumers to exercise extreme caution when using Internet payday loan sites, where loans due by the next payday can cost up to $30 per $100 borrowed and borrowers typically face annual interest rates (APRs) of 650%.

—Robert Longley

First, let's look at automobile title loans. What happens in the case of an automobile title loan is that you literally use your car title to secure a high-interest loan, usually no longer than 30 days. This means that if you as the borrower cannot repay the loan within 30 days, the lender can take your car and sell it to get the loan money back. Many title lenders will not make the loan if you owe anything on your car.

Auto title lenders often target people with bad credit, low-income individuals, military members, and elderly people—in other words, people who are vulnerable and may be desperate to borrow money. These lenders make money from high-interest loans and by selling cars they have repossessed from customers who cannot repay their loans. If you are desperate for cash, an auto loan may seem like a good idea, but this is a short-term solution and the effects can be devastating (South Carolina Appleseed Legal Justice Center, 2010).

If the borrower can't pay the loan on the due date, many lenders will roll it over, which compounds the problem because the high rate of interest continues to build. The paperwork may show that you borrowed the money at 25 percent (which is exorbitant), but this rate over a year is actually 300 percent. This is worse than highway robbery! Unless you are willing to pay the highest kind of interest rates and risk losing your car, you should avoid these loans at all costs.

Payday loans are simply more bad news. These loans are extremely expensive cash advances that must be repaid in full on the borrower's next payday to keep the personal check required to secure the loan from bouncing. The average payday loans cost 470 percent annual interest. Cash-strapped consumers run the risk of becoming trapped in repeat borrowing due to triple-digit interest rates, unaffordable repayment terms, and coercive collection tactics made possible by check holding. In one state almost 60 percent of the loans made are either same-day renewals or new loans taken out immediately after paying off the prior loan.

Tips for Managing Your Credit

- Don't borrow or spend more than you can afford.

- Pay the full balance on your credit card bill each month. If you can't, at least pay more than the minimum amount due.

- Pay bills as soon as they arrive. In addition to incurring late-payment charges, a late payment can result in higher rates on all your other accounts. Creditors can check your credit report regularly, and seeing a late payment may give them reason to raise interest rates.

- Call and have the due date changed if a payment falls at a time of the month when you may be short on cash.

- Opt out of special services that credit card lenders offer, such as fraud protection, insurance, travel club, as so on. Turn down free trial offers that will be billed automatically to your credit card if you forget to cancel.

- Once a year, order your credit report. Check it for accuracy. If any information is inaccurate, dispute it immediately.

- Build a payment history beyond your credit history by using the services of PRBC. Once you enroll, PRBC will keep a payment history of your rental, utility, and other recurring bill payments and provide that information to the three credit reporting bureaus. To learn more, visit www.payrentbuildcredit.com (State of New York Banking Department, 2011).

Payday lenders use coercive tactics to collect their money in many cases. They might threaten you with negative credit ratings on specialized databases and credit reports. Consumers can lose their bank accounts if they have a record of bouncing checks used to get payday loans. Some lenders will threaten criminal charges or court martial if military personnel fail to cover their loans (PayDay Loan Consumer Information, 2010).

Internet payday lending businesses are just as bad as payday lenders, if not worse. By borrowing money on the Internet, you run the risk of security and fraud. In some cases, loans are directly deposited into the borrower's bank account and electronically withdrawn the next payday. Many of these loans are structured to automatically renew every payday, with the exorbitant finance charge electronically withdrawn from the borrower's bank account. Be aware that these loans are often offered with a clever rebate scheme to circumvent states' laws regarding this type of loan (PayDay Loan Consumer Information, 2010).

Check cashing services should be avoided like the plague because they charge astronomical fees. They charge you a high fee to "hold a check" until payday comes around. We know that sometimes your money may not last until the end of the week or month, but getting involved in this vicious cycle only means losing more of your hard-earned, much-needed money. In a recent phone call to several payday loan and check cashing centers, the fee to "hold" a check for $100 for one week averaged $16.50. Therefore, after one week, the amount owed would be $116.50.

That doesn't sound too bad, but if something happened and you had to have them "hold" the check for a while (that is to say, if you had to wait a month or two to pay them back) then this really becomes "a loan" and the $16.50 actually represents an annual percentage rate (APR) of 430 percent. That figure is not a typo: four hundred and thirty percent! The highest APR for even the most expensive credit cards averages only 21 to 30 percent. Again, we use the word *astronomical.*

If you need extra cash until payday, make every effort to borrow it from a friend or family member. In the long run, this will cost you much less. Payday loans, auto title loans, and check cashing services are highly controversial companies that continue to face many legal battles as well as negative perception by the public. The reason they operate is a simple fact: they are highly lucrative businesses that make money by preying on people who are desperate and can't get money anywhere else. If at all possible, avoid these services at all costs!

> 41% of workers often live paycheck to paycheck. More than half said they would need $500 more per paycheck to live comfortably.
> —CareerBuilder.com

THE ALL-IMPORTANT FICO SCORE

Do You Know What Affects Your Credit Score?

You need to know the score—the FICO score! FICO stands for Fair Isaac Corporation. Financial guru Suze Orman (2007) says, "Just about every financial move you will make for the rest of your life will be somehow linked to your FICO score. Not knowing how your score is calculated, how it is used, and how you can improve it will keep you broke long past your young-and-fabulous days. The way the business world sees it, your FICO score is a great tool to size up how good you will be at handling a new loan or a credit card, or whether you're a solid citizen to rent an apartment to." If you have a high FICO score, you will get better interest rates. Your FICO score can affect everything from your ability to finance a house to being able to get reasonable automobile insurance premiums.

So what is this thing called a FICO score? This carefully researched information based on your credit history, income, and ability to repay your debts is a score that determines your level of future credit risk. Your FICO score is a three-digit number based on your borrowing and bill-paying history and is an important component of your overall financial profile. In general, a credit score can range from a low of 300 to a high of 850. Most scores fall in the 600 or 700 range (Consumers Union, 2007). "Generally speaking, a score of 750 or higher is considered in the top tier. Anything below 650 is at the other end of the spectrum" (Slade, 2011). "How important is all of this? The Consumer Federation of America estimates that someone with a bad credit score would be charged more than $5000 than someone with a good score on a five-year $20,000 car loan" (Slade, 2011).

You may also hear this score referred to as your **credit report**. Your credit report is a detailed collection of your entire credit history.

There are three major credit scoring companies in the United States: TransUnion, Equifax, and Experian. The following information explains how you can get your FICO score.

When You Can Obtain a Free Copy of Your Credit Report

- Once every year
- If you have been denied credit in the previous 60 days
- If you have been denied employment or insurance in the previous 60 days
- If you suspect someone has been fraudulently using your accounts or your identity
- If you are unemployed and plan on applying for employment within the next 60 days
- If you are on public assistance
- When applying for a mortgage

Request your free annual credit report from each of the three major agencies every year and check it carefully for suspicious activity. Order all three reports online at www.annualcredit report.com or by calling 1-877-322-8228. You will go through a simple verification process, and your reports will be mailed to you (State of New York Banking Department, 2011).

Your credit score will be based on several criteria, including how much debt you have, how many credit cards you have, how many of your credit cards carry balances, how long you have had outstanding debt, your debt-to-income ratio, how many late payments you have made, how much credit you have available, and your overall history of paying your debts on time. One of the most important factors in your credit score is how much available credit you have (Consumers Union, 2007).

FICO scores are checked when you try to purchase a car or a house, and increasingly for a variety of other reasons. It is common now for potential employers to check credit scores before extending a job offer, so it is important to know what your credit score is and to take steps to build an acceptable score. If your credit score falls in the low 600s, you might be considered for a loan with a higher rate of interest, sometimes known as a subprime loan, if you are considered at all. You will be required to pay a higher rate of interest, assuming your loan is approved, because you would be considered a high risk. Consider the information in Figure 3.4.

If you are turned down for a loan, you are entitled to get a free copy of your credit report, provided you ask for it within six months of being rejected (State of New York Banking Department, 2007).

If you have already done things that cause you to have a low credit score, you can rectify that by beginning to change your habits now. We highly recommend that you request a copy of your credit report to determine your FICO score, to see if you may have a problem, and to determine

Figure 3.4 The Impact of FICO on Buying a Home

FICO Score	Interest Rate	Payment	30 Years of Interest
500	9.3%	$1651	$394,362
560	8.5%	$1542	$355,200
620	7.3%	$1373	$294,247
675	6.1%	$1220	$239,250
700	5.6%	$1151	$214,518

what the concerns are. In fact, we recommend that you get a credit report from each of the three of the major credit bureaus. Different companies report to different agencies, and you need to get the entire big picture. If you find that a mistake has been made on your credit report, you should notify the credit bureau and dispute the information. The credit bureau is required to investigate. A helpful place to begin is to check out the tutorials at www.bankrate.com under "Debt Management."

Getting the best FICO score possible is very important to your bottom line and can be the difference in paying $100 more a month on your car payment or getting a 6 percent mortgage rather than 7.5 percent. You can obtain a credit report from one or all three companies. The addresses and contact information for all three major companies are located below (Consumers Union, 2007). Use this information to complete the following exercise.

> *I have enough money to last me the rest of my life, unless I buy something.*
>
> —*Jackie Mason, comedian*

Equifax	**Experian**	**Transunion**
P.O. Box 740241	P.O. Box 2002	P.O. Box 1000
Atlanta, GA 30374-0241	Allen, TX 75013	Chester, PA 19022
800-685-111	888-322-5583	800-888-4213
www.equifax.com	www.experian.com	www.transunion.com

Go online to one or all of the companies listed above and request a credit report. If you find erroneous information that could damage your credit, call the reporting company to see what you can do about it. You can receive one free credit report per year by logging onto www.freecreditreport.com.

Summarize the findings of your credit report:

_____

_____

_____

_____

_____

After obtaining a copy of your credit report, determine how you can improve your FICO score or keep your FICO score high.

_____

_____

_____

_____

Keeping Your FICO Score Healthy

According to Orman (2007), there are several key ways to improve your FICO score:

- Pay your bills on time. (This shows you are responsible.)
- Manage your debt-to-credit-limit ratio. (This is the sum of what you owe compared to what banks think you can afford to borrow.)

Everett Collection/Alamy

How can financial television programs and books, such as those by Suze Orman, improve your financial I.Q.?

- Protect your credit history. (Rather than canceling credit cards that you have a good history of paying, just destroy the cards and stop using them; you have not destroyed the history.)
- Create the right credit mix. (Lenders want to see a reasonable mix of credit cards, retail cards, and installment loans. This does not mean that you should accept every credit card that is offered to you!)

Protect Yourself from Identity Theft

The FBI calls identity theft one of the fastest-growing crimes in the United States and reports that 500,000 to 700,000 Americans are victims each year. Identity theft is a federal crime that happens when someone assumes another person's identity. This occurs when someone's name, social security number, or any account number is used for unlawful activities (Federal Reserve Bank of Boston, 2011).

Identity thieves frequently open new accounts in someone else's name. They often apply for new credit cards using another person's information, make charges, and leave the bills unpaid. It is also common for them to set up telephone or utility services in someone's name and not pay for it. Some victims have found that identity thieves applied for loans, apartments, and mortgages using their information. These thieves may also access your existing accounts and take money from your bank accounts, make charges on your credit cards, and use your checks to make down payments on cars, furniture, and houses.

Be especially careful of "pretexting," a method of identity theft that is on the rise. The identity thief poses as a representative of a survey firm, bank, Internet service provider, employer, landlord, or even a government agency. The thief contacts you through the mail, telephone, or e-mail, and attempts to get you to reveal your information, usually by asking you to "verify" some data.

> *Your identity is arguably your most valuable possession . . . but most people pay more attention to securing their car than protecting personal data. Identity theft last year struck 9.9 million Americans, costing businesses and individuals $53 billion, according to a survey commissioned by the Federal Trade Commission.*
>
> —David McGuire,
> *The Washington Post*

Victims of identity theft often find that someone they know has committed the crime. Roommates, family members, and landlords all have access to your home, and it is possible for them to access private information. If you are ending a relationship with a roommate, significant other, or spouse, you need to be especially careful as identity theft often occurs around these breakups. Thieves have many ways of accessing your information, including your mailbox, trash, and directly from postal workers. Home computers can be infected with viruses that transmit your data to thieves. **Be careful about opening e-mails from someone you do not know.**

Group identity has also become a major problem for consumers. This happens when a thief gains access to a place that keeps records for many people. Targets can be car dealerships, schools, hospitals, stores, fitness centers, and even credit bureaus. Thieves may use the information themselves or sell it to other criminals (Federal Reserve Bank of Boston, 2011). They may even copy your personal information from courthouse records.

As you can tell, identity theft is a very serious problem for the victims. Here are some ways to help prevent identity theft:

- Carry only the credit cards and identification that you need at any given time.
- Never carry your social security card or birth certificate in your wallet or purse.
- Sign all new credit cards immediately and write across the back of the card in permanent ink, "Check ID."
- Do not make Internet purchases from sites that are not secured. (Check for a padlock icon to ensure safety.)
- Do not write your PIN, Social Security number, or password on any information that can be stolen or that you are discarding.

- Try to memorize your passwords instead of recording them on paper or in the computer. Never give anyone access to your passwords no matter how much you trust them.

- Have the post office hold your mail in your absence.

- Destroy all copies of documents you don't need.

- Be aware of "shoulder surfers." Shield your numbers when using an ATM.

- Avoid providing your social security number to any organization until you have verified their legitimacy.

- Check your credit card file periodically by requesting a copy of your report.

- If you lose your driver's license, notify the state office of the Department of Motor Vehicles, place a fraud alert on your license number, and request a new driver's license with a new number.

- Until you get to know new roommates, colleagues, or neighbors very well, protect your personal data.

- Shred all mail that contains your name and address. (Identity Theft and Fraud, 2005)

MAKING WISE FINANCIAL DECISIONS BEYOND COLLEGE YEARS

How Do I Stay on Track to Build Financial Stability?

After you graduate from college, many of your financial decisions will change. Instead of trying to figure out how to pay for books and tuition, you will most likely be focused on buying a car, purchasing a house, saving for retirement, supporting a family, and making wise investment decisions. In order to make good decisions, you need to fully understand your paycheck and the tax system.

Plan Today for Tomorrow's Retirement

While preparing to graduate from college and immediately after you graduate, you will be faced with many decisions. If you have not done so already, you will have to make decisions about which job to accept, what area to live in, what kind of home you can afford, whether you should keep a car you own now or purchase a new one, whether to get married now or in the near future, whether to have a roommate or to live alone— the list goes on and on.

Most college graduates deal with this list of decisions, and most make reasonable decisions. This list, however, does not include one of the most important priorities: financial management. Most people fail to give the same kind of attention to financial matters that they do to other major areas of their lives. The average person spends more time deciding which programs to watch on TV than on which financial choices to make. Young college graduates often assume that they do not have enough money to manage, and these decisions will be important only when they are much older. Nothing could be further from the truth! The first day you go to work is the day you should start planning for retirement and financial security!

Before you accept a job, find out what options you have for retirement. Does the company offer a guaranteed pension (not many companies do

BIGGEST INTERVIEW Blunders

John interviewed with ACE Design Company and accepted the job without asking anything about the retirement plan. Later he learned that ACE offered neither a guaranteed retirement plan nor a 401(k). The Design It Right Company, on the other hand, offered a guaranteed pension and a 401(k). Too late, John realized that he turned down a better job even though the salary was higher at the job he accepted. What can you learn from John's mistakes?

LESSON: When considering two or more job offers, give consideration to the benefits package, which may save you a great deal of out-of-pocket cash.

> *Money does grow on trees—
> the trees of patience.*
>
> *—Proverb*

anymore)? Do they offer a 401(k)? Do they offer any matching funds based on the amount you are saving yourself? Planning for retirement is one of your most important decisions. Start immediately when you get that first permanent job! This decision is much too important to ignore or put off until later! If you don't understand the program, get an appointment with a human relations manager in the company and ask questions. You can work hard all your life and end up with nothing unless you are smart now!

Understand Your Paycheck

Many new college graduates are not prepared for the amount of taxes that are deducted from their paychecks. Unless you have worked and paid taxes, you may be in for a big surprise. You will have deductions made for federal and state taxes, FICA (Social Security taxes), as well as other deductions for benefits to which you must contribute.

When you begin a new job, you will be asked to complete paperwork that details the number of dependents, or the number of individuals you are supporting, that you want to claim. If you have only yourself, you might want to claim none. This will help ensure that enough taxes are deducted from your paycheck so that you don't owe money on April 15; instead, you might be fortunate enough to get a refund. The more dependents you claim, the more money flows to you with each paycheck.

> *Did you ever notice that when you put the words "The" and "IRS" together, it spells THEIRS?*
>
> *—Unknown*

You may complete your own tax return or you may seek the services of a qualified tax preparation service to assist you in preparing your tax return. Regardless, you should set up a file at the beginning of each fiscal year and keep your documentation for expenses. If you don't know anything about filing a tax return, you need to talk to someone who can provide detailed advice.

You will need to hold onto your W-2 form, which declares how much your income and taxes for the year were. Your employer will send the W-2 to you or distribute it at work. You should have file folders for medical bills, insurance, taxes (cars and house), home office (if you are eligible to declare one), and any other areas that you might need for completing your tax return. Keep records of taxes that you paid on your house or cars. If you purchased a house during this year, certain parts of those expenses are deductible. Of course, children are deductible as dependents, as is child care. Most charitable gifts to churches, the Red Cross, United Way, and many other charities are deductible.

If you keep your papers filed and organized all year, it will take you much less time to get your tax information together and you are much less likely to overlook something you could deduct or need to report. Take advantage of every write-off you can by keeping good records.

Buying Your First Car

Most people love a new car, and many love fancy, expensive cars. Regardless of how much you like them, cars are not one of the best places to spend your money. Unless you live in a big city with good transportation services, however, a car is a necessity for getting back and forth to work and for recreational purposes. Buying a car can be a very confusing and frustrating experience for anyone, especially someone who knows very little about the lingo and sales techniques used by many auto salespeople. One of the first things to do is to make up your mind that you aren't going to fall in love with a car and buy it until you have done extensive homework. If you know very little about buying a car, comparing one brand to another, finance charges, and the like, take someone with you who does.

Smart money tip: Never buy a new car! Buying a new car is a very poor use of your money. As soon as you drive the new car off the dealership lot, the value plummets. Rather than buy a new car, search for a very good used car that is one to three years old. You can usually purchase an extended

Can you really afford this car and have money left for essential expenses?

Shutterstock

warranty on a pre-owned car. You will get a car that most likely looks like the current model, you will save lots of money, and most people will not know if it is new or used. Not only will the price be lower, but so will the taxes and insurance.

Here are some major points that you should consider when buying a car:

- Do your homework! This is too important a decision to take lightly. Research, research, research! Go to a website like Consumer Guide (http://consumerguideauto.howstuffworks.com) to search for prices or J. D. Power to check on consumer satisfaction.

- Know how much you can afford each month before you even start looking. Should you buy or lease? A deal that allows you to buy a new car for $160 a month may sound good, but what is the residual fee at the end? What happens if you go over the allowed 12,000 miles? Can you live within a prescribed number of miles? If you lease, you will typically have a lower down payment and a lower monthly payment, and you can drive a newer car every two to three years. But you don't own the car, you don't accumulate equity, and you have a limited number of miles you can drive. Leasing is usually more expensive in the long run. Wear and tear on the car can change the residual value (what the car is worth at the end of your lease) and cost you more money when it is time to turn the car in to the dealership.

> The more confused you are, the better chance the auto salesperson has at making a fat profit off of you. Auto dealers are kings of creating confusion.
> —Suze Orman, author and TV host

- Use a payment calculator to help you determine the real costs.

- Take the car for a test drive: Does it have blind spots? Is it noisy?

- Depending on your family needs and your budget, should you buy a sport utility vehicle, a sedan, a subcompact, a compact?

- What is the EPA rating? This is a good indicator of how much gas your car will use.

- How much are the insurance and taxes? If you buy a "hot" car, your insurance premiums will cost you more! If you have traffic violations, your insurance will be higher.

- For what kind of interest rate do you qualify?

- Should you consider a hybrid?

- How well does each model retain its value?

- What kind of service charges can you expect? Some are very high, so find out!

- If you are buying a used car, have it carefully inspected by your mechanic.

- Set your price before you start looking. Don't forget the added fees of title, tag, and so forth.

- Negotiate! Don't ever take the first price offered to you.

- Wait 24 hours before you sign anything!

- Look at all the financing options. They are not all created equal. Credit union financing is often better than many others. Dealer financing is often higher.

- Above all—be prepared to walk away if you don't get the deal you need and want. If anything appears fishy or if the salesman seems shifty, keep looking. (Ciminillo, 2010)

Based on the points discussed above, describe the car that you think you should consider buying. Research information about this car and compare it to others in its class. Include price, costs of insurance and taxes, description, model, and year and justify your decision.

PUTTING IT ALL TOGETHER

Some of the points mentioned throughout this book will have a major impact on your life and your lifestyle, but none will be more important than making wise financial management decisions. These decisions include daily budgeting, credit card choices, retirement options, savings programs, and benefit packages. Making the right financial decisions requires taking time to educate yourself about the options. You cannot afford not to prepare yourself to make wise financial decisions!

DIGITAL BRIEFCASE

ESTIMATING INCOME AND EXPENSES

Now that you have become familiar with the terms and the process of budgeting, assume you have a new job and that you want to begin living on a budget right away. A comprehensive budget planning exercise follows that will help you learn to manage your money carefully.

For purposes of this exercise, you will estimate all your income and expenses. Later, you can plug in the actual amount and determine the difference in what you estimated and the actual amount. All sections of the Personal Budget Planner will not be applicable to you at this point, but they will as your income grows and your personal situation changes.

Use the following steps to identify and estimate your sources of income. For purposes of this exercise, we are going to assume that your beginning salary is $35,000 and that you have no other income. (It should be interesting to you to determine beginning salaries in your major as a part of this budgeting experience.)

- Assume that you are earning $35,000 annually with your first job. This is known as gross salary and is the amount of money you make before taxes and other items are deducted.

- For purposes of this exercise, assume you are contributing 5 percent of your gross income to a tax-sheltered individual retirement account, although you might contribute up to 10 percent. An individual retirement account, often called an IRA, is a self-directed, tax-deferred retirement investment account established by employed workers who earn a salary, wage, or self-employment income. Using the amount of $35,000 as your gross salary, take 5 percent of this number and subtract it from the gross amount of your salary. Taxes will be based on this amount. You would figure your IRA contribution amount like this:

$$\begin{array}{r} \$35{,}000.00 \\ \times \qquad .05 \\ \hline \$1{,}750.00 \end{array} \text{ (amount contributed to IRA)}$$

- Now, subtract the amount contributed to an IRA and you will have your gross salary after the tax-sheltered amount has been deducted. This is the amount on which you will figure taxes.

$$\begin{array}{r} \$35{,}000 \\ -\ 1{,}750 \\ \hline \$33{,}250 \end{array} \text{ (gross salary after IRA has been deducted)}$$

■ Now, estimate your net salary. Net salary is the amount you have left after taxes. Assume you are in the 28 percent tax bracket, that your state income taxes are 8 percent of your income, and that your FICA taxes (Medicare and Social Security) are 5.65 percent.

■ Using the $35,000 salary in the example above and considering that you have already subtracted the tax-sheltered amount, you would multiply .28 times $33,250 to determine your federal taxes.

$$\begin{array}{r} \$33{,}250.00 \\ \times \quad .28 \\ \hline \$9{,}310.00 \text{ (federal taxes)} \end{array}$$

■ Enter this amount in Section Two of the Personal Budget Planner under Federal Income Tax, Estimated Amount.

■ Then you would multiply 8 percent (.08) times $33,250 to get your state taxes and enter this number under State Income Tax, Estimated Amount, in Section Two of your Personal Budget Planner.

$$\begin{array}{r} \$33{,}250.00 \\ \times \quad .08 \\ \hline \$2{,}660.00 \text{ (state taxes)} \end{array}$$

■ Finally, you would multiply 5.65 percent (.0565) times $33,250 to determine your Social Security and Medicare taxes and enter this number in the Social Security/ Medicare Tax column in Section Two of your Personal Budget Planner.

$$\begin{array}{r} \$33{,}250.00 \\ \times \quad .0565 \\ \hline \$1{,}878.00 \end{array}$$

■ Now that you have figured all your taxes, add them together and subtract from $33,250 to get the net take-home pay for this example.

$$\begin{array}{r} \$9{,}310 \\ 2{,}660 \\ + \quad 1{,}878 \\ \hline \$13{,}848 \text{ (total taxes)} \end{array}$$

■ Now, subtract your total tax deductions in Section Two from your total estimated income in Section One, and you arrive at your spendable income.

$$\begin{array}{l} \$33{,}250 \text{ (gross salary after IRA deduction)} \\ \underline{- 13{,}848} \text{ (total taxes to be deducted)} \\ \$19{,}402 \text{ (net take home pay after taxes, or spendable income)} \end{array}$$

Spendable income is the amount you can actually budget.

■ This is the amount after all taxes and deductions have been made. For the $35,000 salary in this example, the net take home pay would be $19,402. Enter $19,402 under estimated amount for Net Salary in Section One of your Personal Budget Planner.

■ It is much easier to manage a budget if you set it up on a month-to-month basis. Now that you have determined your income after taxes and deductions, you can divide this amount by 12 to get the amount you can actually budget.

$19,402 ÷ 12 = $1,616 (This is your monthly spendable income and the amount you must divide among your expenses.)

PERSONAL BUDGET PLANNER

Using the information you learned in the previous paragraphs about figuring taxes, Social Security, and other items, complete the Personal Budget Planner below:

Personal Budget Planner
Section One: Income and Income Taxes Section—Annual

INCOME	ESTIMATED AMOUNT	ACTUAL AMOUNT	DIFFERENCE
Net Salary and Bonuses (after tax income)			
Interest Income			
Part-Time Jobs Income			
Investment Income			
Miscellaneous Income (gifts, etc.)			
Total Income			

Personal Budget Planner
Section Two: Income Tax Withheld

INCOME	ESTIMATED AMOUNT	ACTUAL AMOUNT	DIFFERENCE
Federal Income Tax			
State Income Tax			
Local Income Tax (may not be applicable)			
Social Security/Medicare Tax			
Income Taxes Subtotal			
Spendable Annual Income			

In the case of the previous example, this person would have $1616 per month. Right away you can see that this person most likely needs a roommate to share expenses and that he or she will have to budget carefully to cover expenses until they earn more money.

Now proceed to Section Three of the Personal Budget Planner and estimate your expenses for each category that is applicable. This section of the Personal Budget Planner allows you to track how you are spending your money.

Certain expenses will be paid biannually or annually. Convert these expenses to monthly amounts for budgeting purposes so you can be saving toward the date when they will come due. If they are annual payments, divide by 12 to determine the monthly amount. For example, if your car insurance is $658 for one year, your monthly cost is $658 ÷ 12 or $54.83 per month.

When you have completed this exercise, you will have a comprehensive picture of your annual and monthly income and expenses, and you will be able to determine if you have a surplus or a shortage and can make decisions accordingly. You were provided assistance for the first two sections of your Personal Budget Planner. Using the amounts provided as monthly take-home pay, you should now plan a budget using Section Three.

Now that you have completed this exercise, you should have a much better idea of how to manage your money on a monthly and annual basis.

Personal Budget Planner
Section Three: Estimated Annual/Monthly Expenses

CATEGORY	ANNUAL	MONTHLY (Divide by 12)	COMMENTS
Savings			
Investments			
Retirement (your IRA investment goes here)			
Housing			
Homeowner's/Renter's Insurance			
Property Taxes			
Home Repairs/Improvements			
Food (includes groceries, lunches, snacks, eating out)			
Transportation (includes car payments, gas/oil, etc.)			
Automobile Insurance			
Automotive Maintenance Fees, Repairs, Tolls			
Public Transportation			
Telephone—Cell			
Utilities (electricity, gas, water, sewer)			
Internet/Cable			
Student Loans			
Other Loans			
Credit Cards			
Medical Expenses			
Dental Expenses			
Fitness (gym, yoga, massage)			
Entertainment			
Vacations			
Pets (food, veterinarian, grooming)			
Day Care			
Education			
Clothing			
Insurance			
Miscellaneous (toiletries, household products, grooming, hair, makeup)			
Total Expenses			
Surplus/Shortage (your spendable income minus your expenses equals your surplus or shortage)			

REFERENCES

Ciminillo, J. (2010). Ten tips for buying a car. Retrieved April 2007 from www.howtojoinacu .org/services.tentips.cfm.

College Board. (2011). Student loan comparison calculator: Private/alternative loans. Retrieved March 15, 2011, from http://apps.collegeboard.com/loancompare /loancomparisonintro.jsp.

Consumers Union Organization. (2007). What is a credit score? Retrieved April 17, 2007, from www.consumersunion.org/creditmatters/creditmattersfactsheets/001633.html.

Daskaloff, A. (1999). *Credit card debt: Reduce your financial burdens in three easy steps.* New York: Avon Books.

Federal Reserve Bank of Boston. (2011). *Identity theft.* Retrieved from www.bostonfed.org /consumer/identity/idtheft.pdf.

Fowles, D. (2011). Five smart money moves for new college graduates. Retrieved April 14, 2007, from http://financialplan.about.com/od/college/a/SmartMoves.htm.

Geyer, J. (2011). What is credit card debt? Retrieved March 15, 2011, from http://hubpages .com/hub/What-is-Credt-Card-Debt.

Greentree Gazette, Federal Student Loan Consolidation Program. May 2009.

Identity Theft and Fraud. (2005). Money Matters 101, p. 9.

IRA Online Resource Guide. (2007). Information about Roth IRAs. Retrieved April 14, 2007, from www.irs.gov/retirement/article/0..id=137307.00.html.

Larson, A. (2011). Finding a good credit counseling service. Retrieved April 10, 2011, from www.expertlaw.com/library/finance/goodcreditcounselor.html.

Orman, S. (2007). *The money book for the young, fabulous, and broke.* New York: Riverhead Books.

PayDay Loan Consumer Information. (2010). Retrieved August 5, 2007, from www .paydayloaninfo.org/facts.cfm.

South Carolina Appleseed Legal Justice Center. (2004). Auto title loans and the law.

Slade, D. (March 13, 2011). Don't gamble with your credit score. *The State.*

State of New York Banking Department. (2011). Using credit wisely: What you need to know. Retrieved March 16, 2011, from www.banking.state.ny.us/brcw.htm.

Stephen F. Austin State University. FFELP loan program lender information. Retrieved April 9, 2011, from www.sfasu.edu/faid/programs/lenderlist.asp.

Torabi, F. (2011). Presentation at Pearson's Conference. Savannah, Georgia.

chapter four

GROW

BUILDING A LIFE PLAN
THROUGH GOAL SETTING

Success and happiness are not accidents.
They are created by conscious effort and actions.
—Cecile Peterkin

PART ONE: MANAGING YOU

Why read this chapter?

Because you'll learn...

- How to write a personal mission statement
- To list your key values and the role they play in your life
- To write goals with deadlines and measurements

Because you'll be able to...

- Eliminate roadblocks to your success and understand the importance of risk taking
- Understand the role your comfort zone plays in your life

PROFESSIONALS from the Field

Name: C. Steven Spearman

Business: Vice President, J. P. Morgan/Chase

Years ago when interviewing for a new position, the interviewer asked me, "*Where do you want to be in five years and what is your ultimate career goal.*" My response was, "*I'd like to move to the next level.*" He looked at me with a surprised face and said, "*Don't you want to be President of this bank one day?*" I was shocked. I had never thought that far into the future. At that time, I did not have any goals beyond Friday. My advice to you as you enter your career is to think in the long term—plan for five, ten, fifteen years down the road and do things today that will get you there. Learn all you can, act responsibly, lead with ethics, and your future goals will come true.

MyStudentSuccessLab

MyStudentSuccessLab (www.mystudentsuccesslab.com) is an online solution designed to help you "Start strong, Finish stronger" by building skills for ongoing personal and professional development.

WHY I AM HERE

What Is My Main Mission and Purpose in Life?

First, an important statement: This chapter can change your life! But you have to remember this key fact: Nothing works unless you work. Vince Lombardi, the famous coach of the Green Bay Packers, made this statement: "The only place success comes before work is in the dictionary." We can almost guarantee you that you will have a more rewarding life, a more successful life, and a more eventful life if you will follow the instructions given here. We can also guarantee you that you will have to work hard and stay focused. For everything worth having, you will pay a price. You have to decide what is worth the price in your one lifetime. If you truly want to and are willing to work very hard, you can create the life of your dreams. In this chapter, we will teach you to write a personal vision statement, a personal mission statement, and an action plan made up of long-term and short-term goals.

Trying to decide exactly why you exist and what you want to do with your life is hard work, but it is an important first step in determining what goals you want to accomplish. We should tell you that most people never take this important step, and they never come close to realizing their potential. If you ask a group of 1000 people, "Are you as good as you can be?" chances are very good that not a single hand will be raised. And if you continued to talk to the group, you would find that most think they are using very little of their abilities. So why does this happen? The truth is that most people simply don't stop and think about who they want to become, what they want to have, where they want to go, what they want to do, and what kind of life they want to build. We encourage you to take the following advice very seriously and get ready to see significant changes in your life.

Pushing Yourself Out of Your Comfort Zone

If your personal mission statement and goals are worthwhile and worthy of your efforts, you are going to get pushed out of your *comfort zone*. What is a comfort zone, you may ask? This is that place where you are very relaxed, not challenged or stretched, just moseying along with no direction and not making much effort. You can easily do what you have to do when you are stuck in your comfort zone. Well, we are going to make a radical statement: *If you are comfortable, you are not doing anything but wasting your time and your life.* We want you to start *today* pushing yourself out of your comfort zone every day. Imagine a set of concentric circles like the ones in Figure 4.1. Consider each circle to be a step out of the comfort zone.

To accomplish anything worthwhile, you absolutely have to push yourself out of your comfort zone, and you must enlarge your comfort zone every day.

Bananastock

How can your friends, classmates, and peers help you achieve your goals?

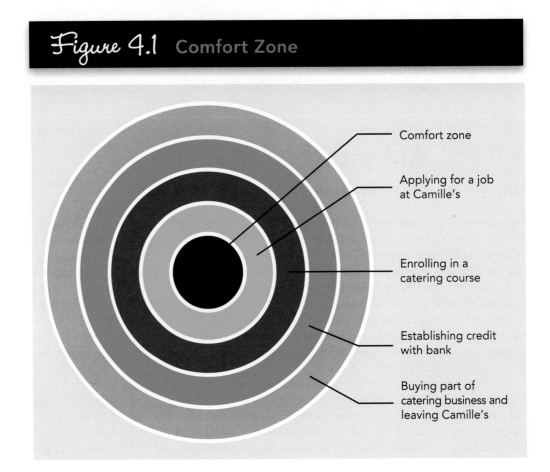

Figure 4.1 Comfort Zone

- Comfort zone
- Applying for a job at Camille's
- Enrolling in a catering course
- Establishing credit with bank
- Buying part of catering business and leaving Camille's

WORKING HARD AND WORKING SMART

How Can You Change Your Life Through Goal Setting?

Have you ever known people who worked hard all their lives and never accomplished very much? The reason for this is that they did the same thing every day, and all along, they kept thinking something magical was going to happen. Their ship was going to come in. They were going to win the lottery. Someone was going to leave them a fortune. You need to know right now that those things rarely ever happen. If they do happen to you, great! But just in case they don't, you need to make something happen in your life. Your future success is up to you. You need to work hard and you need to work smart. And most likely, you need to change.

Someone once said, "Insanity is doing the same thing day after day and expecting a different result." Change means doing something different! Reaching goals means you have to change what you are doing now to something that is more focused and rewarding. Change means focusing on who you are now and who you want to become and then doing something about it. Most people spend more time deciding what they are going to wear to dinner on Friday night than they do deciding where they want to go with their life. As a result, they feel like a rudderless ship adrift on a sea of frustrations.

People who have no goals live lives of grinding monotony and low fulfillment. They have no direction in their lives, and they become very frustrated at the lack of progress they are making. They wonder, "Why am I making so little progress when I am working so hard?" Goal setting encompasses both working hard and working smart—you can't do one without the other. Goal setters have a vision for their lives, and they have formulated an action plan to accomplish that vision. Because of this vision, they know where to concentrate their time and efforts, and they learn to recognize distractions that deter them from becoming who they want to become or having what they want to have.

What Do You Really Value?

Take a little time and think about what and who are truly important to you. What and who make a difference in your life? Your next assignment is to list the things that you value. This list could include family, education, prestige, fame, money, home, beauty, belonging, contentment, daring, faith, harmony, opportunity, risk taking, romance, optimism, love, honor, religion, peace, joy, fun, sports, recreation—the list can go on and on indefinitely—but only some of these are at the top of your personal list. Before you can decide what you want out of life and what you want to become, you have to decide what you value, what really matters to you. After you think about this assignment very carefully, in the space below, write a list of the top 10 things you value in your life.

My Top 10 Personal Values

1. _____
2. _____
3. _____
4. _____
5. _____
6. _____
7. _____
8. _____
9. _____
10. _____

Before you begin writing your personal vision and mission statements, we want you to think about the end of your life, hopefully many, many years from now. Pretend you are an old man or woman and someone is writing your obituary. What would you want said about you?

As you begin to write, just say whatever passes through your mind. Just start writing. Don't worry about spelling, grammar, or sentence structure. For now, you are to think only about the end of your life and what you wish you could have accomplished.

- What did you achieve?
- Who did you influence or help? Why did you do this?
- What kind of character did you develop over all these years?
- Were you highly respected for your integrity?
- What kind of family did you have? Did they love and adore you?
- What did you accomplish at 40, 50, 60, 70?
- What were your passions?
- Did you travel?
- What legacy did you leave for your family and friends to remember you?

Think big! Stretch your imagination! Dream of what you could become by the end of your life, and think of all the good you could do!

Now, in the space below, write your obituary. The sky is the limit!

_____

_____

_____

_____

_____

_____

_____

_____

_____

_____

_____

_____

_____

_____

_____

_____

How can a vision statement help you stay focused and working hard?

IndexOpen

VISION—THE BIG PICTURE

Where Do I See Myself Going?

We want to provide the tools for you to build and lead a powerful, fulfilled life. One of the tools you need is a **personal vision statement.** This is the "big picture" of your life and what you want it to become. To write a vision statement, you have to think of yourself in the future and imagine how you are going to look, feel, and act. "See the person you are; what you are doing, who you are with, what you have accomplished, what is important to you, and how people relate to you. How does it feel to be you? Feel the person you are, your true self. Now, open your eyes and see your life and yourself in the present, through those eyes. You will begin to notice the changes you need to make to honor this vision and lead a powerful life" (Peterkin, 2003).

We want you to become your true self—who you were meant to be, the person you are comfortable with—and to be able to be this person all the time. That takes work! Your personal vision statement should encompass all the important things you want to build for your future life. "Although your personal vision helps you to see into the future, it must be grounded in the present. It is a statement of who you are, and who you are becoming. It is the framework for the process of creating your life. Your vision is where you are headed; how you get there is your mission statement" (Peterkin, 2003). Your vision statement should flow from things you enjoy doing, people you enjoy being with, things you are good at, what you want to become, and how you want to feel about yourself.

Throughout these exercises on writing vision statements, mission statements, and goals, we are going to have you follow Samantha Hawthorne and to be involved with her as she works through her future plans and goals. Samantha's personal vision statement follows:

> I have graduated from college and have the job of my dreams. I am working as the manager of Camille's and am well on my way to owning my own restaurant. I have created a successful part-time catering business. My life is connected to many wonderful people with whom I have positive relationships. My spiritual life is rewarding and calming and provides a compass for my decisions. I am in a great personal relationship with the one I plan to marry. I have become involved in community service through an organization called Sister Care, on which I hope to model my own shelter in the future. I am earning $65,000 a year and am well on my way to achieving my personal mission and goals. I feel happy, joyful, optimistic, and blessed. I can see myself becoming exactly the person I have dreamed of becoming. In most of my interactions with people, I am truly myself. I try to be respectful of other's feelings, but I first try to be true to myself.

Now it's your turn to dream. In the space below, write your personal vision statement.

My Personal Vision Statement

Shutterstock

Can you see yourself accomplishing your dreams?

_____

_____

_____

_____

_____

_____

_____

_____

_____

_____

_____

_____

_____

_____

Once you have the "big picture" solidified, you are ready to make it come true by writing your personal mission statement.

POSITIVE HABITS *at Work*

Colleen began her new job this past week. As soon as she was acclimated to her surroundings and responsibilities, she reviewed the corporate strategic plan and the organization chart. She then started her personal career plan, including her vision statement, mission statement, and long- and short-term goals. Colleen believes she has a much better chance of being successful and of moving up rapidly if she is focused and goal oriented.

PERSONAL MISSION STATEMENT

What Do I Want to Do with My One Lifetime?

Your personal mission statement is your plan for making your personal vision statement come true. Many expert life coaches believe that creating a powerful personal mission statement is one of the best ways to change your life. It is important to get it right because your goals and plans for the future will emanate from this mission statement.

Your personal mission statement should be focused on these things:

1. What is the purpose of my life?
2. What do I value, believe in, and stand for?
3. What action plan do I need to put in place to complement my purpose in life?

Important components of mission statements can be answered with the following three questions: **What do I want to be, what do I want to do, and what do I want to have?**

Samantha might answer the be, do, and have questions like this:

I would like to be a fine-dining restaurant owner, an owner of my own catering business, a wife and mother, a good daughter to my parents, a good sibling to my brother and sister, and a good community servant to people who need help.

I would like to do exciting things with my life, like travel to all the continents and visit all the major cities in this country. I would like to take my family and parents to Broadway plays and scenic vacations. I would like to sponsor homeless children for camps.

I would like to have my own restaurant and later three more of different types. I would like to have my own catering business that will support my charitable efforts. I would like to have a nice home for my family on 10 acres of land with horses and a pond. I would like to have Samantha's Women's and Children's Happy Place, where battered women and children could find a new start. I would like to have financial security when I am old and retired.

Now, you should answer these questions carefully and truthfully. You should please you—not someone else.

What do I want to *be?*

_____

_____

What do I want to *do?*

_____

_____

What do I want to *have?*

_____

_____

When writing personal mission statements, you should begin with the end in mind. Look way down the road and imagine you have come to the end of your life. What will you want to have accomplished? In whose life will you hope you made a difference? What character and values do you want to be known for? Who do you want to be as a person, employee, spouse, parent, colleague, friend? What do you dream of having and doing? If you have ever thought about what makes you happy, who brings you joy, what you value, what you enjoy doing, or what you dream about, you were actually taking some of the first steps in tying down your personal mission statement.

Now that you have determined what is really important to you, you are ready to begin writing your personal mission statement. This might take some time and you may want to continue to edit and adjust it for several days; you might even change this statement months from now. But get started *now!* You need to start with a statement and fill in the blanks with the things you value. Think about what is most important to you. Imagine yourself living a much more enlarged life than you are leading now. Remember, no one can put boundaries on you but you. Don't worry about what anyone else will think about your ambitions and purpose. People around you have no idea how hard you are willing to work or how big your dreams are.

Shutterstock

Do you have a guiding statement for your life?

Having a personal mission statement is like having a compass with you at all times to guide your decisions. You are always pointed in the right direction, and you don't wander around lost. Samantha's mission statement follows. As you can see, it is more specific about what she is actually going to do than her vision statement, which focused a great deal on her feelings.

> I want to start my own business and own several restaurants and a catering business. My plan is to employ homeless people and people who have lost their jobs and give them a chance to own part of the business. When I have established four successful restaurants, I want to build a women's and children's shelter called Samantha's Happy Place. I will use this shelter to teach women how to work in the restaurant and catering business and help them get jobs so they can take care of their children. I want to change lives, make a difference, and be an example to my own children. I want to marry my soulmate and live in the country in a nice home with our children. I want to travel to all the continents with my husband and children, and I want to retire financially secure.

Some other examples of personal mission statements using values follow:

- I want to use my love of physical fitness to start a family-oriented gym with programs for people of all ages. I want to live a clean, healthy life and raise a family with children who are proud of me and who I am as a person. My goal is to help other people learn to eat healthy foods and exercise frequently. I would like to take my programs into schools, and I hope to make videotapes to sell that will help me help others.

- I want to start a plumbing company and own the largest company in Oklahoma City. I want to be able to take my family on international trips and provide them with a good living. I want to buy my mother a nice home and make her life comfortable. I would like to provide scholarships for deserving children who have grown up on Native American reservations.

- I want to use my talents of singing and playing the guitar to become a famous country and western artist. When I am wealthy, I want to use my fame and money to help educate children from the inner-city area of New York. I want to be remembered as one who gave more than I took.

None of these may relate to you—and they don't have to. This is *your* mission statement, so make it belong to you; make it appealing and exciting enough that you want to spend your life working toward accomplishing it. Now write your personal mission statement using the values you listed previously and your be, do, and have statements. Remember, you can erase and change and edit as much as you want to—just make it yours! You can start on this today and finish it next month. The important thing, however, is to think about it every day until you get it right for you.

My Personal Mission Statement

_____

_____

_____

_____

_____

_____

_____

_____

_____

_____

_____

When you have defined your mission, you are ready to set long- and short-term goals, the building blocks and the foundation to a well-lived life.

TAKING THE ALL-IMPORTANT STEP OF WRITING GOALS

Why Do I Need to Write Goals?

Few people take the time to sit down and think about where they are going with their lives when it is a proven fact that having a clear, well-defined, personal mission statement and written goals makes a major difference in how much one accomplishes in life. Most people tend to drift around aimlessly with little purpose in what they do. They simply get up every day and do the same thing over and over again and wonder why their lives seem empty and meaningless and why they never seem to get ahead. They may go backward as often as they move forward. Life is a series of choices, but most people just make decisions without thinking about the ramifications to their lives and the lives of their families. Choose! Choose intentionally! We want you to make conscious choices about what you are doing and where you are going.

Some people have loosely configured goals in their minds and a general direction of where they are headed with their lives, but the roadmap has not been clearly defined, so they detour frequently and rarely ever get to their hoped-for destination. You might compare life with no direction to taking a trip with no destination. You don't have any idea what route you should take. You have no idea what stops you should make along the way. You don't know how much money you will need. You don't know how long it will take. You don't know what to pack in your luggage or what tools you might need on your journey. You don't even know when you get there because you have no idea where you are going.

> _A goal properly set is halfway reached._
> —Abraham Lincoln

> _Experts estimate that only 5 to 10% of people bother to think about their goals on a regular basis, and only 1% to 3% have clearly written goals._
> —Rodger Constandse

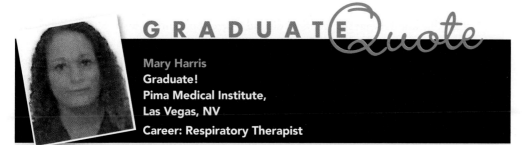

Some reasons for writing goals follow:

■ Writing goals makes you clarify what you really want in life. You have to be specific and you have to set deadlines. You have to do *something!*

■ To be successful, you have to write your goals and take action on them. You need to post them where you can see them several times a day. Goals should not be written as an academic exercise and put on the shelf. You need to see them and live with them and think about them all the time.

■ Putting direction in your life using a list of goals will often bring other associated opportunities. You may even have to rewrite your goals and specify bigger ambitions, and this is fine. Just get started now!

■ Putting definition in your life will help you overcome inertia and the urge to just lie on the couch and watch another mindless television show. You have to do the work associated with goals if you are going to be successful. Merely writing them down is not enough.

■ When you write goals with deadlines and you actually accomplish something, you begin to feel good about yourself and where you are going. You are no longer just doing the same thing day after day, but you are actually moving forward and making conscious choices. Accomplishing goals gives you reason to celebrate! You are enlarging your life!

Writing Long-Term and Short-Term Goals

In the beginning, you should write a rather short list of goals. A shorter list will enable you to experience success that will be motivating to you. As you grow and learn, you will alter your goals and increase your list to fit your current circumstances. **Long-term goals** are exactly what they appear to be—they take time to accomplish. Long-term goals may take a year, five years, or even 20 years. Because they do take a long time, we tend to get discouraged, so we need to set **short-term goals** that are like intermediate steps en route to the bigger goals. Some people refer to short-term goals as *enabling goals*—they enable you to take the steps that help you reach your long-term plans. Short-term goals are based on your long-term goals and should be the steps that lead you to accomplishing the long-term goal. Review Samantha Hawthorne's personal mission statement and then study a portion of her long-term and short-term goals:

The tragedy of life doesn't lie in not reaching your goal. The tragedy lies in having no goals to reach.

—Benjamin Mays

■ **Long-Term Goal 1:** I will own a fine dining restaurant in Portland, Oregon, within five years. (Notice that Samantha said "I will." She knows what she wants to do and where she wants to do it. She described the type of restaurant specifically.)

- **Short-Term Goal 1 (related to long-term goal):** I will secure a job in a fine-dining restaurant, preferably Camille's, and begin learning how to operate this type of restaurant by August 15.
- **Long-Term Goal 2:** I will own my own catering business, Samantha's Catering, within three years.
  - **Short-Term Goal 1:** I will enroll in the online catering program through the local community college and begin learning this business by August 15.
  - **Short-Term Goal 2:** I will work part-time in my neighbor's catering business to learn how to operate and manage this type of business and will begin within one month of finishing my catering certificate.

- **Long-Term Goal 3:** I will purchase a facility and equipment for my first restaurant within 4½ years.
  - **Short-Term Goal 1:** I will save 15 percent of my salary to use as a down payment in purchasing a facility and equipment and will begin as soon as I go to work. I will save all the money I make from catering to use in purchasing my first restaurant.
  - **Short-Term Goal 2:** By September 30, I will begin establishing an excellent credit record with First State Bank by borrowing a small amount of money, paying it back, and borrowing again to be in a position to get a loan.

- **Long-Term Goal 4:** Within 10 years, I will build a women's and children's shelter and involve the women and older children in the catering and restaurant business.

  - **Short-Term Goal 1:** By January 1, 20XX, I will begin volunteering at the Portland Homeless Shelter to learn how to best assist women and children in need of shelter and employment.

As you can see, Samantha has a plan. She knows where she is going and how she is going to get there. There will be no wandering around lost for Samantha! This is just a portion of Samantha's list of goals. Of course, Samantha will add additional long- and short-term goals from other areas that are discussed later as she begins to accomplish some of these goals.

Long-Term Goals

You are probably saying, "Long-term goals? Are you crazy? I don't know what I need to do tomorrow." The reason you don't know is that you have not yet put direction in your life. This is what broad long-term goals do for you. They serve as a compass to guide your rudderless ship. They are like a full moon on a dark night. Figure 4.2 defines areas where you need long-term goals and provides questions you need to answer en route to making these important decisions.

Decide you want it more than you're afraid of it.
—Bill Cosby

After you have identified and solidified your long-term goals, you are ready to think about short-term goals, which are really action plans that you do every day en route to your lifetime achievements. Before you do that, let's focus on writing SMART goals. The acronym SMART is a mnemonic that has been around for quite some time and has been used by many organizations and individuals. Each letter in SMART indicates one criterion of a well-written goal. You can probably locate several versions of this plan, but for our purposes, we are going to define SMART as follows:

- **S—SPECIFIC AND SIGNIFICANT:** SMART goals are detail oriented and will make a significant difference in your life if you achieve them. Unless something is going to make a major difference in your life, why are you wasting time on it?
- **M—MEASURABLE:** You might have heard the phrase, "What gets measured, gets done." This is true of goals. You have to have a plan of how well you are going to do something or how much you are going to accomplish.

Figure 4.2 Long-Term Goal Categories—Seeing the "Big Picture"

Categories of Goals	Questions to Answer
Career	Exactly who do I want to be when I grow up? What do I want to achieve in my career? What level of position do I plan to reach? Have I established a career path that allows me to grow? What new skills and knowledge do I need to develop in order to progress?
Personal	What do I need to do to become a better person? What values do I need to change? How can I improve my attitude and optimism? What work do I need to do on my character?
Romantic Relationships	Who am I looking for as a romantic partner? If I have one, how can I improve my relationship? What are the characteristics I would like to have in a spouse or partner? Who would be an ideal soul mate for me?
Friends/Relationships	What do I need to do to be a better friend and colleague? How can I enlarge my circle of friends? Who needs my help and attention?
Education	Is there another degree or certification I need to earn? What journals and books do I need to read? What seminars do I need to identify to help me gain appropriate knowledge? How can I learn to adapt and function in a changing world economy?
Family	What do I need to learn to be a better parent? How can I find ways to be a better spouse or partner? Who do I need to spend more quality time with? What future needs do I need to help my family plan for? What kind of relationship do I want to build with my children? What kind of parenting style do I want to develop?
Spiritual/Emotional	Do I need to find balance in my life? Do I need to take more time for "joy breaks" with my family and friends? Do I need to meditate and have quiet time to think and rejuvenate? Do I need to attend a religious service? Could I establish a better atmosphere in my home for my family?
Financial	How much money do I need to live comfortably when I retire? How can I discover additional revenue streams? How much do I need to save for college for my children? How can I get rid of credit card debt and student loans? What financial lessons do I need to teach my family? Do I need to take my lunch and put that money into a savings plan for emergencies?
Physical	What steps do I need to take to ensure that I will have long-term good health? Do I need to establish a program of physical exercise? What health problems do I have that I need to work on? Do I need to lose weight in order to be healthy? Do my family and I need to prepare more meals at home and eat healthier snacks? What do I need to teach my children to be healthier?
Service/Community/ Legacy	Do I want to make a difference for a particular group—Girl Scouts, Big Brothers, Boys Club, homeless children, battered women? Could I coach a team for young children? Could I chair a fundraiser for a group? Could I collect bicycles and other toys for children? What do I want to be known for? How can I involve my children in service to the community?

- **A—ACTION-ORIENTED AND ACHIEVABLE:** You have to do something to make goals happen, so action is required. These actions have to be under your control.
- **R—REALISTIC AND RELEVANT:** Goals need to be realistically achievable so you don't get frustrated and quit. They need to be just out of reach so you have to stretch and grow to attain them. Do you believe you can do this?
- **T—TIME STRUCTURED OR TRACKABLE:** Goals need to be guided by a sense of urgency—you don't have forever to make something happen. So give yourself a realistic deadline for reaching your goals.

Characteristics of Attainable Goals

The following characteristics will help you in your quest to bring about change through effective short-term goal setting. Goals should be:

- **Reasonable:** Your goal should be a challenge for you, but also within reason based on your abilities.
- **Believable:** To achieve a goal, you must really believe it is within your capacity to reach it.
- **Measurable:** Your goal needs to be concrete and measurable in some way. Avoid such terms as "earn a lot" or "lose some."
- **Adaptable:** Your goals may need to be adapted to changing circumstances that may be happening in your life.
- **Controllable:** Your goals should be within your own control; they should not depend on the whims and opinions of anyone else.
- **Desirable:** To attain a difficult goal, you must want it very badly. You should never work toward something just because someone else wants it.

> *Whoever wants to reach a distant goal must take small steps.*
>
> —Helmut Schmidt

BIGGEST INTERVIEW Blunders

Latisha had worked in hospitals since she was a freshman in college. Finding a position in Mercy Hospital had always been her goal after she completed her nursing degree. The big day had arrived, and Latisha was being interviewed by the supervisor of nursing at Mercy Hospital. She was excited but calm because she knew she was highly qualified and had good experience. After a few questions, the supervisor asked Latisha this question: "What are your long-term goals in the nursing profession?" Latisha had never thought about this question before, and her answer was not impressive. Fortunately, her other qualifications overshadowed this mistake and she got the job, but she learned an important lesson about being prepared.

LESSON: Before going on an interview, be sure you have anticipated potential questions and that you have thought about career goals, because most interviewers will ask you something about your goals.

How to Write Your Goals to Bring about Positive Change

"I will prepare in every way possible to get my dream job when I interview in three weeks" is an example of a short-term goal. "I will purchase my first home in seven to ten years" is an example of a long-term goal. Goals can be lofty and soaring, but excellent and meaningful goals can also be as simple as "I will spend two hours at the park with my children tomorrow afternoon."

Well-written, exciting, and effective goals include:

- A goal statement with a target date
- Action steps
- A narrative statement
- An "I Deserve It" statement
- A personal signature

The **goal statement** should be specific and measurable—that is, it should entail some tangible evidence of its achievement—and it should have a **target date,** or a timeline for accomplishing your goal. Your goal statement must also use an action verb. An example of a goal statement with an action verb and target date is: "I will lose 10 pounds in six weeks" or "I am going to join a professional organization and get involved by the end of this month." This is a much more powerful statement than: "I am thinking about joining an organization" or "I wanna have a new car."

After you write the goal statement, you'll need to create **specific action steps** that explain exactly what you are going to do to reach your goal. There is no certain number of steps; it all depends on your goal and your personal commitment. An example of action steps for weight loss might be: (1) I will join a gym within two weeks; (2) I will meet with a personal trainer this week; (3) I will join my neighbors who walk a mile at 6:00 every morning; (4) I will . . .

The next step is to write a **narrative statement** about what your goal accomplishment will mean to you and how your life will change because of reaching this goal. For example, if your goal is to lose 30 pounds, paint a "verbal picture" of how your life is going to look once this goal has been reached. Your verbal picture may include statements such as: "I'll be able to wear nicer clothes," "I'll feel better," "I'll be able to ride my bicycle again," "My self-esteem will be stronger," or "I'll be able to do more activities with my children." If your goals don't offer you significant rewards, you are not likely to stick to your plan.

Next, write two reasons why you deserve this goal. This is called your **"I Deserve It" statement.** It may seem simple, but this is a complex question. Many people do not follow through on their goals because deep down, they don't feel they deserve them. The narrative statement helps you understand how your life will look once the goal is met, but your "I Deserve It" statement asks you to consider *why* you deserve this goal.

Finally, **sign your goal statement.** This is an imperative step, because your signature shows that you are making a personal commitment to see this goal to fruition. This is your name. Use it with pride. Before you write a goal statement of your own, review Samantha's first short-term goal statement, which is related to her long-term plans and mission and vision statements (Figure 4.3).

Once you have reviewed Samantha's Goal Sheet, use the goal sheet in Figure 4.4 to build your goals. To help you get started, use this goal-setting sheet as a template for this and future goals.

Figure 4.3 Samantha's Goal Sheet

Name Samantha Hawthorne

Goal Statement (with action verb and target date)
I will secure a job in a fine-dining restaurant, preferably Camille's, and begin learning how to operate this type of restaurant by August 15.

Action Steps (concrete things you plan to do to reach your goal)

1. I will get an application to Camille's by Friday, July 10.

2. I will send my application, cover letter, and resumé to Camille's owner by July 15.

3. I will call Mr. Robinson, who knows Camille's owner, and ask him to talk to her about me and my work ethic by July 15.

Narrative Statement (how your life will look when you reach your goal)
My life is going to be happy and I will feel fulfilled because I will have taken the first step toward reaching my long-term goal of owning my own fine-dining restaurant.

I deserve this goal because:

1. I am hard working and focused, and I know what I want in life.

2. I have earned very good grades in my college courses and have planned for this day all during my college career.

3. When I am successful, I will do good things to help other people. I will always be a "giving back" person.

I hereby make this commitment to myself.

Samantha Hawthorne   June 15, 20XX

My Signature   Date

Shutterstock

What exactly is it going to take to achieve your biggest, most important goals?

Figure 4.4 My Personal Goal

To help you get started, use this goal-setting sheet as a template for this and future goals.

Name _____

Goal Statement (with action verb and target date) _____
_____
_____

Action Steps (concrete things you plan to do to reach your goal)

1. _____

2. _____

3. _____

Narrative Statement (how your life will look when you reach your goal) _____
_____
_____
_____
_____
_____

I deserve this goal because:

1. _____
_____

2. _____
_____

I hereby make this commitment to myself.

_____   _____
My Signature   Date

Reflections:
PUTTING IT ALL TOGETHER

The transition from one place to another is seldom easy, even when the change is what you want. Going to work will give you the opportunity to assume new roles, develop new friendships, meet new people, work under different circumstances, and perhaps adjust your lifestyle. It is an opportunity to improve on who you are at this moment or to build an entirely new person. Work helps you do this. Going to work gives you the opportunity to reflect on your strengths and consider areas where you might need to change. If you begin your career as a goal setter, you will accomplish so much more than you will if you just drift along and accept what happens to you. As you reflect on this chapter, keep the following pointers in mind:

- Evaluate your reason(s) for choosing your career and what it can mean for you.
- Use goal setting to help you direct changes in your life.
- Don't just let change happen; get involved in your own life and learning.
- Focus on the positive by eliminating your negative self-talk.
- Keep your sense of humor.
- Be courageous by facing your fears before they derail you.

DIGITAL BRIEFCASE

WRITING A SOLID MISSION STATEMENT

Although you have already practiced writing a mission statement, you can find more excellent assistance by accessing www.franklincovey.com/msb. Follow the steps on this site and build a mission statement that you can use as you begin your career.

REFERENCES

Covey, F. Building a mission statement. Retrieved June 12, 2011, from www.franklincovey .com/msb.

Peterkin, C. Writing your personal mission statement. Retrieved June 14, 2011, from www .selfgrowth.com/articles/Peterkin3.html.

chapter five

PRIORITIZE

STRATEGIES FOR MANAGING PRIORITIES AND STRESS

*If you want to make good use of your time,
you've got to know what's most important
and then give it all you've got.*
—Lee Iacocca

Why read this chapter?

Because you'll learn...

- The relationship between time management, your value system, and self-discipline
- How you spend your time and develop a "to do" list based on your findings
- How to deal with the major stressors in your life

Because you'll be able to...

- Simplify your life
- Avoid distractions, interruptions, and procrastination in your daily life

PROFESSIONALS from the Field

Name: F. Javier Ortiz B.

Business: Assistant VP, Citigroup

I have 40 people who report to me. I am responsible for completing my own job duties, but I must also do a performance review on all 40 employees every month. If I do not manage my time to do this accurately and fairly, I am not meeting my own position requirements. Time management is extremely important—from showing up on time to being able to manage multiple projects at the same time. My advice to you would be to watch your deadlines carefully so that you do not get overwhelmed. If you get overwhelmed, your job performance will suffer and before long, you won't have a job. Time management is that important at work.

MyStudentSuccessLab

MyStudentSuccessLab (www.mystudentsuccesslab.com) is an online solution designed to help you "Start strong, Finish stronger" by building skills for ongoing personal and professional development.

TIME—YOU HAVE ALL THERE IS

Can You Take Control of Your Life and Make the Most of Your Time?

You can definitely say four things about time: ***It is fair. It does not discriminate. It treats everyone the same. Everyone has all there is.*** No person has any more or less hours in a day than the next person. It may seem that Gary or Tamisha has more time than you do, but that's not the case. In a 24-hour span we all have 1440 minutes. No more. No less. There is one more thing you can definitely say about time, too: ***It can be cruel and unrelenting***. It is one of the few things in our lives that we cannot stop. There are no time-out periods, no breaks, and try as we might, we can't turn it back, shut it down, or stop it. The good news, however, is that by learning how to manage our time more effectively, we don't need to slow it down or stop it. We can learn how to get things done and have more time for joy and fun.

So, how do you spend your time? Some people are very productive, whereas others scramble to find a few moments to enjoy life and have quality relationships. According to time management and personal productivity expert Donald Wetmore (2008), "The average working person spends less than two minutes per day in meaningful communication with their spouse or significant other and less than 30 seconds per day in meaningful communication with their children." Think about that for a moment. *Thirty seconds.* If you think that is amazing, consider the following list. As strange as it may seem, these figures are taken from the U.S. Bureau of Labor Statistics (2006). During your ***working years*** (age 20–65, a 45-year span) you spend an average of:

- 16 years sleeping
- 2.3 years eating
- 3.1 years doing housework
- 6 years watching TV
- 1.3 years on the telephone

This totals ***28.7 years of your working life*** doing things that you may not even consider in your time management plan. What happens to the remaining 16.3 years? Well, you will spend ***14 of those years working***, which leaves you with 2.3 years, or only 20,000 hours during your working life, to embrace joy, spend time with your family, educate yourself, travel, and experience a host of other life-fulfilling activities. Dismal? Scary? It does not have to be. By learning how to manage your time, harness your energy and passion, and take control of your day-to-day activities, 2.3 years can be a long, exciting, productive time.

Why is it that some people seem to get so much more done than other people? They appear to always be calm and collected and have it together. Many people from this group work long hours in addition to going to school and taking care of a family. They never appear to be stressed out, and they seem to be able to do it all with grace and charm.

You are probably aware of others who are always late, never finish their projects on time, rarely seem to have time to get everything done, and appear to have no concrete goals for their lives. Sometimes, we get the idea that the first group accomplishes more because they have more time or because they don't have to work or they don't have children or they are smarter or have more help. Some of these reasons may be true, but in reality, many of them have learned how to overcome procrastination, tie their value system to their time management plan, and use their personal energy and passion to accomplish more.

"I can't do any more than I am doing right now," you may say to yourself. But is that really true? One of the keys to managing your time is to consider your values. What you value, enjoy, and love, you tend to put more passion, energy, and time toward. Do you value your family? If so, you make time for them. Do you value your friends? If so, you make time for them. Think about these questions: How much do you value having a career that you find fulfilling and rewarding? If you value your career, you will find time to devote toward making it successful. *We spend time on what we value!*

TIME MANAGEMENT AND SELF-DISCIPLINE

Do You Have What It Takes to "Git 'er Done"?

> *Self-discipline is teaching ourselves to do the things necessary to reach our goals without becoming sidetracked by bad habits.*
>
> —Denis Waitley

Time management is actually about managing you! It is about taking control and assuming responsibility for the time you are given on this earth. The sooner you understand and get control of how you use your time, the quicker you will be on your way to becoming successful in your career and many other activities. Learning to manage your time is a lesson that you will use in all aspects of your life. **You can't control time**, but you can control yourself. Time management is basically self-discipline—and self-discipline involves self-motivation

The word *discipline* comes from the Latin word meaning "to teach." Therefore, **self-discipline** is really about "teaching ourselves" (Waitley, 1997). Self-discipline implies that you have the ability to teach yourself how to get more done when things are going well and when they are not going so well. If you have self-discipline, you have learned how to hold it all together when things get tough, when you feel beaten, and when defeat seems just around the corner. It also means that when you have important tasks to complete, you can temporarily pull yourself away from enjoyable situations and fun times until those tasks are completed. Consider the chart in Figure 5.1 regarding self-discipline. **Self-discipline is really about four things**: **making choices, making changes, using willpower, and taking responsibility.**

Once you have made the **choice** to engage wholeheartedly in your work, stop procrastinating, and mange your time more effectively, you have to make the **changes** in your thoughts and behaviors to bring those choices to fruition. Then, you have to **accept responsibility** for your actions and take control of your life. You have to call on your **inner strength or willpower**—and you *do* have willpower. It may just be hidden or forgotten, but you do have it. You have the ability to empower yourself to get things done. No one can do this for you. You are responsible for your life and your actions. Self-discipline and willpower help you move in the direction of your dreams.

Willpower and self-discipline are all about **re-training your mind** to do what *you* want it to do and not what *it* wants to do. It is about eliminating the negative self-talk that so often derails us and causes us to procrastinate and get stressed out. By re-training your mind and resisting the urge to simply "obey" your subconscious, you are basically re-training your life. Consider the following situations:

- You come home from work, tired and weary, and you still have to finish a report for your boss by 8:00 a.m. tomorrow. Your subconscious mind tells you to sit down, put your feet up, and watch TV for a while. You have to tell your mind, "NO! I am going to take a short walk around the block to get my adrenaline flowing and then I'm going to write that report."

- You look at your desk or study space and you see all of the books and papers you have gathered for writing your report. Your subconscious mind tells you to just ignore it

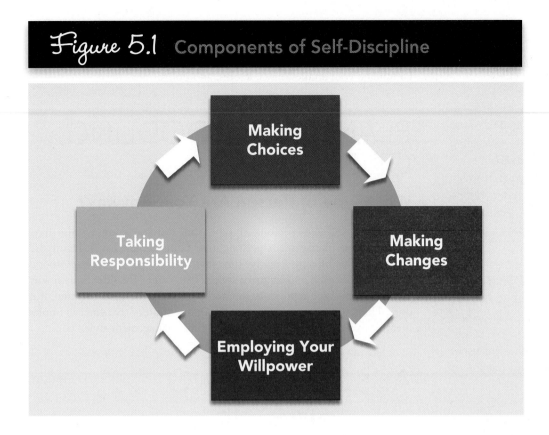

Figure 5.1 Components of Self-Discipline

for a while; there's still time to get it done! You have to tell your mind, "ABSOLUTELY NOT! I'm going to get those materials organized and finish this report before I do anything else so I can get it off my back."

By re-training your mind and paying attention to your subconscious, you can teach yourself to develop the self-discipline and willpower to get things done and avoid the stress caused by procrastination. Willpower gives you strength to stay on track and avoid the guilt associated with putting things off or not doing them at all. Guilt turns to frustration, frustration turns to anger, and before you know it, your negative self-talk and subconscious mind have "won" and nothing gets done. You have the power to change this.

> *Begin doing what you want to do now. We are not living in eternity. We have only this moment, sparkling like a star in our hand and melting like a snowflake.*
> —Marie B. Ray

I'LL DO IT WHEN I HAVE A LITTLE FREE TIME

Is Time Really "Free"?

What is "free time" and when does it happen? We've all used that expression at one time or another: "I'll do that when I get a little more free time," or "I'm going to wait until I find a little more time." Can time be found? Is time free? Do we ever have a moment to call our own? The answer is "maybe," but free time has to be created by you, and it can only be created by getting the things done that must be completed for your success.

Free time is *not* time that you simply create by putting off work that needs to be done. Free time is *not* time that is spent procrastinating. Free time is *not* time that you take away from your duties, chores, studies, family, and obligations. That is **borrowed time,** and if you know the rules of good behavior, you know that anything you borrow, you must repay. When are you going

BIGGEST INTERVIEW *Blunders*

Joaquim interviewed with a business owner of a large plumbing company. The owner interviewed him personally, explaining that he liked to know as much about every employee as possible. He gave Joaquim an intense interview. Joaquim thought he was doing very well until the owner asked him to take a pencil-and-paper test on managing priorities and handling stress. The test required him to prioritize 15 tasks and describe how he would get them accomplished in one day. Joaquim became very frustrated and stressed and finally told the owner that it was impossible to get the entire list done in one day. The owner responded, "This is a typical day's work for our associates; sometimes the work schedule is even heavier." The owner told Joaquim that he appeared to be an outstanding young man but recommended that he work as an apprentice until he learned to manage his time and priorities better.

LESSON: Try to be prepared for real-world activities that might be tested via simulations and other activities. Be sure to familiarize yourself with time and stress management techniques.

> *Time is the most valuable and most perishable of our possessions.*
> —John Randolph

to find the time to "repay" these blocks of time to yourself? Usually, you don't, and that is when and where you get into trouble and your stress level starts to rise. Free time *is* time that you reward yourself with when you have completed your studies, tasks, chores, and obligations.

PLANNING, DOODLING, OR BEGGING

What Type of Person Are You, Anyway?

We all have different personality types, but did you know we also have different time management personalities? Consider the list in Figure 5.2 explaining the different negative time management personalities. Respond YES or NO to each management style. Then, out to the side, explain why you think this type represents you and your daily thoughts on time, if it does. Then, in the last column, list at least one strategy that you can implement to overcome this type of negative time management style.

ABSOLUTELY NO . . . WELL, MAYBE

Do You Know How to Say No?

"No, I'm sorry, I can't do that," is perhaps one of the most difficult phrases you must learn to say when it comes to effective time management, but learning it is absolutely essential." If you continually say yes to everyone and every project, then quickly, you will have no time left for yourself, your family, your friends, and your projects. Many of us are taught from an early age that *no* is a bad word and that we should always try to avoid saying it to others. However, we are not taught that never saying "no" can cause us undue stress and feelings of guilt and frustration, as well as throw our time management plans into disarray. The word *no* needs to become a part of your everyday vocabulary. By learning to say "no" to a few things, you can begin to say "yes" to many other things—things that you want to do, things that you need to do, things that will help others in the long run, and goals and priorities at work that will help you get ahead. "No" is not rude; it is simply a way of managing your time so that you have more time to say "yes" to what is important and useful.

Learning to Say No: It's as Simple as Not Saying Yes

- Think before you answer out loud with an insincere or untrue "yes." Tell the person who is asking that you need time to think about it because you are already stretched pretty thin. Don't make an immediate decision. Buy yourself some time to think before you take on something that is going to stress you.

- Make sure you understand exactly what is being asked of you and what the project involves before you answer.

- Review your schedule to see if you really have the time to do a quality job. ("If you have to have an answer immediately, it is 'no.' If you can wait a few days for me to finish project X, and review my schedule, I'll take a careful look at it.")

Figure 5.2 Time Management Types

Type	Explanation	Do You Have Any of These Tendencies?	What Actions Make You Like This Type of Person?	What Can You Do to Begin Eliminating This Type of Behavior?
The Circler	Doing the same things over and over again and again and hoping for a different result; basically, going around in circles.	YES NO		
The Doodler	Not paying attention to details, doing things that do not really matter to the completion of your project.	YES NO		
The Squanderer	Wasting too much time trying to "get ready" to work and never really getting anything done until it is too late to do a good job.	YES NO		
The Beggar	Expecting time to stop for you after you've wasted time doing nothing or going in circles, then becoming frustrated when you don't have enough time.	YES NO		
The Planner	Planning out your project so carefully and meticulously that by the time you have everything you think you need, there is no time to really do the project.	YES NO		
The Hun	Waiting too late to plan or get things done and then stomping on anyone or anything to get the project done with no regard for others' feelings, time, or relationships.	YES NO		
The Passivist	Convincing yourself that you'll never get it all done and that there is no use to try anyway.	YES NO		

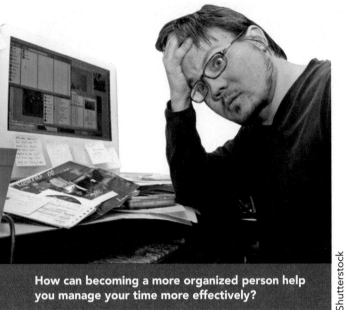

How can becoming a more organized person help you manage your time more effectively?

Shutterstock

- Learn the difference between assertiveness (politely declining) and rudeness ("Have you lost your mind?").

- Learn how to put yourself and your future first (for a change). By doing this, you can say "yes" more often later on.

- Inform others of your time management schedule so that they will have a better understanding of why you say "no."

- If you must say "yes" to an unwanted project (something at work, for example), try to negotiate a deadline that works for everyone—you first!

- Keep your "no" short. If you have to offer an explanation, be brief so that you don't talk yourself into doing something you can't do and to avoid giving false hope to the other person. If the answer is "no" right now and it will be "no" in the future, say so now. Don't smile, because that indicates "maybe."

- If you feel you simply have to say "yes," try to trade off with the other person and ask him or her to do something on your list.

- Put a time limit on your "yes." For example, you might agree to help someone but you could say, "I can give you 30 minutes and then I have to leave."

BEGINNING YOUR DAY WITH PEACE

Can You Start Your Day as a Blank Page and Simplify Your Life?

Imagine a day with nothing to do! That may be difficult, if not impossible, for you to conceive right now. But as an exercise in building your own day from scratch and simplifying your life, think about having a day where you build your schedule and where you do not have to be constrained by activities and projects that others have thrust on you. Think about a day where you are in charge. Crazy? Impossible? Outrageous? Maybe not as much as you think.

Yes, you will need to plot activities such as work, training, and family duties into your daily calendar, but you also need to learn how to schedule time for fun activities, time for silence and peace, and time to be alone with your thoughts. By learning how to build your schedule each evening from scratch, you have the opportunity to plan a day where you simplify your life. There is an old quote that states, "If you want to know what you value in your life, look at your checkbook and your calendar." Basically, this suggests that we spend our money and time on things we value.

12 Ways to Simplify Your Life

- Know what you value and work hard to eliminate activities that are not in conjunction with your core value system. This can be whittled down to one statement: "Identify what is important to you. Eliminate everything else." Match your priorities with your goals and values.

- Get away from technology for a few hours a day. Turn off your computer, cell phone, iPod, and other devices that can take time from what you value.

- Learn to delegate. You may say to yourself, "My family does not know how to use the washing machine." Guess what? When all of their underwear is dirty, they'll learn how to use it. Don't enable others to avoid activities that complicate your life.

■ Make a list of everything you are doing. Prioritize this list into what you enjoy doing and what fits into your value system. If you can only feasibly do three or four of these activities per day, draw a line after number four and eliminate the rest of the list.

■ Do what is essential for the well-being of you and your family and eliminate everything else. Delegate some things to family members of all ages that they can accomplish. Don't waste time saving money. This doesn't mean not to save money—it means not to be "penny wise and pound foolish." Spend money to save time. In other words, don't drive across town to save three cents per gallon on fuel or 10 cents for a gallon of milk. Pay the extra money and have more time to do what you like.

What is most important in your life? Do you spend some of your time with the people and activities that you truly value?

Shutterstock

■ Clean your home of clutter and mess. Make sure everything has a place. Do the same thing at work. Get rid of things you don't need.

■ Donate everything you don't need or use to charity. Simplifying your life may also mean simplifying your closets, drawers, cabinets, and garage. If we are not careful, we are soon possessed by our possessions.

■ Go through your home or apartment and eliminate everything that does not bring you joy or have sentimental value. If you don't love it or need it or use it, ditch it.

■ Clean up the files on your computer. Erase everything that you don't need or want so that you can find material more easily. If you have not used the file in a month, put it on a flash drive for later use.

■ Live in the moment. Yes, it is important to plan for the future, but if you ignore "the moment," your future will not be as bright. Although it is important to plan for the future, it is equally important to live today!

■ Spend a few moments each morning and afternoon reflecting on all of the abundance in your life. Learn to give thanks and learn to do nothing. Count your blessings. (Adapted from Zen Habits, 2008; and Baca, 2009)

In Figure 5.3, compile a list that can help you simplify your life in each category. Add only those things to the list that you can actually do on a daily basis.

THE DREADED "P" WORD

Why Is Procrastination So Easy to Do and How Can You Beat It Once and for All?

It's not just you! Almost all of us procrastinate, and then we worry and tell ourselves, "I'll never do it again if I can just get through this one project." We say things to ourselves like, "If I can just live through this project, I will never wait until the last minute again." But someone comes along with a great idea for fun, and off we go. Or there is a great movie on TV, the kids want to play a game of ball, you go to the refrigerator for snack, and before you know it, you reward yourself with free time before you have done your work. You have to work first; then reward yourself with play.

> If you have to eat two frogs, eat the ugliest one first.
> —Brian Tracy

The truth is simple: We tend to avoid the hard jobs in favor of the easy ones. Even many of the list makers fool themselves. They mark off a long list of easy tasks while the big ones still loom in front of them. Many of us put off unpleasant tasks until our back is against the

Figure 5.3 Ways to Simplify Your Life

Two things I can do to simplify my life at home

Two things I can do to simplify my life at work

Two things I can do to simplify my life with technology (using cell phones, texting, etc.)

Two things I can do to simplify my life with my children, friends, or pets

Two things I can do to simplify my life with my spouse/partner/loved one

Two things I can do to simplify my financial matters

> Don't wait. The time will
> never be just right.
> —Napoleon Hill

POSITIVE HABITS at Work

Make it a habit never to go home from work until you have made your to do list for the next day. Although you may be tired, you will be able to begin work immediately the next morning, and this will put you way ahead of the average employee, who leaves without thinking about the next day. Being prepared and organized is also a great stress reliever.

wall. So why do we procrastinate when we all know how unpleasant the results can be? Why aren't we disciplined, organized, and controlled so we can reap the rewards that come from being prepared? Why do we put ourselves through so much stress just by putting things off?

The biggest problem with procrastination, even beyond not getting the job, task, or paper completed, is *doing it poorly* and then suffering the stress caused by putting it off and not doing our best work. By putting the project off, you have cheated yourself of the time needed to bring your best to the table. Most likely, you are going to hand over a project, *with your name on it,* that is not even close to your potential. If you know your work is not good, so will your boss and your colleagues.

What has procrastination cost you? This is perhaps one of the most important questions that you can answer with regard to managing your time more effectively. Did it cost you an opportunity to look good in the eyes of your boss? Did it cost you money? Did it cost you your reputation? Did it cost you your dignity? Did it cost you your ability to do your best? Did it cost you a friend? **Procrastination is not free.** Every time you do it, it costs you something. You need to determine what it is worth.

In order to beat procrastination, you will also need to consider **what type** of procrastinator you are. Each type requires a different strategy and different energy to overcome, but make no mistake about it, success requires overcoming all degrees and types of procrastination. Which are you? Consider Figure 5.4.

Take a moment and complete the Time Management Assessment in Figure 5.5. Be honest and truthful with your responses. The results of your score are located after the assessment.

Figure 5.4 Procrastinator Types

Chronic Procrastinator	You procrastinate all of the time in most aspects of your life including social situations, financial affairs, career decisions, personal responsibility, and academic projects. Usually, you do not meet any deadlines if you complete the project at all. It is going to take a great deal of thought, planning, and energy to overcome this type of procrastination.
Moderate Procrastinator	You procrastinate much of the time. You usually get things done, but it is not your best work and you create a great deal of stress in your own life. It is going to take a fair amount of planning and energy to overcome this type of procrastination. With some planning, your projects could be much more effective and you could eliminate much stress and guilt.
Occasional Procrastinator	You occasionally put things off. You do not do this often, but when you do, you feel guilty and rush to get the project completed. Sometimes you turn in work that is not your best. You are good at planning most things, but you do need to concentrate on sticking to your plan and not letting unscheduled events obstruct your success.

GETTING THE MOST OUT OF THIS MOMENT

Do You Know the Causes of and Cures for Procrastination?

Below, you will find a list of the 10 most common causes of procrastination and some simple, doable, everyday strategies that you can employ to overcome each cause.

Superhuman Expectations and Trying to Be a Perfectionist

- Allow yourself more time than you think you need to complete a project.
- Allow enough time to do your very best and let that be that. If you plan and allow time for excellence, you can't do more.

Fear of Not Knowing How to Do the Task

- Ask for clarification from whomever asked you to do the project.
- Read as much as you can about the task at hand and ask for help.
- Break up big tasks into small ones.

Figure 5.5   Time Management Assessment

Answer the following questions with the following scale:

1 = Not at all   2 = Rarely   3 = Sometimes   4 = Often   5 = Very often

1. I prioritize my tasks every day and work from my priority list.	1 2 3 4 5
2. I work hard to complete tasks on time and not put them off until the last minute.	1 2 3 4 5
3. I take time to plan and schedule the next day's activities the night before.	1 2 3 4 5
4. I make time during my daily schedule to organize, plan, and get my projects completed so that I can have more quality time at home.	1 2 3 4 5
5. I get my work done before I take fun breaks.	1 2 3 4 5
6. I analyze my assignments to determine which ones are going to take the most time and then work on them first and most often.	1 2 3 4 5
7. I have analyzed my daily activities and determined where I actually spend my time.	1 2 3 4 5
8. I know how to say "no" and do so frequently.	1 2 3 4 5
9. I know how to avoid distractions and how to work through unexpected interruptions.	1 2 3 4 5
10. I do not let "fear of the unknown" keep me from working on a project.	1 2 3 4 5
11. I know how to overcome apathy and/or laziness.	1 2 3 4 5
12. I always tackle the difficult and most important jobs first.	1 2 3 4 5
13. I know how to reframe a project that may not interest me so that I can see the benefit in it and learn from it.	1 2 3 4 5
14. I know how to break down a major, complex, or overwhelming task to get it done in pieces and then put it all together.	1 2 3 4 5
15. I build time into my schedule on a daily or weekly basis to deal with unexpected interruptions or distractions.	1 2 3 4 5

YOUR TOTAL SCORE: _____

RESULTS:

60–75   You manage your time well and you know how to build a schedule to get things done. Your productivity is high. You don't let procrastination rule your life.

45–59   You are good at doing some things on time, but you tend to procrastinate too much. Learning how to build and work from a priority list may help you manage your time more effectively.

30–44   You need to work hard to change your time management skills and learn how to set realistic goals. Procrastination is probably a major issue for you, causing you much stress and worry. Working from a priority list can help you greatly.

29–below   Your time management skills are very weak and without improvement, your career could be in jeopardy. You could benefit from learning to set realistic goals, working from a priority list, and reframing your thought process toward tasks.

Lack of Motivation

- ■ Reframe your attitude to find the benefit in any task.
- ■ Consider how this task will help you reach your overall goals and dreams.
- ■ Take time to do the things you love, creating a healthy balance in your life.

Fear of Failing or Fear of the Task Being Too Hard

- ■ Start the project with positive, optimistic thoughts.
- ■ Face your fears; look them right in the face and make a decision to defeat them.
- ■ Visualize your successful completion of the project.

No Real Plan or Goal for Getting the Task Done

- Set reasonable, concrete goals that you can reach in about 20 to 25 minutes.
- Draw up an action plan the night before you begin the project.
- Look at completing the project in terms of your long-range goals and your overall life plan.

Considering the Task Too Unpleasant or Uninteresting

- Realize that most tasks are not as unpleasant as we've made them out to be.
- Do the hardest tasks first, and save the easiest for last.
- Schedule tasks that you consider unpleasant to be done during your peak hours.

Laziness and/or Apathy

- Concentrate on the rewards of managing yourself and your time more effectively.
- Give yourself a time limit to accomplish a task.

Distractions and/or Lack of Focus

- Close your door and make yourself get started. Turn your desk away from the door, and people are less likely to interrupt you.
- Start on the difficult, most boring tasks first.
- Weed out your personal belongings and living space. Organization helps you manage your time and get to work.

Choosing Fun Before Responsibility

- Reward yourself when you have accomplished an important body of work.
- Don't get involved in too many organizations, accept too many commitments, or overextend yourself. Allow enough time to concentrate on what needs to be done.
- Consider the consequences of not doing what you're responsible for doing.

Waiting for the "Right" Mood

- Avoid whining and complaining, and realize that the right mood can be created by you at any time.
- Just do it! Force yourself to jump into the task.
- Work during your peak hours of the day.

EVALUATING HOW YOU SPEND YOUR TIME

Do You Know Where Your Time Goes?

So how do you find out where your time goes? The same way that you find out where your money goes—you track it. Every 15 minutes for one week, you will record exactly how you spent that time. This exercise may seem a little tedious at first, but if you will complete the process over a period of a week, you will have a much better concept of where your time is being used. Yes, that's right—for a week, you need to keep a written record of how much time you spend sleeping, reading, eating, working, getting to class and back, cooking, caring for children, walking pets, watching television, doing yard work, going to movies, attending athletic events, hanging out, doing laundry, whatever. You will probably be surprised at where your time really goes.

Take your plan with you and keep track of your activities during the day. To make things simple, round off tasks to 15-minute intervals. For example, if you start walking to the cafeteria at 7:08, you might want to mark off the time block that begins with 7:00. If you finish eating

Christian Garcia
Graduate!
UEI College, Ontario, CA
Career: Associate Director of Education,
          UEI College

My advice to anyone in college would be to love what you do. If you truly love what you do, then the old quote is true: "You'll never have to work a day in your life." This is how I feel every day. I actually tell my friends that I stopped working in 1999 because I found my joy—my passion. I would also say that you have to seek opportunities because they usually do not come to you; you have to go to them.

and return to your home at 7:49, you can mark off the next two blocks. You will also want to note the activity so you can evaluate how you spent your time later. Study the example that is provided for you in Figure 5.6.

In Figure 5.7 you will find a daily time log for you to use for this exercise. Remember to take these pages with you and record how you are spending your time during the day. As you progress through the week, try to improve the use of your time. When you finish this exercise, review how you spent your time.

Figure 5.6   How You Really Spend Your Time

7:00	get up	7:00			12:15
	& shower	7:15			12:30
	✕	7:30		Walked to Union	12:45
	Breakfast	7:45	1:00	Ate lunch	1:00
8:00		8:00			1:15
		8:15			1:30
	Read paper	8:30		Talked w/ Joe	1:45
	Walked to class	8:45	2:00		2:00
9:00	English 101	9:00		Went to book	2:15
		9:15		store	2:30
		9:30		Walked to	2:45
		9:45	3:00	my room	3:00
10:00		10:00		Called Ron	3:15
		10:15			3:30
		10:30			3:45
	Walked to class	10:45	4:00	Watched	4:00
11:00	History 210	11:00		TV	4:15
		11:15			4:30
		11:30		Walked to	4:45
		11:45	5:00	library	5:00
12:00		12:00			5:15

Figure 5.7 Daily Time Sheet

Monday		Tuesday		Wednesday	
6:00	6:00	6:00	6:00	6:00	6:00
	6:15		6:15		6:15
	6:30		6:30		6:30
	6:45		6:45		6:45
7:00	7:00	7:00	7:00	7:00	7:00
	7:15		7:15		7:15
	7:30		7:30		7:30
	7:45		7:45		7:45
8:00	8:00	8:00	8:00	8:00	8:00
	8:15		8:15		8:15
	8:30		8:30		8:30
	8:45		8:45		8:45
9:00	9:00	9:00	9:00	9:00	9:00
	9:15		9:15		9:15
	9:30		9:30		9:30
	9:45		9:45		9:45
10:00	10:00	10:00	10:00	10:00	10:00
	10:15		10:15		10:15
	10:30		10:30		10:30
	10:45		10:45		10:45
11:00	11:00	11:00	11:00	11:00	11:00
	11:15		11:15		11:15
	11:30		11:30		11:30
	11:45		11:45		11:45
12:00	12:00	12:00	12:00	12:00	12:00
	12:15		12:15		12:15
	12:30		12:30		12:30
	12:45		12:45		12:45
1:00	1:00	1:00	1:00	1:00	1:00
	1:15		1:15		1:15
	1:30		1:30		1:30
	1:45		1:45		1:45
2:00	2:00	2:00	2:00	2:00	2:00
	2:15		2:15		2:15
	2:30		2:30		2:30
	2:45		2:45		2:45
3:00	3:00	3:00	3:00	3:00	3:00
	3:15		3:15		3:15
	3:30		3:30		3:30
	3:45		3:45		3:45
4:00	4:00	4:00	4:00	4:00	4:00
	4:15		4:15		4:15
	4:30		4:30		4:30
	4:45		4:45		4:45
5:00	5:00	5:00	5:00	5:00	5:00
	5:15		5:15		5:15
	5:30		5:30		5:30
	5:45		5:45		5:45
6:00	6:00	6:00	6:00	6:00	6:00
	6:15		6:15		6:15
	6:30		6:30		6:30
	6:45		6:45		6:45
7:00	7:00	7:00	7:00	7:00	7:00
	7:15		7:15		7:15
	7:30		7:30		7:30
	7:45		7:45		7:45
8:00	8:00	8:00	8:00	8:00	8:00
	8:15		8:15		8:15
	8:30		8:30		8:30
	8:45		8:45		8:45
9:00	9:00	9:00	9:00	9:00	9:00
	9:15		9:15		9:15
	9:30		9:30		9:30
	9:45		9:45		9:45
10:00	10:00	10:00	10:00	10:00	10:00
	10:15		10:15		10:15
	10:30		10:30		10:30
	10:45		10:45		10:45
11:00	11:00	11:00	11:00	11:00	11:00
	11:15		11:15		11:15
	11:30		11:30		11:30
	11:45		11:45		11:45
12:00	12:00	12:00	12:00	12:00	12:00

(continued)

Figure 5.7 Daily Time Sheet (continued)

Thursday		Friday		Saturday		Sunday	
6:00	6:00	6:00	6:00	6:00	6:00	6:00	6:00
	6:15		6:15		6:15		6:15
	6:30		6:30		6:30		6:30
	6:45		6:45		6:45		6:45
7:00	7:00	7:00	7:00	7:00	7:00	7:00	7:00
	7:15		7:15		7:15		7:15
	7:30		7:30		7:30		7:30
	7:45		7:45		7:45		7:45
8:00	8:00	8:00	8:00	8:00	8:00	8:00	8:00
	8:15		8:15		8:15		8:15
	8:30		8:30		8:30		8:30
	8:45		8:45		8:45		8:45
9:00	9:00	9:00	9:00	9:00	9:00	9:00	9:00
	9:15		9:15		9:15		9:15
	9:30		9:30		9:30		9:30
	9:45		9:45		9:45		9:45
10:00	10:00	10:00	10:00	10:00	10:00	10:00	10:00
	10:15		10:15		10:15		10:15
	10:30		10:30		10:30		10:30
	10:45		10:45		10:45		10:45
11:00	11:00	11:00	11:00	11:00	11:00	11:00	11:00
	11:15		11:15		11:15		11:15
	11:30		11:30		11:30		11:30
	11:45		11:45		11:45		11:45
12:00	12:00	12:00	12:00	12:00	12:00	12:00	12:00
	12:15		12:15		12:15		12:15
	12:30		12:30		12:30		12:30
	12:45		12:45		12:45		12:45
1:00	1:00	1:00	1:00	1:00	1:00	1:00	1:00
	1:15		1:15		1:15		1:15
	1:30		1:30		1:30		1:30
	1:45		1:45		1:45		1:45
2:00	2:00	2:00	2:00	2:00	2:00	2:00	2:00
	2:15		2:15		2:15		2:15
	2:30		2:30		2:30		2:30
	2:45		2:45		2:45		2:45
3:00	3:00	3:00	3:00	3:00	3:00	3:00	3:00
	3:15		3:15		3:15		3:15
	3:30		3:30		3:30		3:30
	3:45		3:45		3:45		3:45
4:00	4:00	4:00	4:00	4:00	4:00	4:00	4:00
	4:15		4:15		4:15		4:15
	4:30		4:30		4:30		4:30
	4:45		4:45		4:45		4:45
5:00	5:00	5:00	5:00	5:00	5:00	5:00	5:00
	5:15		5:15		5:15		5:15
	5:30		5:30		5:30		5:30
	5:45		5:45		5:45		5:45
6:00	6:00	6:00	6:00	6:00	6:00	6:00	6:00
	6:15		6:15		6:15		6:15
	6:30		6:30		6:30		6:30
	6:45		6:45		6:45		6:45
7:00	7:00	7:00	7:00	7:00	7:00	7:00	7:00
	7:15		7:15		7:15		7:15
	7:30		7:30		7:30		7:30
	7:45		7:45		7:45		7:45
8:00	8:00	8:00	8:00	8:00	8:00	8:00	8:00
	8:15		8:15		8:15		8:15
	8:30		8:30		8:30		8:30
	8:45		8:45		8:45		8:45
9:00	9:00	9:00	9:00	9:00	9:00	9:00	9:00
	9:15		9:15		9:15		9:15
	9:30		9:30		9:30		9:30
	9:45		9:45		9:45		9:45
10:00	10:00	10:00	10:00	10:00	10:00	10:00	10:00
	10:15		10:15		10:15		10:15
	10:30		10:30		10:30		10:30
	10:45		10:45		10:45		10:45
11:00	11:00	11:00	11:00	11:00	11:00	11:00	11:00
	11:15		11:15		11:15		11:15
	11:30		11:30		11:30		11:30
	11:45		11:45		11:45		11:45
12:00	12:00	12:00	12:00	12:00	12:00	12:00	12:00

ELIMINATING DISTRACTIONS AND INTERRUPTIONS

When Is Enough Really Enough?

If you were diligent and kept an accurate account of all of your time, your evaluation will probably reveal that much of your time is spent dealing with distractions, getting side-tracked, and handling interruptions. These three things account for much of the time wasted within a 24-hour period. In Figure 5.8, you will find a list of some of the most common distractions faced

Figure 5.8 Common Distractions

Common Distractions	My Plan to Overcome These Distractions
Friends/family dropping by unexpectedly at home	
Colleagues stopping by your work space and talking when you are trying to work	
Working on small, unimportant tasks while the big, career-changing jobs go undone or get done poorly	
Spending too much time on breaks and at lunch when you should be working	
Taking time to read mindless e-mails and jokes sent by people who have nothing else to do	
Technology (playing on YouTube, Facebook, iTunes, Google, etc.)	
Constant phone calls that do not pertain to anything of importance	
Not setting aside any time during the day to deal with the unexpected	
Friends/family demanding things of you because they do not understand your schedule or commitments	
Not blocking private time in your daily schedule	
Being disorganized and spending hours piddling and calling it "work"	
Playing with your children or pets before your tasks are complete (and not scheduling time to be with them in the first place)	
Saying "yes" when you need to say "no"	
Other distractions faced by you	

by people who are pursuing a career. Consider how you might deal with these distractions in an effective, assertive manner.

PLANNING AND PREPARING

Is There a Secret to Time Management?

In the past, you may have said to yourself, "I don't have time to plan." "I don't like to be fenced in and tied to a rigid schedule." "I have so many duties that planning never works." Scheduling does not have to be a tedious chore or something you dread. Scheduling can be your lifeline to more free time. After all, if you build your own schedule, it is yours! As much as you are able, build your schedule the way you want and need it.

To manage your time successfully, you need to spend some time planning. To plan successfully, you need a calendar that has a week-at-a-glance or month-at-a-glance section as well as sections for daily notes and appointments. Most companies will furnish a calendar, but it they don't, you can download one from the Internet or create one using Word or another computer program.

Planning and Organizing for Work

Each evening, you should take a few minutes (and literally, that is all it will take) and sit in a quiet place and make a list of all that needs to be done tomorrow. Successful time management comes from **planning the night before!** Let's say your list looks like the one in Figure 5.9.

Next, separate this list into three categories, as shown in Figure 5.10.

Don't get too excited yet. Your time management plan is ***not finished.*** The most important part is still ahead of you. Now, you will need to rank the items in order of their importance. You will put a 1 by the most important tasks, a 2 by the next most important tasks, and so on in each category, as shown in Figure 5.11.

You have now created a plan to actually get these tasks done! Not only have you created your list, but now you have divided the tasks into important categories, ranked them, and made a written commitment to them.

Figure 5.9　To Do List

To Do List

Research procurement project	Exercise
Write report for supervisor— due next week	Go to movie
	Buy birthday card for Mom
Prepare for next training class two days from now	Wash the car
	Take shirts to dry cleaner
Schedule team mtg. at work	Buy groceries
Attend department meeting at 8:00 a.m.	Call Janice about weekend
Meet with supervisor at 10:00 a.m.	

Figure 5.10 Setting Priorities for To Do List

Must Do	Need to Do	Would Like to Do
Prepare for training class	Research procurement project	Wash the car
Exercise	Buy birthday card for Mom	Call Janice about weekend
Schedule team meeting at work	Take shirts to cleaner	Go to movie
Department meeting at 8:00 a.m.	Buy groceries	
Meeting with supervisor at 10:00 a.m.	Write report for supervisor	

Figure 5.11 Ranking Priorities for To Do List

Must Do	Need to Do	Would Like to Do
4 Prepare for training class	1 Research procure-ment project	3 Wash the car
5 Exercise	5 Buy birthday card for Mom	1 Call Janice about weekend
3 Schedule team meet-ing at work	4 Take shirts to cleaner	2 Go to movie
1 Department meeting at 8:00 a.m.	3 Buy groceries	
2 Meeting with supervi-sor at 10:00 a.m.	2 Write report for supervisor	

If these were real tasks, you would now schedule them into your daily calendar (see Figure 5.12). You would schedule category 1 (MUST DO) first, category 2 (NEED TO DO) next, and category 3 (WOULD LIKE TO DO) last. Remember, never keep more than one calendar. Always carry it with you and always schedule your tasks immediately so that you won't forget them.

Great Tips for New Employees

Good time management often boils down to doing a few things extremely well and doing them over and over. When you go to work, the big things count—but so do the little ones! If you have a family, you will need to be highly organized so you can spend quality time with them.

- Break up big jobs into little ones so they don't overwhelm you.
- Allow yourself enough time to complete a task with a few extra minutes, in case there is a glitch. Work expands to fill up whatever amount of time you have, so push yourself to complete the job in a reasonable time frame.

Figure 5.12   Daily Calendar

DAY *Monday*		Priority	Complete?
Time	**Task**		
6:00			Yes _ No
6:30			Yes _ No
7:00	*Study for finance*		Yes _ No
7:30	↓		Yes _ No
8:00	*English 101*		Yes _ No
8:30			Yes _ No
9:00	↓		Yes _ No
9:30	*Read Pg. 1–10 of Chem. Chapter*		Yes _ No
10:00	*Management 210*		Yes _ No
10:30			Yes _ No
11:00	↓		Yes _ No
11:30	*Finish Reading Chem. Chapter*		Yes _ No
12:00			Yes _ No
12:30	↓		Yes _ No
1:00	*Meet w/Chemistry group (take lunch)*		Yes _ No
1:30	↓		Yes _ No
2:00	*Work*		Yes _ No
2:30			Yes _ No
3:00			Yes _ No
3:30			Yes _ No
4:00			Yes _ No
4:30			Yes _ No
5:00			Yes _ No
5:30			Yes _ No
6:00	↓		Yes _ No
6:30	*Dinner/run by grocery store*		Yes _ No
7:00			Yes _ No
7:30	*Internet Research for speech*		Yes _ No
8:00			Yes _ No
8:30	↓		Yes _ No
9:00	*call Janice @ w/end*		Yes _ No
9:30			Yes _ No

- If you are still taking courses or working on another degree, set up a regular time to study and stick to it.
- When you have a project, set reasonable goals that you can meet in 20- to 25-minute blocks.
- Take short breaks; get up from your computer and move around. Leave your desk for lunch and breaks; you'll come back refreshed. Don't ever eat lunch at your desk unless you have to.
- Allow yourself longer than you think you need for a project so you don't have to stay up all night.
- Avoid having to cram for school or work projects by starting early.
- Don't get too involved with outside organizations and commitments that steal your time and make you look slack at work.

- Start on the most difficult, boring jobs first. Reward yourself with something you enjoy after you have completed a good block of work.

- Weed out personal belongings; get rid of clutter that takes your time. Streamline your house, your workspace, your home desk, and your garage.

- File things as you go; don't pile them in stacks. Don't allow yourself to be one of those people who would rather "pile than file," because you will never be able to find important documents.

- If you have children, give each one a workspace with his or her own supplies. Give each child a file drawer or box to keep important papers that he or she will need again. You are teaching your children time management and organization skills.

- Handle paperwork immediately and only once.

- Organize your workspace and designate a specific place for your supplies. Keep supplies on hand so you don't run out at a crucial time.

- Prepare to be successful at work or school by getting ready the evening before. Decide what you are going to wear; press your clothes if they need it; polish your shoes.

- Keep a Rolodex file, iPod, or other system for important phone numbers and addresses you use frequently.

- Organize as effectively at home as you do at work.

- Plan a rotation schedule for housework. Clean one room each day.

- Organize your closets and dresser drawers, ridding yourself of clutter and things you don't use anymore.

- Fill up your gas tank the night before to avoid stress in the morning.

- If you are a perfectionist, get over it! Some things need to be perfect, but most don't.

- Take time to do things you love and create a healthy balance in your life. If you reward the completion of a big job by immediately beginning another big job, you have a good chance of becoming a workaholic.

- If you have children, schedule at least one hour a week with each one. Make this a happy, special time. Sunday nights are great for family night.

- Make family meals happy. Sit down together at least three times a week. Let the children help prepare the meal and set the table. Allow each person to tell about his or her day.

- Put fun days on your calendar and keep them sacred.

- Put family days on your calendar and have everyone help get things done so you can have a great family event.

STRESS? I DON'T HAVE ENOUGH TIME FOR STRESS!

Do You Feel Like You're Going to Explode?

The word *stress* is derived from the Latin word *strictus,* meaning "to draw tight." Stress is your body's response to people and events in your life; it is the mental and physical wear and tear on your body as a result of everyday life and all that you have to accomplish. Stress is inevitable, and it is not in itself bad. It is your response to stress that determines whether it is good stress (**eustress**) or bad stress (**distress**). Positive stress

iStockphoto

Do you find it difficult or easy to simplify and de-clutter your life? Why?

improves productivity, provided it doesn't persist too long. Negative stress, on the other hand, can affect you both physically and mentally.

Good stress can help you become more motivated and even more productive. It helps your energy level, too. It is only when stress gets out of hand that your body becomes distressed. Some physical signs of distress are:

Headaches	Muscular tension and pain	Fatigue
Coughs	Abdominal pain and diarrhea	Mental disorders
Dry mouth	Hypertension and chest pain	Insomnia
Impotence	Heartburn and indigestion	Suicidal tendencies
Twitching/Trembling	Abdominal pain	Apprehension
Jitters	Diminished performance	Decreased coping ability

If you begin to experience any of these reactions for an extended period of time, your body and mind are probably suffering from undue stress, anxiety, and pressure. This can lead to a very unhealthy situation. You may even require medical attention for hypertension. Take the stress assessment in Figure 5.13 to determine the level of distress you are currently experiencing in your life.

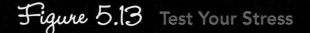

Figure 5.13   Test Your Stress

Check the items that reflect your behavior at home, work, or school, or in a social setting.

☐   1. Your stomach tightens when you think about your work and all that you have to do.

☐   2. You are not able to sleep at night.

☐   3. You race from place to place trying to get everything done that is required of you.

☐   4. Small things make you angry.

☐   5. At the end of the day, you are frustrated that you did not accomplish all that you needed to do.

☐   6. You get tired throughout the day.

☐   7. You need some type of drug, alcohol, or tobacco to get through the day.

☐   8. You often find it hard to be around people.

☐   9. You don't take care of yourself physically or mentally.

☐ 10. You tend to keep everything inside.

☐ 11. You overreact.

☐ 12. You fail to find the humor in many situations others see as funny.

☐ 13. You do not eat properly.

☐ 14. Everything upsets you.

☐ 15. You are impatient and get angry when you have to wait for things.

☐ 16. You don't trust others.

☐ 17. You feel that most people move too slowly for you.

☐ 18. You feel guilty when you take time for yourself or your friends.

☐ 19. You interrupt people so that you can tell them your side of the story.

☐ 20. You experience memory loss.

Total Number of Check Marks

0–5   Low, manageable stress

6–10   Moderate stress

11+   High stress, could cause medical or emotional problems

I DON'T THINK I FEEL
SO WELL

What Is the Relationship Between Poor Time Management, Monumental Stress, and Your Health?

There are probably as many stressors in this world as there are people alive. For some people, loud music causes stress. For others, a hectic day at the office with people demanding things and equipment breaking down causes stress. For others, that loud music and a busy day at the office are just what the doctor ordered—they love it and thrive off of the energy and demands. For some people, being idle and sitting around reading a book cause stress, whereas others long for a moment of peace walking on the beach or just sitting out in the backyard with a good book. One thing is for sure: poor planning and running out of time are on most people's list of major stressors. Medical research has shown that exposure to stress over a long period of time can be damaging to your health.

Consider the following tips for dealing with and reducing stress in your life:

- Become a dedicated goal setter and list maker and follow your plans carefully. One of the greatest causes of stress is floundering, not knowing where you are going.
- Reduce intake of alcohol, which can cause your moods to fluctuate and can make you edgy.
- Eat well. Certain foods give your body energy, while others drain your vitality. Reduce sweets and carbohydrates, and increase proteins such as lean baked turkey. Put more fruits and vegetables in your diet.
- Exercise! Physical exercise actually takes stress out of your body. If you feel yourself getting uptight, stop what you are doing and take a brisk 15-minute walk. Do the same thing for your children with homework. If they are getting frustrated, take the entire family on a walk.
- Get rid of all the clutter in your life. Sometimes we can become "possessed by our possessions."
- Use relaxation techniques such as visualization, listening to music, and practicing yoga.
- Get enough rest. You may not need eight hours, but your body needs a certain amount of sleep to regenerate itself.
- Let minor hassles and annoyances go. Ask yourself, "Is this situation worth a heart attack, stroke, or high blood pressure?"
- Don't be afraid to take a break.
- Learn to relax, and even take a little nap if it helps renew your energy.
- Laugh often! Laughter has been shown to increase learning and retention by 800 percent! Joy and laughter are great stress relievers.

Other physical symptoms include *exhaustion,* in which one part of the body weakens and shifts its responsibility to another part and causes complete failure of key organ functions. *Chronic muscle pain* and malfunction are also affected by unchecked stress. "Chronically tense muscles also result in numerous stress-related disorders including headaches, backaches, spasms of the esophagus and colon (causing diarrhea and constipation), posture problems, asthma, tightness in the throat and chest cavity, some eye problems, lockjaw, muscle tears and pulls, and perhaps rheumatoid arthritis" (Girdano, Dusek, & Everly, 2009).

As you can see from this medical research, stress is not something that you can just ignore and hope it will go away. Examine Figure 5.14.

Figure 5.14 Three Types of Major Stressors in Life

Cause	What You Can Do to Reduce Stress
Situational	
Change in physical environment	■ If at all possible, change your residence or physical environment to better suit your needs. ■ If you can't change it, talk to the people involved and explain your feelings.
Change in social environment	■ Work hard to meet new friends who support you and on whom you can rely in times of need. ■ Get involved in some type of activity outside of work. ■ Join a group activity or sports team.
Daily hassles	■ Try to keep things in perspective, and work to reduce the things that you allow to stress you out. ■ Allow time in your schedule for unexpected events. ■ Find a quiet place to relax and think.
Poor time management	■ Work out a time management plan that allows time to get your work complete while allowing time for rest and joy, too. ■ Create to do lists.
Conflicts at work and home	■ Read about conflict management and realize that conflict can result in stress. ■ Avoid "hot" topics such as religion or politics if you feel this causes you to engage in conflicts. ■ Be assertive, not aggressive or rude.
People	■ Try to avoid people who stress you out. ■ Put people into perspective and realize that we're all different, with different needs, wants, and desires. ■ Realize that not everyone is going to be like you, and not everyone is going to like you.
Relationships	■ Work hard to develop healthy, positive relationships. ■ Move away from toxic, unhealthy relationships and people who bring you down. ■ Understand that you can never change the way another person feels, acts, or thinks.
Death of a loved one	■ Try to focus on the good times you shared and what they meant to your life. ■ Remember that death is as much a part of life as living. ■ Talk about the person with your friends and family—share your memories. ■ Consider what the deceased person would have wanted you to do.
Financial problems	■ Cut back on your spending. ■ Seek the help of a financial planner. ■ Determine why your financial planning or spending patterns are causing you problems.
Psychological	
Unrealistic expectations	■ Surround yourself with positive people and work hard to set realistic goals with doable time-lines and results. ■ Expect and anticipate less.
Loneliness	■ Surround yourself with people who support you. ■ Call or visit home as often as you can until you get more comfortable. ■ Meet new friends at work or in your neighborhood.
Fear	■ Plan and execute carefully to help you feel more confident. ■ Visualize success and not failure. ■ Do one thing every day that scares you to expand your comfort zone.

Cause	What You Can Do to Reduce Stress
Psychological *(continued)*	
Anxiety over your future and what is going to happen	■ Put things into perspective and work hard to plan and prepare, but accept that life is about constant change. ■ Don't try to control the uncontrollable. ■ Try to see the big picture and how "the puzzle" is going to come together.
Anxiety over your past	■ Work hard to overcome past challenges and remember that your past does not have to dictate your future. ■ Learn to forgive. ■ Focus on your future and what you really want to accomplish.
Biological	
Insomnia	■ Watch your caffeine intake. ■ Avoid naps. ■ Do not exercise two hours prior to your normal bedtime. ■ Complete all of your activities before going to bed (working, watching TV, e-mailing, texting, etc.). Your bed is for sleeping.
Anxiety	■ Laugh more. Share a joke. ■ Enjoy your friends and family. ■ Practice breathing exercises. ■ Talk it out with friends. ■ Learn to say "no" and mean it. ■ Turn off the TV if the news makes you anxious or nervous.
Weight loss/gain	■ Develop an exercise and healthy eating plan. ■ Meet with a nutrition specialist. ■ Join a health-related club or gym.
Reduced physical activities	■ Increase your daily activity. ■ If possible, walk to work or lunch instead of driving. ■ Take the stairs instead of the elevator.
Sexual difficulties/dysfunction	■ Seek medical help in case something is physically wrong. ■ Determine if your actions are in contradiction with your value system.

TIME, STRESS, DEPRESSION, AND ANXIETY

What Does One Have to Do with the Other?

Most people never make the connection, but not managing your time properly can cause more than stress—it can cause depression, anxiety, and a host of other mental, emotional, and physical problems. When you're rushing around trying to complete a project at the last moment, your stress level rises, and with higher levels of stress, depression and anxiety begin to creep in. Many of our mental and emotional issues can be addressed by allowing ourselves enough time to do a project well and not stress out over it. Yes, there are many causes of depression and anxiety, but managing your time well can help with reducing the levels of both.

SILENT PROBLEMS OF THE MIND
How Do You Control Depression and Anxiety Disorders?

Depression is a term used to describe feelings ranging from feeling blue to utter hopelessness. The use of "I'm depressed" to mean "I'm sad" or "I'm down" is a far cry from the illness of clinical depression. Depression is a sickness that can creep up on an individual and render that person helpless if it is not detected and properly treated.

There are several major types of depressions. They include the following:

- **Situational depression.** Situational depression is a feeling of sadness due to disappointments, bad news, daily frustrations, or "people problems."

- **Clinical depression.** Clinical depression is major depression and is characterized by the inability to enjoy life, loss of interest in things you once loved doing, self-hatred, feelings of utter worthlessness, and suicidal thoughts. Clinical depression is diagnosed when these feelings last at least two weeks.

- **Dysthymia.** Dysthymia is classified as mild to moderate depression and can last a long time—two years or more. There are times that you can't remember not being depressed and it is hard to enjoy life, family, or friends.

- **Seasonal depression.** Seasonal depression is caused by the weather or by the changing seasons of the year. Some people are depressed by rain; others are depressed by a lack of sunshine.

- **Postpartum depression.** Postpartum depression, sometimes called "the baby blues," occurs after the birth of a child. It can be a very serious condition where the mother avoids the child or even wants to cause harm to the child. It can occur up to a year or more after birth.

- **Anxiety.** According to the Anxiety Disorders Associations of America, anxiety disorders are the most common mental illness in the United States—with more than 13 percent of adults suffering from some form of anxiety disorder. Learning to cope with anxiety allows you to focus and maintain balance in your health and academic welfare. There are several ways to proactively approach dealing with anxiety: relaxation techniques such as yoga, music or dance therapy, and meditation; cognitive behavior therapy or other forms of therapy; and medication.

If you are feeling depressed or your anxiety has reached a level where you cannot control it, but your depression seems minor or situational, try some of these helpful hints for picking yourself up out of the blues:

- Get physical exercise—it releases endorphins, which help to stimulate you and give you a personal high.
- Spend time talking with a good friend; share your thoughts and feelings.
- Control your self-talk. If you're feeding yourself negative words, change to positive thoughts.
- Do something special for yourself: Take a long walk in the park, watch a favorite movie, listen to a special song, or visit a friend.
- Nurture yourself by doing things you love and enjoy and that bring you peace.
- *Never* be afraid or ashamed to seek professional assistance.

Reflections: PUTTING IT ALL TOGETHER

Managing your time and reducing your levels of stress are two skills that you will need for the rest of your life. By learning to avoid procrastination and taking the time to enhance the quality of your life, you are actually increasing your value as an employee. Technological advances, fewer people doing more work, and pressure to perform at unprecedented levels can put your life in a tailspin, but with the ability to plan your time and reduce your own stress level, you are making a contribution to your own success.

DIGITAL BRIEFCASE

LEARNING TO USE A SOCIAL MEDIA MONITORING SYSTEM

Assume you have accepted a job with a startup company, headed by a young, ambitious technology guru. The company has been financially backed by angel investors (look up the definition for this term) and is under a great deal of pressure to produce quick results. The CEO and her management team are trying to maximize the use of social media for marketing, data collection, feedback, and other purposes.

Most people know how popular Facebook and Twitter are for personal use, but companies have caught on quickly that social media tools are also for business and creating lasting relationships with customers. Your boss is being pushed hard by his managers to increase the use of social media and to have employees actively engaged in constantly researching and finding new ideas and solutions to grow the business. As a member of this team, your job is to help find solutions and to generate new business using social media. You have found that tracking related websites is very time consuming, so you are seeking software that will help you track data while simultaneously helping you manage your time. Your job is very stressful and high pressure, so it helps to manage your time well.

Access the website www.omillion.com. Activate the free demo and learn the main points of this social media monitoring system. Write a two-paragraph report for your busy supervisor explaining how this software works and why it would be good for employees in your department. You can create fictitious information if you need to. In this report, explain the terminology "single dashboard" and "social media monitoring."

REFERENCES

Baca, M. (2009). *Get More Done*. Retrieved January 3, 2011, from www.getmoredone.com.

Girando, D., Dusek, D., & Everly, G. (2009). *Controlling stress and tension* (8th ed.). Boston: Benjamin Cummings.

U.S. Bureau of Labor Statistics. (2008). *Education and training pay.* Washington, DC: U.S. Government Printing Office.

Waitley, D. (1997). *Psychology of success: Developing your self-esteem.* Boston: Irwin Career Education Division.

Wetmore, D. (2008). Time management facts and figures. Accessed December 1, 2008, from www.balancetime.com.

Zen Habits. (2008). Simple living manifesto: 72 ways to simplify your life. Retrieved July 20, 2011, from http://zenhabits.net.

chapter six

SOCIALIZE

AVOID WORKPLACE LAND MINES AND PERFECT YOUR PERSONAL IMAGE

Never go to bed at night wondering if you were a conversational gun in the slandering of a person's character or the endangerment of his/her future.
—*Letitia Baldridge*

Why read this chapter?

Because you'll learn...

- To recognize and avoid "water cooler" gossip groups
- To be careful when dealing with office politics and workplace romances
- To select a classic business wardrobe, including business casual

Because you'll be able to...

- Work a room or a cocktail party like a pro
- Dine with dignity in any setting

PROFESSIONALS from the Field

Name: Lee Templeton

Business: Supervisor, Rush's

One of the biggest workplace land mines and conflicts can arise from hearsay, rumors, and gossip. Often, unfounded rumors are spread about how managers treat one employee one way and others a different way. Untrue rumors begin about relationships and workplace romances. Hearsay begins about favoritism. This almost always leads to conflict and causes unrest. When you assume a leadership role, it is extremely important to treat everyone equally, show respect to all, and avoid sharing private information. It will also be vitally important to never spread rumors or hearsay—not on the job, not in a social setting with coworkers or employees, not anywhere for that matter. While you can be empathetic and offer professional assistance, treat everyone equally and avoid the rumor mill at all costs.

MyStudentSuccessLab

MyStudentSuccessLab (www.mystudentsuccesslab.com) is an online solution designed to help you "Start strong, Finish stronger" by building skills for ongoing personal and professional development.

NAVIGATING LAND MINES

How Do I Avoid Problems from Day One?

From the first day on, it is very important to perform your duties in an outstanding manner and convince your bosses that they made a good decision in hiring you. You should perform at your highest level every day and be willing to learn. Sometimes this means being willing to do the "dirty work" that no one else wants to do. It might mean arriving early and staying late at times. It will almost certainly mean that you will be sitting in classes or studying some phase of company regulations in front of a computer screen as you become oriented to the company.

In some cases, you will be on probation for a certain period of time, usually 90 days, so it is imperative that you perform at the top of your game during this time. The majority of companies conduct regular, formal performance appraisals. Ask for a copy of the evaluation instrument, study the items on which you will be evaluated, and be sure you are performing all of them at a high level. You don't want any surprises when the boss evaluates you. It is not unusual for employees to think they are doing what is expected of them only to learn at evaluation time that they have missed the mark. Although doing your job well is key, it is also important to be looking toward a promotion and your next career opportunity. Observe people in leadership roles who have done well and are respected by their colleagues: What is their educational background? How do they communicate? What do they do that sets them apart? Study the trends in your industry. Read good books, business journals, and trade journals in your field. What can you learn from books and journals that you can apply to your own work and perhaps do a better, more creative job?

"WATER COOLER" GOSSIP GROUPS

How Much Can a Little Gossip Hurt?

There are very few people who don't like to gossip. The workplace is no exception to this rule. Rumors fly around all the time, many of which have no real substance whatsoever; in fact, some people love to take a little tidbit of information and embellish it until there is no truth whatsoever. The problem with this little exercise is that it hurts the people who are the subjects of this unfounded gossip. The other problem is that everybody knows who the rumormongers are, and nobody trusts them. It's not hard to tell who goes up and down the halls spreading malicious gossip. A sure way to damage your personal reputation is to become one of these people. A good thing to remember is that stepping on one's feelings is as painful as stepping on one's toes, and it lasts a lot longer.

Never Speak Negatively about Your Boss or Former Employer

Think about this quote: "If you work for a man, work for him, or find another job." This is good advice whether your boss is a man or woman! While it is absolutely certain that some bosses won't earn your respect or

POSITIVE HABITS at Work

Do everything possible to make your boss look good. Find out what your boss is trying to accomplish and do everything you can to help him or her be successful. Bosses typically reward people who work hard, try to help in reaching the organization's goals, and are loyal. Avoid getting involved with the gossipers and naysayers.

BIGGEST INTERVIEW *Blunders*

Marie Hanson went on a job interview and was asked to describe her current boss. She proceeded to blast him with a stream of negative comments. Marie was highly qualified for this position based on her education and skill sets, but she didn't get the job. She made the classic mistake of bad-mouthing her former boss.

LESSON: Never say anything bad about your former boss or anyone else at your former company no matter how much you dislike him or her. People at the company where you are interviewing will assume that you will do the same about your new colleagues.

deserve your loyalty, he or she is the boss nevertheless. Not every boss is a good supervisor, but he or she is still the boss. You will be very fortunate if you get a boss who is visionary, fair, honest, ethical, and caring, and who tries to help all employees grow and to learn. Even if you have a lousy boss, if you are going to take the paycheck, you need to give a good day's work for a good day's pay.

Many bosses will tell you that the number one quality they value is loyalty. This doesn't mean that you can't disagree with the boss. It just means that you disagree with him or her in person and that you do it respectfully. Should you choose to disagree with your boss, you need to choose your words carefully and say something like this: "Mrs. Brown, I know you have so much more experience than I do, and I may be way off base, but it seems to me that the decision to close that branch might be a little premature. Are you aware that XYZ company is getting ready to build a big plant within half a mile of that branch?"

Never make the boss look bad in front of anyone to show how smart and clever you are. If you have a boss who truly encourages speaking up and disagreeing in meetings—and these are rare—be sure that even then you use a respectful tone of voice and that you don't say or do anything that causes the boss to lose face. No one—including a boss—ever forgets being embarrassed in front of his or her colleagues.

Figure out what is near and dear to the boss's heart and work hard to make it happen. This is not being underhanded; it's just using good sense. Don't let your boss hear bad news from someone else if you know about it. Bosses don't like surprises. They especially don't like to hear about it from their own bosses.

When you go for an interview, never say anything bad about the company or your present or former boss. Even if he or she deserves to be attacked, the person interviewing you will assume that you will be negative when you go to work with the new company, and most likely, you won't get the job offer.

Paying Attention to Workplace Politics

Politics is rampant in the workplace! You will see "kissing up," "brown-nosing," lying, bullying, exaggerating, people taking credit for others' work—the list goes on and on. The secret is to know what is going on without being a participant in the negative aspects of office politics. Most people know which colleagues are spreading the rumors, attacking others, playing up to the boss, and so on. You can't stop politics, so don't waste your time trying.

The only way you can avoid politics is to go to work in the middle of a forest and never see anyone else. The good news is that not all politics are bad. You don't have to change who you are to be successful at office politics. Nice guys do finish first most of the time. J. W. Marriott, CEO of Marriott Corporation, said, "The closer you get to the top, the nicer people are." You can be thoughtful, sincere, considerate, and interested in others, and your chances of succeeding are far better than those who choose to use dirty politics.

Some people believe that office politics are only played by people who can't get ahead by any other means, but according to Herminia Ibarra, associate professor at Harvard Business School, "You don't have to be a jerk to make things happen. Integrity can be a source of power." Lou DiNatale, senior fellow at the McCormick Institute of Public Affairs at the University of Massachusetts, says, "Real political power is about pulling other people to your ideas, and then pushing those ideas through to other people." Today it seems that people value knowledge and skills far more than they do negative politics. Politics will only take you so far, and if your power is attached to someone else's, when he or she falls from grace, so will you, especially if you have been a backstabber to other people.

There will always be a grapevine. It has been said that 80 percent of what comes down the grapevine is true. If you are the boss, you need to put the truth down the grapevine as often as you can. If you hear a rumor and you know it is not true, simply say, "That's not true. I was in that meeting, and Mr. Carter didn't say that. This is what he said."

Politics will always exist. Know what is going on around you at all times, but refuse to be a player in underhanded, dirty politics. Practice honesty, integrity, fairness, and decency, and if you are good at your job, you will succeed. Take time to get to know people on a personal level; don't judge them based on what anyone else says. Just because one person has a problem with a colleague doesn't mean you have to.

What does this statement mean?

Never judge another person through someone else's eyes.

_____

_____

_____

_____

Avoid Backstabbing and Trampling on Others

There are many ways to trample on others' feelings, and you will probably encounter or observe most of them. The important thing is for you to avoid participating in such behavior. Some of the typical behaviors that people hate most are:

- Having someone take credit for their work
- Colleagues who don't perform their work well and on time so someone else falls behind and looks bad
- Unfounded rumors, such as untrue accusations about having an affair
- Schmoozing those at the top and scorning those below them
- Spreading rumors about people to cause animosity with the idea that the gossiper will come out on top
- Resisting requests for information that a person needs to do his or her job
- Bullying by loud, intimidating colleagues
- Laughter at some off-color or inappropriate joke that hurts another colleague
- Being left out of the loop intentionally on things that should be common knowledge

Just as these behaviors hurt you, they also hurt other employees. You will be respected if you refuse to participate in these games. If someone mistreats you, gather your courage, go to his or her office, and say something like, "I was told that you were spreading a rumor about me that isn't true, so I decided to ask you if you did this. Did you say I was having an affair with Mr. Kendall?" Since most people who trample on others and backstab their colleagues are chickens underneath their loud exteriors, the person will probably deny having said it and probably won't say it again. You can respond, "Well, I didn't think you were that kind of person, and I'm glad to know you aren't doing such a despicable thing. So we don't have a problem." The chances are good that this person will not target you again.

One in five employees reports being bullied at work.
—Valerie Cade, Bullyfree Workplace

WORKPLACE ROMANCES

What's Love Got to Do with It?

Is it something in the air? Or is it the music that plays constantly in many offices? Or is it the close proximity of office cubicles? No one seems to know what causes so many office romances, but "almost half of us have been romantically tied to someone from work, and many more would like to find amour in a neighboring cubicle" (Vault.com, 2010). Office romances seem to be rather common today. After all, employees spend up to one-third of their time at work in close quarters with other people. While office romances are not as taboo as they once were, for best results, cupid is best left out of the office.

What does your company's policy say about office relationships? Read this as soon as possible, before an office romance is even remotely possible. Before you jump into a romantic relationship with a coworker, you really need to think about it carefully. This may seem like the love of your life, the soulmate you have longed for. But what happens if this romance goes sour? What have you got to lose if it doesn't work out? Or even if it does work out?

In a worst-case scenario, you could lose your job. Some companies' corporate regulations forbid romantic relationships. You could damage your professional reputation, and in some cases, even be charged for sexual harassment if you get your life tangled up with the wrong person. Certainly, you know by now that everyone is not honest and ethical, much less responsible. If you have a relationship that doesn't work out, naturally, it would be much easier if this took place somewhere besides your office.

According to Joni Johnston, president and CEO of WorkRelationships.com, "Most dating relationships end. Think of the number of people we date and the number we end up marrying—the odds are not good." Is this relationship worth the gossip that will surely go on around you? (Remember, there are very few secrets at work.) Could you become involved in some kind of jealous triangle? Are the quarters too close for comfort to keep an office romance going? You have always heard the old expression, "Look before you leap." This is one of those times when you really need to weigh all the consequences before jumping in and getting in way over your head.

All that said, and even if it is not a good idea, it is virtually impossible to stop love from happening. Because you obviously have similar work interests, it stands to reason that you might share other mutually rewarding interests in hobbies, sports, movies, and the like. You might even have a group of friends to which you both belong, and perhaps you all go out together after work. One thing leads to another, and you find yourself in an office romance.

While we highly recommend not getting involved romantically at work, it would be wrong to say that everything is negative about a workplace romance. Because you work with the person, you can observe his or her behaviors frequently and determine if this person is a good match for you. You could have the opportunity to go to lunch or work out together in the company exercise facility. You can get an idea if this person is a good love interest or simply a wolf in sheep's clothing.

> *There is no greater hatred than the hatred between two people who once loved.*
>
> —Sophocles

You need to maintain a good balance between romance and work. Review the pointers in Figure 6.1 that might help you as you deal with office relationships.

While office romances may bring happiness, they have the potential to bring just as much sadness and anger, and at the same time, damage your career. Try very hard to avoid compromising situations. Proceed with caution, maturity, and wisdom.

DON'T PARTY AT THE COMPANY PARTY

Is It Really Worth Ruining Your Professional Reputation?

The company party is not the place to party! You should be seen, be sociable, and be gone. You should arrive a little late and leave a little early. If everyone else is staying very late and drinking too much, this is a good reason for you to excuse yourself and leave. You should never have more than one drink at a company function. Nurse that drink as long as you are there, and refrain from drinking simply because the liquor is free. This is not the place for you to have too much to drink and make a fool of yourself. You don't have to drink more than anyone else just because the drinks are free.

Figure 6.1 Tips for Managing Workplace Relationships

- Never have a relationship with your boss or a subordinate! You increase the risk of a sexual harassment lawsuit, you damage morale in the office, and you might get accused of preferential treatment. If you are a colleague competing for promotions, salaries, and other perks, naturally, people will say that you get better treatment. Managers tend to lose respect if they are caught dallying around with a subordinate. What about evaluations? How can a boss be unbiased in evaluating a love interest? "Just don't date anyone in your direct chain of command. Just don't do it," according to Taylor (2005).

- Never get involved with a married person—at work or anywhere else. You will quickly ruin your reputation. If this person will cheat on his or her spouse, he or she will cheat on you.

- If you sense that a work relationship is getting too serious, spend less time working and more time doing things that take your mind off this person. Go to places where you might meet someone with similar interests; spend more time working out; look up old friends.

- If you fall in love and you think you absolutely must have this person, one of you needs to move to another department or even to another company. Is this person worth giving up your job?

- If you become involved with a colleague, move very slowly into a serious relationship. It takes very mature people to handle a romantic relationship in the office.

- Kersten (2002) offers good advice: "Once you enter into a relationship, there are two people contributing to the way you are perceived in the company. It doesn't matter if you're being professional, if that other person is not, it's still going to impact you." What if your love interest shares intimate information with a colleague and it gets out around the watercooler?

- Do your homework. Does your company forbid interoffice dating? Are there unwritten rules that everyone seems to follow? What is the policy on harassment? Does your relationship with this person pose situations that may be harmful to the company? Are there any older, long-term employees in relationships with colleagues? Do you have very conservative bosses? Are other peers dating, and how has this affected their standing with their colleagues and bosses? If you were discussed in the same way as they are, could you live with it? How would you feel toward your romantic interest if the relationship cost you a promotion or your job?

- If you do get involved, make some hard-and-fast rules that you both will follow. No contact at work, no discussion of dating, no physical contact, and no talk of love. Perhaps the most important rule to agree on is this one: How will you treat each other if the relationship doesn't work out? Of course, there is no guarantee that either of you will live up to these promises. Can you be sure of what will happen if things don't turn out well? In extreme cases, one person or the other can't turn loose of their love interest, and it creates a bad scene at work, even resulting in violence and loss of job.

- Don't fall in love, get all starry-eyed, and stop paying attention to your job. You need to go to work, be prompt, meet deadlines, and handle your assignments in an excellent manner so your work doesn't suffer. Avoid e-mailing on company computers, and don't spend lots of time text-messaging when you should be working. Your computer at work belongs to the company, and anything you write can be examined by someone above your head if he or she chooses to do so. If this prince or princess doesn't work out, you still need your job and your reputation.

- If you break up—and you most likely will, according to statistics—handle it with maturity. Don't say bad things about your love interest; don't jump into another relationship at work or anywhere else right away; cool off. No one gets over a broken heart easily, but this is one of those times when you must deal with it in a very mature manner.

Wear something that is in good taste. This is a work function—not a laid-back social gathering with your best buddies. Women certainly want to look attractive, but not overly sexy. Women in upper management are not likely to dress in skimpy, tight clothes. You want to fit in with them. Men should also dress like the company executives do. They won't have on jeans and t-shirts.

If you are attending a pool party, don't swim. You will look like a drowned rat while everyone else is still fresh and attractive. Don't parade around in a swimsuit even if you look like a movie star. Neither men nor women will win friends by insisting on showing off a great body. This is not the place!

At every party there are two kinds of people—those who want to go home and those who don't. Trouble usually follows those who don't.

—Unknown

Figure 6.2 How to Work a Room Like a Pro

- Survey the room before you enter to get "the lay of the land."

- If you have a drink, hold it in your left hand so your right hand is free to shake hands. Don't have more than one drink!

- Avoid eating. It is difficult to talk, eat, balance a plate, and shake hands. Eat before you go! You are there to do business, not eat. The worst thing you can do is to load up your plate and act like this is your last meal.

- Don't cluster in the corner with the only person you know! Move around the room, shaking hands and introducing yourself. Take the initiative. Most people will be glad you did.

- Focus on the other person. Smile and be friendly. Talk for a few minutes and move on.

- Sell yourself with a sound bite—something interesting about yourself. For example: "I'm John Martin, the new admissions coordinator at Marion Hospital."

- Don't look around the room or over the other person's shoulder while you're talking to someone. Look at the person as though he or she is the most interesting person in the room. Use the person's name.

- Don't talk about politics, make fun of a state, or tell religious or ethnic jokes. You never know whom you might offend.

- Don't talk about your health. People find this very boring. No one wants to hear about your operation or extensive details about your vacation.

- Converse a few minutes, excuse yourself, and move on. The idea is to meet people and network.

How to Work a Room

As a businessperson, you probably will attend cocktail parties. You should consider them an extension of work. You are there to make contacts, make a good impression, network, expand your client base, and generally represent your company in a positive manner. In other words, you should work the room. Consider the basic tips in Figure 6.2 for working a room.

Business parties, receptions, and cocktail parties should be treated as an extension of work. You should look your best, present yourself well, and consider these events as a great opportunity to network.

ALCOHOL AND SUBSTANCE ABUSE

What Is the Cost to Companies and Individuals?

Alcohol and substance abuse by employees creates expensive problems for business and industry, including injuries on the job, increased premiums for health insurance, and missed work that affects others' jobs. "The loss to companies in the United States due to alcohol and drug-related abuse by employees totals $100 billion a year, according to the the National Clearinghouse for Alcohol and Drug Information (NCADI). These staggering numbers do not include the cost of diverting company resources that could be used for other purposes, toward addressing substance abuse issues. Nor does it include the 'pain and suffering' aspects, which cannot be measured in economic terms" (Buddy, 2011). Costs add up quickly in terms of expense of absenteeism, injuries, health insurance claims, loss of productivity, employee morale, theft, and fatalities.

According to NCADI statistics alcohol and drug users:

- Are far less productive.
- Use three times as many sick days.

- Are more likely to injure themselves or someone else.
- Are five times more likely to file worker's compensation claims.

One survey found that nine percent of heavy drinkers and 10 percent of drug users had missed work because of a hangover, six percent had gone to work high or drunk in the past year, and 11 percent of heavy drinkers and 18 percent of drug users had skipped work in the past month. (Buddy, 2011)

There is no doubt that alcohol and substance abuse create serious problems at work and can cause you to lose your job. You are urged to use good judgment related to any type of substance abuse for your health, as well as your career.

People abuse substances such as drugs, tobacco, and alcohol for many complex reasons, but our society pays a terrible price because of these abuses. People harm themselves and others, work suffers, families are adversely affected, relationships are ruined, and many people end up in prison due to substance abuse. There is a strong correlation between drug dependence and crime. While the use of cocaine has declined, use of other drugs such as heroin and "club drugs" has increased (Daly & Richards, 2007).

Friends, family, and coworkers may see some of the signs of substance abuse in people they know and care about listed in Figure 6.3.

While we cannot go into great depth on the issue of substance abuse here, suffice it to say that it is an increasingly serious problem among U.S. workers, and many people are not well-educated on the potential harmful effects of substance abuse. Many people, for example, have the mistaken idea that marijuana is harmless and non-habit-forming. According to Hoffman and Froemke (2007), "The odds of marijuana dependence in adulthood are six times higher for those who start using pot before the age of 15 than for those who begin after 18." Residual damage from substance abuse includes unwanted pregnancies, sexually transmitted diseases, and driving fatalities and accidents.

How would getting hooked on prescription drugs affect your career?

Shutterstock

> The estimated number of users of illicit drugs in the United States is about 13 million. About 10% of the population is dependent on alcohol and 25% of Americans smoke cigarettes.
> —National Household Survey

Figure 6.3   Signs of Substance Abuse

- Showing a decline in grades or work performance
- Using room deodorizers and incense to hide odors
- Using drug paraphernalia such as baggies, pipes, or rolling paper
- Giving up hobbies and sports that he or she used to enjoy
- Getting drunk or high on a regular basis
- Lying about how much he or she is consuming
- Appearing rundown, hopeless, depressed, or suicidal
- Driving while under the influence of alcohol
- Avoiding friends and family to get drunk
- Hiding alcohol or drinking alone
- Becoming aggressive or hostile
- Getting suspended from school or work because of substance abuse–related incidents
- Getting in trouble with the police

Source: Adapted from Daly and Richards, 2007.

Eighty-five percent of the U.S. prison population either meets the medical criteria for substance abuse or addiction, or had histories of substance abuse; were under the influence of alcohol or other drugs at the time of their crime; committed their offense to get money to buy drugs; were incarcerated for an alcohol or drug law violation; or shared some combination of these characteristics.

—"Behind Bars II: Substance Abuse and America's Prison Population"

Binge drinking is drinking for the primary purpose of getting drunk. Cooper (2002) reported that 61 percent of men who binge drink practice unprotected sex, as compared to only 23 percent who do not binge drink. Forty-eight percent of women who participate in binge drinking practice unprotected sex, compared to 8 percent of women who do not practice binge drinking.

A substance abuse dependency started in college is very likely to carry over into the workplace. Many companies today will require a drug test before they will hire you. We offer the concerned advice of being very careful not to develop a substance abuse problem that can affect you for the rest of your life. If you have a problem or know of someone who does, get help at your earliest convenience.

PERFECT YOUR PROFESSIONAL IMAGE

How Do You Dress and Dine to Be Remembered for All the Right Reasons?

Should I use the shortest fork for my appetizer or the salad? Should I wear French cuffs on an interview? Should I extend my hand to be shaken or wait until a hand is offered?

Many people have the mistaken idea that everyone knows how to dress, how to dine properly, and how to demonstrate good manners. Some even believe that these qualities are not important. The truth is that these things are not taught at home as much as they once were, and many people grow up not knowing these basic points. However, do not be mistaken—first impressions, manners, etiquette, and basic grooming remain very important.

Several years ago, John Malloy, an "image guru," said, "As much as one-third of your success depends on what you wear." In Malloy's opinion, your appearance, image, and presence contribute greatly to your overall success in your career. When you combine a powerful first impression, professional dress, good basic manners, excellent dining etiquette, proper language skills, and add a winning smile, you have all the makings of an outstanding professional package. More and more colleges and schools are providing educational experiences in all these areas for their students. The professional package is the "icing on the cake" that helps students secure the job they want and then move up rapidly in the ranks.

What Is Image, Exactly?

What do we mean by image? And why do you have to have one? Image is the mental picture that people have of you when you pass through their minds. Image is what people see when they think of you. Whether you like it or not, you have an image. Take a minute right now if you can, and go stand in front of a full-length mirror. Pretend this person who is looking back at you is someone other than you. Try to look at your image with an unbiased eye. What do you see? Are you dressed well? Are you clean and pressed? Does your hair look well groomed? Are you smiling? Are your clothes altered correctly and professionally? Do you think you present an upper-middle-class image? If not, you have work to do, because image has a great deal to do with how people treat you and respect you.

Your image and attire combine to make up one component of your overall ability to practice good judgment. You want to dress like you have good judgment and demonstrate an image that makes people look at you as a professional. Knowing how to dress for work can be challenging and confusing. Because dressing can be daunting, many people, especially women, fail at making the right selections.

First, you should determine if your company has a dress code. If so, get a copy from your HR department and abide by the policies. Second, consider your long-term career goals and dress for the position you aspire to rather than the one you are in today. Third, pay attention to how the company leaders dress and take your cue from this group of successful people. Fourth, determine if your position dictates what you wear. If you are in accounting, for example, you might need to wear dark suits, blazers, and other professional outfits. Finally, consider your business wardrobe an investment. It should last for years if you buy classic clothing and avoid putting too much money into fads.

Dress to Impress

Many people like to demonstrate their own style and pay little attention to what constitutes appropriate dress at work. Frequently, companies today don't spell out exactly what they are looking for in employee dress, so you need to pay attention to what the successful people are wearing. Even if you are required to wear a uniform, notice how others present themselves. Is the uniform clean and pressed? Does it fit well?

You have to be able to determine for yourself what looks good on you, what is over-the-top dressing for your particular environment, and what is considered dress that will impress your superiors, colleagues, and customers. Look carefully at the people who have already made it and those who appear to be on a fast track. What do they wear to work? Are they overly casual? Do they wear jeans to work on casual day? Do you see any of them with earrings, tongue studs, or bright red streaks in their hair? Do you find any who have tattoos on their necks, heads, and other conspicuous places? Companies are hiring you to represent them, and they want a positive appearance from all their employees. The appearance that was appropriate at school and in a casual environment may not be acceptable in the work environment.

Women's Dress

Women have so many more choices than men—and so many more ways to get it right or wrong. Getting it right can be a great asset to someone thinking about promotions or making positive impressions. You have many choices that can complement your individual style and body type and still present you in a positive light. You should use dress to reinforce how serious you are about your work and your career.

Whatever your profession, you want to look the part. You don't necessarily want to wear clothes that make you stand out; rather, you want to look good so that people will respond to you appropriately. The mark of a well-dressed woman is that she always looks professional and well-dressed, but you don't necessarily remember exactly what she had on. If you stand out, you have to be sure it is for the right reasons—perhaps a flair for color, style, jewelry, or the ability to mix styles.

If you need to (or are required to) wear business suits, they should be dark colors and preferably should be natural fabrics like wool or linen. Shoes should be stylish, but comfortable, preferably leather, and jewelry should be well-made, preferably gold or silver. Women's professional shoes should not have open heels or toes, straps, platforms, or high spike heels.

Clothes should always be cleaned, pressed and immaculate—no spots, safety pins, or hems or cuffs that are in bad repair. Purses and belts should be leather and in good repair. Your blouses should be tailored; you should avoid busy prints, frilly lace, and sexy garments. Likewise, you should avoid pastel colors for major pieces of your wardrobe, especially light pink (which screams "baby girl") and bright, garish colors. Appearance is a cultivated practice, and you can learn to look and act successful, which will go a long way toward making you successful. To get an idea of how people dress in your profession, purchase magazines or journals that have pictures of people who work in your profession. You might also consider visiting an office where you would like to work and observing the dress of the women who work there. You want to have an image that says "understated elegance."

Shutterstock

If you saw this person at lunch, would she impress you as a professional?

Fashions fade, style is eternal.
— *Yves Saint Laurent*

Although pants are acceptable in most business offices, women should typically stick to pantsuits that have matching blazer and pants. The pants should be hemmed at the proper length according to what is in style. Sleeves should be hemmed so they do not extend below the wrist. Most clothes require some alterations. Avoid buying clothes off the rack that do not fit well or wearing them without having them altered properly to fit you. No matter what salespeople tell you, clothes off the rack almost always need alterations.

The information presented previously primarily relates to business dress for women who are working in business offices. Naturally, if you are working in aviation mechanics, you can't wear pumps and a business suit. Likewise, if you are working in a cubicle as a computer programmer, you will find that most of your colleagues aren't wearing dark business suits. Some positions, such as nursing, will require you to wear a uniform. When it comes to dress in non-traditional fields and fields other than business, you should observe what others in your position or department are wearing and follow suit. No matter what your position or dress code, you should always wear clean, pressed clothes in good repair. Some universal dress tips are presented in Figure 6.4.

Figure 6.4 Universal Dress Tips for Women in a Business Office Environment

Remember that you cannot be sexy and professional in the same outfit—so make up your mind what you want to be known for. No one will take you seriously if you dress provocatively at work.

- The best colors for business suits are navy, black, gray, burgundy, olive, tan, and khaki.

- Pantsuits should preferably have a matching blazer and pants, should be hemmed to the right length, and should never be too short.

- Sleeves should be hemmed so they do not extend below the wrist.

- If you wear a skirt, it should come at least to the top of your knees, even if very short skirts are in style—fashions may dictate changes in skirt lengths, but they should never be too short at work. When you sit, your thighs should be covered.

- Business dresses and pantsuits are fine for most days, but if you have an important meeting, wear a business suit with a skirt. If you wear a dress, wear a blazer or jacket over it.

- Your clothing should not be louder than your voice or personality.

- Avoid overpowering perfume that may be offensive to others. Some people are allergic to strong perfumes.

- Your hair should be clean, well-groomed, and fashionable and should not distract from your overall appearance.

- Avoid clothes that are too tight, see-through, or have long slits in the front that expose too much leg.

- Have your clothes altered to fit well.

- Avoid all extremes such as trendy clothes; bleached hair; or unnatural hair colors such as green, blue, or bright red streaks.

- Have no visible tattoos.

- Avoid any kind of body piercings that are obvious, especially facial piercings or multiple earrings.

- Jewelry should be simple—gold or silver is best.

- Wear no more than one ring on each hand, except for wedding and engagement rings.

- A nice gold watch and one bracelet are nice touches at work.

- Hose should coordinate with your outfit, but usually a barely black or suntan color works for most business occasions. You should always wear hose in the winter.

- Avoid colored, fishnet, and patterned hose at work.

- Carry a cordovan briefcase and no purse so you don't look like a pack horse when you go to an important meeting.

- Carry a briefcase or leather portfolio even if you have nothing in it. It is the image you are going for—a professional with her accessories.

- If you carry a purse, organize it, and don't be seen digging around in it searching for an item.

- Walk briskly and act like you know where you are going. Never drag around at work. This behavior becomes part of your image.

Your image should match your ambitions. If you were going to work today, would your wardrobe reflect your ambitions? Would you look chic and stylish, or would you appear frumpy and nondescript? Would you look like a student or like a professional? What would people say about your grooming? What does your body language say about you? Image is a complete package, and anyone can improve personal image. Some people are naturally more attractive than others, and some are more graceful and charming, but anyone can learn to develop presence and build a better image.

Women: Considering all the tips for dress and image improvement that we have shared with you, list several things about your typical dress that you think you could (and should) improve so that your appearance more closely matches that of your potential coworkers and your career goals.

_____

_____

_____

_____

_____

_____

_____

Men's Dress

One of the best ways for men to stand out is by dressing in an outstanding manner. The typical male does not give a great deal of attention to his appearance, so when a man does it right, he gets a lot of positive attention. As stated earlier, women have many more choices than men—and many more ways of making bad decisions. Any man can become a very good dresser if he is willing to work at it.

While you may not work in a job that requires a suit, you need at least one nice suit and preferably two, especially for the interview. You want interviewers to think they are getting a bargain in you. The best times for men to buy suits are after Christmas and after the Fourth of July, when most nice men's stores put their suits on sale. You might also look for warehouse sales, which often provide excellent bargains if you know how to shop for them.

Many suits can be worn year-round, except perhaps on the coldest or hottest days. If you live in the South or Southwest, you don't need heavy wool clothes—you will get very little wear from them. Regardless of where you live, however, the fabric in your suits should contain wool because it helps suits keep their shape better after cleaning. If you are taking a traveling position, you need clothes that won't wrinkle badly.

Certainly, the rules of dress for a business office do not apply to many professional careers such as plumbing, electrical engineering, auto mechanics, computer programming, and medical assistant positions. In such positions, men should observe what others at their level are wearing and dress accordingly. If you are a computer programmer, for example, you may be allowed to wear jeans and a golf shirt. If this is the case, be sure your jeans are clean, pressed, and do not have holes or frayed cuffs, even if this is a fashion statement.

Review the tips for men's dress presented in Figure 6.5.

Shutterstock

Do you think a company would be interested in hiring this man?

Figure 6.5   Universal Dress Tips for Men in a Business Office Environment

- If you are going to work in a company where you need to wear suits, start building a good wardrobe now. Suits and blazers are expensive and should be accumulated over a period of time.

- Most men need to own at least two suits—navy and charcoal gray work well for most men and fit in well in most companies.

- As a new graduate, you can interview in a blue blazer and charcoal gray slacks if you don't have a suit. A nice sport coat is a good wardrobe addition.

- If you are required to wear dress shirts to work, you should own at least 6–10 of them, including several white shirts and at least two light blue shirts. French blue is also a versatile color that can be worn with most of the colors mentioned above. Of course, you can gradually accumulate this collection.

- The only color shirt to wear to an interview is white, and it should be starched and immaculate.

- Dress shirts should be starched—always! Do not rely on permanent pressed because they always look unkempt if not pressed.

- Dress shirts should always be long-sleeved, even in the summer. Never wear short-sleeved dress shirts—especially to an interview!

- A small monogram on your left cuff is a nice touch.

- You might want to consider at least one shirt with French cuffs and cufflinks.

- Suits should either be two- or three-button. Stay away from trendy suits that will go out of style soon.

- Purchase black and brown belts and shoes; they will look good with almost everything.

- The dressiest shoe a man can wear is a lace-up wing-tip, but young men can wear tasseled loafers or cap-toe lace-up shoes just as well. If you don't understand these terms, ask a shoe salesperson to explain them to you.

- Heels of shoes should not look worn, and shoes should always be polished and shined.

- Socks should be black if worn with gray, navy, or black. Bare leg should not show if you cross your legs, so buy long socks.

- Never wear white socks with a business suit or sport coat. Patterned socks are the mark of a well-dressed man if they are coordinated well.

- Ties should be stylish and bought with careful consideration. If you don't know how to choose a tie, get help from a salesperson at a nice men's store. Unless she has excellent taste, don't let your girlfriend or your wife choose your ties.

- Ties should be made of silk in a stylish width and should have no spots on them.

- Men should learn to tie a knot that is in style. The bottom part of the tie should reach right below your belt. Do not wear a tie that sits on your stomach and indicates that you do not know how to dress professionally.

- Men should wear a mild, non-offensive cologne.

- Remove fat wallets, large key rings, and excessive change from your pockets. You want to look streamlined and put together.

- Buy a nice leather briefcase, and use it even if you have nothing in it but your lunch!

GRADUATE Quote

Jonathan T. Ellis
Graduate!
The University of South Carolina, Columbia, SC
Career: Network Administrator, The University of South Carolina

The most important lesson I learned was this: Perfect your capacity to articulate your abilities and skills because you never know what employers are really looking for. Never be discouraged. Your dream position is out there.

Dress for interviews should be based on the kind of job you for which are interviewing. If you are dressing to be machine technician, you would dress differently from someone interviewing for a position in allied health. "The first judgment an interviewer makes is going to be based on how you look and what you are wearing" (Doyle, 2011).

Men: Considering all the tips we have discussed with you, list several things about your dress that you think you could (and should) improve so your dress more closely matches that of your potential coworkers and your career goals.

_____

_____

_____

_____

_____

_____

Business Casual—The Type of Professional Dress That Stumps Many Men and Women

The important thing to remember about business casual is this: "While casual may be optional, looking professional is not. Exercising poor work attire choices can convey an unfavorable message to your superiors and colleagues and ultimately stunt your growth within an organization" (Zuri, 2011). Business casual should be crisp, clean, neat, and pressed. You should feel well-dressed even if you bump into the president.

Many businesses allow employees to "dress down," especially on Friday. Dressing down does not mean "anything goes." Some people really mess up with casual dress, and they stand out for all the wrong reasons because they don't take it seriously enough.

Although you don't want to overdress when others are casual, you don't want to go to great extremes with your casual dress either. Actually, it is just as expensive to dress well for casual occasions as it is to dress for business—and more difficult for many people because they fail to take it seriously. A general rule of thumb for dressing for success is this: Observe what others, including your supervisors, are wearing.

Some basic tips for business casual dress are listed below:

■ On casual days, men should wear a good pair of dress slacks and a golf shirt or a knit shirt with a blazer.

■ Men can also wear a button-down shirt with slacks and a blazer. Women can wear simple slacks that are pressed, the right length, and not too tight.

■ Under no circumstances should you wear t-shirts and wrinkled khakis or unpressed jeans. Tennis shoes, sandals, or hiking boots are never appropriate.

Shutterstock

Does this man pass the test as a well-dressed professional?

- Showing cleavage for women is never appropriate, no matter what you see on television or in magazines.
- Facial hair should be worn only if higher-ranking company executives do so, and should be well-groomed.
- Makeup should be conservative and natural looking. Nails should be groomed and cleaned. Women should avoid very bright polish for business. Likewise, they should avoid all the fashion design nails done by salons for work.

DINE WITH CLASS

Who Cares If I Don't Use the Right Fork?

The mark of a very polished person is the ability to use outstanding dining etiquette, to order food and beverage with confidence. The finer points of dining etiquette need to be studied and used as you enter your career and consider moving up. No one is exempt from needing to know how to sit and eat a meal with dignity and grace. No one! Read a good etiquette book and take it seriously. Research shows that only about 12 percent of new hires are skilled in the social graces. In fact, many companies hire consultants to teach their employees how to practice good etiquette. Etiquette or the lack of it may mean the difference between success or failure. Excellent manners will set you apart early in your career. Manners will also make a positive impression on almost everyone, especially your customers and clients!

We assume you know the basics, such as chew with your mouth closed, keep your elbows off the table, pass food to the right, cut your meat only one piece at a time, and butter only one small piece of bread at a time—but many people don't know these rules! You also need to know the following basic rules of good etiquette and dining:

Do these employees look dressed professionally for work on business casual day?

Shutterstock

- A utensil that has been used should never be placed on a tablecloth. Place it on the edge of your plate.
- If you use a sweetener or other item that has been wrapped in paper, slip the paper under your bread plate. Don't leave it on the table in a conspicuous manner.
- Remember LR, LR, LR—liquids to the right. This means that you should only drink from or use the glasses on your right. Solids, such as bread plates, are always on your left.
- As part of your interview, you may be taken to a nice restaurant. People will be observing to determine if you can represent them well.
- Order something that is easy to eat and not the most expensive thing on the menu. A good rule is to follow the price range of the host who is taking you to dinner.
- Avoid messy foods. Spaghetti is difficult to manage, soup might drip on your clothes, and ribs can't be eaten easily.
- If you eat soup, dip your spoon away from you, rather than towards you.
- Do not push food onto your fork with your knife or a piece of bread.
- If the host orders dessert, you can do so, but you should not if he or she does not.
- Under no circumstances should you drink or smoke, even if others at the table do. If your host orders wine, you may have one glass of wine if you would like to, but you should not have any more.

■ If you share foods—and this is not advised on an interview—do not pass your plate back and forth. Using a clean, unused utensil, place a portion on your bread plate and pass it to the person for whom it is intended or ask your server for a small plate.

Figure 6.6 is a diagram of a formal table setting. Study it carefully so you will know what to do if you are dining at a formal restaurant. Starting at the outer edge, use the appropriate fork with each course. Again, the rule to remember is: Solids on the left, liquids on the right; in other words, your personal bread plate is on the upper left hand side of your plate, and your drink will be on the right. If you can't remember this, wait and watch others at the table, then do what they do.

If you leave the table, place your napkin on your chair; do not put it on the table until the meal has been completed and you are leaving the restaurant. When you finish your meal and are leaving the table, fold your napkin loosely and place it back on the table.

When women approach or leave the table, men should stand. If it is a business occasion, women should stand at the beginning of the meal and shake hands as the men are doing. Women do not need to stand when someone leaves the table or returns. A man should help the woman to his right with her chair and then help the woman on his left if no one else is doing so. Take your seat from the right side of the chair.

You may be saying to yourself, "Who cares?" or "What difference does it make which fork I use?" The answer is simple and complex—no one and everyone. However, consider this: It is always better to have knowledge and skills and not need them than to need them and not have them. You will use this often!

There is much to learn en route to developing a professional presence, and you might make some mistakes. Learn from them and keep working until you are comfortable in any setting.

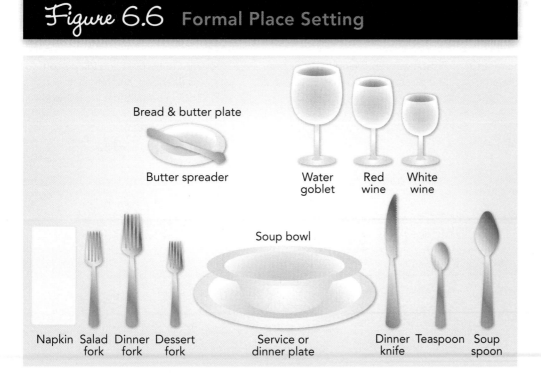

Figure 6.6   Formal Place Setting

Bread & butter plate

Butter spreader

Water goblet

Red wine

White wine

Soup bowl

Napkin   Salad fork   Dinner fork   Dessert fork   Service or dinner plate   Dinner knife   Teaspoon   Soup spoon

Reflections:
PUTTING IT ALL TOGETHER

Avoiding workplace land mines can be quite tricky, but it's just a part of going to work every day. If you go to work with the right attitude, give your best, support your boss, and build a network of people who have goals and dreams like yours, you will be able to navigate the mine field.

In the beginning, you may have difficulty learning to dress well, to dine correctly, or simply to avoid office politics, but you will learn if you put your mind to it, and you will be surprised how much all these little things contribute to your big picture.

DIGITAL BRIEFCASE

CONDUCTING A POLL AND REPORTING DATA

Use Poll Everywhere (www.polleverywhere.com) and set up a poll that queries your social media friends on the "mistakes" they have seen people make, such as posting negative remarks about their boss or company, sending e-mails that contain obscenities on a company computer, sexting, posting pictures of drunken parties on Facebook, and others.

Also, ask them to describe in detail what the offense was, what the consequences were, and if this mistake can be rectified. Then make a three-column table with the headings "Offense," "Consequence," and "How to Resolve the Problem." Report what you learned using a chart similar to the one below. Research and write two brief paragraphs on "Avoiding Poor Choices Using Social Media."

Offense	Consequence	Resolution (if possible)
Sent offensive e-mail based on race to friend, who forwarded it to others.	Person was reprimanded by his boss and placed on probation because of violation of company policy.	Apologize to his boss and the person who was offended, and refrain from ever sending e-mails that are not work-related at work.

Offense	Consequence	Resolution (if possible)

REFERENCES

Behind bars II: Substance abuse and America's prison population. (2011). Retrieved May 14, 2011, from www.casacolumbia.org/templates/PressReleases.aspx?articleid=592&zoneid=79.

Buddy, T. (2011). Substance abuse in the workplace: A dangerous and expensive problem. Retrieved June 2, 2011, from http://alcoholism.about.com/cs/work/a/aa990120.htm.

Cooper, M. (2002). Alcohol use and risky sexual behavior among college students and youth. *Journal of Studies on Alcohol, 63*(2), 101.

Daly, K., & Richards, J. (2007). Substance abuse. Retrieved July 18, 2011, from www.emedicinehealth.com/substanceabuse/articleem.htm.

Doyle, A. (2010). How to dress for an interview. Retrieved July 18, 2011, from http://jobsearch.about.com/od/interviewattire/a/interviewdress.htm.

Hoffman, J., & Froemke, S. (2007). *Addiction: Why can't they just stop?* Emmaus, PA: Rodale.

Kersten, D. (2002). Office romances can be risky. USA TODAY. Retrieved July 21, 2011, from www.usatoday.com/money.jobcenter/workplace/relationships/2002-11-12-office-romance.

Taylor, D. (2005). The intuitive life blog. "Why are office romances such a bad idea?" Retrieved May 18, 2011, from http://www.intuitive.com/blog/why_are_office_romances_such_a_bad_idea.html

Vault.com. (2010). Office Romance Survey 2010. Retrieved May 19, 2011, from www.vault.com/wps/portal/usa/vcm/detail/Career-Advice/Office-Romance/Office-Romance-Survey-2010?id=5519&filter_type=0&filter_id=0

Zuri, I. (2011). How to dress for work for women. Retrieved May 15, 2011, from www.ehow.com/how6223951dress-work-women.html#ixzz1MQBf9L4M.

chapter seven

MANAGE

NAVIGATING THE HUMAN RESOURCE MAZE

The only place where success comes before work is in the dictionary. —Vince Lombardi

PART TWO: MANAGING YOUR LIFE

Why read this chapter?

Because you'll learn...

- The functions of human resources departments
- The differences in corporate benefits and which ones best serve you
- How companies are organized and where you fit in the structure

Because you'll be able to...

- Select benefits that protect you, your family, and your future
- Discuss various benefit packages and understand their importance to your future.

PROFESSIONALS from the Field

Name: Tina Petrie

Business: Director of Salary Administration and Benefits, The College of Southern Nevada

Your human resources (HR) office will be your center of information from application to retirement. Often, people think of HR as a place that hires and fires, but my advice would be to lean on your HR department for things like tax and estate planning, health spending accounts, medical plans, career path advice, professional development, and group discounts to large chains and entertainment venues. The HR department can also help you gather data to complete projects for your own department. Basically, use your HR department to leverage your benefits, information, and life planning.

MyStudentSuccessLab

MyStudentSuccessLab (www.mystudentsuccesslab.com) is an online solution designed to help you "Start strong, Finish stronger" by building skills for ongoing personal and professional development.

OVERVIEW OF THE HUMAN RESOURCES DEPARTMENT

How Do They Manage All These Requirements?

Human resource management (HRM) is engaging people (employees) in a variety of ways and at different levels to accomplish an organization's goals and objectives. Human resource managers and employees work on a diverse array of responsibilities, ranging from recruiting to staffing to training to compensating to evaluating employees. This department is in charge of annual leave and vacations, sick leave, discrimination policies, social security deductions, taxes, retirement funds, and employee privacy. In addition, they must comply with government laws and rules such as safety regulations, and they must oversee internal corporate policies and procedures. At times, HR professionals must deal with unions and labor relations and negotiations. The illustration in Figure 7.1 shows the major functions in the HR process.

"In a large corporation, the *director of human resources* may supervise several departments, each headed by an experienced manager who most likely specializes in one human resources

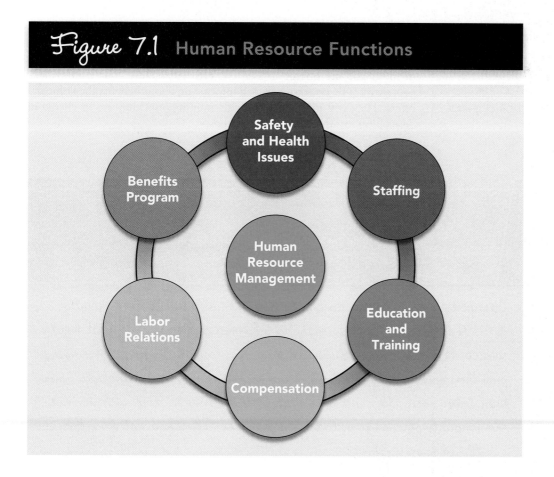

Figure 7.1 Human Resource Functions

activity, such as employment and placement, compensation and benefits, training and development, or labor relations. The director may report to a top human resources executive" (U.S. Department of Labor, 2010–2011). In small companies, the HR department may consist of a manager and a few employees with multiple responsibilities.

Changes in HR Functions

Although the divisions of HR departments remain rather static, the functions are changing dramatically with shifts in technology and the global economy. "The world economy is going through a seismic shift from capital investment to intellectual capital. This shift, along with the change in the pace of business dynamics, is leading to compelling changes in the way people are managed. The boardroom has moved into the HR function, and most CEOs now don the hat of the Chief Talent Officers. As the workforce gets younger and the businesses increasingly become global and virtual, the challenge that HR faces is to engage the diverse workforce and align them to the business's objectives" (Murali, 2011). Today the HR department is heavily involved in using technology to recruit, receive and review resumés, conduct interviews, educate employees, and keep people informed about new rules and regulations.

GETTING ORIENTED AT YOUR NEW JOB

Will Someone Help Me Understand All These Rules and Regulations?

> *Research indicates that workers have three prime needs: Interesting work, recognition for doing a good job, and being let in on things that are going on in the company.*
> —Zig Ziglar, *motivational speaker*

From the very beginning of your contact with a company, you will be dealing with some aspect of HR. Someone from HR might interview you in addition to managers from the area where you are trying to find employment. If you are offered a position, HR will handle your employment paperwork. HR professionals will inform you about benefits the company offers. They will most likely provide training, and they are in charge of developing forms for evaluation purposes.

GRADUATE *Quote*

William Paddock
Graduate!
Louisville Technical Institute, Louisville, KY
Career: IT Security Specialist, First Technology

Completing your degree does not complete your learning—especially in fields that change rapidly, such as information technology and health science. Learning never stops. If you stop learning, you stop growing and then no one will hire you. You have to continually upgrade your knowledge base. You will also need to learn how to deal with the massive amounts of change in today's workplace. If I had not done this, I would not have survived.

One of the first ways you might be engaged with the HR department staff is through the company's orientation program for new employees. During this time, you will be provided a great deal of information about the company, including the company's history, the products and services it provides, policies and procedures, and financial data. You will most likely be provided information relative to the company's organizational structure, vision statement, mission statement, and goals and objectives. You will learn the names of people on the executive team. You may hear from a higher-level executive at some point in the process, and you might be given information about the company's primary competitors, clients, and market region.

In addition, you will complete a number of forms related to the hiring process. These forms will include a W-4, which informs HR how to withhold your taxes. At this time, you will also be informed about the company's benefits program. If your company requires that you wear an identification badge, this will be given to you. You might also be given keys to certain areas to which you will need access. At some point during the orientation process, you may be given a copy of the employee handbook. An HR person will go over some of the most important points, but you should read the entire handbook and keep it in your work area as a reference. You will probably need to refer to it often as you become familiar with your new position.

You may feel a little overwhelmed when hearing all of this data in a short period of time. Take good notes and take home any information provided to study it carefully. Do not hesitate to ask questions if there is anything that you do not understand. One of the most important areas for you to comprehend is the benefits section. It is much better to ask questions than to make a major mistake in selecting benefits.

UNDERSTANDING AND SELECTING BENEFITS

How Can I Get the 411 on My 401(k)?

Even in economic downturns, employers are always looking for ways to attract high-quality employees. Offering an outstanding benefits program is one way of attracting good people. Employers are always looking for unique ways to reward employees in order to retain their services. When you are interviewing for a new position, one of the areas you need to examine most closely is the benefits program, and after you accept a position, you really need to pay close attention. Benefits are **indirect compensation** (financial rewards that are not included in your paycheck such as paid holidays, medical insurance, or child care). Another name for benefits is "perks," and you might hear it mentioned in the workplace.

According to the U.S. Bureau of Labor Statistics, the cost to companies in supplying benefits to their employees has risen sharply. Many companies provide thousands of dollars in benefits to each employee annually. "U.S. businesses pay an average of $7.40 per hour that each employee works. The average cost of health care benefits is approximately $8424 annually per person" (Mondy, 2010). Because of the extraordinary costs of providing employee benefits, some companies are taking a less paternalistic approach and shifting more of the responsibility to employees themselves. Rather than provide retirement programs, more and more companies are moving to 401(k) programs to which employees contribute and manage themselves.

Usually only full-time employees receive benefits, although some companies provide limited benefits for part-time employees. You should consider benefits as part of your compensation package, and you should weigh their value very carefully when making an employment decision. Benefits are very expensive if you have to pay for them yourself. For example, if you have small children and your company provides child care as a benefit, this can save you thousands of dollars every year, plus give you the satisfaction of knowing your children are taken care of while you work.

> *People are definitely a company's greatest asset. It doesn't make any difference whether the product is cars or cosmetics. A company is only as good as the people it keeps.*
>
> —Mary Kay Ash, founder of Mary Kay Cosmetics

Full-time employees usually receive **direct benefits** (monetary value) and **indirect benefits** (such as sick leave and vacation). Due to rapidly rising costs, many companies are reducing the amounts of some of their benefits and eliminating others altogether. The list of potential employee benefits offered by companies usually includes a retirement plan, 401(k) plan, vacation, sick leave, personal leave, health insurance, life insurance, dental insurance, disability insurance, employee stock ownership plans, maternity leave, paternity leave, vision plans, and parking.

Some benefits such as paid vacation and holidays are considered company paid. Benefits to which the employee contributes are considered employee paid—employees are usually required to make a contribution to the cost of their health insurance, for example, because it is so expensive. Study Figure 7.2 for information on 10 of the most frequently provided benefits.

Benefits such as unemployment insurance, worker's compensation, social security, and family and medical leave are mandated by the federal government. "Approximately 95 percent of the workers in this country pay into and may draw Social Security benefits" (Mondy, 2010). The looming retirement of the "baby boomers" has endangered the solvency of social security if it continues on its current path. Congress has to find solutions and make changes in the next two decades or the program will not be able to pay full benefits.

> *The flatter the corporate hierarchy, the more likely it is that employees will communicate bad news and act upon it.*
>
> *—Bill Gates*

Figure 7.2 Understanding Benefits Programs

Type of Benefit	Explanation
Health Care	The most expensive benefit provided. Includes **HMOs** (exercises control over which doctors and facilities you can use); **PPOs** (encourages employees to use services specified by the system, with out-of-system services costing more); **defined contribution health care plans** (provides employees a specified amount of money, which they can use to purchase health insurance of their choice); and **major medical** (designed to cover large medical expenses brought about by long-term illness or serious diseases or accidents).
Dental and Vision Care	The costs provided for these benefits vary by company, but they usually require a small deductible before paying approximately 50 to 100 percent of the costs for dental preventive services. Some plans cover partial costs of orthodontics. Vision plans may cover the costs of eye examinations and all or part of the cost of glasses.
Retirement Plans	**Defined benefit plans** provide a fixed amount of money each month to retired employees and are usually based on years of service and an average of the employee's salary during the last years of work. Employees know exactly how much money they will receive each month under this program. Because of extraordinary costs, this type of program is declining, and the burden of planning for retirement is now on the employee. In **defined contribution plans,** employers make specific contributions to employees' retirement programs. The amount of money available to the employee at retirement under this plan will depend on how well investments made by the employee performed. **401(k) plans** fall under this category.
Paid Vacations	A very popular program with employees that allows them to rejuvenate and rest. Usually, the number of days increases with seniority.
Sick Leave	Employees who are too sick to come to work are still paid for a certain number of days each year.
Employee Stock Options (ESOP)/Profit Sharing	Companies who offer this benefit contribute shares of stock to employees based on their salaries. Some people believe that ESOP participation causes employees to work harder and to be more concerned about productivity. The downside to ESOPs is that employees cannot sell their stock until they retire, meaning that they cannot capitalize on an upswing in the stock market.

Type of Benefit	Explanation
Life Insurance	Many companies provide life insurance for employees in the amount of 1½ times their salaries, with options to purchase more for their themselves and their families.
Child Care	For employees who have small children, this is a very important benefit. Usually, the child care program is not paid 100 percent, but is subsidized, thus reducing the very expensive cost of child care. Some companies provide emergency care for children when babysitting services are not available on a temporary basis.
Education Reimbursement	Many employers will pay for employees to go back to school. Benefits vary but usually reimburse expenses based on achieving a certain grade. Some will pay only for courses or programs related to an employee's work.
Flextime or Flexible Scheduling	For many employees, this is a great benefit because it gives them the opportunity to choose some of the hours they work, and they can fit their work around family needs. Usually, employees are required to be at work during a core time (for example, 10:00–2:00) but are allowed to choose to come in early or stay late.

Choosing the Right Benefits

In some companies, all employees are provided the same basic benefits. In other companies, a **cafeteria benefits plan** is used. This type of plan allows employees to select certain benefits. Some companies provide the basic benefits such as health insurance for everyone in addition to the ones selected by the employee; others allow employees to choose from the cafeteria plan for all their benefits. An employee who has small children might select child care, whereas an employee who is taking care of older parents might select elder care. Employees select benefits based on their current stage of life and on what their individual needs are.

The following is a list of benefits your employer may offer:

Retirement plan	Child care	Parking
401(k) plan	Educational assistance	Company car (provided for certain positions)
Prescription drug program	Scholarships for dependents	Free meals in the cafeteria
Dental insurance	Vision care	Chiropractic visits
Family medical program	Legal assistance	Relocation benefits
Major medical insurance	Elder care	Flextime schedule
Flexible spending medical account	Paid vacation	Telecommuting
Medical insurance	Paid holidays	Compressed work week
Dental insurance	Paid personal days	Employee stock options
Life insurance	Company discounts	Health center

As you review the extensive list of benefits above, think about how your choice of benefits might change according to your age and family status. If you were going to work today and were offered a cafeteria plan for all your benefits and could choose only five to seven from the list, which ones would benefit you most? List them below:

1. _____

2. _____

3. _____

4. _____

5. _____

MAKING AN IMPORTANT CHOICE

How Do I Decide Which Job to Accept?

One of the most effective ways to make a decision is to use a numerical scale to actually assign a "grade" to each choice before you. This exercise is designed to help you make a choice between two job offers in relation to benefits. Of course, benefits are not the only major factor you have to consider when choosing between two jobs, but it is one of the most important components. This decision chart works in the following way:

- **Create an Element (benefit) column.** This column lists the aspects of the decision that are important to you, such as pay, potential for growth, joy of work, and so on.
- **Create a Rating of Importance column.** This column gives each element a rating that *you* assign. Using a scale of 1 to 10, you will decide if a particular benefit is very important (an 8, 9, or 10) or if it is not very important (a 1, 2, or 3).
- **Create a Choice 1 column.** This column will list the numerical calculations for your first job offer. You will decide how good this company's benefits program is in terms of a specific benefit and then multiply that number by your importance rating.
- **Create a Choice 2 column.** This column will list the numerical calculations for your second job offer. You will decide how good this company's benefits program is in terms of a specific benefit and then multiply that number by your importance rating.

Once you have created your columns (see Figure 7.3), you will work through your decisions using your head and your heart. Assume Samantha has been offered two jobs. Review how she

Figure 7.3   Samantha's Decision-Making Chart

The following example shows a decision-making chart between two job offers for Samantha. The Element (benefit) column lists the items that are most important to Samantha in selecting a new job.

Element (benefit)	My Rating of Importance 1–10	Choice 1 Job at Mercy Hospital	Choice 2 Job at Grace Hospital
Health insurance	10	Rating = 5 $10 \times 5 = 50$	Rating = 8 $10 \times 8 = 80$
Child care	10	Rating = 9 $10 \times 9 = 90$	Rating = 7 $10 \times 7 = 70$
Flexible schedule	7	Rating = 2 $7 \times 2 = 14$	Rating = 5 $7 \times 5 = 35$
Retirement plan	9	Rating = 9 $9 \times 9 = 81$	Rating = 5 $9 \times 5 = 45$
Paid vacation	8	Rating = 8 $8 \times 8 = 64$	Rating = 6 $8 \times 6 = 48$
		TOTAL SCORE = 299	TOTAL SCORE = 278

Figure 7.4 Decision-Making Chart

Element (benefit)	My Rating of Importance 1–10	Choice 1	Choice 2
		TOTAL SCORE =	TOTAL SCORE =

rated each benefit for the two different companies to help her make a decision about which job to accept.

As you can see, Samantha's best option in terms of benefits is Mercy Hospital. A numerical score may not be the ultimate way to make a decision, but at least you have taken the time to think about what is important to you, what is offered within the choices, and how it ranks in importance to you. By using this system, you are calling on your head and your heart to make decisions that could affect your life for a very long time.

Now, using the top five benefits that you selected above, insert them into the Decision-Making Chart in Figure 7.4. For purposes of this exercise, you can make up information about the two jobs.

PERFORMANCE APPRAISALS

How Do I Earn a Good Score?

Performance evaluations make everyone a little nervous, but there are ways to prepare for them that should relieve you of worry. When you are in an orientation program, find out when you will be evaluated and by whom. You will probably be evaluated at the end of your probationary period and thereafter on an annual basis. Ask for a copy of the appraisal instrument and go over it carefully to be sure you are doing everything that falls under your job description. You may be doing a great job in almost everything but get a low rating in one category because you simply ignored it.

Some companies will have you complete a **self-appraisal** prior to the one conducted by your supervisor. Self-appraisals are documents that are completed by the employee in advance of the formal evaluation and are designed to inform the boss. Most people tend to evaluate

BIGGEST INTERVIEW *Blunders*

Quan landed an interview with a company that was seeking a person for her dream job. She prepared carefully, dressed well, and arrived on time. But only a few minutes into the interview, Quan interrupted the interviewer to ask about benefits, telling the interviewer, "Benefits are my main consideration in accepting a position." Quan should have waited until the second interview to bring up benefits, or she should have given the interviewer time to introduce the subject during the interview. Because Quan appeared to be much more interested in her own compensation than she was in doing a good job for the company, she did not get the job.

LESSON: Wait until the second interview to mention salary and benefits. The interviewer knows you are interested and will most likely discuss it with you before you have to ask.

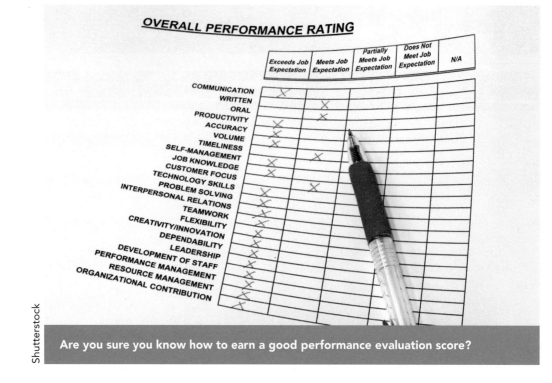

Are you sure you know how to earn a good performance evaluation score?

themselves fairly accurately and are often tougher on themselves than their bosses are. A self-appraisal is a good opportunity to make sure your boss knows everything you have been doing. Remember, your boss is very busy and does not always know exactly what you are doing or how hard you are working. Tell the truth and do not be overly critical of yourself. This is a time to "toot your own horn" in an appropriate manner. Attach a list of major accomplishments that you have achieved since the last evaluation period. If you are not asked to complete a self-appraisal form, provide the list of accomplishments to your boss in a memo prior to the formal evaluation.

There are numerous appraisal methods and systems, including the rating scale method, the critical incident method, the work standards method, the forced distribution method, and the popular 360-degree feedback evaluation method, to name a few. The important thing is to find out exactly how you will be evaluated, get a copy of the instrument, evaluate yourself periodically, and be sure you are performing all aspects of your job in an outstanding manner.

MAXIMIZING PRODUCTIVITY

What Makes a Company Run?

Many people go to work and just try to learn only their own job. Most entry-level jobs are rather narrow in scope, and if that is all you learn, you are not likely to progress very fast. You should go to work with the idea that you "own the company" and that you want to learn everything you can possibly uncover. Ideally, you have already learned a great deal about the company when you were preparing to interview, but now you are on the inside and there is so much more to grasp. Pay attention to what the top executives do. What do they wear? How do they conduct themselves? What are their goals? Ask questions, read company documents, and observe carefully. Your eyes should be like little cameras—clicking, clicking, clicking, and storing up knowledge and information to help you be more productive and efficient.

Some of the things you need to familiarize yourself with are the company's **mission statement** (the purpose of the company, which answers the question, "Why does this company exist?"), **vision statement** (where the company is trying to go, which might be described as a picture of the company in the future), and **core values statement** (a guide for the company's internal conduct, which determines its relationship with the external world).

A mission statement should be clear and brief so that everyone in the company can quote it from memory. An example of a mission statement follows. This one belongs to Aflac:

Mission Statement

To combine aggressive strategic marketing with quality products and services at competitive prices to provide the best insurance value for consumers.

There is no doubt as to the purpose of this company. The employees know what they are trying to accomplish, the customers can understand what the company stands for, and the marketing and advertising are geared to match the mission.

Examples of vision statements follow:

> **Disney:** To make people happy.
>
> **Walmart:** Worldwide leader in retail.
>
> **Ritz Carlton:** We are ladies and gentlemen serving ladies and gentlemen.

There is no doubt in anyone's mind what these companies are trying to accomplish.

An example of a core value statement follows.

1. **Accountability.** To accept responsibility for all our actions and all subsequent effects upon the community.
2. **Community.** To be an organization that gives back to the community, both with the services we provide and the charitable work we do.
3. **Diversity.** To appreciate the richness of a diverse staff and strive to build a team that reflects the diversity of the community we serve.
4. **Ethics.** To foster a workplace environment in which honesty and integrity are valued.
5. **Excellence.** To perform our services better than any of our competitors.
6. **Profit.** To give our valued shareholders the return they deserve by being financially successful.
7. **Leadership.** To provide visionary leadership that includes employee development.

A company's administrators and leaders typically develop the **strategic plan,** which might be described as a roadmap that flows from the mission and vision statements. This plan encompasses the strategy, the action plan, and the deadlines of how the company will accomplish its vision. Each department within the company will have certain **goals and objectives** to carry out that are part of the master plan. Goals are broad statements that are connected to the mission statement, and objectives are more clearly defined statements that detail exactly what the company plans to do. Figure 7.5 provides a visual illustration of what a strategic plan is all about.

When you go to work, ask for copies of the mission, vision, and core values statements. If possible, secure these documents and read them before you interview with a company. Take time to study them and strive to work in such a way as to help your company's leaders accomplish their goals for the business, employees, and customers. Some companies do not distribute the entire strategic plan, but if yours does, read it carefully. You'll be ahead of most of your colleagues in understanding what your leaders are trying to accomplish and how you can help.

Figure 7.5   Strategic Planning Diagram

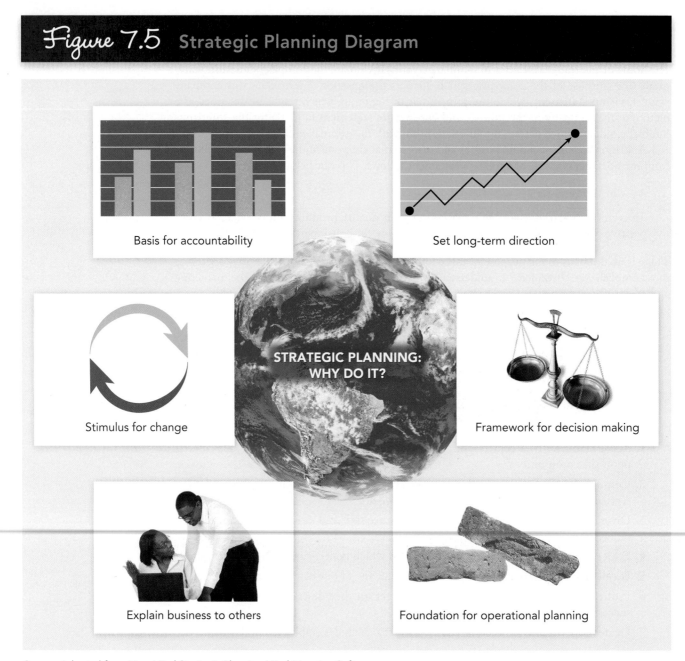

Source: Adapted from NovaMind Strategic Planning Mind Mapping Software.

COMPANY ORGANIZATIONAL STRUCTURE

What Is the Big Picture?

The **organizational structure** of a company is a critical part of corporate effectiveness and internal customer satisfaction. The organizational structure determines how the company uses its resources and how it arranges itself. The structure may be one that divides employees into departments, each of which has a specific function. The organizational structure determines how the **five critical functions of management**—planning, organizing, staffing, leading, and controlling—will be carried out. Figure 7.6 illustrates the five functions of management.

Figure 7.6 The Five Functions of Management

Planning	Organizing	Staffing	Leading	Controlling
Plan strategy, set goals, establish deadlines, and develop action plan.	Decide what has to be done, how it will be accomplished, and who will do it.	Decide how employees will be organized, recruited, trained, and developed.	Determine how to motivate employees to carry out strategic plan, direct employee tasks and projects, and resolve conflicts.	Oversee corporate activities, projects, and plans to ensure satisfactory completion in a timely manner.

Every company has an **organizational chart**. Most people go to work every day and try to do their jobs well, but they don't have a clue as to how their company is organized, where they fit in the big picture, and who reports to whom. You should get a copy of your company's organizational structure and study it carefully. This chart will detail for you exactly what your career path might be as you move up the ladder, as well as other possible options. An example of one type of organizational chart is shown in Figure 7.7. The chart details key functions in this company and shows the lines of authority. Companies are typically organized around the functions that employees carry out. In the case of this company, the business is organized around the functions of marketing, finance, operations, human resources, and information systems.

Companies have a board of directors to which the CEO (chief executive officer and the company leader) reports directly. The board's job is to work with the CEO in developing

Figure 7.7 Organizational Chart

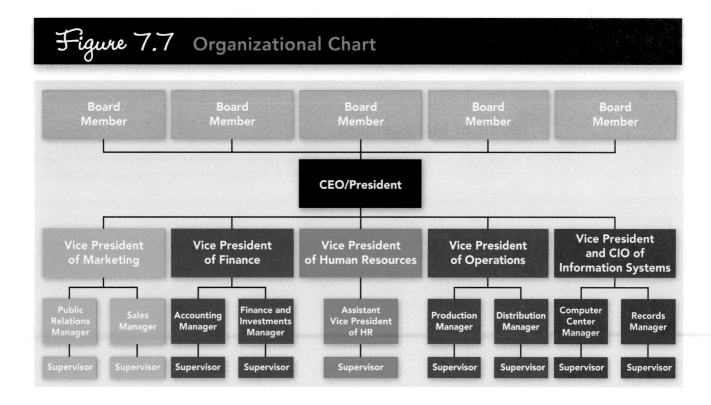

POSITIVE HABITS at Work

When you accept a new job, try to learn everything you can about the company, the executives who make the major decisions, the board members, and the company structure. Read the strategic plan and determine if any of the action items relate to your department and your job specifically. If so, make every effort to contribute to the completion of those action items that relate to you and your job. Continue to learn everything you can about your new company, and you will most likely be much more successful.

Three Rules of Work:
Out of clutter find simplicity;
From discord find harmony;
In the middle of difficulty
lies opportunity.

—*Albert Einstein*

the corporate strategy. The board members are elected to their positions by the shareholders (people who own stock in the company). Some companies have a CEO and a president; in some cases, one person serves as both the president and the CEO. The vice president of information systems is also frequently referred to as the CIO (chief information officer).

Responsibilities of Each Department

The **marketing department** handles the functions of creating the company's image and promoting and distributing the products or services. The **finance department** is responsible for controlling, managing, and growing the company's financial assets. The finance department is also responsible for developing and managing budgets. The **accounting department** handles payroll, incoming and outgoing cash and checks, and invoices and purchase orders. The **human resources department** takes care of all personnel issues, including recruiting, hiring, compensation packages, training programs, promotions, and terminations. The **operations department** is in charge of producing and distributing the products or services offered by the company. The **information systems department** deals with everything related to electronic management of information and all operations having to do with computers, including evaluating, purchasing, installing, and managing new software and computers.

There are many different types of organization charts and ways of organizing a company or institution. You should find your immediate supervisor on the chart and see to whom he or she reports. You should also be able to identify the top corporate officers if you see them in the building or meet them on some occasion, assuming you go to work for a big company and may not know the top officers. An important thing to remember: Do not go over your boss's head to his or her boss. Follow the lines of authority.

Although many corporate structures are organized differently depending on the business of the company, most will have a similar structure to the one that follows in Figure 7.8. Each level of employees has a specific function to perform, again depending on the nature of the company's business.

Levels of Management

Companies typically have three levels of management, including the top level (senior executives), the middle level (managers and directors), and the lower level (supervisors and assistant managers).

TOP LEVEL.   The top level consists of the board of directors, chief executive officer, president, or managing director. The top level of management has the authority to make major decisions, to manage goals, and to develop policies for the company. The top level considers strategic decisions, controls activities of all departments and employees, provides leadership for the company, and has a responsibility to shareholders to manage the company in such a way as to make a profit.

MIDDLE LEVEL.   Middle managers consist of managers and directors who report to top management and are responsible for all functions of their department, division, or area. Their jobs are considered tactical in nature, meaning they tie the strategy to the department's day-to-day

Figure 7.8   Corporate Structure

CORPORATE STRUCTURE

Board of Directors

President/CEO

Executive Team Vice Presidents

Middle Management Team Directors, Managers

Operations Team Supervisors, Assistant Managers

functions. They are primarily involved in organizing and directing functions for the area for which they are responsible. This group of managers must follow company policies, provide training for their subordinates, carry out directives from top management, write reports and send critical data to top management, evaluate employees' performance, and provide leadership for their division.

LOWER LEVEL.   The lower level of management is the operations level, or the level where the actual day-to-day work is performed. Managers at this level may be called supervisors, assistant managers, foremen, or superintendents. They are concerned with getting the job done and use the direction and controlling functions of management. Their job consists of assigning jobs and tasks to employees, providing guidance as to how to perform a task, ensure quality control, make recommendations to higher level managers, provide training to new employees, procure the products needed to do the job, prepare and deliver reports to higher levels of management, and discipline and motivate employees (Management Study Guide, Columbia College).

> *I'm a great believer in luck, and I find the harder I work the more I have of it.*
> —Thomas Jefferson

Reflections: PUTTING IT ALL TOGETHER

Learning everything you can about your company makes you a better and more engaged employee. When you go to work, try not to focus only on the narrow aspects of your particular position. Instead, try to understand how what you are doing fits into the big picture. What is happening around you? Who is doing what? Who is performing extraordinarily well and would be someone to emulate? Who might be a good mentor for you? How does the expansion into international markets affect you, and what opportunities does it offer? What new degrees or courses could you take to enhance your career opportunities? Turn yourself into an inquisitive, involved, and concerned employee who is career oriented and at the same time, willing to give 100 percent back to the company that writes your paycheck.

DIGITAL BRIEFCASE

COMPLETING A W-4 FORM

Access the website www.irs.gov/pub/irs-pdf/fw4.pdf for a copy of the W-4 form that you will have to complete on employment. This form is interactive and will provide practice for you. By completing this form, you will learn what you do not understand and will know how to ask questions before you have to complete this form at a real job.

REFERENCES

Management Study Guide, Columbia College. (2010). Levels of management. Retrieved May 9, 2010, from www.managementstudyguide.com/managementlevels.htm.

Mondy, R. W. (2010). *Human resource management.* Upper Saddle River, NJ: Prentice Hall.

Murali, D. (2011). The changing landscape of technology in HR. Retrieved June 6, 2011, from www.thehindu.com/business/Industry/article2076741.ece.

U. S. Department of Labor. (2010–2011). *Occupational outlook handbook.* Human resources, training and labor relations managers and specialists. Retrieved June 4, 2011, from www .bls.gov/oco/ocos021.htm.

chapter eight

SERVE

MAXIMIZING CUSTOMER SERVICE AND PRODUCTIVITY IN THE WORKPLACE

PART TWO: MANAGING YOUR LIFE

• OIL CHANGE • BRAKES • TUNE-UPS • SPRINGS • SHOCK

SHOP

INSPECTIO

• AUTO
ALARMS
• REMOTE
STARTERS
• PAGING
ELECTRICAL

The goal as a company is to have customer service that is not just the best, but legendary.
—Sam Walton, founder of Walmart

Why
read this chapter?

Because you'll learn...

- To identify the components of the customer service triangle
- To develop relationships that lead to excellent customer service
- To identify and understand the statements and components that drive productivity

Because you'll be able to...

- Deliver better customer service in person and online
- Read and understand an organizational chart

PROFESSIONALS
from the
Field

Name: Hade Robinson

Business: Personal Stylist Manager, Nordstrom

Nordstrom is known for its outstanding service to our internal and external customers. We pride ourselves on being friendly, outgoing, and available to help our customers. My advice to anyone going to work today is to be prepared to work with all kinds of people from all walks of life. We have many different nationalities and ethnic groups among our employee and customer base. This is not going to change, so I advise you to open up your mind and grow from the experience. At Nordstrom we believe in excellent customer service, and you will find that any good company will have that same core value. Learn to take care of your customers, and they will take care of you.

MyStudentSuccessLab

MyStudentSuccessLab (www.mystudentsuccesslab.com) is an online solution designed to help you "Start strong, Finish stronger" by building skills for ongoing personal and professional development.

THE IMPORTANCE OF CUSTOMER SERVICE

How Do You Put the "WOW" Factor in Customer Service?

Most jobs today are service centered. Since the mid-fifties, the U.S. economy has gradually shifted from a manufacturing economy to a service economy, making customer service extremely important to all businesses and all employees.

All successful businesspeople understand a simple fact: Providing excellent customer service is absolutely essential to building a thriving business, whether it be health care, public safety, or solar technology! Customer service is about being so good at taking care of customers that they want to come back to your business. The definition of excellent customer service in a nutshell is this: Bring the customers back for more, and do what it takes to send them away happy. It sounds simple, but it takes dedicated, caring employees to make excellent customer service happen. As an employee, you want to be so good at taking care of customers that you personally are known for putting the "WOW" factor in customer service. You do this by carefully paying attention to your customers; listen to what they are saying, and they will tell you what they need to be happy. Good customer service is essentially all about building relationships.

To be successful in providing excellent customer service, a company must make a commitment to relentlessly pursue a system that exceeds customers' expectations. The customer service philosophy of a company must include all aspects of the **service triangle** (see Figure 8.1), as defined by Albrecht and Zemke (2001). According to these authors, every company should have a **service strategy** that distinguishes it from the competition. Most companies delivering the same services and products have only one way to distinguish themselves—service. Further, Albrecht and Zemke state that companies should have **service systems.** Systems are the points at which services actually get delivered. It could be the telephone, a drive-through window, an ATM, or a face-to-face meeting with a front-line employee. The mistake that companies make, according to Albrecht and Zemke (2001), is that they make systems convenient for themselves and forget about their customers.

Finally, companies should focus on **the people.** The people are the deliverers of service, the ones who make or break a company's reputation. The hard part about the people component of the service triangle is that this group is usually the lowest paid and often the least trained group in most companies. The people are also the most important part of the service triangle. "Companies that have earned a reputation for service excellence understand the employees interacting with customers every day are the true ambassadors of their brands. As a result, finding the right people and putting them in a position to succeed is key" (Business Wire News Releases, 2011).

"Our primary focus is on hiring the right people and just letting them be themselves," states Aaron Magness, senior director of brand marketing and business development at Zappos.com. "You can't hire someone and teach them to provide great customer service, but you can hire people who are committed to providing great customer service" (Business Wire News Releases, 2011). All employees—top to bottom—must be so well-trained that customer service is on their minds at all times.

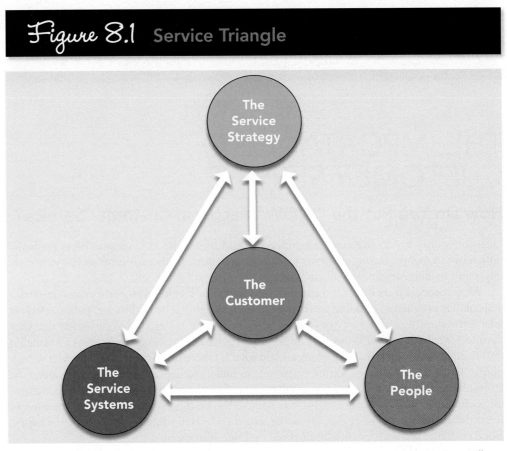

Figure 8.1 Service Triangle

Source: Albrecht, K., & Zemke, R. (2001). *Service America in the new economy.* New York: McGraw-Hill. Copyright © Karl Albrecht. All rights reserved. Used with permission. Website: KarlAlbrecht.com.

How Do Customers Judge Customer Service?

"Getting service right is more than just a nice thing to do; it's a must do," said Jim Bush, Executive Vice President, World Service for American Express (Business Wire News Releases, 2011). Although nine in ten Americans (91%) consider the level of customer service important when deciding to do business with a company, only 24 percent believe companies value their business and will work hard to keep it. Most feel businesses could do much more to keep them as customers.

According to the American Express Global Customer Service Barometer (2011), a majority of Americans report that quality customer service is more important to them in today's economic environment (61%). Seventy percent will spend an average of 13 percent more when they believe a company provides excellent service. However, it appears that many companies are not paying attention to their customers' needs, because six in ten customers feel companies are helpful but don't do anything extra to keep their business. Twenty-six percent feel companies are actually doing less to keep their business than they did the previous year.

- 21% believe that companies take their business for granted.
- 27% feel businesses have not changed their attitude toward customer service.
- 28% say that companies are now paying *less* attention to good service.

This report does not bode well for U.S. businesses.

American consumers are willing to spend more with companies that provide outstanding service. They will tell, on average, twice as many people about bad service than they will about good service. Ultimately, great service can drive sales and customer loyalty.

—Jim Bush, executive VP for American Express

The same study conducted by American Express revealed that customers use the following criteria when making a buying decision:

- Value for the price
- Overall quality of customer service
- Knowing the company will be there to resolve any problems
- Benefits the product or service provides
- Convenience
- The way the product or service makes them feel

"Customers appear to think that the three most influential factors when deciding which companies they do business with include personal experience (98%), a company's reputation or brand (92%), and recommendations from friends and family (88%)" (Miller, 2010).

© Shutterstock

What would you say to a customer to make her feel that you care about her personally?

Customer Service Is All about Relationships

So how do you go about building good relationships? You do what you say you are going to do no matter how difficult it is. You don't make promises you can't deliver. It is often said, "Under promise, over deliver." In other words, do more than you said you would do, and people will not only be pleased, they will be amazed. Even more important, they will tell other people. The best advertisement is a satisfied customer who can't wait to tell someone how good your service is and how much he or she likes you personally.

One of the best ways to build relationships is to learn people's names and use them. Say things like, "Welcome back, Mrs. Smith. We are happy to have you with us again today. How can I help you?" Later, during the conversation, you might ask a question about someone in her family that she has mentioned to you. "How is your daughter doing in college?" Or "How is that adorable little granddaughter who was with you last time?" By all means, be sincere. Nothing is worse than false compliments or pretending to be interested. Customers value sincerity.

GRADUATE *Quote*

Erica R. Harrison
Graduate!
Lincoln College of Technology, Cincinnati, OH
Career: Medical Administrative Assistant,
    Pediatric Associates of Fairfield

The most important advice that I can give you is to believe in yourself. I know that sounds trivial, but it is vitally important. You have to believe that your degree and experience will provide you with a better life. You can't sit around waiting for the future to get better, for someone to wave a magical wand and give you your dream job. You have to make your own future. Your training and degree are the first steps in making your own future. Use them and never look back.

> *In the United States, 74 percent of the gross domestic product and 79 percent of jobs are derived from the performance of services rather than the production of jobs.*
> —Karl Albrecht and Ron Zemke

Some of the best people at handling customer service actually keep a file on their best customers. After they leave, they write information to use when calling them on the telephone or when greeting them in the business. For example, Mr. Aamann might have mentioned to you that his son is in the Navy SEALs. You can inquire about his son and how he is doing. You can't possibly keep all this information in your head, so you need to make notes about pertinent facts. A simple index card file can be used, or you may use a computer program such as Microsoft Office vCards or create a customer service database using software such as FileMaker.

There are many definitions of customer service. Some excellent definitions follow:

- Doing ordinary things extraordinarily well
- Going beyond what is expected
- Adding value and integrity to every action
- Being at your best with every customer
- Discovering new ways to delight those you serve
- Surprising yourself with how much you can do
- Taking care of your customer like you would take care of your grandmother (Carlaw, 1999, p. 4)

Study the points about excellent customer service in Figure 8.2. Then consider customers' wants in Figure 8.3 as you think about excellent customer service.

Figure 8.2 Top 10 Customer Service Commandments

1. Implement a customer service plan, and be sure every employee has been properly educated in how to deliver outstanding service. Everyone in the company should understand the first rule of doing business: The customer is the boss. All employees need to grasp the fact that customers pay their salaries and without them, there will be no jobs. Good customer service is added value for your business. The best customer service is delivered *before* the customer even knows there is a problem. All employees should be so attuned to solving problems that they are alert and take care of problems before they magnify. One bad apple can mess up things for a lot of others. Unhappy customers are said to tell at least 18 other people about their bad experience.

Employees should never discuss their political or religious views with customers. You have no idea what individual customers believe, and you can offend them without even knowing you have done so.

2. Answer the telephone on the first ring if possible. The phone should never ring more than three or four times before someone answers it. *Someone*—not an answering machine! Nothing is more frustrating than getting a long list of connection possibilities that lead to another long list of possibilities, none of which answers

the question that you need answered, especially if you are in a hurry. Answer politely, completely, and with a smile in your voice. When you are talking on the telephone, all you have to use to communicate are your tone of voice and your words. So smile, literally, and it will come across in your voice. Never put anyone on hold unless you absolutely have to. Then ask the person if he or she minds being put on hold. Say something like this: "Would you mind holding for just a moment, please?" Then get back to the person as quickly as you can. Time passes very slowly when waiting.

3. Know the answers to the most frequently asked questions. Every employee should know the answers to the top 25 questions that customers are likely to ask. If you don't know the answer, respond politely, "I don't know, but I will find out, and I will call you back immediately." Then do exactly what you said you would do. Go find out and call the customer back immediately.

4. Keep your promises. If you tell the customer her new carpet will be installed on Monday, she is going to be expecting you to deliver. And if you don't, she is going to be upset. Not only will she be upset, she will tell everyone with whom she comes in contact that day and every day until you install the carpet. One unhappy customer can cause you a world of hurt! If you think you might need until Tuesday, schedule her for Tuesday. If you are able to install the carpet on Monday, call her and give her that option. Chances are, the customer will be happy and impressed. You have under promised and over delivered.

5. Listen to what your customers are saying. Listen, listen, listen! So many employees don't pay any attention to what the customer is telling them. Then they have to ask again or they get the order wrong. Look at your customer; nod to indicate that you are hearing what he or she is saying; take notes so you don't forget; ask questions so you get the order right. Make customers feel good about being your customer by doing things that let them know that they are valued and appreciated. If you are taking the customer to be helped by someone in another department, introduce him or her; "Jack, this is Mr. Redmond. He is one of our favorite long-term customers. Please take good care of him."

6. Handle complaints quickly and carefully. This is called "damage control," and if it is done properly, it can keep customers for life. Conversely, it can lose customers forever. People who are unhappy are going to complain. They will complain to the company, and they will complain to anyone else who will listen. This is known as the *multiplier effect.* Consumers who are unhappy about their customer service experience will tell twice as many people (18 or more) as they do about a good experience (9 people). "Customers who have a fantastic service experience say friendly representatives (65%) who are ultimately able to solve their concerns (66%) are most influential" (Business Wire News Releases, 2011). Every interaction with customers is crucially important to a company.

First of all, thank the person for bringing the complaint to you so that you can solve it. Do not argue with the customer and say that he or she is wrong. Apologize for the inconvenience, and explain how you are going to take care of the problem. How can you solve the problem so the customer leaves happy and loyal even though he or she has been inconvenienced? If you don't act like you care, no solution will make the person happy.

Try to find ways to say "yes." Naturally, you can't give away the store, and you have to make a profit, but you can find other ways to say "yes." If you can't negotiate on the price of a big-ticket item, for example, you can throw in a few inexpensive extras that make the customer feel like you cared and that you tried to make him or her happy. If the customer has had a bad experience, what can you do to make up for it? Can you give him or her a coupon? Can you add some small item to the order to show that you are sincere?

When you have finished, thank the customer again for letting you know about the unsatisfactory experience. Say something like this, "Once again, I am so sorry you had this problem. This is not like us because we strive to be 100 percent correct all the time. We appreciate your helping us get better." Remember, you want customers to come back. You cannot build a business on one-time customers, especially if they go away unhappy. You want customers who are so loyal that they stick with you for a lifetime. Excellent service builds this kind of business and attracts this kind of customer.

7. If someone has a problem that you can solve easily, do it, do it now, and do it for free. Maybe a customer needs a copy made or some simple solution. Just do it for the customer and smile while you are helping him or her. You may not make any money from that customer today, but who knows how much he or she might spend during the next visit to your business. Say something like, "It is my pleasure." Little things bring big results.

8. Give more than is expected by going the extra mile. Go out of your way to be helpful. Don't point to where an item or a person is. Get up and go with the customer to the right place. Everyone is in a hurry, and this will let your customer know that you care enough to be helpful. Because the future of all companies lies in keeping customers happy, think of ways to elevate yourself above the competition. Consider the following:

- What can you give customers that they cannot get elsewhere?
- What can you do to follow-up and thank people even when they don't buy?
- What can you give customers that is totally unexpected? (Friedman, 2011).

9. Try to establish a pleasant environment throughout the business. Today's employees are overworked, overstressed, and sometimes underpaid, so it is difficult to get excellent customer service from everyone. Although establishing an excellent work environment where internal customers (employees) feel valued has to come from the top, you can do your part by coming to work with a great attitude and doing everything you can to be supportive of your colleagues. Leave your personal problems at home—no one really wants to hear whiners and complainers. Bring your "I feel great" attitude to work and share it with everyone. In the long run, excellent customer service on your part will pay off because some satisfied customers will tell your boss how much they appreciate you.

10. Know your business. Customers want to feel like they are talking to someone who knows what he or she is talking about and can answer questions about the products. For example, if a customer asks you a question about a computer, he or she expects you to know the answer. If you can't answer questions about your products or services, the customer will lose interest and go somewhere else. Learn everything you can about your job. Then learn everything you can about the rest of the company. The more you know, the more likely you are to get promoted.

Figure 8.3 What Customers Want/What Customers Don't Want

What Customers Want	What Customers Don't Want
They want you to smile when you greet them.	They don't want you to use company jargon that they don't understand.
They want fast, courteous service, and they want you to acknowledge them and let them know you see them waiting.	They don't want to stand in long lines without being acknowledged while employees act oblivious.
They want you to know their names and use them.	They don't like loud music, horseplay, gum chewing, and personal conversations that have nothing to do with business.
They want you to know your products.	They don't like phones that are not answered promptly or being put on hold.
They want good, competitive products and services.	They don't like flippant, disrespectful attitudes.
They want employees who demonstrate initiative and make things happen.	They don't like employees who can't work one minute past quitting time to finish up their business and take their money.
They want to be respected.	They don't like negativism between employees.
They want you to treat them like they are somebody.	They don't want to hear about your grandchildren, gallbladder surgery, or vacation—but they want to tell you about theirs.
They want you to listen and solve their problem.	They don't like rude, inattentive employees when they have a problem.
They want you to stay cool, even when they lose theirs.	They don't want you to promise what you can't deliver.
They want effective follow-up.	They don't want you to forget to call them as you promised.
They want to do business with a company that has a progressive, successful image.	They don't like employees who bad-mouth their own business or their boss.
They want you to act like you are interested in taking their money and that you understand that their money pays your salary.	They don't like for you to keep working and not stop and look up at them. They want you to give them your undivided attention.
They want you to smile and thank them.	They don't like for you to take their money and not thank them.

DEALING WITH DIFFICULT CUSTOMERS

How Do You Manage Challenging Situations?

Some people are just naturally difficult, but most people are reasonable if you listen to them and try to understand them. People who lose their temper might just hang up on you, or they might ask to speak to your supervisor. Many will threaten to switch their business to a competitor. If you are on the receiving end of an irate customer's anger, it can be unpleasant, but there are ways to handle this kind of customer and, in most cases, turn a bad situation into a good one. Some tips on dealing with difficult people follow:

Success is never final.
—*Winston Churchill*

■ **Even if the customer is wrong, make up your mind not to argue.** Stay calm and relatively quiet. Be patient and let him or her vent. You can't fight fire with fire! You'll both get burned!

■ **Listen to what the irate customer is saying.** Stay calm and try to uncover why he or she is upset. There may be a legitimate complaint that someone needs to hear and correct.

■ **Watch your body language as well as the customer's.** If the customer indicates that he or she is getting out of control, excuse yourself and give the individual time to get control. Get assistance if you think you need it.

■ **Do not take the customer's anger personally.** Chances are good that the person is just having a bad day, and you are an easy target. If you stay calm and demonstrate sincere concern, the other person will typically calm down and might even apologize. But if you meet anger with anger, the situation will escalate into an unpleasant situation.

■ **If the customer appears to be capable of violence, excuse yourself and get a supervisor.** You want to solve as many problems personally as you can, but occasionally it is best to ask for help. You do not have to take unwarranted abuse. Cursing, yelling, threatening, and other forms of aggressiveness do not have to be tolerated. Walk away.

© Alamy

How would you diffuse a customer's anger?

■ **Use calming phrases** such as, "I understand, Mrs. Jenkins. You have a right to be upset. This is not like our company, so please give me a chance to get this corrected. Why don't you have a cup of coffee and give me a few minutes to solve this problem?"

■ **Solve the problem and do so immediately if you can.** If the person has been dishonest or has damaged the product, you may want to discuss the matter with your supervisor before providing an answer. If there is no reason for you not to take care of the problem, get it done as urgently as you can.

■ **Learn your company's policies and procedures.** You cannot do anything that your company's policies don't allow you to do. Some customers don't want to hear this and will tell you, "I don't care about your policies. This television isn't any good, and I want my money back." Some will say things like this after they have used an item well beyond the warranty. Many are just fishing and hoping you will give them a new item even though they know the warranty has expired. Depending on company policy and your supervisor's decision, you may be able to offer the customer a good discount on a new item or make some other concession that might make him or her happy.

■ **Strive to build a good relationship with every customer, even the difficult ones.** It may take time, but you can usually win over most people. Give it your best shot; make it your mission to get this person on your side and turn him or her into a dedicated, loyal, lifelong customer. There will be days when you have to face an irate person face-to-face or on the telephone. Try to remain calm, use a soothing voice, give the person a chance to vent, and do everything you can to solve the problem in a satisfactory manner. The goal is to keep the customer and to turn him or her into a nicer person.

BIGGEST INTERVIEW *Blunders*

Jeremy had an appointment to interview with a major company as a customer service representative. When asked how he would handle a customer who grew angry and yelled at him on the telephone and demanded that he refund his money, Jeremy replied, "I wouldn't take his abuse. I'd tell him to take his business elsewhere and then I'd slam the phone down." Needless to say, Jeremy did not get this job.

LESSON: Unless a customer is extremely abusive, you should consider the customer to always be right. You are trying to build repeat business, so you need to try to find a solution to the customer's complaint.

CUSTOMER SERVICE FOR ELECTRONIC AND MOBILE COMMERCE

What Are the Advantages and Disadvantages?

Information technology and communications technologies have converged to create e-commerce, bringing advantages and disadvantages for consumers and businesspeople alike. One thing is certain, however—businesses must have a web presence today, and many have only a web presence. Some people refer to companies who have both physical plants and a

Figure 8.4 Advantages and Disadvantages of E-Commerce as It Relates to Customer Service

Advantages of E-Commerce as It Relates to Customer Service	Disadvantages of E-Commerce as It Relates to Customer Service
Business can be conducted 24/7; the physical storefront does not have to be open to do business.	Someone has to be paying attention 24/7 for technological problems or customers' questions.
The business can market worldwide and have access to a global marketplace.	Worldwide communications often come with language barriers and shipping costs and problems.
Catalogs, ads, and brochures can be delivered instantly.	Because speed of delivery is instant, customers expect quick responses.
The business can use customer outsourcing (meaning that many of the tasks typically performed by employees are done by customers) and shift some of the costs to the customers.	Many customers need assistance and they expect it immediately.
Customers can pay online, and the business can have instant access to their funds.	Paying online is troublesome to some customers, and they may decide not to buy because they are concerned about having their identities stolen or credit cards abused.
Nonperishable goods can be sold directly to the consumer.	Perishable goods often cannot be satisfactorily shipped and leaves room for problems and complaints.
A website provides some very good sensory information for sight and auditory.	A website cannot provide certain sensory information such as smell or weight, and the consumer may not be able to see the item from all angles.
Customers can buy products without having to go to a brick-and-mortar facility.	Customers have to wait for their products and cannot take them home immediately.
People are beginning to trust online businesses as orders have increased dramatically.	Returning goods can be a problem: customers are not sure if products will reach the source, don't want to pay return shipping, or are concerned about getting credit for returned goods.
A customer service phone number can be posted so customers can reach a live person to answer questions.	The business is not conducive for very large or very small orders because of shipping costs, especially overseas.
The business can respond by phone or e-mail to customers' questions and do so immediately.	Customers may not be sure if the business is legitimate or is some kind of bogus operation that might take their money and deliver no goods.

web presence as using "clicks and mortar." Your first job might very well be working with a web-based company, especially if you are good with technology. Although customer service may be delivered differently, it is still just as important. In fact, delivering excellent customer service via the Internet might be even more important, because chances are almost 100 percent that you will never see or talk to your customer.

Consider the advantages and disadvantages of customer service delivered electronically that are detailed in Figure 8.4.

Friends do business with friends.
—J. W. Marriott

Reflections: PUTTING IT ALL TOGETHER

The information contained here is very important to your success as a professional. No business can function without customers, and the best way to attract and retain customers is to provide excellent customer service. One way for you to gain positive attention from your supervisors is to take care of your company's customers, because many of them will tell your boss how you went out of your way to help them.

Understanding your company's organizational structure, the top management's strategy and vision, and the lines of authority as they affect your job gives you an advantage over those who don't take time to become informed. You can never know too much about your company and its directions!

DIGITAL BRIEFCASE

EXPLORING ONLINE CUSTOMER SERVICE TECHNIQUES

E-mail at least five of your friends on Facebook and have them send you one customer service mistake or offense that they have personally encountered in the past few months. Select five complaints from the complete list and develop a customer service technique to respond to each problem. Format your list and solutions in a Word chart and send it to your Facebook friends who helped you with the list.

Customer service techniques are somewhat different for online companies as compared to storefront businesses, but they are still vitally important. In fact, they may be even more important because the customer is interacting via computer rather than face to face. When customers walk into a small specialty store in a mall, usually someone greets them. When customers access an online business, they usually have one or two ways to get information about products and to have their questions answered: an online chat, in which both parties type their questions and answers, and a video chat, in which a live person answers questions and shows you products if you desire.

Go online to the Lands' End website (www.landsend.com) and Amazon's Help page (www.amazon.com/gp/help/customer/display.html/ref=gwmbhe?ie=UTF8&nodeId=508510) and explore how they interact with their online customers. You might try accessing each type of service and asking a question to determine how satisfactory each type of service is. After you have examined both live video chat and online service, make a chart that details the advantages and disadvantages of each type of service.

Sixty eight percent of customers quit shopping at a business because they are dissatisfied with the attitude of a company employee.
—U.S. Small Business Administration and U. S. Chamber of Commerce

REFERENCES

Albrecht, K., & Zemke, R. (2001). *Service America in the new economy.* New York: McGraw-Hill.

American Express Global Customer Service Barometer. (2011). Market comparison of findings. Retrieved April 24, 2011, from http://about.americanexpress.com/news /docs/2011x/AXP_2011_csbar_market.pdf

Business Wire News Releases. (2011). Good service is good business: American consumers willing to spend more with companies that get service right, according to American Express Survey. Retrieved May 8, 2011, from http://finance.boston.com/boston/news /read?GUID=18338537.

Carlaw, P. (1999). *Big book of customer service training games.* New York: McGraw-Hill.

Fontaine. C. W. (2007). Organizational structure: A critical factor for organizational effectiveness and employee satisfaction. White paper. Northeastern University.

Friedman, S. (2011). The ten commandments of great customer service. Retrieved May 8, 2011, from http://marketing.about.com/od/relationshipmarketing/a/crmtopten.htm.

Management Study Guide, Columbia College. (2010). Levels of management. Retrieved on May 9, 2010, from www.managementstudyguide.com/managementlevels.htm.

Miller, R. (2010). Do companies really value their customers? Retrieved May 8, 2010, from http://customerservicezone.com/cgi-bin/links/jump.cgi?ID=1284.

chapter nine

COMMUNICATE

EFFECTIVE COMMUNICATION FOR THE SOCIAL MEDIA GENERATION

The way we communicate with others and with ourselves ultimately determines the quality of our lives.
—Anthony Robbins

Why read this chapter?

Because you'll learn...

- The key elements of the communication process
- How to make a positive first impression
- The difference between formal and informal communications

Because you'll be able to...

- Engage in appropriate verbal and nonverbal communication
- Compose a variety of written communication documents

PROFESSIONALS from the Field

Name: Leo G. Borges

Business: CEO/Founder
Borges and Mahoney, Inc.

Successful businesses are built on communication. There is no substitute for it. There is no way around it. And there is no excuse for not doing it well. One of the most important things you will encounter in any business, small or large, is how strong communication plays a vital role not only in the big strategic plans of a company but also in the day-to-day workings between people. Lack of clear and strong communication skills can cost you dearly in the workplace and I would encourage you to learn everything you can about communicating well in writing, orally, nonverbally, and online. Then, practice it!

MyStudentSuccessLab

MyStudentSuccessLab (www.mystudentsuccesslab.com) is an online solution designed to help you "Start strong, Finish stronger" by building skills for ongoing personal and professional development.

THE IMPORTANCE OF COMMUNICATING WELL

How Does It Affect Your Life?

Effective communication skills are constantly rated among the top five attributes that employers seek in today's workforce. According to the National Association of Colleges and Employers (2011), verbal communication skills topped the list of soft skills companies seek in college graduates. Good communication skills set you apart from others.

Communication is not something we do **to people**; rather, it is something that is done **between people.** Communication encompasses every aspect of your personal life, your work life, and your social life and takes up most of your time—in fact, the typical person spends up to 75 percent of every day communicating. Even though this process is so important, most of us were never taught to communicate properly; therefore, many go through life feeling frustrated, misunderstood, involved in conflicts, and not measuring up to their potential simply because they didn't learn to communicate well.

Communication involves what you are thinking and saying, but just as important, it involves what the other person is thinking and saying. To become a good communicator, you have to put yourself in the other person's position. This chapter will discuss the communications process and will show you how to co-create better outcomes with people in all aspects of communications. To co-create good communication outcomes, you have to take responsibility not just for what you are saying or writing, but also for how the other person interprets your messages. Quite often we think we have communicated something to another person, and they interpreted the message in an entirely different way from what we intended. It is a mistake to assume that the other person understood your message exactly as you meant it.

When you go to work, you will be communicating all day—talking on the phone; responding and generating e-mails; meeting face-to-face; using social media; attending meetings; interfacing with customers; working with colleagues; writing memos, letters, and reports; and interacting with your supervisors. In other words, everything you do will be affected by how well you speak, write, listen, interpret nonverbal communications, and make good decisions about what is communicated to you by others.

> The single biggest problem in communication is the illusion that it has taken place.
> —George Bernard Shaw

> You can have brilliant ideas, but if you can't get them across, your ideas won't get you anywhere.
> —Lee Iacocca, former CEO of Chrysler Corporation

THE COMMUNICATION PROCESS

How Does Communication Work?

Basically, the communications process involves **six elements:** the source, the message, the channel, the receiver, barriers, and feedback. Consider Figure 9.1.

Barriers (represented by the lines in Figure 9.1) are factors that can interfere with the source, the message, the channel, or the receiver. Barriers can occur anywhere within the communication

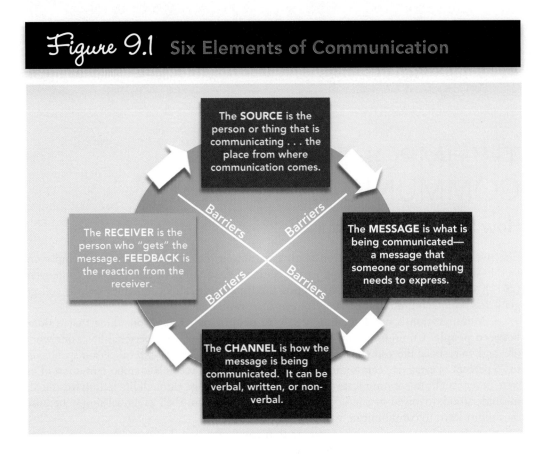

Figure 9.1 **Six Elements of Communication**

The **SOURCE** is the person or thing that is communicating . . . the place from where communication comes.

The **RECEIVER** is the person who "gets" the message. **FEEDBACK** is the reaction from the receiver.

The **MESSAGE** is what is being communicated— a message that someone or something needs to express.

The **CHANNEL** is how the message is being communicated. It can be verbal, written, or non-verbal.

Barriers Barriers Barriers Barriers

process and can include external noise (others talking, cell phones, and traffic) and internal noise (self-talk, doubt, and questioning). Your emotions, past experiences, social norms, communication expectations, and prejudices can also be barriers to effective communications. **Feedback** is the verbal and nonverbal responses the receiver gives you.

MAKING AN IMPRESSIVE FIRST IMPRESSION

How Do People Judge You Face-to-Face?

You never get a second chance to make a good first impression. So what do you need to do to impress people? First, remember that the impression starts the moment someone sees you, hears you on the telephone, or receives your written communication. You may not like it, but first impressions stick, and they are very hard to change and virtually impossible to erase. So you need to get it right the first time!

According to Susan Bixler and Nancy Nix-Rice (2005), "Books are judged by their covers, houses are appraised by their curb appeal, and people are initially evaluated on how they choose to dress and behave. In a perfect world, this is not fair, moral or just. What's inside should count a great deal more. And eventually, it does, but not right away. In the meantime, a lot of opportunities can be lost." If you don't make a good first impression, you may not get a chance to make another one.

It doesn't take long to make an impression. "You have about 30 seconds, at the most. When someone first sees you, they will be deciding about your education level, competence and success, personality, level of sophistication, confidence, trustworthiness, sense of humor and social heritage" (Bixler & Nix-Rice, 2005). People may not even realize they are judging you, but it is a natural human reaction to do just that.

So exactly what do people notice when they meet you? From several feet away, they first see you. They notice if you are standing tall or slouching, neatly groomed or sloppy, smiling or frowning, walking briskly or dragging along, acting confident or shy. The person meeting you sees all these things at once. Their eyes are like little cameras, snapping picture after picture and saving them. They are deciding if you are likeable, assertive, and friendly. They are drawing conclusions about your ability, communication style, manners, etiquette, and attitude—and they haven't even met you yet!

Then the person hears your voice and makes another judgment. Is your voice well modulated? Is it pleasant? Is it too loud or too soft? Do you use good grammar? Do you have an accent? Is there a smile in your voice? Do you appear to be educated? All of this is taken in by the other person in an instant.

And finally, you shake hands with the other person and he or she notices immediately if you have a firm handshake or a "cold fish" grip. So, in less than 30 seconds, you have made a first impression that will be very difficult to change. Not only are overall impressions, dress, and grooming significant factors when getting a job and working with clients and colleagues, they are also very important when it comes to being considered for a promotion. That's why all of this is important!

Do yourself a big favor. Take a few minutes, look in the mirror, and judge yourself as though you are looking at someone else. Use the questions in Figure 9.2 to assess your first impression profile.

In the space below, identify the one thing you need to work on most to improve your first impression profile.

_____

_____

_____

Employers expect you to have an excellent professional appearance and behavior because you are representing their company. When you interview looking your best and presenting yourself as a professional, it's like "money in the bank." Employers pay more for people who look and act professional. When you greet clients with a smile, a firm handshake, and appropriate dress, you are representing yourself and your company well and making a lasting positive impression. Because of technology, we have fewer face-to-face meetings, making the ones that we do have all the more important.

Figure 9.2   First Impression Profile

- If you are honest, what do you really see when you look in the mirror? What can you improve?
- Is something about your appearance holding you back? How are your grooming and hygiene? Do you need to change anything?
- What do your posture and facial expressions say about you? Do you smile or frown often?
- Do you dress appropriately for a person about to enter the business world, or do you need to spruce up your wardrobe?
- Are you friendly and engaging? Are you nice to everyone you meet?
- Do you shake hands firmly and confidently?

Making a Good Impression on the Telephone

Later, you will learn about nonverbal communication and the importance of body language. When talking on the phone, you lose the power of body language, including facial expressions. All you have to represent yourself is your voice. How you sound is more important than what you say. When you answer, put a smile in your voice and make the other person feel that you are glad he or she called. Identify yourself properly, speak clearly with a well-modulated tone of voice, and provide accurate and timely information. If you say you will get back to someone by a certain time, do it! If you don't know the answer to his or her questions, say, "I don't know, but I will find out and get back to you right away." If the person calling is irate, do not return anger. Perhaps he or she is just having a bad day. If you stay calm and polite, the other person will often apologize for being rude.

Making a Good Impression in Written Documents

If you have never met someone or talked to them on the telephone, all they have to judge you on when they receive a document from you is the document itself. This is what he or she will automatically notice: Is the document professional? Is it formatted correctly? Is the paper of good quality? Are the spelling and grammar correct? Were you polite, clear, and concise?

It is very important to remember that you are always making impressions on people, and they are saving them like pictures in an album. Most people really don't know you, but they have an opinion of you because of what you choose to let them see. The good news? You can shape those opinions and impressions.

Is the woman likely to make a good first impression? Why or why not?

Shutterstock

FORMAL AND INFORMAL COMMUNICATION

Why Is It Important to Understand the Difference?

At work we communicate to share information for several different purposes: persuading, influencing, motivating, or informing. Information is delivered in two basic ways—**formal** and **informal.** Formal communications flow through an organization's lines of authority. You receive information based on your role in the company and where you are located on the organizational chart. This information is distributed through formal networks in order to get action from everyone who needs to be involved.

Formal information may come through your direct supervisor, a division supervisor, or a company officer. This type of important information can be delivered either vertically or horizontally and is important for keeping employees informed. Formal messages flowing through the organization need to be carefully planned, because such information may have a dramatic impact on employees. **Formal vertical information** often flows from the top down—from executives and directors to managers and then to staff—and may be delivered in oral messages, company newsletters, procedures manuals, policy directives, or management decisions. Formal vertical information can also flow up the organizational chart in the form of reports, budgets, and suggestions from staff to managers to directors to executives. It is important for you to follow the chain of command when communicating formal information. **Formal horizontal information** usually occurs between people or departments who work closely together and are located near each other on the organizational chart.

The second major type of communication is **informal.** This type of communication is not planned or managed in an organized manner but is nevertheless very important. Informal communication follows no lines of authority and tends to be spread by word of mouth. This information can spread quickly throughout a department and even a company because no one is restricted from hearing it and no formal lines of communication are used.

Frequently, you will hear informal communication referred to as *the grapevine.* This type of information may be considered as gossip or rumors. Grapevine messages usually escalate when employees feel threatened or vulnerable about their jobs or a policy that they think is coming down from the top. If situations are ambiguous or uncertain or if big changes are being planned without employees having enough knowledge, the grapevine will kick into high gear. Rumors can spread information very quickly, and the danger is that exaggerations and deletions happen as the story is passed from one person to another.

Regardless of whether the grapevine is accurate or not, it cannot be eliminated. People simply cannot be stopped from talking, but wise managers can learn to understand and influence it. After conducting a survey about informal communications, Carol Gorman (2005) concluded: "Formal communication focuses on messages the company wants to deliver, with a scope management feels is appropriate, and at a time management feels is right. The reason the grapevine plays such an important role is that it delivers the information employees care about, provides the details employees think they should know, and is delivered at the time employees are interested." According to Gorman (2005), "80 percent of information coming down the grapevine is true."

Answer the questions in Figure 9.3 to determine how well you are helping to co-create effective formal and informal communication.

How does informal communication such as the "grapevine" affect the work environment?

Figure 9.3 Taking Responsibility for Co-Creating Effective Communication

- Am I sure I understood how the other person interpreted my message?
- Did I make the other person feel acknowledged and important?
- Did I really hear the other person, or did I show some reaction that caused me not to get the right message?
- Did I speak in the other person's language/communication style to make him or her feel comfortable?
- Was I open, honest, and sincere in my message?

- Did I prejudge the other person for any reason that may have caused me not to understand his or her message?
- If I asked someone to do something, was I clear in my expectations and deadlines?
- Did I make the other person feel that his or her viewpoints were appreciated and respected?
- Did I listen well enough to get a better understanding of the other person's feelings and positions?
- If the conversation did not go as I wished, did I gain anything from the conversation that will help me improve my relationship with the person?

VERBAL COMMUNICATION

Are You Sending the Right Message?

Verbal communication includes any type of interaction that uses the spoken word. Knowing a great deal of information is important, but the ability to use words and enthusiasm to bring those ideas to life is highly valued in the business world. You will need to be able to use effective verbal communication in business meetings, staff meetings, interactions with customers, telephone discussions, and informal conversations with colleagues.

Learning to deliver powerful and considerate oral communication messages can be very important to your career, as well as in your personal life. Communicating verbally can be a little tricky. If you use basic words or slang, you may not appear to be well-educated; on the other hand, if you use big words that most people don't understand, you may be considered arrogant, and you probably won't be understood.

It is better to remain silent and be thought a fool than to open one's mouth and remove all doubt.
—Abraham Lincoln

The goal of verbal communication is to be heard and understood, so you have to think about your listener. How old is the receiver of your message? How well educated is the person? What is the person's mood at the time? Listen to what is not being said, as well as what is. Look at the person and be sure you are establishing eye contact. Do you sense anger? Is it better to leave things unsaid for now?

Speak with Authority and Clarity

While nonverbal communication is extremely important, you cannot ignore that what you say and how you say it matters, too. The "power of words" is staggering. They can make a person's day or break a person's spirit. They change nations, free masses, and even start wars. The most interesting thing about words is that they must have a medium—they must be written or spoken—and here is where you come into the picture. In truth, the phrase "the power of words" is a misnomer. Words have little power until they are used by humans. *You* determine how words and phrases are to be used, and in turn, you determine their power.

If you have to deliver bad news, remember the lesson you probably experienced when you were a child: When you had to take bad medicine, it went down easier when it was in orange juice. Wrap up bad messages in "orange juice" by sharing a compliment first, which should make your words more palatable for the receiver.

Your ability to speak with confidence, clarity, and sincerity will be paramount to your success. To improve the *quality* of your oral communication skills when interacting with others or interviewing, use these simple strategies:

- Be sincere and honest
- Be clear, accurate, and detailed
- Mean what you say and work hard to say what you mean
- Choose your words carefully
- Use examples to clarify your point
- Ask for feedback during the discussion
- Get to the point as quickly as possible
- Make sure you emphasize your main points
- Pay attention to others' feelings and emotions
- Respect others' opinions
- Don't use language that is threatening or demeaning to you or others
- Try to put other people at ease
- Remember the power of silence; force yourself to listen

Think about your own communication efforts at this point in your life. Below, make a list of three positive communication strategies you now use. An example might be, "I am very good at making my point clear."

1. _____

2. _____

3. _____

Now consider the areas where you may need improvement. List three areas and at least one strategy for improvement in each area. Example: "I am not a very good listener." Strategy for improvement: "I plan to make it a point to stop talking when others are talking."

1. _____

Strategy for Improvement: _____

_____

2. _____

Strategy for Improvement: _____

_____

3. _____

Strategy for Improvement: _____

> The real art of conversation is not only to say the right thing at the right place but to leave unsaid the wrong thing at the tempting moment.
> —Dorothy Nevill

Dealing with Language Diversity in the Workplace

"When the 2000 census results were publicized, many customer service companies received a jolt: Hispanics now made up nearly 13 percent of the U.S. population and had surpassed African Americans as the largest minority group in the country" (Holmes, 2003). In 2011 over 16 percent of the population, the Hispanic population has continued to thrive in this country and is expected to increase to 30 percent of the U.S. population by 2050. Because of the rapid growth of the Hispanic population and other nationalities, the language of business has changed.

Astute companies are bringing the Spanish language to their English-speaking employees through in-house classes while simultaneously teaching English as a second language to their Spanish-speaking employees. In response to increased diversity in the workplace, companies are making Spanish ATMs available, providing call centers with Spanish-speaking employees, and introducing Spanish-language credit cards. Several other minority cultures have grown significantly in recent years and are making their mark on the U.S. workplace as well.

Communication among employees and between employees and customers and clients is critical in any well-run business, but it is complicated when you are dealing with a culturally diverse workforce. Language diversity can be a serious problem in the workplace. On the other hand, used properly, language diversity can be a great asset because a business can relate more directly to large populations. Communicating well with all employees affects employee morale, improves understanding of safety regulations, helps build good relationships with a diverse customer base, and exposes all employees to a rich internal corporate culture.

If you are a native-born U.S. citizen, you have the advantage of understanding the language and the culture, and you can be very helpful and accommodating to non-English-speaking employees in helping them understand the culture. If you are viewed as a friendly, helpful team player, this will bode well for you in terms of getting promoted.

Some people say the United States has no real culture, that we are merely a conglomeration of cultures from other worlds. "There are many reasons why it is important to remember that America does have a culture. The first reason, quite simply, is a question of pride. Having cultural self-awareness gives us all, regardless of our culture, a sense of identity and core values that allows us to function more successfully in both our personal and professional lives. Equally important, however, is that knowing our own culture makes it possible to more accurately interpret the needs and behaviors of colleagues, patients, and families who might be new arrivals to this country" (Thiederman, 2011). Our pride, culture, and language are all important to us. We need to remember that the same can be said of people who come to this country from other countries.

NONVERBAL COMMUNICATION

Does Your Body Language Match Your Words?

The typical working adult spends about 75 percent of waking hours communicating knowledge, thoughts, and ideas to others and making an effort to transfer information to another person. Most of us, however, do not realize that a large part of what we communicate to each other comes through nonverbal communications or body language.

> *The most important thing in communication is to hear what isn't being said.*
> —Peter Drucker

> *What you're doing speaks so loudly I can't hear what you're saying.*
> —Anonymous

Nonverbal communication includes facial expressions, tone of voice, body posture and motions, eye contact, and positioning within groups. It may also include the way we wear our clothes or the fact that we remain silent or how we use space. It could be a look, a glare, a wince, a pulling back, or a crossing of arms. You need to be very aware of this fact: As much as 90 percent of what you are saying is not coming from your mouth.

Because we function in a global society today, it is important to remember that nonverbal communication is powerful in any language or culture. Some researchers believe that facial expressions convey 55 percent of a message. Facial expressions are similar in many different cultures. A smile, for example, is universally understood.

Study Figure 9.4 carefully for information about different aspects of nonverbal communication.

Understanding all kinds of communication is very important to your career and personal success, but perhaps none is more important than nonverbal communication.

WRITTEN COMMUNICATION

Did I Get My Message Across?

Although written communication is not used as much as verbal communication or nonverbal communication, it is very important to your career success. The forms of written communication used in business include letters, reports, e-mails, memos, and notes. These documents can be printed, handwritten, or sent electronically. All business documents should be typed, unless you are writing a personal note such as a thank you or a congratulatory note.

One of the major differences in written and verbal communication is that the document alone conveys the message—you are not there in person to smile, be friendly, or listen and answer questions. When the recipient gets your written document, he or she will automatically judge you on the appearance and the content. If you wrote a letter, what kind of stationery did you use? Was it heavy bond paper or did you scrawl it on notebook paper? Did you use correct grammar and spelling? Is the document formatted well? Is the content clear and complete? Were you respectful of the other person? All these points matter when you are communicating in writing.

Study the tips for written communication in Figure 9.5.

Figure 9.4   The Important Messages of Nonverbal Communications

Eye Contact	Eye contact is one of the most powerful communication tools. Eyes convey emotion; they may signal when to start or finish and may show anger, disgust, friendliness, happiness, or sadness.
Facial Expressions	Facial expressions often convey the attitude of the person. This could be a smile, a frown, a sneer, a yawn, a raising or lowering of the eyebrows, a doubtful look, squinting the eyes, or a blank stare.
Voice	The quality and tone of your voice and how fast or slow you speak conveys a message. Your voice should be pitched deep; you should speak with a strong voice; and you should speak fluently and knowledgeably to be believable.
Gestures	Gestures are often a reflection of the individual and may be somewhat difficult to understand. Some gestures, such as a raised, clenched fist, are universally understood and some, such as pointing, are considered rude and unmannerly. Gestures include waving the arms, crossed arms, tapping the fingers, and cracking knuckles.
Space	Respect the other person's space. The distance you stand away from someone may indicate attraction, the intensity of the conversation, or status of the person. Pulling back from someone might mean that something has been said or done that the other person finds offensive.
Kinesics	People's movements while they are talking sometimes convey hidden messages.
Forward, Backward, and Vertical Movements	It is considered good practice to lean slightly forward in an interview, as it conveys interest. Similarly, it is considered positive to stand up straight and tall when you are meeting someone or greeting someone at an interview. Slumping conveys a message of laziness or a lack of self-confidence.
Handshake	A firm, full handshake is considered extremely important as you interview, meet people, or greet clients.
Tactile	Touch can convey much more than mere words if used correctly. A gentle touch on the arm, an arm around the shoulder, or a firm handshake can be positive nonverbal communications. On the other hand, improper touching and invading someone's personal space can be harmful.
Personal Space	Personal space varies according to each person's needs. Some people are not offended if you stand close, while others are. You have to judge how the person responds and guards his or her personal space. Because of their status, executives are afforded more space than others. The president can put his or her arm around an employee, if done properly, but the employee most likely should not invade the president's personal space.
Environment	The way you arrange your office conveys a message. Is your desk neat or messy? Do you have pictures of your family on your desk? The size of one's office or desk, the number of windows, or a corner office may convey one's status in the organization. Some people recommend putting your professional items on your desk and personal items such as children's pictures behind the desk on a credenza or bookcase.
Silence	You do not have to be talking to convey a message. The fact that you remain silent may indicate that you disagree or that you are thinking. It is better to remain silent if you are not sure of your opinions at the moment. You may need to say, "I need to think about this more" to indicate that you have heard the other person.
Appearance of Documents	The appearance of your written documents sends a nonverbal message. Are your documents well-written? Are they reader-friendly and courteous? Do you have spelling and grammatical errors? Are your documents too brief or too wordy?

Figure 9.5 Important Tips for Writing Business Documents

1. Be very careful what you put in writing and what you promise in writing because it might become a legal document.

2. Write a draft first, especially if it is a very important document. Read and edit the draft carefully.

3. Be very specific about the goal of your written document.

4. Select the best and most appropriate communication form, and include all necessary details—dates, times, and places.

5. Tell the person who is receiving your communication exactly what you want him or her to do. Include contact information and give the reader a deadline so he or she knows how to help you.

6. Be clear about any benefits to the reader if he or she does what you ask.

7. Be succinct and respectful of the reader and of his or her time.

8. If appropriate, establish your credibility in a modest way. Avoid overusing "I," "my," and "our."

9. Send the document to everyone who needs the information, but avoid sending out blanket messages to busy people who are not involved. Be sure to keep your supervisor informed and do not leave out anyone who might be offended if he or she did not receive a copy.

10. If you are angry or upset, do not send the document until you have calmed down and had time to rewrite your message. A good rule to remember is to send good news in a written document and deliver bad news in person. If possible, avoid putting bad news in written form, especially if you are angry.

How to Write a Business Letter

A business letter is a formal document that is written to someone outside your company, such as a person in another organization, a customer, a vendor, a member of the local community, or a company with which you conduct business. Business letters are written for a variety of purposes, including to extend an offer, accept an offer, provide information to a customer, and extend or cancel a contract.

Since business letters represent your company, as well as yourself, you want to be sure that they are well written, error free, and grammatically correct. Your formal business letters should be typed on the company letterhead using a quality paper and professional font (such as Times New Roman), formatted correctly, and signed by you. Check to be sure you have made it clear what follow-up response by the recipient is needed. Always proofread letters before you mail them; if the letter is very important and contains binding information such as prices or quotes, you might want to get someone else to proofread it as well.

Figure 9.6 shows the correct format for writing a business letter.

The Business Envelope

The envelope for your letter makes the very first impression so it, too, needs to be done correctly. Number 10 envelopes (9.5" x 4" in size) are used by most businesses. The recipient's name, title, and address are typed in the middle of the envelope and the writer's name, title, and address are typed in the upper left-hand corner. Be sure names and addresses are typed correctly and that your envelope is formatted properly.

Figures 9.7 and 9.8 show examples of a correctly written and formatted business letter and envelope.

BIGGEST INTERVIEW Blunders

Jocelyn was in a rush and did not proofread her cover letter very carefully. To her horror, she discovered later that the letter had several typos and grammatical errors and that the interviewer's name was spelled incorrectly. Needless to say, she didn't get an interview. Interviewers believe you put your best foot forward before an interview; if you have errors in your resumé and cover letter, they tend to think you will be careless at work.

LESSON: Never mail any written document without carefully proofreading and correcting errors.

Figure 9.6 Format for Business Letters

The information at the top is the company letterhead

Type the date about two inches from the top of the page

The inside address should include the recipient's name, title, company, and address

The salutation should include the person's title and last name. Use a colon after the name.

Begin all lines of the document at the left margin.

"Sincerely" is the best way to end a business letter. It is followed by a comma.

The writer's full name and title should be typed four spaces below the closing.

If someone other than the writer types the letter, his or her initials should be here. "Enclosure" or "Attachment" is used only if something else is included with the letter.

VISION COMPUTER COMPANY
4568 Main Street
Columbia, SC 29087

April 15, 2012

Mr. Jack Rogers
President
Skyler Electronics
58 Main Street
Columbus, OH 38765

Dear Mr. Rogers:

The first paragraph of your letter should tell the reader why you are writing. If you do not know the person, you may want to introduce yourself or tell where you met the recipient.

The second paragraph (and sometimes a third, if necessary) should provide the details of why you are writing. The main reason you are writing should be detailed here.

Use the last paragraph to end your letter in a respectful manner. If you need to include a deadline or contact information, it should be done in this paragraph.

Sincerely,

Mary S. Thompson

Mary S. Thompson
General Manager

jku
Attachment

Figure 9.7   Sample Business Letter

SKYLER ELECTRONICS
58 Main Street
Columbus, OH 38765

April 20, 2012

Ms. Mary S. Thompson
General Manager
Vision Computer Company
4568 Main Street
Columbia, SC 29087

Dear Ms. Thompson:

Thank you for your recent letter inviting me to meet with you and your sales representative for a demonstration of your new XJZ printers. I was very impressed with your products when I saw them at the trade show in Myrtle Beach. Your salesman, Jamaal Greenwood, did a very good job convincing me that I should take a look at them.

My staff and I will be able to meet with you on the date you requested, May 16, at 10:30. I will invite all six of our department managers to be present for your demonstration. We will allow one hour for your demonstration and questions followed by lunch in the conference room for further discussion.

I look forward to your and Jamaal's visit and hope that our managers will be as impressed with your printers as I was. I am enclosing directions to our facility. If you need additional information, please call me at 404-555-5555. Please give my regards to Jamaal.

Sincerely,

Jack Rogers
Jack Rogers
President

mjk
Enclosure

Figure 9.8   Sample Business Envelope

President
Skyler Electronics
58 Main Street
Columbus, OH 38765

Ms. Mary Thompson
General Manager
Vision Computer Equipment
4568 Main Street
Columbia, SC 29087

How to Write a Business Memo

Business memoranda (or memos) are used for interoffice correspondence between employees in one location or between employees who work in different branches of a company. They are used to share ideas, inform people of decisions, or make announcements or requests. Memos are considered less formal than a business letter but are usually more private and important than an e-mail. As with all business documents, memos communicate a nonverbal message about you; therefore, the content should be given the same attention as a business letter although the format is less formal. You should be sure to include all the necessary details for your recipients while being as brief as possible. Refrain from writing volatile information in a memo or anything that might be misconstrued by those receiving it. As with any written document, some things are better said face-to-face rather than putting them in writing.

Figure 9.9 shows an example of how to format and write a business memorandum. Figure 9.10 shows an example of a business memo that is correctly written.

How to Write a Business E-Mail

E-mails have become a mainstay of business communication and are by far the most frequently used form of internal and external communication. Writing an e-mail is quicker, easier, and more efficient than writing a formal document, making this type of communication very acceptable in the business community.

E-mails are usually brief and informal, but this doesn't mean you can relax your standards of good grammar, composition, and spelling. You are judged by the quality of your e-mails just as you are by your formal letters. E-mails may be written in a more relaxed, informal manner, but you should still be careful to demonstrate professionalism. Write the purpose of the e-mail

---

Figure 9.9   Format for Business Memoranda

Some people like to type "MEMORAN-DUM" at the top, but that is a matter of preference. If it is confidential, type "CONFIDENTIAL MEMORANDUM."

Begin the actual memo about one to one and a half inches from the top of the page. Bold the headings but not the information that follows. Write your initials above your typed name to indicate that you have read the memo and approve. Capitalize all words in the subject line.

Add an extra line space between headings and paragraphs. Single space the body of the memo.

Add initials of the typist if someone else typed it, and add "Attachment" or "Enclosure" if you attach or enclose anything.

THE SILVER EMPORIUM
MEMORANDUM

TO: Kenneth Rosemond, Vice President
FROM: Carmella Esperanza, Sales Manager
DATE: July 14, 2012
SUBJECT: Format for Memorandum

Memoranda (memos) are documents that are sent within the company or to employees in other branches of the company. They provide a record of a variety of company actions, policies and procedures, meetings, and other items.

Many companies used printed forms that are saved and retrieved when needed to ensure a uniform look and to save time for employees. Your word-processing software has a memo template that can be used, if you prefer. Some companies prefer that the company name be typed or printed at the top of the memo.

jkl
Enclosure

Figure 9.10   Sample Business Memo

THE SILVER EMPORIUM
MEMORANDUM

TO: Kenneth Rosemond, Vice President
FROM: Carmella Esperanza, Sales Manager
DATE: July 14, 2012
SUBJECT: Sales Report for June, 2012

The sales figures for June 2012 were up 18 percent over June 2011. Our internal and external sales forces did an outstanding job. The American Silver Eagle coins have been an amazing product for us during this past few months, and demand continues to increase steadily.

The entire sales force is looking forward to having you attend our next meeting on July 21 at 10:00 in the main third-floor conference room. Thank you for your support and leadership. We are all proud of our division and glad to be working for you.

---

in the subject line. If you know the person well, you can write as though you are speaking to him or her. Avoid the temptation to use emoticons, smiley faces, or other unprofessional inserts that may take away from your document's message and your professionalism.

While it is very tempting to share stories, jokes, and cartoons with your colleagues, you should refrain from doing so. First, you are on company time, and managers frown on having people waste time. Second, if you are constantly forwarding this type of information, you will not be taken seriously by anyone. You also need to be aware of the fact that your work computer belongs to the company, and anything on that computer can be accessed by high-level corporate officers if they feel the need to do so. Further, a court of law can subpoena your documents if the need arises, so you should never put anything on a work computer that you would mind being made public.

Finally, you need to remember that anything you write in an e-mail can be forwarded to anyone else. Be especially careful not to put anything in an e-mail that you would mind seeing passed along to others. By all means, do not forward anything that might be offensive to a colleague or customer, and do not forward anyone else's e-mail without asking their permission. Figure 9.11 shows an example of a proper business e-mail.

Professionalism in Social Media

Social media such as Facebook, Twitter, LinkedIn, Jing, Bing, Hulu, YouTube, Google+, and blogs have taken the younger generation—and many of the older—by storm! Many people use social media only for personal communications and entertainment, but the business world has caught on to the benefits of using social media to promote their products and services. Your ticket to a good job might very well be your ability to use social media for professional reasons.

Most big companies and many smaller ones now have a social media strategy. Social media in business is used primarily for marketing and promotions. One of the major differences in traditional marketing and social media marketing is that social media belong to the consumers. People don't just receive messages from social media; they create them and respond to them and interact with them. This form of communication is not a one-way street. "Social media is multiple online mediums all controlled by the people participating within them, people who are

Figure 9.11 Example of a Business E-Mail

From: Xia Guang
To: Marketing Department
cc: Jill Henderson, President
Subject: Marketing XJS5 Mainframe

Please plan to meet with me on July 14 from 10:00 until noon in my conference room to discuss promotion options for our new XJS5 mainframe computer, which will be released in November. I realize that this meeting is longer than our typical meetings, but I want us to get a head start on the promotion package because the XJS5 is going to be marketed heavily in international markets as well as domestic. Baahir Boparai will address the group at 10:30. Baahir is an expert on the Indian domestic and corporate computer markets and will share his expertise with us as we prepare to move into that arena.

Lunch will be served following the meeting.

busy having conversations, sharing resources, and forming their own communities" (Kabani, 2010).

There are many social media platforms, but here we will focus on four of the major platforms: Facebook, Twitter, LinkedIn, and blogs. Since social media have become important in so many arenas, both social and professional, it is important for you to demonstrate professionalism and etiquette when communicating via media such as Facebook, Twitter, and LinkedIn. Many of the rules of netiquette apply to social media.

Facebook is one of the most popular social media sites and now boasts over 600 million users. Marketers use Facebook to attract customers to their websites. "Facebook is like a coffee shop. Everyone is there for his or her own reasons, but it is a great place to strike up a conversation" (Kabani, 2010). Facebook allows you to create a profile and promote it online. This is an opportunity for you to create your own identity, so develop it carefully.

A Facebook profile is a good way to make yourself known, but you want to be sure that you are known for the right reasons. Pictures you think are amusing today may not be so funny five years from now when they show up on YouTube or some other medium. Employers searching your Facebook profile will not be impressed with pictures of you and your friends partying—and many do check your profile. Be selective in posting photos for the world to peruse. You don't want to look like "Good Time Susie" who appears to do nothing but party.

You should avoid putting anything in writing that you would not want to see in the headlines of the newspaper. Don't use language on Facebook or any other social medium that you would not want your grandmother to read. If your boss is one of your friends on Facebook, he or she can read what you post about him or her, so you have to use good judgment. Many people have been fired for posting inappropriate remarks on social media. Many interviewers check Facebook pages today, so you want to have a professional image in case your profile is checked. Likewise, you should refrain from sending any sexually explicit messages or pictures via any form of social media—you have no control over where the receiver might forward your message or pictures. The boyfriend or girlfriend of today may not even be a friend next year, and who knows what may happen with your personal messages and photos at that point!

We suggest that you invest in a professional photo to use on your Facebook profile along with pertinent information that you want to share. You may want to protect your personal information from everyone except those you choose to accept as friends. Be very careful what you put on Facebook that might attract the wrong kind of people.

What happens in Vegas stays on Facebook, Twitter, and other Social Media.

—*Social Media Revolution 2*

Twitter is another rapidly growing and popular social medium. "Twitter is like a giant, colorful bazaar" (Kabani, 2010). Marketers use Twitter to attract customers directly, and it is also a very popular social interaction platform. You can send direct "tweets" (messages limited to 140 characters each) to friends as well as reply to other people's tweets. Begin by selecting a short Twitter name and posting an attractive headshot. Capture attention with your profile, for which you are allowed 160 characters. You might say something like this: "Soon-to-be college graduate with excellent social media marketing experience. Seek full-time position with progressive company in Atlanta region."

Perhaps the most helpful social medium for career purposes is **LinkedIn,** a network for professionals. The main purpose of LinkedIn is to give businesspeople a platform for connecting. While it is important to be professional on all social media sites, it is crucial that you put your best foot forward on LinkedIn. This might be the source of your first big job if you can connect with the right person.

LinkedIn is much more formal than Facebook or Twitter. You might consider LinkedIn as an interactive online resumé. As with other social media, use a good headshot. Ask your references to post recommendations that might attract an employer who is searching for someone with your skills. Your summary is very important and should be written to impress and attract professionals who might read it. It should be professional and truthful. Use keywords that make it easy for other professionals to locate you, such as *social media expert.*

Text language (LOL, OMG, BFF, :-(BTW, FYI) is fine when texting or IMing with your friends, but not for e-mails (or class/work projects). Use them sparingly. Proofread your summary carefully to be sure your grammar and spelling are perfect.

As part of your LinkedIn network, you might want to connect with previous colleagues and bosses, former customers, vendors, and bloggers who may be related to your field. You will be surprised how quickly your network of professionals grows.

Finally, you need to understand blogs. A blog is a personal website that can be updated anytime you want. You might want to experiment with developing your own blog, using directions from many sources on the Internet. If you have a blog, you need to refresh it with new content fairly often if you want people to keep coming back. Blogs are used for many purposes and can be recognized by the following characteristics:

- They resemble websites, but not all websites are blogs.
- A blog can be accessed using a web address.
- Blogs usually consist of posts, which are like miniature articles.
- Readers can read blogs and post their comments and reactions.

As with all social media, you should be sure your blog represents you well as a professional and that you post nothing that others may find offensive.

How to Write Thank You Notes and Congratulatory Notes

One of the most important of all written communications is the handwritten note. Nothing grabs an employee's attention more than a sincere, handwritten thank you note from the boss. People who get notes from their bosses usually save them and read them several times. On the other hand, bosses are people, too, and they also like to get an occasional thank you note. For example, if your boss recommended you for a nice raise, you should take time to write a sincere thank you note. If someone does something thoughtful or nice for you, take a few minutes and write the person a note. If a colleague achieves an unusual accomplishment or gets a promotion, write a sincere note congratulating him or her. Thank you notes and other similar notes should be brief and handwritten on note paper. Figure 9.12 demonstrates the correct format and main parts of a thank you note.

POSITIVE HABITS *at Work*

Go to work every day with the attitude that you are going to be nice to everyone you meet, that you are going to look your best, that you are going to smile and be friendly to colleagues and customers, and that you will make a good first impression on new coworkers and customers. Resolve to do all these things even when you don't feel well or are in a bad mood. Resolve to use positive communication in your personal relationships as well as your verbal and nonverbal communication.

Figure 9.12   Sample Thank You Note

Write the date at the top of the paper.

Use an appropriate salutation, along with the person's name.

Tell the person how his or her actions made you feel, and extend your thanks specifically for what he or she did.

Use an appropriate closing and remember to sign the note.

August 18, 2012

Dear Jacquelyn,

Thank you so much for the lovely flowers you sent me while I was in the hospital! What a thoughtful surprise! When I awoke on Wednesday afternoon, I was so pleased to see the beautiful arrangement of my favorite flowers. They lasted several days, and I enjoyed them immensely.

You are a wonderful colleague, and I am fortunate to call you friend.

Sincerely,
Jamie

THE IMPORTANCE OF INTERPERSONAL COMMUNICATION

Do You Have Good People Skills?

Interpersonal communication is your personal interaction with other people. This form of communication is very complicated because it comes with so many variables. "Theorists note that whenever we communicate there are really at least six 'people' involved: 1) who you think you are; 2) who you think the other person is; 3) who you think the other person thinks you are; 4) who the other person thinks s/he is; 5) who the other person thinks you are; and 6) who the other person thinks you think s/he is" (King, 2000).

As you have already learned, communication can take on a variety of forms, such as oral speech, the written word, body movements, and even yawns. All of these actions communicate something to another person. When thinking about your interpersonal communication encounters, remember this—communication is continuous and irreversible. Communication happens all the time; you can't take back words you have said because they have already made an impact. People judge us on our actions, not our good intentions. Consider the tips about interpersonal communications in Figure 9.13.

How to Make a Powerful Business Presentation—Prepare, Prepare, Prepare

The secret to a good presentation is to begin with a specific goal that you want to accomplish and then prepare to the point that you are comfortable with your remarks. While you may not have to speak to hundreds of

The #1 Rule for Effective Interpersonal Communication:
Be nice. Be nice. Be nice.
—Patricia G. Moody

Figure 9.13 General Tips for Interpersonal Communication

- You never know what type of day, month, year, or life a person has had—act accordingly. Everyone you meet is carrying a burden of some type. Be kind.

- Ask people about themselves. This puts them at ease.

- Interpersonal communication involves a great deal of trust on your part.

- Never try to diminish another's self-worth, because you diminish yourself when you do.

- Try to greet and treat everyone as if he or she was your personal friend.

- Show empathy for others and, most of the time, you will be treated the same.

- Always choose your words carefully. They are immensely powerful tools.

- Pay very close attention to your nonverbal communication, including gestures, facial expressions, clothing, proximity, posture, touch, and eye contact.

- Understand that first impressions are not always correct. Get to know the person and the situation.

- Remember to listen very carefully and read between the lines. Listen to what is not being said.

- Eliminate distractions such as cell phones, other conversations, and outside noise.

- Never use your power or position to control a person just because you can.

people, you will most likely have to present information to your colleagues, your managers, or your customers. Regardless of how relaxed a speaker might appear to be, almost no one is born with the innate ability to speak in front of a group without being nervous. The more you speak, the better you will get and the more confident you will become. A list of important points about making a business presentation follows:

- Prepare, prepare, prepare. Get ready to do a good job.
- Prepare three major parts to your presentation: the opening, the body, and the ending. Plan for a powerful opening, such as a story, a question, or an example. Deliver the main message in the body of your presentation. End powerfully, again with a story, a question, or a quote. You want to touch your participants' emotions so they will remember your remarks.
- Do your homework. Find just the right illustrations to make your presentation interesting.
- If humor is appropriate (and don't overdo it), find the perfect story to complement your presentation. Never use off-color, ethnic, or religious jokes; they are sure to offend someone.
- Make an outline but speak from the heart. Never read your presentation!
- Speak clearly and distinctly and use professional language.
- State the purpose of your presentation and use major points to support the purpose.
- Avoid uncomfortable sounds like "Uh," "umm," or "you know." You do not have to fill up every second with words.
- Be aware of your nonverbal communication. Establish eye contact with your audience. Look up—not down at your notes. Get an "eyeful" and look up.

GRADUATE Quote

Eric Despinis
Graduate!
ITT Technical Institute, Levittown, PA
Career: System Administrator/Project Manager

In my field of information technology, there is something new that comes along every day. Every day! Without my training and education, I would not be able to process all of the changes that are required to be successful. I would not be able to keep up. My education taught me how to expect the unexpected and know the unknown. Use every tool in your box to be able to meet the demands of your position. Never stop learning. Never stop growing.

- Do not lean on the podium, if you are using one.
- Wear an outfit that makes you feel confident. Avoid loud colors and/or patterns that may be distracting.
- Choose supporting visual content carefully. If you are using presentation software, do not overdo it with too many graphics, tables, cartoons, pictures, or page after page of small print. Limit the number of words you put on one slide. Never read word for word from your screen! Visual content should support your presentation, not dominate it.
- Test all equipment before you begin. If it malfunctions, it may not be your fault, but it's your problem.
- If you have activities designed to engage your audience, think them through carefully to be sure they will work as you want them to. Provide simple, complete directions.
- If you use a handout, include activities that involve the audience as you proceed through your remarks. If not, distribute the handout at the end so as not to distract the participants during your presentation.
- Be brief, be good, and be gone. Never drag out a presentation until everyone has glazed over with boredom.

Reflections: PUTTING IT ALL TOGETHER

As you prepare to go to work, nothing will be more important to your success than improving all aspects of your communication profile. Begin now by learning to make a good first impression—this will serve you well when interviewing and later when you are in the workplace. Hone your speaking and writing skills by focusing more attention on all your writing and speaking and intentionally thinking about improving.

DIGITAL BRIEFCASE

OPENING A FACEBOOK ACCOUNT

This exercise is designed to walk you through the steps in registering for a Facebook account and learning to use some of the simpler options available. Even if you already have an account, you should be able to learn some new things by completing this exercise. Follow the steps below:

1. **First, register your account.** Go to www.facebook.com. In the top right of the screen, on the blue taskbar, click on "Register." This will take you to the registration screen. Type in your name, identify what you do for a living if you are working, and enter a valid e-mail address. Facebook needs your e-mail address to contact you and occasionally send updates on new things. Then, follow instructions to choose a secure password, agree to the terms and conditions, and click "Register now."

2. **Confirm your e-mail.** Open the e-mail sent to you by Facebook and click on the link that will take you to your new Facebook profile.

3. **Next, personalize your Facebook profile and find friends.** All you have to do is enter your e-mail address, and Facebook will search for your friends for you. You have the option of selecting the people you want from the "friends" Facebook locates for you. Click on the box to the left of each person you want to add as a friend. This means they will have access to you and your postings. Then you'll be given the option of befriending others who are not in your e-mail address book. You can send e-mails inviting them to join and be your friend.

4. **You can search for coworkers by clicking on "Search for coworkers."** Write the person's company and the name of the person for whom you are searching. Then click on "Search for coworkers," and Facebook will search for you.

5. **Next, click on your name in the upper right corner to access your profile.** Here you will find empty sections waiting for you to complete. You can enter your sex, if you are interested in men or women, your relationship status, and why you are accessing Facebook (for dating, friendship, etc.). Then enter your birthday, hometown, state, and religious views, if you so desire. When you like what you have done, click "Save changes."

6. **The next step is to click on "Contact Information" under "Info" on your profile.** You can now enter a screen name and a telephone number, if you want to. You can click on "Personal" and enter activities, interests, music, sports, TV shows, books, and the like. You can tell things about yourself if you choose to. You might want to keep this short, because people tend not to read long items. You can also enter your educational background and your work information.

7. **You do not have to complete every field unless you want to.**

8. **You can upload a picture from your hard drive for your profile picture. Click on the "Photo" tab to upload a picture.** Now that you have registered and completed your profile, your assignment is to create a group. On the left side of the screen, under "Groups," is a tab called "Create a Group." Click on this tab and create a group of 10 people. This group can be a study group, a group of colleagues at work, or a group of friends. Once you have created the group, ask each member to send in one tip for using Facebook safely and professionally. Then share the list with the group.

REFERENCES

Bixler, S., & Nix-Rice, N. (2005). *The new professional image: From corporate casual to the ultimate power look.* Avon, MA: Adams Media Corporation.

Gorman, C. K. (2005). I heard it through the grapevine. Retrieved April 3, 2011, from www.communitelligence.com/clps/clprint.cfm?adsid=329.

Holmes, T. (2003). Diversity in the workplace: The changing language of business. Retrieved April 18, 2011, from www.boston.com/jobs/diversity/062003.

Kabani, S. H. (2010). *The zen of social media marketing.* Dallas: BenBella Books, Inc.

King, D. (2000). Four principles of interpersonal communication. Retrieved April 7, 2011, from www.pstcc.edu/facstaff/dking/interpr.htm.

National Association of Colleges and Employers. (2011). Job outlook report for 2011. Retrieved July 25, 2011, from http://www.naceweb.org/s04142011/job_outlook_spring_update/

Thiederman, S. (2011). American culture: Knowing yourself in order to understand others. Retrieved February 18, 2011, from www.diversityworking.com/diversityManagement/americanc-ulture.php.

chapter ten

RELATE

RELATIONSHIPS, DIVERSITY, AND MULTIGENERATIONAL DISTINCTIONS

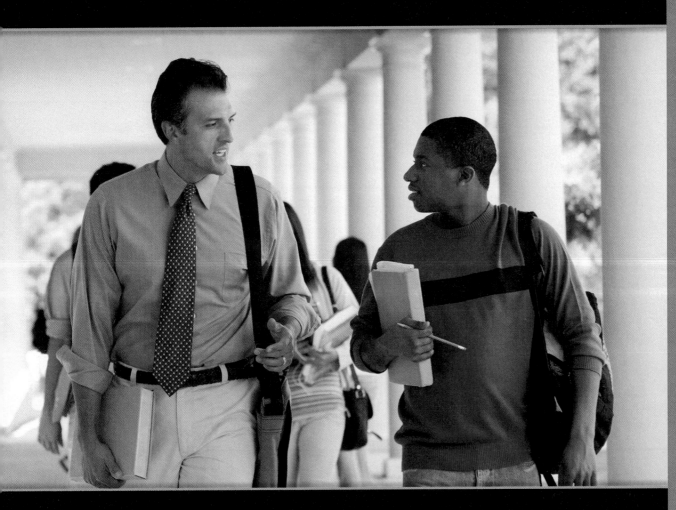

We must learn to live together as brothers or perish together as fools.
—Martin Luther King, Jr.

Why read this chapter?

Because you'll learn...

- Why it is important to respect people from diverse backgrounds
- To respect opinions that are different from yours
- The concept of globalization and the impact on personal and work relationships

Because you'll be able to...

- Work more effectively in a company that has a diverse, multigenerational workforce
- Determine the type of workplace culture in which you feel most comfortable

PROFESSIONALS from the Field

Name: Bert Pooser

Business: CEO, IMIC Hotels

I have been in the hotel business for many years and have learned that the ability to build good relationships with all kinds of people is one of the most important skills you can have. When we are hiring new employees, we look for personalities whom we think will be engaging and friendly with our customers. We can teach someone to use a computer and work at the front desk, but we can't teach them how to be personable, friendly, helpful, and willing to serve our customers so these are the qualities we seek when interviewing. We also look for people who can interact with a very diverse customer base. We have people of all ages, from all parts of the world, from many different religious backgrounds, and who represent a great variety of ethnicities. Our employees have to be able to relate to all of them and to treat them as our respected guests.

MyStudentSuccessLab

MyStudentSuccessLab (www.mystudentsuccesslab.com) is an online solution designed to help you "Start strong, Finish stronger" by building skills for ongoing personal and professional development.

DEVELOPING STRONG WORKPLACE RELATIONSHIPS

How Do You Build Relationships at Work?

Building solid relationships is one of the most important jobs you have in the workplace. If you cannot get along with other people, you will not be promoted and you certainly will not be placed in a management position. There are so many ways to work and play well with others, and many are detailed here. There is one rule you can apply consistently—you need to be nice, be nice, be nice to everyone with whom you come in contact. Civility will go a long way toward building positive relationships. Do the little things—send a sympathy or get well card, write a congratulatory note, do something for someone's children, buy donuts for the department occasionally, smile often, and learn to give sincere compliments and accept them in return.

Working and playing well with others can be spelled out in hundreds of simple ways that make a difference in people's lives. Simple actions done over and over again build good relationships. Some of these actions are listed below:

- Catch people doing good things and tell them about it—in front of others if you can.
- Compliment someone on making a difficult decision and having the character to do the right thing.
- Be a good listener and a good confidante. If someone shares their personal feelings with you, they trust you and have paid you a high compliment.
- Accept feedback even when it is painful, and try to learn from it.
- If you must criticize, wrap the criticism up in praise. Deliver the criticism quickly and let it drop.
- Take time for yourself, but also take time for others. Do the little things that make a big difference in others' lives.
- If you harm someone, apologize quickly and sincerely. Admit when you are wrong.
- Always treat others fairly, even when it is not the best thing for you.
- Be generous with your praise for others and be sincerely happy for them when good things happen.
- Tell the truth, even when it is painful and not to your advantage.

> The closer you get to the top, the nicer people are.
> —J. W. Marriott

Think about this discussion and add a few simple, powerful actions to the list that you can do for your colleagues in your workplace:

Why Is It Important to Understand People Who Are Different from You?

A truly educated person knows how to listen to others, learn from many different people, and grow from others' experiences and cultures. This chapter will provide a chance for you to rethink and evaluate some of your long-held beliefs and offer a challenge to open yourself and your thinking to new possibilities regarding diversity, different generations of coworkers, and relationships with a variety of people—indeed, to learn to celebrate differences and to relate to and enjoy all kinds of people.

Today's workplace requires interactions with people from all walks of life. You may have a boss who is different from you in many ways, and you will certainly have colleagues who think differently from you. You will probably serve on committees and teams with people who have diverse backgrounds. Although you don't have to love everybody at work, you have to be able to work with all of them—even the difficult ones. The sooner you begin learning how to build strong workplace relationships with all kinds of people, the more successful you will become.

Few things will do more to make you an educated, sophisticated, and competitive person than to expand your thinking about diversity and to be able to build lasting and rewarding relationships with people from many walks of life. Many people think diversity is only about culture and race, but diversity encompasses so many more differences than just those two areas. You will be working with people who are different from you in many respects: They may be older; they may be from a different country; their religion may be very different from your personal beliefs; they may come from a different part of the country; their sexual orientation may be different from yours; their social status may differ. The list of differences is very long, and your job is to learn to relate to all types of people who embrace different backgrounds, philosophies, and beliefs than yours and to learn to work with them.

UNDERSTANDING YOUR COMPANY'S WORKPLACE CULTURE

What Kind of Personality Does Your Company Have?

Workplace culture means the same thing as *corporate* or *organizational culture*—you will see all of these terms used. *Corporate culture* seems to infer big, multinational companies, so we prefer *workplace culture.* "Corporate culture, sometimes also called organizational culture, refers to the shared values, attitudes, standards, codes, and behaviors of a company's management and employees. Some would argue that the corporate culture extends to the broader circle of relationships a business maintains, such as with customers, vendors, strategic partners, and so forth. Corporate culture is rooted in an organization's goals, strategies, structure, and approaches to business activities" (Encyclopedia for Business, 2011).

Workplace Cultures—How We Do Things Around Here

Workplace cultures can be very diverse. Some would describe it simply "as the way we do things around here." You might say that workplace culture is what life is really like at work; it is the glue that holds the company together. Workplace culture can be very difficult to define, but everyone who works at the same place soon understands exactly what it is. The culture is usually established by upper management but can be heavily affected by employees. The values and expectations of the management group tend to trickle down to the employees until everyone "gets it" and operates using unwritten rules.

Workplace cultures can be casual, friendly, and fun-loving; they can be stiff, closed, and formal; or anything in between. Employees may feel free to take a break and discuss a project in a room with comfortable furniture and a pool table, or they may be restricted to cubicles with little or no communication. In some organizations, lower-level employees have a great deal of interaction with higher-level executives, whereas in others, there is very little contact between ranks. Employees may come to work in jeans and tennis shoes or they may be required to have on dress clothes. In hospitals and in some small businesses, employees may be required to wear uniforms, either for a consistent look or because of the nature of the work. In some companies, employees may be asked to share their opinions and ideas, or they may simply be expected to follow orders from their boss. The company may value innovation and togetherness or they may have high regard for structure and working alone. No two companies have exactly the same workplace culture. A large corporation's culture will be very different from a small business environment where everyone knows each other and works closely on a daily basis.

> *Every company has two organizational structures; the formal one is written on the charts; the other one is the everyday relationship of the men and women in the organization.*
> —Harold S. Geneen, former CEO of ITT Corporation

Part of your job when interviewing is to check out the workplace culture and see if you are a good fit for a particular environment. Observe carefully as you walk around, and ask questions that give you information but are not offensive. Every business has a personality, and it is important for you to find the one that matches your goals, skills, and temperament.

Remember, you are there to interview the company while they are interviewing you. Study the checklist in Figure 10.1 and use it to evaluate a company's workplace culture as it relates to you and your needs and goals.

After studying Figure 10.1, write a brief statement about your personal needs in a corporate culture. Not every company will be a good match for you.

_____

_____

_____

_____

_____

_____

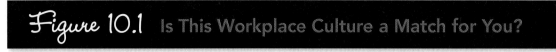

Figure 10.1   Is This Workplace Culture a Match for You?

Workplace Observation	YES	NO	COMMENTS
Do you like the size of the company?			
Would you be able to get to know everyone?			
Is the company so small that everyone would know your business?			
Do people seem friendly and engaged with each other?			
Is it a cold, formal environment?			
Are the company's values readily visible in the way employees act and perform?			
Is the basic dress formal?			
Do the people wear uniforms?			
Is the workforce diverse in terms of generations, ethnicity, and other important categories?			
Does the company have many layers of managers in its organizational structure?			
Do you see opportunities for advancement?			
Are the working hours fairly routine?			
Is the heaviest part of the work seasonal, requiring you to work longer hours?			
Does the company appear to embrace work/life balance?			
Do the company and employees appear to value customers, both internal and external?			
Do you feel tension between individuals and/or groups?			
Does the company appear to value independent thinking?			
Does the work you would be doing require field work and travel?			

Workplace Observation	YES	NO	COMMENTS
Do you think power is invested in only a few people?			
Do you think this is an adaptive company that can change quickly if necessary?			
Does the benefits package reflect the fact that owners/managers value employees?			
Is there a 401(k) or other retirement package?			
Does the company provide child care, break room, exercise facility, or play rooms?			
Is the atmosphere quiet and sterile as is necessary in some medical settings?			
Is the atmosphere lively and informal as in some technology companies?			
Does management interact with employees?			
Do supervisors travel with and train new employees if the company is a small business, such as an air-conditioning company?			
Does the company provide a comprehensive educational program?			
If the company is a small business, such as electrical installation, does it provide an apprentice program?			
Do people seem to enjoy coming to work?			
If the company is a relatively small business, such as an automobile dealership, do the mechanics have enough time to do a good job?			
Do you know what a typical day at work would be like for you?			
Do employees seem to have a can-do spirit?			
Can you tell if the company appears to be based on long-term goals that include caring for employees, as opposed to short-term, profit-based goals?			
Do you think this company can provide the kind of opportunity you are seeking?			

CELEBRATING AMERICA'S DIVERSE HERITAGE

How Can You Strengthen Relationships with a Diverse Workforce?

The U.S. culture is the most diverse of any on earth! We are a nation of immigrants that still welcomes people from all over the world to our shores. This fact is one of our greatest strengths—ideas from all over the world can come together in an environment that allows anyone to pursue his

How comfortable would you be working with a diverse group?

iStockPhoto

or her dreams and ambitions. On the other hand, all this diversity is accompanied by the problems of throwing so many people from diverse cultures together and expecting them to function together as one society.

Although U.S. society is called the "melting pot," it is not so simple to mix all these people together and not have problems. Perhaps the best way to think of U.S. society is not as a melting pot but as a mixed salad, with each item remaining intact but still complementing each other. Regardless of what we symbolically call ourselves, this country offers the greatest opportunities of any on earth. As we grow as a nation and as individuals, we must all seek to become so good at dealing with differences that it really doesn't matter that we are not alike. In fact, we should learn to celebrate differences as strengths and as unique opportunities to expand our thinking.

LEARNING TO THINK GLOBALLY WHILE MAKING LOCAL APPLICATIONS

Is It Really a Small World after All?

iStockPhoto

"Think globally, act locally" was a phrase that emerged from an international conference on environmental issues in the early 1970s. In today's world, that phrase encompasses so much more than just the environment. Today we are connected by technology and economics, as well as social networks. Because we are so mobile and interconnected, what happens in another part of the world can have immediate implications for our part of the world. For example, war in a Middle Eastern country can interrupt oil supplies and thus affect our economy. As we have seen, a meltdown in U.S. financial markets can severely affect the world markets because other countries' citizens own a significant portion of U.S. stocks and bonds.

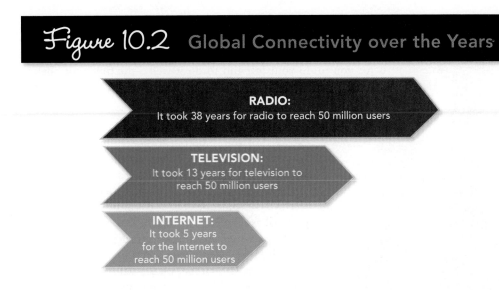

Figure 10.2   Global Connectivity over the Years

RADIO:
It took 38 years for radio to reach 50 million users

TELEVISION:
It took 13 years for television to reach 50 million users

INTERNET:
It took 5 years for the Internet to reach 50 million users

Because of technology, primarily the Internet, we are now connected with people all over the world. "Internet users are roughly 35 percent English and 65 percent Non-English with Chinese at 14 percent. Google's Index now stands at over 8 billion pages. Today we have over a billion internet users, and that number is growing rapidly" (Internet in Numbers, 2011). Consider the statistics in Figure 10.2.

Technology has opened the doors to the world and brought with it amazing opportunities and difficulties. But it has also brought a new set of problems and concerns as it exposes our differences to a greater degree than in the past and pits us against each other as competitors for jobs, business ventures, and tourists. So we all have work to do to become good global citizens in this brave new world. As a citizen and an employee, you will need new skills and knowledge to function at your best capacity. Some ideas to consider as you begin to ***think globally and act locally*** are:

> *I am not a citizen of Athens or Greece but of the world.*
> —Socrates

- To act with compassion and understanding for people who are different from you
- To develop a good understanding of the different cultures, beliefs, and issues embraced by people from locations all over the world
- To travel internationally and experience first-hand people from other parts of the world
- To examine multiple viewpoints and philosophies and make decisions that are respectful of many types of differences
- To listen carefully, think differently, and solve problems that emerge in the workplace and in communities because of cultural differences
- To study historical perspectives to grasp reasons for tensions between different cultures

> *We don't see things as they are; we see things as we are.*
> —Anaïs Nin

RELATING TO YOUR SUPERVISOR

How Can I Best Support My Supervisor?

Supervisors come in all sizes and shapes and bring with them a great diversity of personalities, likes and dislikes, and expectations. Some are warm and friendly; others are distant and cool. Some are hard-driving and goal-oriented; others are laid back and nonchalant. Some are supportive; some are tyrants. Some supervisors want people to love each other and work together as a team in an open and relaxed environment; others don't care if you like each

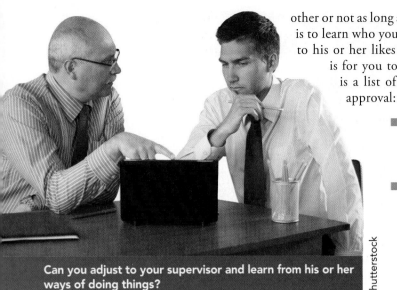

Can you adjust to your supervisor and learn from his or her ways of doing things?

Shutterstock

other or not as long as you get the job done. So the first thing you have to do is to learn who your supervisor is as a person, and then you have to adjust to his or her likes and dislikes. The main things most supervisors want is for you to do your job and to do it well—the first time. Below is a list of ways to support your supervisor and win his or her approval:

- Know exactly what your job duties are and what is expected of you. Find out if there is anyone to whom you can delegate or if you should do everything yourself.
- Always be sure to get your job done before you volunteer to help someone else. You will be judged on your personal assignments, so they have to come first. Once your supervisor learns that you are dependable, you will most likely be given bigger and more important tasks. Let the boss know that you are willing to learn more and that you don't mind taking on more responsibilities. Supervisors love people who are willing to do whatever it takes to get the job done.

- Keep your supervisor informed of what is going on around the office. Bosses don't like surprises, and they certainly don't want to be surprised by hearing negative information from their bosses. You don't have to be a sneak or a tattletale, but supervisors need to know certain things before they get out of hand. Some people may have hidden agendas and will actually work against the boss. This is the kind of thing the boss needs to know. You need to be absolutely sure you are right and have concrete evidence before you share such information with your boss.

- If you can't meet a deadline although you have worked overtime, tell your supervisor before he or she comes to you. Ask for more time, and then focus on getting that task completed quickly and well.

- If you have questions, make a list of things you want to discuss with your supervisor and get an appointment. Get answers to all your questions so you don't have to keep going back again and again.

- If you uncover a problem, let the boss know, but also give him or her a potential solution to the problem. Supervisors have a lot on their plates, so they value people who can solve problems.

- Above all, be loyal to your supervisor. Do everything you can do to make your boss look good. Supervisors know who is really on their team, and they will reward loyal, hard-working employees.

RELATING TO YOUR COLLEAGUES

How Can I Please All These People?

The first thing to understand is that you simply can't please everyone all the time, but you can always treat everyone professionally and respectfully. You will really like and relate to some colleagues; others will seem complicated and unlike you. Nevertheless, you still have to find a way to work with them. Since you will spend so much time at work, you are likely to be more productive if you are happy with your relationships. Some helpful hints follow that will guide you in "playing well" with others.

- **Use good manners with everyone.** Be as nice and friendly to the janitor as you are the CEO. Use e-mail properly and refrain from using your cell phone during work hours. Avoid all personal business at work unless you have to take care of something; then do it quickly and efficiently.

- **Be friendly and engaging.** Take time to inquire about how your colleagues are doing. Don't be nosy about their personal business. If someone shares something personal with you, treat it as confidential information. If someone asks you how you are doing, the only answer is "I feel great!"

- **Avoid engaging in gossip.** Don't be snared by the head gossip who talks about everyone and is loyal to no one. Stay away from the areas and offices where malicious gossip often takes place. Be seen as someone who is there to work, not gossip.

- **Manage your time and priorities well.** Meet your deadlines, and be sure you don't inconvenience someone else by not doing what you are supposed to do.

- **Deal well with the unexpected.** Sometimes things happen suddenly and everyone needs to stop what they are doing and pitch in to handle a crisis. Be one of the first to go to work to solve the problem.

- **Stay away from certain topics.** There are so many different viewpoints about religion and politics that you should refrain from discussing them at work. You are sure to offend someone even if you are careful. Don't ever tell off-color or race-based jokes, and don't forward offensive e-mails.

- **Do not forward anyone's e-mail message unless you ask permission.** If someone sends you an e-mail message, assume it is meant only for you unless you ask.

- **Do not discuss your personal business or problems at work.** Everyone has problems and issues, but they do not belong at work. When you have problems, discuss them with friends with whom you do not work. Never put your personal business "on the streets." Some people will be glad you have a problem and others will use it against you. Only your close personal friends should know your business.

- **If you make a mistake, admit it and don't pass the blame to someone else.** Everyone makes mistakes sooner or later. Admit the mistake and fix it as quickly as you can. Apologize to everyone concerned and don't do it again.

- **If you are really sick, stay at home; if you just feel bad, go to work.** No one wants to be around people who have the flu or a virus, so stay at home. If your head hurts or you feel groggy, take some medicine and go to work. Go to bed early that night so you can recover for the next day.

- **Dress appropriately and in a manner that reflects well on you and the company.** You should always dress neatly and appropriately at work. Some jobs may have specific requirements about what you should wear, while others will allow you to use your judgment. Regardless of what you choose or need to wear to work, look your best. Your clothes should be clean and pressed, and you should be well-groomed. People judge us on what they see, so it is up to you to shape your business image.

- **Limit the amount of time you spend socializing with work colleagues.** You can't avoid spending some social time with colleagues, but your best friends should be outside of work. If you get promoted over a friend, he or she may be jealous or expect certain favors. If you have a disagreement, it will be magnified at work.

- **Make a good impression at business meetings.** Be prepared by studying the agenda. Make at least one constructive suggestion or ask one thought-provoking question. If you are very new to the company, listen more than you talk. Never text while in a business meeting or allow your cell phone to ring.

- **Make a good impression on customers by going out of your way to serve them.** Customers pay your salary, so try to always provide good service. If you don't know the answer, get up and find it. Return calls in a timely manner. Always deliver more than you promise.

LIVING AND WORKING IN THE BRAVE NEW WORLD

What Are the Dimensions of Diversity?

Both managers and employees must learn to work and manage in an environment that includes great diversity in terms of ethnicity, age, and gender. Older workers are staying longer because they are living longer, and many cannot afford to retire. "The U.S. workforce is in the midst of a transformation. From 1980 to 2020, Caucasian workers in the United States will decline from 82 percent to 62 percent . . . the non-Caucasian portion of the workforce is projected to double from 18 percent to 37 percent, with the Latino portion almost tripling from 6 percent to 17 percent" (Meister & Willyerd, 2010). In the future, as many as five generations will be working side by side in the workplace. This means that everyone—managers and employees alike—will have to learn to work together productively.

The kinds of diversity you might encounter include race, religion, gender, age, ethnicity, nationality, culture, sexual orientation, social class, geographic region, and physical ability (see Figure 10.3). It is important for you to become open and accepting of individuals in all categories of diversity. The most significant thing you can do is to think of people who are different from you as individuals, not as groups. Some of you will need to make bigger changes in your overall belief system than others; it all depends on what kind of background you come from and what experiences you have had. An explanation of some major types of diversity follows.

Figure 10.3   Dimensions of Diversity Wheel

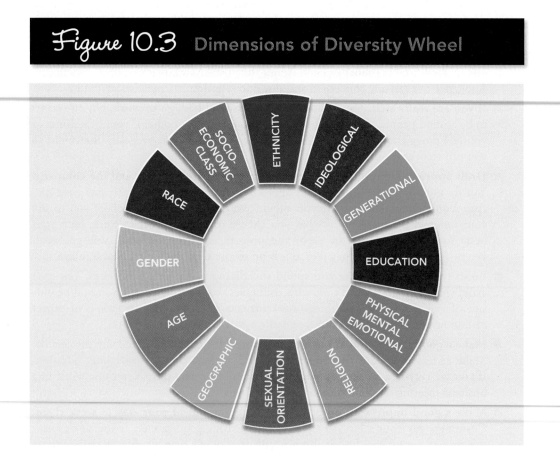

Racial Diversity

Racism is a prejudice that exists when an individual has a negative attitude about any race or ethnic group. Racism can be institutionalized in actions such as racial profiling or refusal to hire certain races except for menial manual labor. It can also mean that certain races are charged higher interest rates when borrowing money or have to pay more for an automobile than another race. Racist language usually implies that an individual or group is inferior in some way. In many cases, races that are discriminated against have been relegated to inferior positions in society due to economic and political oppression.

Religious Diversity

Many religions are practiced in this country and around the world. Ranging from orthodox practices that have been in place for hundreds of years to newly formed religions, people who practice each of these forms of worship are sensitive to unkind remarks about their beliefs. There are actually three major beliefs about other religions: *exclusivism*, *inclusivism*, and *pluralism.* Those who believe in exclusivism think that other faiths are in grave error and often view them as opponents. Those who practice inclusivism believe other faiths have some truth in them, but are only partly developed. Finally, those who believe in pluralism think that all faiths are legitimate and valid—when viewed from within their particular culture.

The biggest problem, quite simply, is that people tend to believe their religion is the only right one and is superior to all others. Such a position can also be dangerous, as wars frequently break out over religious differences. The terrible events that took place on September 11, 2001, were perpetrated by individuals who no doubt believed they were martyring themselves in the name of their religion. You live in a free country where you are free to worship as you choose. We must all grow to the point that we can allow others the same choice without judgment or hate. Regardless of what your religion is, you should not discuss it at work, nor should you try to recruit colleagues to your religion.

Gender Diversity

Since the 1960s and the women's rights movement, women in the United States have made steady gains toward being treated equally to men. However, there are still biases to be found among some institutions and certainly with some individuals. The fact that Hillary Clinton was a strong contender for the 2008 Democratic Party presidential nomination and that Sarah Palin was named as the Republican vice presidential candidate marks the fact that women have made significant gains. There are still a large number of both men and women, however, who will make the statement, "I just can't vote for a woman for president."

Just a few years ago, boys were expected to grow up to be masculine and to pursue certain types of careers, whereas girls were expected to be

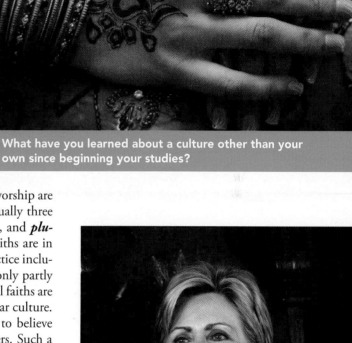

iStockPhoto

What have you learned about a culture other than your own since beginning your studies?

Zuma Press/Newscom

What are your personal feelings about diverse groups of people succeeding in areas where there were previous limitations?

feminine and perhaps pursue a role as a homemaker, nurse, or teacher. Many of the women who ventured out and did become involved in the business or academic world ran up against the "glass ceiling." Today men and women are attending college in record numbers, with more women actually in attendance than men. Although dramatic progress has been made to improve gender bias, there is still some confusion regarding "women's roles," as well as stigma attached to certain careers for men, such as nursing.

What do you think a person older than you could teach you about the world and about work?

iStockPhoto

Age Diversity

In your coursework, you have probably had classmates of all ages, so you have had some experience dealing with age diversity. In today's workforce, you will experience a community with people of all ages, and you need to learn to relate to and work with all of them. Older people are very much like other employees of all ages. They want to be treated with respect; most want to laugh and have fun; some want to see the latest movies; many are likely to enjoy sporting events; some will enjoy travel; and they want to be included in discussions. Study Figure 10.4 to determine how to work with diverse age groups.

List two other ways to work with a diverse age group of colleagues:

_____

_____

Figure 10.4 Working with Diverse Age Groups

- Learn to mix well with all age groups.
- Treat people of all ages and backgrounds with respect.
- Do not restrict your group of closest company colleagues only to people of your age.
- Seek the advice of older colleagues and those who have been with the company longer.
- Be sure to watch your language carefully at work. You might easily offend people of older generations as well as younger workers.
- Invite colleagues of varying ages and backgrounds to lunch. It is an asset for you to be seen as one who brings diverse groups together.
- If a group is going to lunch or for drinks after work, you might extend an invitation to your immediate supervisor.
- Take time to listen to people of all ages and backgrounds. This is the nicest compliment you can give anyone, and it will help you form positive relationships at work.

Ethnic Diversity

The word *ethnic* is derived from the Greek work *ethnos,* meaning "nation"; some people refer to ethnic groups simply by the country from which they originated. Scholars don't always agree on exactly what constitutes an ethnic group. An ethnic group is considered by some to be a social group that is typically distinguished by race, religion, or national origin. These groups may be marked or identified by distinguishing features and physical characteristics. But in some cases, they can be identified by their religion or language even when physical differences do not exist. Ethnicity might mean to others simply national origin. According to Feagin and Feagin (2008), an ethnic group is "a group socially distinguished or set apart, by others or by itself, primarily on the basis of cultural or national-origin characteristics."

Sexual Orientation Diversity

In your workplace, you will most likely encounter people of a variety of sexual orientations. Actually, work is not the place for this topic to be openly discussed. A person's sexual orientation is really no one else's business. Regardless of your personal sexual orientation, this should be a private matter. If other people choose to discuss their personal business with you, you should not share this with others, and you are not required to discuss your own personal business because they did. Ideally, all sexual orientations are respected in the workplace and people are treated as individuals rather than a member of a group. Actually, there are intelligent, engaging, attractive people of all sexual orientations—people who can become good friends and colleagues if you are open to accepting them and open to being accepted.

Social Class Diversity

Socioeconomic status or social class can be defined using the parameters of a person's income, education level, type of work, and family heritage. Someone may have social status because his or her grandfather was a senator, yet still not have large wealth. In the United States, the following terminology is generally used: upper class (wealthy), middle class (people who have jobs requiring considerable education or who own businesses that afford them a certain level of income), and lower class (people who are unemployed or hold low-level jobs that do not provide them with a good standard of living).

If you follow our advice and consider people as individuals rather than part of a class, you will meet great people from all classes. Wealth and status certainly provide opportunities and advantages not enjoyed by everyone, but you can find outstanding people in all classes to add to your personal community.

Generational Diversity

While you may have heard of many different types of diversity, you are less likely to have been informed about generational diversity. Different generations have been labeled with names such as the "Traditionals," "Boomers," "Generation X," and the current generation, "Generation Y" or "Millennials." You do need to remember that just because a person fits a particular age group, it does not mean that he or she will automatically embrace all the characteristics of that generation. A good rule to remember when considering all types of diversities is to treat people as individuals. Figure 10.5 explains the categories for age groups of different generations.

For the first time, four distinctly different generations, each with their own loyalties, priorities, and expectations, are working side by side in the workplace (Glenn, 2007). Naturally, with such a wide range of ages and different viewpoints, there are conflicts over how work should be processed, what constitutes company loyalty, how many hours one should work after closing time, and how best to communicate.

Figure 10.5   The Multigenerational Workforce

TRADITIONALS OR VETERANS

They believe in following the chain of command and are typically very loyal to their company and bosses. They may not function as well in collaborative efforts as some of your younger colleagues. They are not very tech savvy, as a rule, and usually prefer formal memos or phone calls rather than text messages or e-mail. They don't believe in accumulating large debts.

- Born between 1927–1945
- Most have retired, but some are still in the workforce
- Strong work ethic
- May not have strong technology skills

- Respect experience
- Believe in following the chain of command
- Very respectful of their bosses

BOOMERS

Boomers are often thought of as "climbers," and they tend to be ambitious. They are usually more tech-literate than people older than they are and handle voicemail and e-mail well. They know about social media and texting but are not likely to use them very often. They tend to believe in "face time" at work and don't put much faith in people working from home.

- Born between 1946–1964
- Very hard working
- Motivated by prestige and position
- Tend to handle their business in meetings

- Like to feel valued by their supervisors and colleagues
- Tend to be optimistic about their future

GENERATION X

This generation is fairly savvy when it comes to using technology. They are not overly fond of face-to-face meetings. You might hear them grumble after a meeting, "This could have been handled in an e-mail." They tend to be independent and don't necessarily enjoy working in groups. Many of them were reared as "latchkey" children, so they value family time. Because they grew up in times of recession, they tend to be savers.

- Born between 1965–1980
- Smaller in numbers than other generations
- Independent thinkers

- Many suffered through the recession and limited job market
- Value informality and fun at work
- Enjoy freedom to work in their own way

GENERATION Y/MILLENNIALS

Having been in school more recently, they are usually tech-savvy and especially enjoy social media. Their favorite way of communicating is texting, and they are very attached to their smartphones. They do not care for e-mail or phone calls, but are very adept at using the Internet. They usually exhibit a strong degree of confidence and tend to be social. They went to school at a time when tuition was on the rise, and many have big student loans.

- Born in mid-1980s
- Fastest-growing group in workforce
- Technology savvy
- Work to make money so they can spend freely
- Like to work with creative people

- Tend to be good at multitasking
- May be more tolerant of people who are different from them
- 96 percent of them have joined a social network
- Spend 16 hours a week online

You may very well go to work with an older person from the "traditional" generation who is very focused on a chain-of-command approach. In the same group, you might have a "boomer" who believes strongly in visibility or face time at the office and equates that as time spent working. Your team might include a member of Generation X who believes that his or her time is as important as money and that it doesn't matter if you don't work overtime as long as you do the job and do it well. If you work with Generation Y employees, you may find them to be focused on technology and finding a job that makes them happy.

Geographic Region Diversity

As strange as it seems, there are some who are prejudiced against people from certain geographic regions in this country. It is true that there are people in all parts of our country who have very different ideas from the masses; however, we should not label an entire section of the country based on the actions of a few. In the case of geographic regions, as in all cases, you should determine the characteristics of an individual rather than judge him or her as a member of a group. You might find that a friend from California could open up all kinds of new ideas and thinking for you, a friend from the South could show you beautiful beaches and golf courses, or a friend from New York could introduce you to Broadway or Central Park. As you expand your personal community of friends, make a special effort to get to know people from other regions of the country and learn to consider their character rather than where they came from.

Physical, Mental, and Emotional Diversity

You will encounter a number of colleagues who suffer from physical, mental, and emotional challenges. They could be visually impaired, deaf, or confined to a wheelchair. Quite a few people have depression, and others deal with bipolar disorders. Research shows that around 15 to 20 percent of all people experience some kind of learning disability such as dyslexia (National Institutes of Health, 2010). We assume that people who are labeled legally blind cannot see, when in fact, 80 percent can read large or regular print books. They may have a problem in only one eye. Truthfully, these colleagues are just like everyone else, except they have a physical problem that makes life a little more difficult. They have feelings just like the rest of us; they want to be included in social life and activities, and they don't want to be treated as disabled, different, and unable to participate. Consider getting to know a physically, mentally, or emotionally challenged person and bringing this person into your social network.

Ideological Diversity

The fact that we all have different opinions and ideas that are rooted in our family backgrounds, socioeconomic status, religious beliefs, cultural experiences, political beliefs, educational levels, and travel experiences creates great diversity and can cause difficulties between individuals and groups of people. "Individuals tend to come to more extreme views if they deliberate a given issue with like-minded people" (Kallock, 2009). In other words, internal diversity tends to be squelched by the forces of group polarization. People tend to remain moderate in expressing their beliefs until they are confident that others agree with them, and then they tend to become more extreme in their beliefs. These personal beliefs

BIGGEST INTERVIEW *Blunders*

When Jack Richardson interviewed with a large international company, he was interested in a position in logistics. During the interview he was asked this question: "Our logistics division employee base is made up of people from many different nationalities, many of whom have excellent computer skills. How do you think you will function working in an environment with Asians, Hispanics, Indians, and others?" Jack made a crucial mistake when he answered: "I'm from a small Midwest town where most people were Caucasian, so I think I might fit in another department better." The interviewer then told him that all their departments were highly diverse, and that they were proud of this fact and how well their employees worked together. Jack learned that day that he had a great deal of growing to do and that he needed to open up his mind to being able to work with people from a wide variety of backgrounds if he was going to be successful.

LESSON: When you go to work, you are unlikely to work in a company where everyone has the same background, race, and religion that you do. Learn to be open to relating and accepting all kinds of people. Judge them on their character and work ethic.

iStockPhoto

How could your ideological differences cause you a problem at work?

create diversity in thoughts, reasoning, ideas, and creativity. Political beliefs, for example, can be quite polarizing between individuals and groups. As an educated, enlightened individual, you will need to practice patience and understanding of other people's viewpoints and why they believe them even when you are diametrically opposed to their beliefs.

THE LAW PROTECTS PEOPLE FROM DISCRIMINATION AT WORK

What Is EEOC and What Does It Have to Do with You?

The Equal Employment Opportunity Commission (EEOC) is a part of the sweeping civil rights legislation passed after President Kennedy was assassinated. This legislation was actually being debated when he was assassinated, and President Johnson picked up the torch and managed its passage in 1964. The EEOC is charged with the responsibility of protecting people from being discriminated against in many different areas of employment, including recruiting, hiring, unlawful terminations, wages and salaries, and promotions. "The Equal Employment Opportunity Commission (EEOC) is an independent federal law enforcement agency that enforces laws against workplace discrimination. The EEOC investigates discrimination complaints based on an individual's race, color, national origin, religion, sex, age, perceived intelligence, disability and retaliation for reporting and/or opposing a discriminatory practice. It is empowered to file discrimination suits against employers on behalf of alleged victims and to adjudicate claims of discrimination brought against federal agencies" (Wikipedia, 2011).

If you experience discrimination, your first step is to read the legislation and be sure that you have a legitimate case. Then contact your human resources division and seek their help in resolving the problem.

> *Everything we shut our eyes to, everything we run away from, everything we deny, denigrate or despise, serves to defeat us in the end. What seems nasty, painful, and evil, can become a source of beauty, joy, and strength, if faced with an open mind.*
>
> —Henry Miller

If that fails, go to the EEOC in your state and ask for assistance in resolving the problem and in determining if your situation is a legitimate claim.

UNDERSTANDING STEREOTYPES AND PREJUDICE

Why Is Having an Open Mind So Powerful?

As you seek to develop an open mind and become an educated citizen, you need to be aware of the terms ***discrimination*** and ***prejudice***. If you discriminate against someone, you make a distinction in favor of or against a person on the basis of the group or class to which the person belongs, rather than according to an individual's merit. For example, you might discriminate against a person who is highly qualified for a job because he or she is of a certain race or religion, rather than consider his or her qualifications. Prejudice, on the other hand, is an unreasonable opinion or feeling formed beforehand or without knowledge, thought, or reason; it is a preconceived opinion of a hostile nature regarding a racial, religious or national group (*Webster's College Dictionary,* 1995).

If you discriminate against someone, it is because you are prejudiced against him or her for preconceived ideas that are based on insufficient knowledge, irrational feelings, or inaccurate stereotypes. As you can see, prejudice is usually not based on reason or knowledge, but on opinions most likely shaped by someone who influenced you or a region of the country where you grew up. Finally, prejudice is not an illegal act, whereas discrimination is illegal in employment, housing, loans, and many other areas outlined in the Civil Rights Act of 1964.

To receive the benefits of knowing someone, you need to enter all relationships with an open mind. If you have a derogatory mindset toward a race, an ethnic group, a sexual orientation, or a religion, for example, you have internal barriers that can keep you from getting to know who a person really is.

POSITIVE HABITS at Work

You will be expected to interact and work well with people from many different backgrounds. From the beginning, take time to get to know people who are different from you. Accept them as individuals, rather than judging them as members of a larger group. Ask people who have different viewpoints from you to go to lunch, and make an effort to understand their perspectives. Go out of your way to be known as a person who is not prejudiced or biased toward anyone. The more engaging and open you are to other people, the more open they will be to you.

Reflections: PUTTING IT ALL TOGETHER

Remember, we are motivated by what we value. As you establish your career and work toward personal and professional growth and change, consider the following ideas:

- Examine your personal values and beliefs to determine if cultural adjustments are needed.
- Listen to people and try to understand them before you form opinions.
- Stand up against intolerance and bigotry of any kind.

- Help others understand the importance of organizing against hate crimes.
- Develop relationships with people from a variety of backgrounds.
- Learn to appreciate and celebrate differences.
- Maintain close friendships with people who share your values and beliefs, as well as others who bring new and different ideas to the mix.

DIGITAL BRIEFCASE

ADJUSTING TO A GLOBAL ECONOMY

One of the many ways you can grow at work is to educate yourself on issues resulting from a global economy. Regardless of what position or workplace you are in, you will be affected by what is happening in other parts of the world. A good place to begin is to learn as much as you can about what is happening in China and India, two of our fastest-growing international competitors—and sometimes partners.

Access YouTube and identify several videos that show how employees in China work. As you view these videos, try to determine how their workplace differs from yours. Do you see any advantages Chinese businesses have over U.S. businesses because of a difference in regulations and laws? What reasons can you find that would cause U.S. businesses to ship certain jobs overseas to China rather than keeping the jobs here at home?

REFERENCES

Encyclopedia for Business. (2011). Corporate culture. Retrieved May 17, 2011, from www .referenceforbusiness.com/encyclopedia/Con-Cos/Corporate-Culture.html.

Feagin, J. R., & Feagin, C. B. (2008). *Racial and ethnic relations.* Upper Saddle River, NJ: Pearson/Prentice Hall.

Glenn, J. M. L. (2007). Generations at work: The new diversity. *Business Education Forum* (62)1.

Kallock, A. (April 16, 2009). Sunstein: Lack of ideological diversity leads to extremism. *The Harvard Law Review.*

Meister, J. C., & Willyerd, K. (2010). *The 2020 workplace.* New York: HarperCollins.

National Institutes of Health. (2010). Learning disabilities. Retrieved October 27, 2011, from http://www.nichd.nih.gov/health/topics/learning_disabilities.cfm.

Royal Pingdom. 2010. "Internet 2010 in numbers." Retrieved July 28, 2011, from http://royal.pingdom.com/2011/01/12/internet-2010-in-numbers.

Webster's College Dictionary. (1995). New York: Random House.

Wikipedia. (2011). Equal employment opportunity commission. Retrieved May 16, 2011, from http://en.wikipedia.org/wiki/Equal_Employment_Opportunity_Commission.

chapter eleven

LEAD

TEAMWORK—HOW TO LEAD AND HOW TO FOLLOW

Leadership is a potent combination of strategy and character. If you must be without one, be without the strategy.
—Gen. H. Norman Schwarzkopf

Why read this chapter?

Because you'll learn...

- The characteristics of a good leader
- The types of power
- The steps in becoming a good follower

Because you'll be able to...

- Discuss how to work in a virtual team
- List steps in effective delegation

PROFESSIONALS from the Field

Name: Mike Collins

Business: CEO and founder, IMI Living

Learning to lead and to follow are equally important. There are times when I need to step up as the CEO of my company and lead my colleagues with a clear vision and motivational strategy. There are other times when I need to sit back and let someone else who may be more of an expert in a particular area take the lead. I advise you to learn to lead a good meeting—one that has a clear agenda, that is focused, moves quickly and decisively, has good complementary visuals and graphs, and ends with a clear action plan. You also need to be a good meeting participant—do your homework and come prepared to make valuable comments or ask questions that focus the group on the right targets. I also encourage you to learn about the different kinds of power—some of which you have as a new employee—and to use power wisely and effectively. You should never abuse power just because you have it.

MyStudentSuccessLab

MyStudentSuccessLab (www.mystudentsuccesslab.com) is an online solution designed to help you "Start strong, Finish stronger" by building skills for ongoing personal and professional development.

LEADING WITH PASSION, POWER, AND PROMISE

How Do I Find the "Right Stuff" to Lead?

Everyone recognizes good leadership and strong leaders. Sometimes we refer to leaders as having "the right stuff." We observe outstanding leadership in dynamic corporate presidents, in good teachers, in football stars, and in effective politicians. Leadership qualities can be found in class presidents, military platoon leaders, or organizations' officers. At times we can almost see leadership as it is happening. Certainly, we feel the presence of a great leader, but leadership remains somewhat intangible.

Before we go further, we need to define *leadership*. There are many definitions, but the one we like best is this one: Leadership is the ability to establish a culture where people can make contributions, use their unique talents, and feel that they have been part of something bigger than they are. The influence potential of leaders is determined largely by how well they get other people to willingly and enthusiastically do what they want them to do.

Leadership is not playing a role, acting a part, wearing a uniform, or holding an office. Leadership is caring about people and an organization, putting others' needs ahead of your own, giving more of yourself than just enough to get by, and working as hard on "dirty work" as on "glory work." Leadership is knowing when to follow, sharing successes, understanding people's innate needs to achieve and to feel good about themselves, and helping others develop their potential. Finally, leadership is having the ability to craft a vision that is bigger than any one person's goals, and that, when accomplished, is worthy of having done the work to get there. We will discuss leading and following here to help prepare you for your future leadership roles, as well as for your role as a member of a team—both very important to your career.

You may be thinking, "I'm not interested in being a leader, and my degree won't lead me to a leadership role." However, you will be working in teams and with others in every position, and there will be times when you may have to lead in order to complete a task, help others, or just keep your job.

> *If your actions inspire others to dream more, learn more, and become more, you are a leader.*
> —John Quincy Adams, sixth President of the United States

Embrace Outstanding Leadership Qualities

The leader's job is to secure the cooperation of a group of followers, stimulate them to work together for common goals, guide them using previous experience, encourage them to become a dedicated member of the team, and set such a positive example that people willingly do what the leader wishes. You can only teach what you model yourself; if you don't do what you are telling everyone else to do, they won't do it. Leadership should never be confused with power, adoration, and seizing recognition for oneself. Although good leaders come in many shapes and sizes and rise from a multitude of backgrounds, they share common characteristics.

Major points for becoming an outstanding leader are listed in Figure 11.1.

> *Remarkable leaders never build pyramids in their own backyards.*
> —Wes Roberts

Figure 11.1   Qualities of Outstanding Leaders

Outstanding Leaders:

- Have the ability to shape a vision that is compelling enough to make other people believe in it and see themselves participating in making it happen.

- Are goal oriented and demonstrate direction in their own lives. Leaders must never allow their personal goals to supersede the goals of the organization, nor should an organization be used as a vehicle to serve the leader's personal ambitions. Goals must be jointly shared by the leader and the people.

- Can establish a climate of success, where people feel they can achieve and find fulfillment. This climate is inviting, encouraging, and rewarding to individuals. Leaders are able to involve all people and make them feel a part of an organization.

- Have a strong system of values and morals. As a leader, one must be an example for others to follow, meaning that one must be a decent, ethical, honest, and trustworthy person and must treat people consistently and fairly.

- Are great communicators. They are outstanding listeners as well as talkers. They know how to communicate up and down the chain of command, and can deliver a compelling inspirational message.

- Help others feel good about themselves, assist others in sharing in successes, and help others be a part of something bigger than themselves. A good leader is a diplomat who can navigate through the difficult situations confronted by decision makers.

- Know the basic underlying truth of leadership: leaders serve others. They meet the needs of others ahead of their own. Albert Schweitzer, Mother Teresa, and Martin Luther King, Jr., are all recognized as great leaders because they were servant leaders.

- Understand that leadership is caring about people and an organization, putting others' needs ahead of your own, and giving more of yourself than just enough to get by.

- Know that they must step aside and let others lead sometimes. They realize that they may be leaders today and followers another day. They know that they must first be good followers and good teammates in order to become a leader.

- Must be courageous, decisive, bold, imaginative, creative, and strong. They must be able to develop plans that are daring and different, and then they must have the strength and staying power to make them happen. Good leaders are "can do" people.

- Are able to display confidence in themselves and others. They must look, act, and speak like leaders. The ability to speak well is a great asset to anyone trying to lead. Leaders must look and act the part if people

are going to follow them. They must stand tall, walk briskly, and speak decisively.

- Must be courageous and able to stand adversity. They must be able to look at a bad situation and find a way to capitalize on it and overcome it.

- Do what they say they will do. Good leaders "keep their promises and follow up on their commitments" (Berko, Welvin, & Ray, 1997). They honor their word.

- Are able to compromise on some issues. One cannot always get everything he or she wants. People who are unyielding, unbending, and uncompromising will accomplish very little. The leader's job is to get the group to reach a consensus and then implement the plan.

- Must be open-minded and able to hear competing viewpoints and separate the good ideas from the bad. Leaders must be able to keep arguments from getting personal. No members should be allowed to attack other individuals. The leader's job is to give everyone a forum in which to express ideas and opinions, bring the group to a satisfactory conclusion, get disagreeing members to accept the compromise, and not take criticisms of an idea too personally.

- Are willing to share the victory! This can be accomplished by celebrations that involve everyone and by making statements such as, "This was a great team effort. We all made sacrifices and worked very hard. This is a victory for all of us, and I am proud to be a part of this team."

- Praise people and present awards publicly. Make people feel good and recognize them when they have worked hard and made outstanding contributions. Leaders know how to "make a difference in the lives of others—and liberate the leader in everyone" (Berko, Welvin, & Ray, 1997).

- Know that winning nobly and with class is a must. Leaders don't gloat or take the credit when they win. They are humble and always share the credit. The more you give credit away, the more it comes back to you.

- Are cheerleaders for their team members. Leaders write notes of personal congratulations; they thank people sincerely in front of groups; they tell people, "I appreciate you." Leaders spend a great deal of their time cheering others' accomplishments and no time cheering their own. If you are good, you don't have to tell people; they will know.

- Have the ability to get along well with all kinds of people and see the best in all people. They don't judge people by their race, religion, color, ethnic background, sexual orientation, or level of education. They cherish diversity! Leaders must be passionate about their vision, their followers, and their goals.

A positive attitude will help you so much more than a negative attitude when it comes to reaching your goals and working at your best. When you face challenging times, dig in and hold on. If you let negative thoughts and self-talk derail you, you won't survive in this world. Approach every day in your position as a chance to learn something new and help someone along the way.

GOOD LEADERS USE POWER CAREFULLY

How Can I Use Power Without Being Heavy Handed?

Many people confuse management with leadership, just as many confuse power with force. Real leadership power and respect must be earned. They cannot be bought, inherited, or bestowed on someone. The strangest thing about power is that the less you use it, the more you seem to have. Power is a precious commodity that few people know how to use. Conversely, if you have power, you must use it at times when a hard decision has to be made, or people will lose their respect for you and you will lose your power. The worst leaders are those who use their power for trivial reasons, personal gain, or vindictiveness. Weak leaders use force rather than leadership. Remember, leadership is the ability to get people to follow you voluntarily. Good leaders use their power to develop other leaders and take pride in seeing people they have led become successful.

> *Nearly all people can stand adversity, but if you want to test their true character, give them power.*
>
> —*Abraham Lincoln*

Categories of Leadership Power

Power comes to us through a variety of means. Specifically, we can view the acquisition of leadership power in six categories, illustrated in Figure 11.2. Each category is numbered in increasing order of significance in acquiring power for a leadership role. Category 1 is the weakest and most short-lived, whereas Category 6 is the strongest and most long-lasting. However, Categories 1 through 5 are actually part of Category 6. Each one builds on the other and strengthens Category 6. Viewed separately, we can describe each category as such.

CATEGORY 1: WHAT YOU HAVE. Category 1 is the weakest category for acquiring power. Many people are drawn to materialistic goods and place people who have a variety of these goods on a pedestal. Some people who are wealthy and have valuable property, spacious homes, or other commodities viewed as "important" use these objects to attract and gain temporary power. Unfortunately, some people are swayed by "things" and will step back and let wealthier people

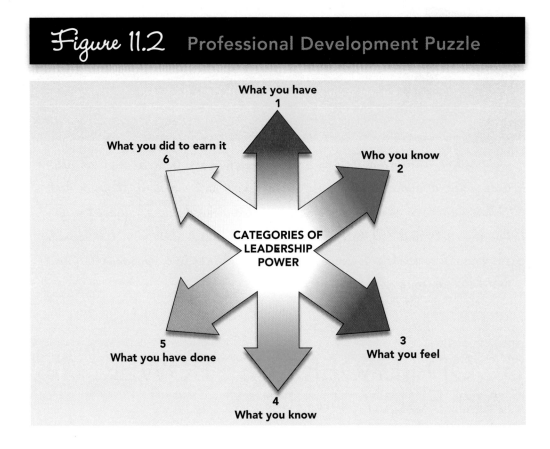

Figure 11.2 Professional Development Puzzle

make all the decisions. If a person's power base is built only on material objects, his or her power base will soon crumble.

CATEGORY 2: WHO YOU KNOW.   Who you know is Category 2. You probably have heard the expression, "It's not **what** you know, but **who** you know." In today's workplace, this is often true. Networking and making contacts are of ultimate importance to most employees today. Nevertheless, a power base built only on "who you know" is weak. Managers, supervisors, and leaders who acquired their positions because they "knew the boss" are familiar to us. Many people who acquire power this way quickly learn that the boss or the owner can make you a supervisor or assign you a title, but they cannot give you real power. True power is earned through the respect of the people you lead.

CATEGORY 3: WHAT YOU FEEL.   What you feel, Category 3, is much more abstract than what you have or who you know. Acquiring power by what you feel can be summed up as "leading with a soul." People respect leaders who are reflective and thoughtful. When leaders make decisions with their souls, those who are being led know the difference. This is the beginning of earned power. People begin to respect and appreciate that the leader has taken the time to look at every option, explored many solutions—and taken the human side of matters into consideration. Earning true power begins with soul leadership. This category includes leaders who care about the people they are leading; they feel their pain and frustrations and try to help them overcome their problems. Leaders who care also try to help people get promoted and find their strengths so they, too, can become leaders. Leaders with soul build other people.

CATEGORY 4: WHAT YOU KNOW.   What you know, Category 4, goes a long way with people who are being led. Sometimes older people have difficulty being led by younger people. The younger person feels threatened and sometimes uses too much force, and the older person sees the younger

Surround yourself with the most brilliant, talented, and optimistic people possible.
—Steve Brannon

leader as a "hotshot" fresh out of college with no real life experience, just "book knowledge." To a large extent, leadership power is gained through competence, experience, and expertise. When people know that the leader is intelligent, bright, studious, resourceful, clever, and concerned about them, respect and earned power follow. It is important to understand that good leaders with real power are knowledgeable students, too. They continue to learn from their surroundings, and they learn from the people they lead. If you are a young leader, it is wise to ask older people for their advice and suggestions. If you are an older leader, it is wise to learn the new ideas that young people bring to the table. In all cases, good leaders must keep people informed of what they know that needs to be shared. What people are not up on, they are down on.

CATEGORY 5: WHAT YOU HAVE DONE.   What you have done, Category 5, might be referred to as life experience. Used properly, life experience is one of the most powerful tools in leadership and can earn you great respect and power. Leaders should be careful, however, not to rely too heavily on the past and, in doing so, overlook current trends and new options. Using what you know is one of the strongest tools for gaining respect and acquiring power. People like working for leaders who have experience, knowledge, background, and training. They also like working with leaders who know how to use past situations to develop solutions to current problems. People also admire and respect leaders who stay up to date and are always looking forward and learning emerging trends and tools that will help them compete.

CATEGORY 6: WHAT YOU DID TO EARN IT.   What you did to earn power, Category 6, is the most important category. Coming full circle, true power is always earned. Power may come from what you have, who you know, what you feel, what you know, and what you have done, but, ultimately, true power is earned. Power can be earned by:

- Respecting other people
- Appreciating the work that people do and what they know
- Making good, solid, fair decisions that people respect
- Demonstrating a genuine interest in colleagues and their families
- Appreciating and calling on others' life experiences
- Being courageous and willing to take calculated risks
- Giving others the power to help themselves (empowering and enlarging)
- Remaining calm and getting the facts in the face of crisis
- Being a positive, optimistic, and engaging force
- Using creativity and asking for help
- Providing employees with the tools, support, and training to help them do the best job possible
- Living the motto, "I am a part of a bigger picture."

Powerful leaders enable others to be the very best they can be. They enlarge other people and their abilities. They encourage others to explore options and to create new paths. Last, powerful leaders are not challenged or threatened by people who excel, but they learn from them and celebrate their successes.

The Use of Power from Leaders' and Followers' Perspectives

Power is the ability to make things happen or to prevent things from happening. Power is also the ability to cause people to act in certain ways. People sometimes label power as being a bad thing, but power, in and of itself, is not bad. The issue is how someone gets power and how he or she uses it. Actually, everyone has some form of power, although some people don't understand how to use the power they have. Study the types of power illustrated in Figure 11.3.

> Power is like being a lady. If you have to tell people you are, you aren't.
> —Margaret Thatcher, former Prime Minister of England

Figure 11.3 Power from Leaders' and Followers' Perspectives

Types of Power	From Leader's Perspective	From Follower's Perspective
Reward	Has power because he or she has control of the finances and resources—can reward through money, promotion, increased visibility	Complies in order to get the resources that he or she believes a person has
Coercive	Has power because he or she can deliver punishment	Complies to avoid punishment by the person he or she thinks can wield it; fears the consequences of not following this person's orders
Legitimate	Has power based on one's position or title; given by the company and carries authority to make decisions	Believes power is granted by the company and he or she must carry out the directives given by this person
Expert	Has power because this person is an expert at something that is valued in the company (for example, technology knowledge)	Admires this person's knowledge and thus assigns him or her power
Referent/Charisma	Has power that is gained from charm, humor, and engaging personality that causes people to want to emulate him or her	Complies because he or she wants to be liked by this person and accepted in his or her circle of friends
Information/Knowledge	Has power that is gained from special knowledge that others need; related to skills, practice, experience, expertise	Believes that this person has information he or she needs and therefore, must stay on his or her good side
Connection	Gains power through the legitimate power of others (for example, an executive assistant to the president has the power to allow people in to see the boss); has the ear of powerful people	Believes this person has access to someone who is powerful and therefore, he or she must be obeyed
Support	Has ability to gain support from peers, subordinates, superiors, and customers outside the formal organization	Complies because he or she perceives this person to have internal and external power
Ethical/Character	Has respect and thus power because his or her word can always be trusted; treats everyone with respect and dignity; when this person speaks, he or she usually has something worthwhile to say	Complies from respect of who this person is and how well he or she is respected in the company

OUTSTANDING FOLLOWERS AND TEAM PLAYERS

How Do You Become a Great Team Member?

It has been said that "power corrupts and absolute power corrupts absolutely." In so many cases, this statement proves to be true. In the space below, explain that statement:

_____

_____

_____

_____

If you become a leader/manager of people, what can you learn from this statement and how can you avoid becoming corrupt simply because you have power over people?

Certainly, you must have a great leader to accomplish major goals, but great leaders cannot lead without great team members. According to Maxwell (2002), "Team players are enlargers, meaning they have the ability to see their teammates in the best light and make those around them better." If you are an enlarger, you believe in your teammates and want the best for them. You delight in seeing them grow. If you are a good, solid team player, others will work better because of you and your contributions to the team. Good team members who are also good followers care about their colleagues, and they have a burning desire to succeed together. A good team member is committed to giving his or her all to making the team succeed. The characteristics listed in Figure 11.4 are always found in good team members.

> *A team is many voices with a single heart.*
> —John C. Maxwell

Figure 11.4   Characteristics of Great Team Members

- Great team members love to win, to do a job better than any other team, and to win with their teammates. It's not so much that they love to beat someone else; the fact is that they simply love to strive together, to learn and improve together, and to reach goals together. Winning is simply the visible fact that they have worked hard and accomplished something great together. Winning together is bigger than any one of them winning separately.

- Great team members are excellent communicators. They are friendly, engaging, and able to express themselves and their ideas well. They are adept at listening and reading body language. They speak up when they have a point to make; they disagree with their teammates if they feel they should, but they do it in a respectful and careful manner. Great team members speak up candidly and openly, being careful not to offend intentionally. They own what they say and take responsibility for it.

- Great team members are intentional. *Intentional* is a word one hears a lot in business settings today. It simply means that people are acting deliberately, purposefully, and in a calculated manner with intentional goals and motives, rather than wandering around with no direction. They know where they are headed. Team members who act with intention take responsibility for keeping themselves mentally, physically, and emotionally in top condition.

- Great team members are adaptable and flexible. They are able to change directions if they need to, stop what they are doing and pick up something else if they are needed urgently in another place, and keep a lid on their emotions when things get stressful.

- Great team members are able to collaborate and cooperate. They learn to love being together as a team and to value what they can achieve together. Together they create a synergy that none of them has alone, and this is the glue that holds them together and makes them care about each other. They are able to work in a group and give and take on ideas.

- Great team members have a sense of humor. If you really love your work and your colleagues and you are in the right place, work becomes fun. Work is challenging, fulfilling, educational, and rewarding. Everyone loves people who can laugh and have fun, especially at their own expense. Laughter can diffuse tension and anger and cause people to release stress that is building up in their bodies; laughter is healing. A leader or follower who can evoke laughter into the mix has power.

- Great team members are committed to the vision and the goals. They place the team's goals ahead of their own. They know where they are headed and they will not take "no" for an answer. Failure is not an option!

- Great team members are disciplined. They stay and do the job no matter how tired they are. They are determined and tenacious and go above and beyond to be sure they don't let their team down. In a championship playoff game between the Dallas Mavericks and the Miami Heat, Dirk Nowitzski played with a temperature of 102 degrees—he was that committed to his team and to winning with them. Not only did he play, he led a comeback that enabled his team to win the game.

- Great team members are enthusiastic and excited about the team and what they are accomplishing together. They come to work fired up and ready to go to work. They don't drag others down with negativism, whining, and complaining. They bring an "I feel great" attitude to everything they do, and they are a joy to be around.

- Great team members are supportive of their colleagues. No matter how strong or private a person is, everyone needs help at one time or another. Good team members understand this fact, and they take care of each other during good times and bad. If one team member is having a bad day or a particularly difficult time in life, the others step up and take up the slack. It is said about geese that if one is shot or has to fall out of formation, another goose will follow and stay with him until he is OK or until he is dead. Good team members look after each other this way.

LEAD WITH VISION

How Can I Sell the Big Picture?

A vision portrays how the future is supposed to look. It provides people with a framework to help them understand. A leader's vision gives direction and asks: *What* should we be? *Where* should we be? *When* should we be there? *Why* should we be there? *Where* will we concentrate our resources? *How* will our lives be changed?

"Vision, quite simply, is a way of spelling out for your listeners the big picture, to help them understand the effort in which they are engaged, and to win their buy-in" (Barnes, 2005). A good leader must be able to paint a picture that is compelling for the people who are following. The vision must be something that is worth working for together and something that will challenge people to work for a common goal.

> *Leadership is the capacity to translate vision into reality.*
> —*Warren Bennis*

Good leaders understand that there can be no leadership without followers. Leaders and followers ideally bring out the best in each other. A visionary leader must capture the imagination of followers by painting a picture of some worthy achievement. Leaders are the kind of people who draw others to them, often because of the visions they lay out.

Followers are not likely to get excited about a plan that accomplishes very little or that is not much different from what they have always done. In other words, they don't want a leader who "majors in the minors." Big plans and big changes may frighten people, but they also grab them. Being able to comprehend, design, and sell a challenging vision that is built in conjunction with team members is one of the hallmarks of a great leader.

LEADING AND FOLLOWING IN A GLOBAL WORKPLACE

How Do You Work with a Virtual Team?

The use of virtual teams is becoming increasingly popular in today's modern workplace. Team members may work very effectively together while living in different time zones or even different countries. Virtual work teams can be part of an ideal job for people with certain requirements

Shutterstock

How do you think you would function as a member of a virtual team?

Figure 11.5 Guidelines for Virtual Team Members

- Establish a clear system for communicating, taking notes and sharing them in an accessible medium, and a sequence of participating so that everyone has an opportunity and an expectation to participate.

- Take time to get to know each other on personal and professional levels. Have "water cooler conversations" using Skype, WebEx, GoToMeeting, or some other system and pretend you are all together sharing likes and dislikes, hobbies and interests, and special skills and knowledge.

- Use a shared calendar system that allows people to schedule meetings and to have discussions with each other across multiple time zones. Designate core or mutual time slots when everyone must be available to confer. Use systems such as Google Apps and Google Calendar to assist in the scheduling process.

- Use instant messaging instead of e-mail—it is more effective. Some virtual teams always have Skype or some other system running to use for quick conversations.

- Share documents through tools such as Dropbox.

- Plan a "workplace happy hour" where you share new ideas and create together. You might consider using Second Life as a channel for having these meetings. Explore the use of new technologies, ideas that other companies are using, and how you can better work together as a virtual team.

and needs. The major key in making virtual teams work is that everyone is comfortable and productive working in this situation. Certainly, it is not for everyone. Figure 11.5 provides several important guidelines for making this happen.

THINK BEFORE YOU ACT

How Do I Make Good Decisions as a Leader?

Good leaders have to be decisive! Most of the time they don't have to make snap judgments, but at times a leader must make a quick decision. In 1955, Ruth and Eliot Handler, the cofounders of Mattel Toys, bet their company on television advertising when they signed on with ABC's *Mickey Mouse Club* for the sum of $500,000—the net worth of the company at that time. They had only a few hours to make this monumental decision. The payoff was immediate and significant. Orders came in by the sackful, all because of leaders who were willing to take a chance and make a decision at just the right time.

Most decisions won't be this urgent or important. However, sometimes a decision could mean life and death, or it could involve a piece of equipment that is needed right now, or it might be necessary to stop something being done by an employee. Most decisions, however, can wait until you have had time to think about the end results and the process needed to accomplish an objective. Being decisive and able to make a rational decision under pressure is very important, but being smart enough to take your time and weigh all possibilities is smarter if you have the luxury of time.

Here are some points to consider before you act:

- Can it wait so you can have a little more time to think about your decision? (But don't let decisions sit on your desk forever.)

- Do you have all the facts? Or at least most of them?

- Have you asked other leaders how they would handle this situation?

- Have you thought through how your decision will affect everyone concerned?

- Have you heard from everyone the decision might affect?
- Have you talked to members of your team and listened to their opinions? Do you have "buy-in" from them?

The best advice to be offered here is simply, "Stop and think!" Don't make rash decisions that can come back to haunt you. Sometimes you may not have much time to make a decision before you act. You can't hear opposing viewpoints; you can't take a vote; you can't read a good book—you simply have to act. Stay calm, think, and make the best decision you can make. **Remember, however, that not making a decision *is* a decision.**

CREATIVE PROBLEM SOLVING

How Can You Learn to Make Good Decisions Using Creativity and Logic?

> *Nothing is more difficult, and therefore more precious, than to be able to decide.*
>
> —Napoleon

The word *decision* comes from the Latin word *decidere,* meaning to "cut off." In other words, you have decided on something, and all other options have been canceled. Life is a series of choices, and the ones we make affect our lives in many different ways. Therefore, we need to learn to make good, logical, and creative choices.

Decisions mean letting uncertainty enter your life because the results usually happen somewhere in the future. For example, you could decide suddenly, without thinking the decision through, to drop out of school. The result might be that you can't get a good job or that you aren't earning the salary you had hoped for. If you had taken time to think about this decision and weigh all the possible results, you might have decided not to leave school. We all make poor decisions at one time or another, but we can learn to make good decisions most of the time by using the right strategies. The leader's job is to make the hard decisions, the decisions that can't be delegated, and the right decisions. Some decisions are amazingly smart; others are painfully embarrassing, and in hindsight, you wonder how you could have made such a bad decision. The scary part of leadership is that we don't have a crystal ball to see how our decisions are going to turn out.

As you lead and make decisions, approach difficult problems as though you are trying on a new pair of glasses. Try to see things you have never seen before; look beneath people's hidden agendas—secret motives different from the group's agenda—and fears and try to find their strengths; and be sensitive to others' feelings. Consciously try to see things in a new light, and you might be able to devise a new solution.

Here are some things to consider when making decisions:

- Set high standards and have big expectations of everyone. Expect people to perform at their highest level of ability.
- Surmount your anxieties (Useem, 2005).
- Create an atmosphere where information flows freely and decisions are transparent, unless it must be kept confidential to protect employees' rights.
- Use logic to solve problems. Think through your decisions step by step. Analyze the potential outcome and effect on other people. Weigh all the information. Look before you leap, if you have time to study the situation.
- Use creativity to solve problems. Just because it has never been done before doesn't mean it isn't a good idea. Remember that people resist change, even good change.
- "Don't put paint on a rotten board." This means that glossing over a difficult problem or trying to "fix" an incompetent employee is only going to cover up the problem temporarily; it won't solve the problem. Address the problem—not the symptoms!
- Get other people's ideas and tap into their creativity—but you make the decision. You don't have to take a vote or get a consensus if you are the decision maker. The leader makes the call and bears the responsibility, so take charge.

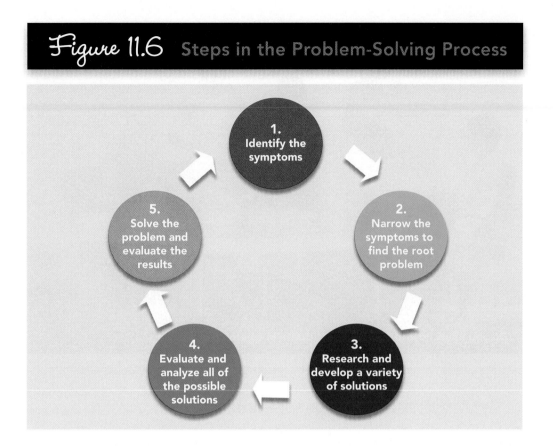

Figure 11.6 Steps in the Problem-Solving Process

- Quit being a perfectionist. Understand that you cannot please everyone. Do what you know in your heart is right.
- Don't become paralyzed with indecision until the decision is made by lack of a decision.
- The decision you make should match with the overall goals of the organization, or with your personal goals if the decision is personal.
- Remember that decisions are very much about "who" rather than "what" (Collins, 2005).
- Once a decision has been made, execution becomes crucially important. Ideas without action don't get the job done. Just do it!
- Forgive yourself when you make a bad decision and move on.

To assist you in solving problems and making difficult decisions, you might want to examine the chart in Figure 11.6

PARTICIPATING IN AND LEADING EFFECTIVE MEETINGS

How Can I Be Sure I Won't Lead a Worthless Meeting?

People tend to hate meetings because so many are poorly planned, accomplish nothing, and waste people's time. If you haven't already done so, sooner or later, you will find yourself at the head of the table discussing an agenda. There is a true "art" to leading (and participating in) an effective meeting. Productive meetings do not "just happen." Good meetings take planning, research, and careful preparation. If you can lead a good meeting in which people can honestly say, "I really got something out of that meeting," you will shine.

Do you know how to lead and participate in an effective meeting?

Shutterstock

Here are some tips for leading and participating in a meeting.

Before the Meeting

■ Prepare to do well by developing a folder with an agenda, supporting documents, minutes, and handouts for each committee or group with whom you have meetings. Before the first meeting, read previous minutes so you will be prepared. Do your homework!

■ Bring all necessary supplies to the meeting (pen, paper, personal calendar, highlighter, and supporting folder).

During the Meeting

■ Take good notes, highlighting any items that require your personal action.

■ Participate in the meeting if you have relevant information.

■ Ask a thought-provoking question to enable your committee to think through critical decisions.

■ Listen twice as much as you talk.

■ Don't make commitments for something over which you have no authority.

After the Meeting

■ Read your notes to ensure that you understand them. Transfer highlighted items that are your assignments to your personal planner so that they become a part of your to do list. Develop an action plan that enables you to complete your tasks prior to the next meeting.

■ Provide an overview of the meeting for your superior in writing, through e-mail, or through a meeting.

Following Good Meeting Manners and Established Protocol

■ Arrive at least five minutes early. Late arrivals irritate some bosses greatly. In any case, it makes you look slack.

- Never smoke or eat in a meeting unless everyone is eating.
- If refreshments are served, choose only items you can eat inconspicuously, and don't talk with your mouth full.
- Choose your seating carefully. The seat to the right of the leader is usually reserved for the next-in-command. Sit close so you can hear. Avoid sitting by people who talk to each other during the meeting. This behavior is rude, and the boss—and everyone else—will notice.
- Never use inappropriate language in a meeting.
- If you have to leave early for any reason, inform the chair prior to the meeting. Leave as quietly and as inconspicuously as you can. Call the committee chair during the day to determine what you missed.
- Leave your seat and work area free of debris. The committee chair is not your mother and will be irritated if he or she has to clean up after you.

> *A stream of decisions over time, brilliantly executed, accounts for great outcomes.*
> —Jim Collins, *Fortune* author

Leading an Effective Meeting

The first thing you must always consider is this: Do we really need a meeting? If you are leading or chairing a meeting, there are several questions you should ask yourself:

1. Do I need the group to accomplish the task, or is this something I could handle by phone or e-mail with a few key people? If you can handle the situation in a satisfactory manner electronically, do it and don't have a meeting.
2. Will a meeting save time by allowing us to accomplish more faster?
3. Do I need the group to meet to allow me to gain their commitment and to be transparent in an important decision?
4. Do I have everything I need to conduct this meeting properly (time, answers to questions, supplies, handouts)?
5. Do my committee members have the time to meet? Will they have enough time to prepare adequately for the meeting?

Before the Meeting

- Set goals and objectives.
- Plan and disseminate an agenda to your committee members in time for them to study and prepare details carefully. People are watching your leadership skills in action.
- Secure meeting space and supplies. Notify members of the meeting and inform them of when, where, what, how, and why.

During the Meeting

- Arrive early for the meeting to be sure everything is ready.
- Conduct the meeting in an organized way. Own the meeting! Take charge!
- Tell the group how long this meeting will last, and end it on time. This helps keep the agenda on track.
- Review decisions and assign tasks to members with deadlines.
- Determine the committee's next meeting time.

BIGGEST INTERVIEW *Blunders*

Wanda wrote on her resumé that she spoke Spanish fluently. When Wanda arrived the interviewer talked for a few minutes and then began conducting the interview in Spanish. Wanda's Spanish was mediocre at best, so naturally she did not perform well on the interview. She did not get the job, and she made a bad impression because she had stretched the truth.

LESSON: You should always tell the truth on your resumé and when you are interviewing. The people in HR departments and others have a great deal of experience in interviewing, and they can usually tell if someone is lying.

After the Meeting

- Have someone transcribe the minutes of the meeting and disseminate them as soon as possible.
- Minutes should include a comprehensive action plan that describes an overview of important discussion items, action items, responsible parties, and due dates.

Participating in and leading impressive meetings gain positive recognition with your bosses and colleagues.

LEARN TO DELEGATE EFFECTIVELY

How Can I Get All This Work Done?

If you cannot delegate, you cannot lead! Many leaders have a very difficult time giving up control. You cannot hold everything close to yourself; you must trust others to help get the work done. When you delegate, you simply hand work over to someone else, usually someone who reports to you and whom you trust. This person needs to be someone on whom you can depend, someone who has proved himself or herself to you by past actions. The opposite of delegation is "dumping," the process of giving bad jobs to someone who has no choice in the matter. Delegation, done properly, should be considered an opportunity to assume more responsibility and to develop leadership skills that will prepare one for promotion. If you view delegation as job enrichment, the chances are good that the person to whom you are delegating will be motivated to do a good job because people like responsible jobs over which they have control.

Many people use this excuse not to delegate: "By the time I could teach someone else to do this, I could have done it twice." That may be true, but the next time you need it done, you already have someone trained to do the task, and a simple review of the steps is all that is required.

People need clear goals. They need their managers to sit down with them periodically and help them understand exactly what is expected of them. Many employees don't have a clue. They may be doing what they think the boss wants, and it may not even be close. If your employees don't know where you want them to go, any road will be fine. You have to lay out the path, especially when you delegate.

Conversely, if you have responsibilities delegated to you, appreciate the opportunity and learn from it. Someone had to have confidence in you in order to decide to delegate to you.

Here are steps in delegating work to someone else:

1. First, remember that you are still responsible for getting the work done. If it doesn't happen, the responsibility is still yours. Likewise, if it is done poorly, you will be held accountable by your boss.

2. When you delegate a task, delegate authority to get it done along with the responsibility. For example, if you ask someone to collect data from all your colleagues, you have to make it known that you, as the boss, have asked this person to collect data.

3. When you delegate a task to someone, begin by telling the person that you have a job that you need help with and that you need him or her to help get this done. Make the person feel that you value what you are asking him or her to do, not dumping a bad task. Tell the person you trust him or her and believe he or she has the skills to do the job well. Be positive.

POSITIVE HABITS *at Work*

If your boss delegates a job to you, consider it an opportunity to showcase your abilities. Meet and exceed all deadlines and do more than expected. Check with your boss intermittently, even if he or she does not contact you to be sure you are on track. Sometimes your boss doesn't know exactly what you are doing—in this case, the boss will know exactly how well you are doing.

It is better to lead from behind and put others in front, especially when you celebrate victory when nice things occur. You take the front line when there is danger.

—*Nelson Mandela*

4. Let the person know that you look on this as an opportunity for him or her to grow and that these are the kinds of tasks that he or she will need to be able to do in order to move up the ladder. In other words, you are grooming this employee to be promoted. Be careful, however, not to go overboard, since promotion may not be imminent and may not be your decision.

5. Once you have described the task, you then need to work with the employee to set realistic goals and deadlines. Set intermediate steps to achieve, deadlines, and checkpoints.

6. It may be necessary to provide training to the person to whom you are delegating to ensure that he or she is able to do the job according to your expectations. Discuss the quality that is expected.

7. If the employee is not meeting deadlines and not doing quality work, constructive criticism and more direction needs to come as soon as you are aware of the problem.

8. Establish a timeline. Set an ending date that allows you time to recover if the assignment is not completed or done to your expectations. Remember, your name is on the line!

9. Establish intermediate checkpoints to be sure the person is on target, especially if this is a big, time-consuming task.

10. Encourage the delegatee to ask questions if concerns arise.

11. Evaluate the project and provide feedback to the person who did the job.

12. When the job is completed, give the person the credit for doing the job. Praise him or her openly in front of other colleagues.

> *Everybody wants to be somebody.*
> —Patricia G. Moody

Reflections: PUTTING IT ALL TOGETHER

You may be thinking, "Leadership? I'm just trying to find a job and survive." That may be true, but never doubt that you, your talents, your communication skills, and your overall decorum are constantly being evaluated by your superiors.

There will always be a need for effective, fair, honest, and hard-working leaders and followers in the workplace. You may be the next leader of a team, a department, a division, an entire shift, or even a company. It is never too early to begin thinking about your leadership abilities. Being a good follower will always be important throughout your career.

DIGITAL BRIEFCASE

WORKING COLLABORATIVELY IN A VIRTUAL TEAM

Select two people to work on a virtual, collaborative team that you will lead. They can be members of your class or two friends. Using Google Docs, Dropbox, or another collaborative program, work together to write a brief, two-page, double-spaced paper on teamwork. As the leader, you should furnish the outline and begin the draft. Assign one part of the outline to each participant. Give your teammates a deadline for making any adjustments to the draft before you finalize it as the team's leader.

REFERENCES

Barnes, J. (2005). *John F. Kennedy on leadership: The lessons and legacy of a president.* New York: AMACON/American Management Association.

Berko, R., Welvin, A., & Ray, R. (1997). *Business communication in a changing world.* New York: St. Martin's Press.

Collins, J. (2005, June 27). Jim Collins on tough calls. *Fortune.*

Maxwell, J. (2002). *The 17 essential qualities of a team player.* Nashville, TN: Thomas Nelson Publishers.

Useem, J. (2005, June 27). Decisions, decisions. *Fortune.*

chapter twelve

RELATE

MANAGING CONFLICT AND
DEALING WITH DIFFICULT PEOPLE

*Good leaders first get the right people on the bus,
the wrong people off the bus, and the right
people in the right seats.*

—Jim Collins, Good to Great

Why read this chapter?

Because you'll learn...

- To identify sources of conflict in the workplace
- To understand how the amygdala functions
- To assess how well you manage conflict

Because you'll be able to...

- Resolve certain types of conflict
- Deal with different types of difficult people

PROFESSIONALS from the Field

Name: Dr. Patricia G. Moody

Business: Dean Emerita
University of South Carolina

No matter what profession or job you are in, you will experience conflict, and you will encounter some very difficult people. On the other hand, you will have relationships with many wonderful employees and customers, and fortunately, there are many more nice people than rude ones. As a dean leading a large college at a major university, I have had to deal with rather difficult situations. My advice is to always try to keep your cool; try to make fair and consistent decisions when arguments arise; and try to treat everyone as you want to be treated. Our college prides itself on excellent internal relationships with our faculty and staff and outstanding external customer service and relationships with our students and parents. My goal was to try to take care of internal and external customers, even the difficult ones, in such a way that our employees love working in our college and that our students leave us with a feeling that they were well cared for and respected. It's a tough job at times—but our college does it well!

MyStudentSuccessLab

MyStudentSuccessLab (www.mystudentsuccesslab.com) is an online solution designed to help you "Start strong, Finish stronger" by building skills for ongoing personal and professional development.

CONFLICT—THE MOST AVOIDED AREA IN THE WORKPLACE

Exactly What Is Conflict and What Do You Do about It?

As much as we all hate conflict, it is a natural part of life, and sooner or later, you will experience it in the workplace. Conflict is never pleasant, but the sooner you face this demon, the quicker and more effectively you can resolve it. *Conflict* is from a Latin word, *conflictus*, meaning "to strike together with force." This is basically what happens when two people—or sometimes more—have conflict. Their opinions and ideas and ways of doing things are at direct odds with each other, and conflict arises as a result. Conflict causes some people to be intimidated and withdrawn, brings out the worse in some of us, but actually is not a bad thing if handled properly. When conflict arises at work, someone has to deal with it, and the sooner, the better.

THE AMYGDALA AND ITS ROLE IN CONFLICT

What in the World Is an Amygdala?

The amygdala plays a major role in how each of us responds to conflict. A part of the brain's emotional system, the amygdala, shown in Figure 12.1, can cause us to go into default behavior based on past experiences.

So one of the first steps in understanding conflict is to know that sometimes people are reacting to something in which you had no role—they are just fighting for their emotional survival. They are reacting to a past trauma that has been brought to the forefront by this new experience. In recognizing how the amygdala functions, you will be able to understand the causes of some conflict.

DR. PHIL'S ANALOGY OF WRITING ON A SLATE

What's That Got to Do with Me and Resolving Conflict?

In a television interview, Dr. Phil McGraw, noted television personality, discussed the former Duchess of York's childhood and her difficulty in loving herself and believing she was OK. In the course of this conversation, he described to Sarah Ferguson his belief that we all have a "slate" that we and other people write on all the time. After a while, it begins to be the picture

Figure 12.1 The Amygdala

Don't let this word or concept frighten you. If you have never heard the word ***amygdala*** (pronounced ah-MIG-da-la), you're not alone. Most people have not. But this term and concept are important for you to be able to understand the overall aspects of your emotions. The amygdala, simply a part of the brain's emotional system, can cause us to go into default behavior based on what we remember from a similar experience. Do I use ***fight*** or ***flight***? Basically, the amygdala is there to protect us when we become afraid or emotionally upset. When influenced by the amygdala, everything becomes ***about us***. We become more judgmental. We don't stop to think about differences or the other person's feelings or the relationship. The amygdala can trigger an emotional response **before** the rest of the brain has had time to understand what is happening, and this situation causes us to have problems with others.

The amygdala remembers frustrations, fears, hurt feelings, and anger from our past. The tension from these past experiences causes the amygdala to go into default behavior—we ***feel*** before we ***think***—and this can create a potentially explosive situation. If you had a bad experience several years ago and are placed in a similar situation today, the amygdala will remember and trigger emotions that cause the body to respond. These feelings often cause people to bypass critical thinking (the logical brain) and to respond with angry words or actions (the emotional brain). For example:

- They get angry—you get angry.
- They curse you—you curse them.
- They use physical violence—you use physical violence.

However, if you remain calm and level-headed, you will begin to see that the other person usually begins to calm down, too. He or she will follow your emotional lead, positive or negative, and if you're calm and rational, anger and violence become out of place for most people.

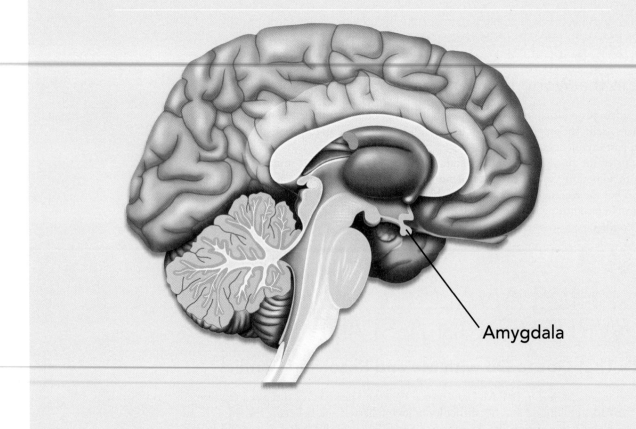

Amygdala

of the person we believe we are. According to reports, Sarah's mother looked nothing like her daughter and would make disparaging remarks such as "Sarah comes from the postman" because of her red hair and blue eyes. When Sarah was 12, her mother left her family and ran away to Argentina with a polo player, and Sarah rarely ever saw her. Sarah Ferguson had it all and lost it because of poor decisions and, according to herself, her "low self-worth." Perhaps if Sarah had had positive things written on her slate, she might have been a much happier person. Certainly, she would not have had as much conflict in her life or caused as much conflict in the lives of her loved ones.

Trinity Mirror/MirroxPix/Alamy

We share this story with you as we discuss conflict and difficult people as a reminder that people are rarely who they appear to be. Many difficult, contrary people are not mean; they are just hurt. Bill Cosby said, "Hurt people, hurt people." In other words, they fight back even when there is no real reason to fight. We have no idea what was "written on someone's slate" that causes him or her to behave in a bad manner. So we begin by encouraging you to listen to people before you make judgments and try to understand why they do the crazy things they do—because there is always a reason.

CAUSES OF PERSONAL CONFLICT

Why Can't People Just Get Along?

What causes conflict between people? "The short answer to the question of what causes conflict is quite simply, life. Bringing people together in social interaction necessarily involves a set of interpersonal dynamics which sooner or later will lead to conflict" (Thompson, 2011). When one considers what a diverse population mix we have in this country, it is easy to see why many conflicts arise. First, we are free to express ourselves, and most of us do. We come from a melting pot of races, ethnic backgrounds, religious beliefs, customs, values, and backgrounds, so sometimes we simply don't see eye to eye. Because we are so different, we are unlikely to co-exist without conflicts, so we have to learn to manage our disagreements in a civil manner and as acceptably to both parties as possible. Conflict is simply a fundamental part of human relationships—often a very misunderstood part.

Conflict is inevitable. But conflict itself is not the problem; the breakdown in organizations' productivity and the inability of people to work together is the dangerous part of conflict. Conflict is difficult, uncomfortable, and stressful, but used properly, as a learning tool, conflict can actually help you learn and grow. Believe it or not—conflict can even be essential to an organization's improvement. An organization that encourages transparency, honesty, openness, and expression of ideas and feelings can expect conflict. On the other hand, an organization that tries to restrict honesty and openness and centralizes all the power within a few people can also expect conflict. Conflict may arise simply from having people view problems or actions from different perspectives. Chances are they may both be partially right, and by combining both opinions, you might arrive at a potentially great idea—but first the people have to calm down and communicate. Communications is key to solving conflict.

Please hear what I am not saying.
—Old Indian Proverb

So conflict is going to happen. How do you deal with it? The first step in dealing with conflict is to determine the root causes—not the symptoms of the problem, but what is at the bottom of the problem. There are many causes of conflict. Sometimes conflict is caused by difficult people (which we will discuss later) and sometimes it can be caused by people who are

GRADUATE Quote

Jennifer Rosa
Graduate!
InterCoast College, Northridge, CA
Career: Alcohol and Drug Counselor

If you were able to have an internship during your college studies, use this experience to best advantage. Always list your internship experience on your resumé and talk about your experiences during the interview. Having real-life, on-the-job experience goes a long way in an interview. If an internship is not required for your degree, try to do one anyway. It will benefit you greatly.

typically calm. There is no "one size fits all" solution to handling conflict. It all depends on the people who are involved, where they are coming from, what past experiences they have had, and numerous other factors.

> *If you are patient in one moment of anger, you will save yourself a hundred days of sorrow.*
> —Chinese Proverb

We all have our "hot buttons"—those touchy topics that make our blood boil and cause us to say things we wish we hadn't. And let's face it—some people just rub us the wrong way. We simply find some people's habits, actions, and demeanor annoying. Maybe they don't carry their load; maybe they act like know-it-alls; maybe they flaunt their possessions and brag too much to suit us. What causes one person to go off the deep end may only slightly irritate another person. We've all experienced the unpleasant feelings that conflict stirs in each of us. It creeps up on us like the flu. We never expected it to happen, but before we know it, in a moment of anger, during a misunderstanding, dealing with a difficult colleague, or in a jealous rage, we lose control, and the door to conflict has been opened. Conflict can happen between any people, even the best of friends.

SYSTEMIC SOURCES OF CONFLICT

Does Anyone Around Here Know What Is Going On?

> *Stepping on someone's feelings and ideas hurts just as bad as stepping on their toes, and it lasts a lot longer.*
> —Unknown

Not all conflict is the result of people not getting along or not liking each other. "Conflict in the workplace is often blamed on personalities and misbehavior, but in reality, much workplace conflict is systemic and endemic to the workplace environment. **Systemic conflict** is conflict that is caused by the system's policies and procedures. **Endemic conflict** is conflict that is common in a particular kind of business or setting. Ineffective organizational systems, unpredictable policies, incompatible goals, scarce resources, and poor communication can all contribute to conflict in the workplace. Workplace conflict causes loss of productivity, distractions, and employee dissatisfaction. However, management can produce positive results by paying attention to and addressing the true causes of conflict in their organizations" (Cardenas, 2011). Management is the key to systemic conflict. Workplaces need highly organized systems and controls and clearly communicated policies that are consistently applied to all people.

Let's give you a chance to try your hand at solving systemic conflict. Assume you are a manager and have been put in charge of solving systemic conflicts. If you were in charge, how would you solve the systemic sources of conflict listed in Figure 12.2? Write your answers in the right-hand column. You may need to do some research to solve some of these problems. The Internet has excellent resources on conflict management.

Now that you have been introduced to systemic causes of conflict, you need to understand some basic causes of personal conflict, as shown in Figure 12.3.

Sometimes it helps to resolve conflict by just being calm and deliberate and thinking things through. Approach conflict with an open mind. This is not about trying to prove one person wrong and another right. The goal is to have a win–win solution. You won't always have that option, but if you do, some good questions to ask yourself are outlined in Figure 12.4.

iStockPhoto

How does conflict hurt your chances of promotion?

Figure 12.2   What Would You Do to Solve Systemic Sources of Conflict?

Systemic Source of Conflict	How Would You Solve the Problem If You Were in Charge?
Competition for scarce resources (people, time, money, space, travel)	
Interdependence conflicts (when one person depends on another who is not producing)	
People who have overlapping responsibilities with no clear delineation	
Two bosses giving conflicting directions and simultaneous deadlines to the same person	
Unequal application of policies with favoritism shown to some	
Unnecessary change that keeps people off balance, irritated, and confused	
Poor communication by management that has the grapevine running wild with rumors	
Skill deficits by some employees	
Conflict among teams because of incompatible goals with no clear vision or leadership from management	

Figure 12.3 Causes of Personal Conflict

- Failure to understand and respect an individual's needs, background, culture, sex, age, or values.

- Competing interests and perspectives.

- Hidden agendas—perhaps someone is fighting against an idea because it introduces a major paradigm change and makes him or her feel threatened and insecure.

- Passive-aggressive communication style and use of sarcasm to make an underhanded "dig" at someone.

- Killing people's ideas without giving them an opportunity to "sell" their thoughts.

- Interpersonal conflicts—sometimes people simply don't get along. Interpersonal communication is complicated; often this type conflict has to be mediated.

- Harsh criticism and lack of appropriate feedback.

- Gender differences that create different ways of looking at things.

- Bullying and intimidation, which are forms of harassment. These sources of conflict are an abuse of power that always cause conflict and unhappiness among employees.

Figure 12.4 Ask the Right Questions When Resolving Conflict

- Does the cause appear to be systemic or personal?

- Is it because you or someone needs a scarce resource?

- Is there a conflict in work and personality styles?

- Is there a communications breakdown?

- Is there a clear picture of what management expects of these people who are involved in conflict?

- Are there conflicting pressures because of two managers' expectations?

- Is the policy clear, and is it being applied consistently to everyone?

Cultivate the Mavericks

Conflict, handled properly, can actually be a good thing for a person or a company. If everyone at your workplace had total agreement, the ideas would become stagnant. There are always "mavericks" at work who frequently take an opposing view to a decision or direction. Although they may be annoying, mavericks are often the people who move the organization faster than it might have moved and in new and rewarding directions. On the other hand, if there is too much conflict, work is disrupted, and people focus on the conflict rather than their work. If you are a maverick, be careful of how you say things; be aware of stepping on other people's ideas; present your ideas in a rational, well-thought-out manner; and don't surprise your boss with something that he or she might not like discussed openly at a meeting before you talk to him or her.

As a result of being forced to work through a situation, good things can actually occur:

- The relationship may become more viable, and both parties' work might actually improve.
- A discussion might clear the air.
- People might examine the issues and develop new strategies and solutions that lead to growth and progression.
- Perhaps both parties can compromise and get most of what they want.
- Talking together and listening to each other can provide a better understanding of each other.
- Communications in the future might be improved.
- Policies might be revamped and made more fair and consistent.
- Stress can be reduced if the conflict is resolved.

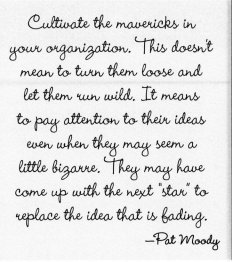

Cultivate the mavericks in your organization. This doesn't mean to turn them loose and let them run wild. It means to pay attention to their ideas even when they may seem a little bizarre. They may have come up with the next "star" to replace the idea that is fading.
—Pat Moody

CONFLICT RESOLUTION

How Can I Settle Disputes and Keep the Peace?

Conflict resolution is a way of settling disputes and disagreements in a peaceful manner through discussions that lead to an understanding of the cause of problems. Ideally, conflict resolution resolves the problem without name-calling, violence, fights, or long-term hostilities. While some conflicts are easy to resolve, others may take months. As a leader, you can be assured that you will be called on to resolve conflicts and disputes.

There is no common denominator for solving conflict issues. Some are very complex, deep-seated, and difficult to eradicate; they may not be resolved quickly or easily. Some may require professional counseling, and in some cases, people have to be terminated because they are such a disruption in the workplace. An extreme example of deep-seated conflict is the conflicts between Catholics and Protestants in Northern Ireland that can be traced back to 1690. While this is an extreme example, it illustrates how conflict can be passed along from one generation to another. Different types of racial conflict in this country, for example, are deep-seated and not easily solved overnight. There are ways, however, to deal with more common conflict situations that arise in the workplace. Figure 12.5 details some of them.

Shutterstock

Can you think of situations where you can create a "win–win" solution?

Dealing with Conflict as a Manager

When resolving interpersonal conflict and incompatibility in a leadership role, you will need to discover ways that all parties can win at least some measure of satisfaction. This is not an easy task! If you have to resolve a conflict, these suggestions should be helpful, whether the dispute is between two other people or between you and someone else:

- Conflict just won't go away. Putting your head in the sand and ignoring it is the worst thing to do. The quicker you face it, the better.
- As the mediator, you need to be objective and show no favoritism. Don't attack either person or let one attack the other.

A leader is needed who can listen to both sides and propose a model for a problem solving session in which both sides come together and mediate a solution.
—Warren Bennis and Joan Goldsmith

Figure 12.5 Ways to Resolve Conflict

- Accept the fact that conflict is a natural occurrence, one that will happen in all areas of your life. Work hard to learn to deal with it and not let it control your life. Remember, no one can control you unless you let them—and you should never allow this to happen!

- Don't be afraid of conflict—if you do, you will always be a victim.

- Provide a forum where people can be heard when conflict arises.

- Allow the other person to vent fully before you begin any negotiation or resolution. Breathe deeply.

- Don't meet anger with anger. Sometimes firmness is required, but be firm, not volatile.

- Try to see the world through the other person's eyes. You have no idea who wrote what on his or her "slate" or who has imprinted negative thoughts on his or her amygdala.

- Try to create win–win situations where everyone can walk away having gained something. It is always best not to have a loser.

- Try to reach an agreement that uses part of both people's ideas, if possible.

- Determine if the conflict is a "person conflict" or a "situation conflict."

- Ask the other person what he or she needs. Try to understand the situation.

- Realize that you (or your company or office) may very well be in the wrong.

- Try to face the conflict head-on and quickly. To avoid conflict only makes it worse. Most conflict will not go away quietly, so deal with it before it escalates.

- Don't become the same type of difficult person as the ones with whom you are dealing. Fighting fire with fire will only make the flame hotter. In most situations, you will need to be the "cool" one.

- Don't take the other person's attitude or words personally. Most of the time, the person doesn't know you or your life. You are his or her sounding board.

- Avoid physical contact with others at every expense.

- If you must give criticism, try to do so with a positive tone and attitude. If possible, provide some positive comments to the person before you offer your criticism.

- Don't save up a list of the person's faults and problems and "sandbag" him or her all at once.

- Never verbally attack the other person.

- Allow the other person to save face. Don't back the other person into a corner and give him or her no way out except to fight.

- If you have a problem with a person or his or her actions, be specific and state your concerns before things get out of hand. The person can't read your mind.

- Ask yourself, "If this were my last action on earth, would I be proud of how I acted?"

- If someone shows signs of becoming physically aggressive toward you, get help early, stay calm, talk slowly and calmly to the other person, and if necessary, walk away to safety.

- Own your words. If you're making a statement, let it come from you, not "them."

- Show your concern for the other person.

- Try with all your might to end on a positive note. It is far better to make a friend—or at least build a relationship with a colleague with whom you can work—than it is to make an enemy who will always be a problem for you.

- Define the conflict. Get to the root of the problems, not the symptoms. Is this a people argument or an issue conflict?

- Try to set up an ending scenario where an agreement can be reached.

- If you are the boss, let the conflicting parties know that you expect them to resolve their differences and be able to work together. The workplace cannot be disrupted by constant conflict.

- Ask them to state their opinions in respectful language. Don't let the parties get off track, accuse each other in threatening tones, or use improper language toward each other.

- Try to avoid having a winner and a loser. You should try for win–win if possible. Both parties will more than likely have to compromise.
- Diffuse anger with humor if possible, but don't make light of the situation.
- Never make a decision without hearing both sides. There are always two sides, at least.
- Provide constructive criticism and feedback to both parties. Avoid accusing and finger-pointing. State feedback in positive terms.
- Your goal is to reach a mutually desirable end. Suggest some possible solutions that do not favor one over the other.
- You cannot change either party; you can only try to get each to see the other person's side.
- Sometimes you have to get people to make trade-offs.
- Occasionally, you have to allow for a cooling-off period before people are able to settle down and perhaps reach an agreement.
- Don't expect someone else to read your mind. You have to state your opinions in a modulated, even voice. Avoid yelling or shrill-pitched words. Stay cool!
- Allow both parties to save face. Humiliation is never a good tactic in any circumstance!
- Try to end the meeting in a positive manner.

iStock

Is there ever a time when one should resort to physical violence to solve a conflict? How can such a situation be avoided?

Resolving conflicts is never easy. It takes a level-headed person who is able to see all sides of a situation and who can use strategies for diffusing the situation and reaching a mutually satisfying conclusion.

The assessment on conflict management in Figure 12.6 will help you determine how well you personally manage conflict.

HARASSMENT IN THE WORKPLACE

What Are These People Thinking?

The most important thing you need to know about harassment is that it is illegal. Exactly what constitutes workplace harassment? "Workplace harassment is any unwelcome or unwanted conduct that denigrates or shows hostility or an aversion toward another person on the basis of any characteristic protected by law, which includes an individual's race, color, gender, ethnic or national origin, age, religion, disability, marital status, sexual orientation, gender identity, or other personal characteristic protected by law. A conduct is unwelcome if the employee did not solicit, instigate or provoke it, and the employee regarded the conduct as undesirable or offensive" (Strategic HR Services, 2010). Any kind of behavior toward another employee that creates a hostile workplace is in violation of the law. Some of the major points you need to know about harassment as an employee and as a potential manager are outlined in Figure 12.7.

BIGGEST INTERVIEW Blunders

James was asked a question that he considered inappropriate; in fact, he thought the question was illegal. Instead of approaching the question calmly or the interviewer respectfully, James barked, "What business is that of yours? I don't have to answer that question." He learned later that the question was legal. While the question may not have been in the best taste, the interviewer had the right to ask the question.

LESSON: Know what questions are illegal and determine in advance how you will respond if someone asks you such a question. Don't be caught off guard and don't be too quick to snap at an interviewer. You might say, "I prefer not to answer that question because I don't see how it is relevant to this job."

Figure 12.6   Conflict Management Assessment

Read the following questions carefully and respond according to the key below. Take your time and be honest with yourself.

1 = Never typical of the way I address conflict   3 = Often typical of the way I address conflict
2 = Sometimes typical of the way I address conflict   4 = Almost always typical of the way I address conflict

#	Question	1	2	3	4
1.	When someone verbally attacks me, I can let it go and move on.	1	2	3	4
2.	I would rather resolve an issue than have to "be right" about it.	1	2	3	4
3.	I try to defuse arguments and verbal confrontations at all costs.	1	2	3	4
4.	Once I've had a conflict with someone, I can forget it and get along with that person just fine.	1	2	3	4
5.	I look at conflicts in my relationships as positive growth opportunities.	1	2	3	4
6.	When I'm in a conflict, I will try many ways to resolve it.	1	2	3	4
7.	When I'm in a conflict, I try not to verbally attack or abuse the other person.	1	2	3	4
8.	When I'm in a conflict, I try never to blame the other person; rather, I look at every side.	1	2	3	4
9.	When I'm in a conflict, I try not to avoid the other person.	1	2	3	4
10.	When I'm in a conflict, I try to talk through the issue with the other person.	1	2	3	4
11.	When I'm in a conflict, I often feel empathy for the other person.	1	2	3	4
12.	When I'm in a conflict, I do not try to manipulate the other person.	1	2	3	4
13.	When I'm in a conflict, I try never to withhold my love or affection for that person.	1	2	3	4
14.	When I'm in a conflict, I try never to attack the person; I concentrate on his or her actions.	1	2	3	4
15.	When I'm in a conflict, I try to never insult the other person.	1	2	3	4
16.	I believe in give and take when trying to resolve a conflict.	1	2	3	4
17.	I understand and use the concept that kindness can solve more conflicts than cruelty.	1	2	3	4
18.	I am able to control my defensive attitude when I'm in a conflict.	1	2	3	4
19.	I keep my temper in check and do not yell and scream during conflicts.	1	2	3	4
20.	I am able to accept "defeat" at the end of a conflict.	1	2	3	4

Total number of 1s _____   Total number of 3s _____

Total number of 2s _____   Total number of 4s _____

If you have more 1s, you do not handle conflict very well and have few tools for conflict management. You have a tendency to anger quickly and lose your temper during the conflict.

If you have more 2s, you have a tendency to want to work through conflict, but you lack the skills to carry this tendency through. You can hold your temper for a while, but eventually, it gets the best of you.

If you have more 3s, you have some helpful skills in handling conflict. You tend to work very hard for a peaceful and mutually beneficial outcome for all parties.

If you have more 4s, you are very adept at handling conflict and do well with mediation, negotiation, and anger management. You are very approachable; people turn to you for advice about conflicts and their resolution.

Figure 12.7 Frequently Asked Questions on Workplace Harassment

1. **What law(s) does workplace harassment violate?**

   Workplace harassment is a violation of Title VII of the Civil Rights Act of 1964, the Age Discrimination in Employment Act, and the Americans with Disabilities Act.

2. **What constitutes sexual harassment?**

   Sexual harassment is any advancement toward another person of a sexual nature that is unwanted and uninvited. "This applies to harassment by a person against another person of the opposite sex as well as harassment by a person against another person of the same sex" (Strategic HR Services, 2010). It includes gender harassment against employees because of pregnancy, childbirth, or any other violations of a related nature. The law also applies to what is known as "quid pro quo" sexual violations, in which a person is promoted, given a raise, or offered other special rewards in exchange for sexual favors.

   Some examples of sexual harassment are verbal abuse or harassment (e.g., dirty jokes, unwanted letters, e-mails, sexually explicit pictures, telephone calls, or written materials); unwelcome sexual overtures or advances; pressure for dates or to engage in sexual activity; remarks about a person's body, clothing, or sexual activities; personal questions of a sexual nature; touching of any kind; or referring to people as *babes, hunks, dolls, honey, boy toy*, and so forth.

3. **How does one know when a violation has occurred?**

   If an employee is required to work in a hostile environment where he or she is intimidated or treated in an offensive manner, a violation has most likely occurred. Employees cannot be discriminated against for any reason, nor can they be retaliated against if they file a complaint or ask for an investigation.

4. **To whom does one report a violation?**

   First, tell the offender directly to stop harassing you and that you will report it if it doesn't stop immediately. To whom you report the offense depends, of course, on who is making the violation. If it is your boss, you can go directly to his or her boss, or you can report it to human resources. You should have the offenses carefully documented and dated. If you can find another person who has experienced the same offense and will go with you, your case will be strengthened. If it is a colleague, go to your boss. The person to whom the offense is reported is required by law to address the violation immediately. Supervisors should report the claim of violation to management immediately. The law requires that all claims of sexual harassment be investigated. File a formal complaint with the HR department.

Is taking a chance on sexual harassment worth losing your job and embarrassing yourself and your family?

5. **Can the employee who commits the offense be held accountable?**

   You most likely will not be successful in suing an individual unless you work in a state that has a statute that authorizes a suit against an individual.

6. **What happens to the person who commits the harassment?**

   The chances are good that the person will be fired if the offense can be proved. Companies do not want the liability of a person who violates others' rights.

7. **What happens if you report an offense and nothing happens?**

   If you believe you have a good case and you have tried to resolve this through proper channels, hire an attorney. Harassment is against the law, and you may have to bring legal charges if necessary.

DEALING WITH DIFFICULT PEOPLE

What Causes People to Be So Ornery?

According to Brinkman and Kirschner (2002), "we all have varying degrees of knowledge and ignorance in our repertoire of communications skills, with their consequent interpersonal strengths and weaknesses." You may get upset with a whiner, while your friend gets upset with a procrastinator. Overly aggressive people may set you off, while a "yes person" may drive someone else crazy. You may not be able to stand people who boast about their accomplishments and belongings. Chances are pretty good that each of us has characteristics that drive someone crazy. The truth is that most people are OK once you get beneath the surface and understand why they do what they do. Of course, that takes lots of time and lots of listening, and you won't ever be able to get to the bottom of every person's reasons for being ornery, so you have to deal with him or her and move on. Honest answers and responses, delivered in a kind, rational manner, often provide the best results. Figure 12.8 provides some insight into how to deal with certain types of difficult people.

Understand, Relate to, and Lead Difficult People

If you are a leader or an employee, you will deal with difficult people. We can all be difficult at times and under certain situations, but some people excel at being difficult. They resist everything; they think every rule is made to get them; they can't get along with their colleagues; they won't carry their loads; they don't get paid enough—on and on the list goes.

As you try to motivate people and give everyone a fair chance, one important principle to remember is this: Reinforce the behavior you want. When someone performs well—even if it's for a day—recognize and praise him or her. Many people have never had praise at work or at home. Having you notice them can be enough to get some people to change their behavior. Say things like: "I really appreciate your staying late to help Jack today. You were a real team player." "I'm very impressed with the way you handle irate customers on the phone. You are making a great difference in helping us resolve problems." Write a personal, handwritten note thanking the person for his or her achievement. Catch people doing something right and tell them about it!

If people don't do well, don't ignore the behavior. Bring the behavior to their attention as soon as you can. If a person is late, for example, let him or her know you know as soon as it happens. Certainly, everyone has a problem sooner or later, but if this becomes a habit, others notice that one person is getting away with it and that the policies are being applied inconsistently and with favoritism. If people need training in order to perform their duties, get it for them. If people are having personal problems and you can provide company counseling, recommend it. Do everything in your power to help the difficult person be successful. First, you try to salvage difficult people, but you need to know that you can't save everyone. Sometimes you have to perform surgery; in other words, you may have to follow company policy, document unacceptable behavior and work performance, and terminate the person.

Difficult people come in all shapes and sizes, all ages and backgrounds. They may have a Ph.D. or they may have a middle school education. They may be loud and obnoxious or sly and underhanded. Regardless of what their tactics and habits may be, they are a disrupting force in the workplace and cannot be ignored. Some tips for dealing with difficult people are detailed in Figure 12.9.

POSITIVE HABITS at Work

Build a reputation as a level-headed thinker who never loses your cool. Stay calm when others are getting out of control, and you will earn respect. Learn all you can about mediating disagreements and managing difficult people, even though it may not be the most pleasant thing to do. Gaining respect from your fellow workers is one way to gain power and be recognized as management potential.

Figure 12.8   Types of Difficult People

	Type of Difficult Person	Behavior of This Type	How to Deal with This Person
	Bulldozer	Loud, obnoxious, bully; delights in intimidating people and getting his or her way.	Stand your ground; show no signs of weakness; take deep breaths; look him or her right in the eye and calmly state your position. You might say, "I'll listen to you when you calm down and treat me with respect." If a superior is bullying you, you may need to take formal action.
	Saboteur	Undercuts colleagues to make him- or her-self look good; stabs people in the back; goes behind your back instead of talking directly.	You want to bring this person out in the open. Ask him or her in front of other people, "Exactly what are you trying to say or do with that remark?" If you don't know who is sabotaging you, ask around. Go to the person's office and confront him or her. Tell the person, "I have a problem with what I hear you or saying or doing." This is another type of bully. Expose the person, and he or she will back off.
	Procrastinator	Can't make a decision; afraid of doing the wrong thing; poor time management skills; occasionally they will use procrastination as a way of getting attention.	Many procrastinators just need coaching on better work habits; some need help in overcoming fear of making a mistake. Negative remarks may have been written on their "slates" in the past. Give them false deadlines so they get their work done on time. Help them be successful and get positive attention. Teach them time management.
	Whiner	Everything is always wrong; bad things always happen to these people; they are overworked but spend most of their time complaining.	Nobody likes to be around whiners. You certainly don't want to listen to them, but try. When you hear anything that you might be able to be positive about, stop them and tell them that is a good idea. Try to find solutions without listening to too much whining. Seek ways for this person to get positive attention so he or she can feel a part of the team.

(continued)

Figure 12.8 Types of Difficult People (*Continued*)

	Type of Difficult Person	Behavior of This Type	How to Deal with This Person
	Exploder	Loses temper all the time over little things; uses explosions to get his or her way; has probably been doing this since he or she was a child.	You may have to raise your voice to be heard. Stand your ground. This person probably has a damaged amygdala and is reacting to something you know nothing about. You just happened to touch the nerve. Don't try to solve the problem today. Give it some time and tell the person you'll resume talking when he or she is under control.
	Pleaser	Agrees with everyone; will never have an opinion; may be passive-aggressive; the consummate "yes" person.	Force this person to make a decision. In a meeting, go around the room and call on everyone. Try to establish a "fail-safe" atmosphere where there are no wrong answers. These people have had others write on their "slates" with negativism so much that they are afraid to even have a decision. Build confidence by helping them have successes.
	Grandstander	Insecure; needs to feel good about himself or herself; knows a little about everything but has no in-depth knowledge on anything.	The know-it-all will try to block your ideas by always having a different idea or finding a reason why something won't work the way you think it will. Remember, this is usually an insecure person, so tread gently and choose your words carefully. You might say, "What if we used this part of your idea and add my idea to it?"
	Doomsayer	Expects the worst and usually gets it.	First, you need to know these people will always be complainers and you can't change that about them. Don't let them change you, because they are always looking for a teammate with whom to gripe and complain. Try saying, "Oh, surely things aren't that bad. Can you name one good thing that has happened to you today?" If you are the boss, you need to tell the person directly that his or her complaining is affecting everyone. Tell the person directly, "Stop complaining!"

© Robert Sherfield and Patricia Moody.

Figure 12.9   Tips for Dealing with Difficult People

- Create a climate where people feel they are heard.

- Assess the situation. Identify the difficult person or people, study their behavior, and see if you can determine why they are causing trouble.

- If someone tells you about the problem, get the other side before making a decision or an accusation. There are always two sides to every story. Remember, some people are very cunning and underhanded, and everyone does not tell the whole story. People usually omit their own wrong behaviors. Don't jump to conclusions. Nothing is ever exactly as it seems at first glance. Never react—act!

- Don't sit around and hope they will change. They won't! Chances are, difficult people have been acting this way for a long time and getting away with it. Wishing for a different behavior will get you nothing and provide no relief. You must confront the person and be very specific about the behavior and your expectations.

- If this is a difficult person for you to get along with personally, ask for a time to discuss the situation and try to resolve it by calling it to the person's attention, letting the person know you want to get along with him or her and to be a good colleague.

- If it is an employee under your supervision, develop a plan that includes exactly what the offensive behavior is, what needs to be done, and what you expect and by when.

- If a difficult person has been getting away with offensive behaviors for a long time, the other employees will appreciate having a boss who takes care of it, and they will respect you for doing so. Take a stand!

- Confront the employee in a private setting. Never embarrass or humiliate anyone in public. They will never forget or forgive you. These people are often fragile and easily hurt and offended—even the bullies. Talk to the offender in private, and you may see a different person. Tell him or her in a strong, assertive, forceful voice that this behavior has been documented, and it has to stop *now*. Remember to address the criticism to the behavior, not the person.

- Stick to the one behavior you are discussing. Don't load up the employee with all kinds of criticisms.

- Let the person explain his or her feelings and reasons. Tell the person how you feel: "I am disappointed that you would say that to your colleague" or "I was shocked that you would say that in an open meeting. What were you thinking?"

- Stay in control of the meeting. If the person gets loud and obnoxious, ask him or her to speak more quietly and to treat you with respect. If the person is not respectful, ask him or her to leave and come back after regaining self-control.

- If the person cries, offer him or her a tissue, and leave the room for awhile.

- Don't let the meeting deteriorate into a gripe session. Explain that the person needs to work more and complain less.

- Try to include the employee in designing a solution. Ask the person to stop the offensive behavior, and give him or her a deadline.

- If a formal disciplinary action is necessary, state the action in writing, following your company's policies. Tell the employee that you are summarizing this meeting and placing a copy in his or her file.

- Monitor the effectiveness of your meeting. Pay close attention to the employee's behavior.

- If you see positive results, praise the employee. Your goal is to salvage the employee, not isolate him or her.

PUTTING IT ALL TOGETHER

Because we are all so different and come from such a variety of backgrounds, it stands to reason that there will be conflict. The major lesson to be learned is that most conflicts can be resolved either by listening and improving communications so you can understand other people, or by fixing something that is wrong with the system. If you are involved in a conflict, try not to let it consume you. Be reasonable and be sure you are not part of the problem. Remember the amygdala and the role it plays in how we act and react. As you work with people, think about what may have been written on their "slates" and how that may be affecting their actions. Sometimes it pays just to be quiet, ask the right questions, and listen.

DIGITAL BRIEFCASE

WHAT KINDS OF CONFLICT HAVE YOU EXPERIENCED?

Access Poll Everywhere at www.polleverywhere.com and click "Create your first poll." Follow the directions at this site and create a series of questions on conflict management that can be answered with "yes" or "no." Then send your poll to five people, record their answers, and share your poll with your friends.

REFERENCES

Brinkman, R., & Kirschner, R. (2002). *Dealing with people you can't stand: How to bring out the best in people when they are at their worst.* New York: McGraw-Hill.

Cardenas, H. (2011). What are the causes of conflict in the workplace? Retrieved June 14, 2011, from www.ehow.com/list5801672causes-conflict-workplace.html.

Stretegic HR Services. (2010). Workplace harassment. Retrieved June 21, 2011, from www.strategichr.com/shrsweb2/harassment01.shtml.

Thompson, N. (2011). How conflicts arise. Retrieved June 17, 2011, from www.humansolutions.org.uk/conflict-1.html.

chapter thirteen

CONNECT
WORKING WITH TECHNOLOGY
IN A KNOWLEDGE ECONOMY

Never before in history has innovation offered so much promise to so many in such a short time.
—Bill Gates, Microsoft founder

Why
read this chapter?

Because you'll learn...

- To define digital workplace, social media, and the knowledge economy
- Qualifications for working in the knowledge economy
- How technology can assist you in all phases of your career

Because you'll be able to...

- Access tutorials to assist you in learning certain programs
- Identify specific programs that you need to know in any workplace

PROFESSIONALS
from the
Field

Name: Cathy Lanier

Business: CEO/President Technology Solutions

Few things are more important to a successful career today than a comprehensive knowledge of technology. Not only must you be adept at using word processing, spreadsheet and presentation software, and e-mail, but effective use of social media is becoming increasingly important for an employee's business profile. In addition to being technology efficient, you must be good at writing effective messages, using appropriate netiquette rules, and making good decisions about what to spend your time on when at work. You also need to learn the technologies that allow you to collaborate and share documents because so much work is now done collectively from a variety of offices all over the world. The basic point you need to know and embrace about technology is this: Technology is always changing, and you have to change with it or you will be left behind in this "brave new world."

MyStudentSuccessLab

MyStudentSuccessLab (www.mystudentsuccesslab.com) is an online solution designed to help you "Start strong, Finish stronger" by building skills for ongoing personal and professional development.

THE KNOWLEDGE ECONOMY

What's It Got to Do with You?

Over the past decade the world has gone through traumatic times—financial crisis, mortgage meltdown, several simultaneous wars, and political stalemates, just to name a few. At the same time, a somewhat silent "event" was taking place in the U.S. workplace. Slowly but surely, the economy has become a knowledge economy as opposed to a manufacturing economy. This new workplace requires a complex set of skills that includes decision making, problem solving, communication, analysis, relationship building, collaboration, and technology abilities. "Today 48 million of the more than 137 million U.S. workers are knowledge workers, making this group the fastest growing talent pool in most organizations . . . 70 percent of all U.S. jobs created since 1998—4.5 million jobs, or roughly the combined workforce of the fifty-six largest public companies by market capitalization—require a set of conceptual tacit skills" (Meister & Willyerd, 2010).

> The global economy is giving more of our own people, and billions around the world, the chance to work and live and raise their families with dignity.
> —Bill Clinton

"Knowledge workers fuel innovation and growth . . . The heart of what knowledge workers do on the job is collaborate, which in the broadest terms means they interact to solve problems, serve customers, engage with partners, and nurture new ideas . . . Those able to use new technologies to reshape how they work are finding significant productivity gains" (Manyika, Sprague, & Yee, 2009). The knowledge economy is all about working smarter and using technology to build an innovative, collaborative, and frequently, global workforce.

This path to working smarter is characterized by:

I. Using technology to enhance the connections between people and establish a collaborative environment to improve productivity and quality,

II. Optimizing workflows to reduce costs and ensure that work gets done by the right person and the right team in the right sequence at the right time,

III. Ensuring that accurate and consistent information about business can be accessed by all who need it, when they need it,

IV. Integrating applications with business processes so they serve the needs of the business, and

V. Creating a continuous improvement in business processes with the help of analytics and metrics. (IBM, 2009)

What does the knowledge economy have to do with you? Everything! Everything about how work is done in this country—from nursing to welding to accounting—is changing rapidly and will continue to evolve. U.S. companies are shifting much of their manufacturing and lower-level tasks to less expensive workers in developing countries while simultaneously creating a wave of knowledge jobs here.

Why would you want to be one of the new breed of knowledge workers? Because these employees "earn a wage premium that ranges from 55 percent to 75 percent over the pay of workers who perform more basic production and transaction tasks" (Manyika, Sprague, & Yee, 2009). Regardless of what career you pursue, you will most likely use a computer and perform at least some tasks of a knowledge worker.

GLOBALIZATION

What Does "It's a Flat World" Mean?

Thomas Friedman, author of *The World Is Flat*, has called today's global economy "a world without walls." The term *flat world* means that the playing field has been leveled because of technological advances. It doesn't matter if you live in a highly developed country or a developing country, because if you can "plug and play," you can compete. Changes are happening so fast and worldwide competition is increasing so rapidly that companies can ill afford to focus on one change at a time; rather, they must address many fronts at once. Headquarters of the world's largest companies have made major shifts in recent years, with the United States losing 38 companies. Many corporations are moving to the so-called BRIC countries (Brazil, Russia, India, and China). "By 2020, the BRIC countries will be the dominant centers of economic influence" (Meister & Willyerd, 2010).

U.S. corporations have reached out all over the world to find employees who have the knowledge and skills to help them become more productive at lower costs. The world's largest corporations and the newest high-tech start-up companies are tapping into a global talent pool as they develop a virtual workforce. Today's employees may become part of a global team with members who telecommute from home. These workers from the "flat world" communicate using innovative technology such as instant messaging, collaborative software, global conference calls, and document-sharing sites. Professional athletic teams have long recruited stars from all over the world. Now businesses are following suit, making the competition for technology jobs even tougher.

As the changing global workplace closes some doors for U.S. workers, it will open new ones for those who are properly prepared. If you can speak a second language such as Spanish or Mandarin, you may have an opportunity to work in an international arena or interface between foreign employees and U.S. workers. A solid language skill could provide an opportunity to be an interpreter, marketer, or salesperson in an international market. As you develop your "personal brand," use every skill you have worked hard to learn. A second language is a major asset.

The good news? You can do this. You can become the marketer of your own brand if you can use technology skillfully, make good decisions, work collaboratively, communicate across language barriers, and think innovatively. Many tutorial programs exist online that are free and easy to use and enable you to teach yourself many of the new programs. Here we will discuss many of the technologies you need to learn and how to access tutorial programs.

You can prepare yourself to become a knowledge worker in a global economy if you are willing to work hard and smart. You can also prepare yourself to be a knowledge worker in a small business in Anytown, USA. Regardless of what field you pursue, you will no doubt, in some ways, become a knowledge worker.

Will the communication habits of today's Millenial Generation carry over into the workplace?

Shutterstock

THE NEW CONNECTIVITY CULTURE

What Role Will You Play?

Today we live in a constantly connected world, and people all over the world are players. You might say, "They are always on, always available." The lines have blurred

Figure 13.1 Who Are the Hyperconnected Players?

- They are located all over the world, but more heavily concentrated in Latin America and Asia Pacific.
- They tend to be clustered in the banking and tech industries.
- They come in all ages, but over 60 percent are under age 35.
- Sixty-three percent of them have WiFi at home.
- They play more networked games than others.
- Their culture includes men and women, but most are men.
- They tend to work in companies that have a high concentration of high-tech equipment and the latest technologies.
- The hyperconnected can be found throughout a company, but most are in management.
- They might be located in any job but tend to work in a high-tech industry.
- They are most likely to live in a city.
- If they leave their homes for 24 hours, they are more likely to take their laptops than their wallets.
- They look at connectedness as normal and tend to blur lines between work and leisure. They are always checking their messages.

Source: Adapted partially from Aducci et al., 2008.

between work and social use of technology, becoming somewhat addictive for many who use multiple devices.

Today's youth are growing up as part of the so-called hyperconnected community. Those who fit this mold are always connected—at the movies, at home, in a restaurant, at work, on a trip—everywhere. If you observe a teenager, you will most likely see him texting on his cell phone, IMing, reading a message on Facebook or Twitter, doing homework with an iPod stuck in his ear, and perhaps interacting with others' avatars in an online video game. Today's youth are always in touch with their family, friends, and coworkers. Exactly who are these hyperconnected people and what are their characteristics? Study Figure 13.1 for a more detailed explanation.

> 96% of Millennials, also known as Generation Y, have joined a social network and 80% of companies use social media for recruitment.
> —Eric Qualman, *Socialnomics*

GRADUATE *Quote*

Lawrence Cain
Graduate!
Lincoln College of Technology, Cincinnati, OH
Career: Customer Representative/Teller Services,
U.S. Bank

You control your own destiny. As long as you know and live by this, you have no excuses. You have to create your own future through goal setting, knowledge, and hard work. There will be people who help you along the way, but basically your future is what you make of it. No one is coming to rescue you. No one is going to save you. You have to save yourself and make your own way.

BIGGEST INTERVIEW *Blunders*

Ramon was excited when he was granted an interview with the largest plumbing company in his city. His goal was to become an entrepreneur and he planned to start his own company after he gained experience. In the interview, Ramon was asked if he knew how to use accounting software such as Quicken or QuickBooks. Without hesitating, Ramon answered, "Oh, I took a course that had a unit on that, but I didn't pay much attention to it because I was primarily interested in just the plumbing courses." The interviewer explained to him that this was a very progressive company. "Our plumbing associates all carry handheld electronic devices that require them to know QuickBooks. Our system requires our associates to submit invoices and other information directly to our central system." Ramon realized he had made a bad statement and quickly added, "Now that I realize how important it is, I'll go back and learn this software, and I'll start immediately." Ramon was fortunate. He got the job, but he learned a valuable lesson: technology is used in almost every job today, and you can never know too much.

LESSON: When you interview and begin work in a new company, be willing to do what needs to be done to be successful. You must always be learning new skills if you are going to be successful in the workforce today.

We are likely to see as much as 40 percent of the labor force in the hyperconnected culture within the next few years.

DEFINING THE DIGITAL WORKPLACE

Are You Ready for the Future?

The digital workplace has become a reality and is expected to grow exponentially in years to come. The digital universe is defined as "information that is created, captured, or replicated in digital form" (Meister & Willyerd, 2010). This revolution is redefining what constitutes work, how we perform work, how we measure work, and how we lead and manage employees who may be working on site or from distant workspaces. Study Figure 13.2 to understand some of these major changes. Regardless of where you work and what job you are doing, your work will be affected in some ways by the digital universe.

In the next few sections, we will introduce you to a number of technology programs that you need to be able to use in today's workplace. You can't possibly learn everything that is available or keep up with all the new programs that are constantly emerging, but you need to always be familiar with the most popular and widely used.

One of the best ways to learn new technology is to use the tutorials that you can find on websites such as YouTube and www.butterscotch.com. You can teach yourself how to use many new programs if you are persistent and patient.

THE SOFTWARE PACKAGE THAT YOU ABSOLUTELY MUST KNOW!

So What Is This Microsoft Office 2010?

Microsoft Office is a proprietary commercial office suite of several popular interrelated desktop applications, servers, and services for the Microsoft Windows and Mac OS X operating systems. This package was introduced by Microsoft in 1989 and has been refined several times since then. The current version for PC is Microsoft Office Suite 2010. Few offices operate today without Microsoft Office, and because it is so dominant, it is a "must know" for anyone entering the workforce.

The major desktop applications are Word (word processing), Excel (spreadsheets), Outlook (e-mail), PowerPoint (presentations), OneNote (digital notebook), and Publisher (desktop publishing). We highly advise you to spend as much time as necessary to become proficient in Microsoft Office. Screen captures of Microsoft Word, Excel, PowerPoint, Outlook, OneNote, and Publisher are shown on the following pages.

Figure 13.2 Impact of the Digital Universe

- More video was uploaded to YouTube in the past two months than if ABC, CBS, and NBC had been airing new content continuously since 1948.
- Launched in 2001, Wikipedia now features over 13 million articles in over 200 languages.
- Newspapers and traditional advertising are in steep decline, but digital advertising is growing rapidly.
- The average American teen sends 2,272 text messages per month.
- The mobile device will be the world's primary connection to the Internet in 2020.
- Ninety-three percent of adults in the United States own a cell phone.
- In February of 2008, John McCain raised $11 million for his U.S. presidential bid. Barack Obama attended no campaign fundraisers but utilized online social networks to raise $55 million in 29 days.

Source: Based on XPLANE, The Economist, Karl Fisch, Scott McLeod, and Laura Bestler, "Did You Know? 4.0" [video]. Retrieved May 28, 2011, from http://www.youtube.com/watch?v=rhe2XUKZ-fU&noredirect=1

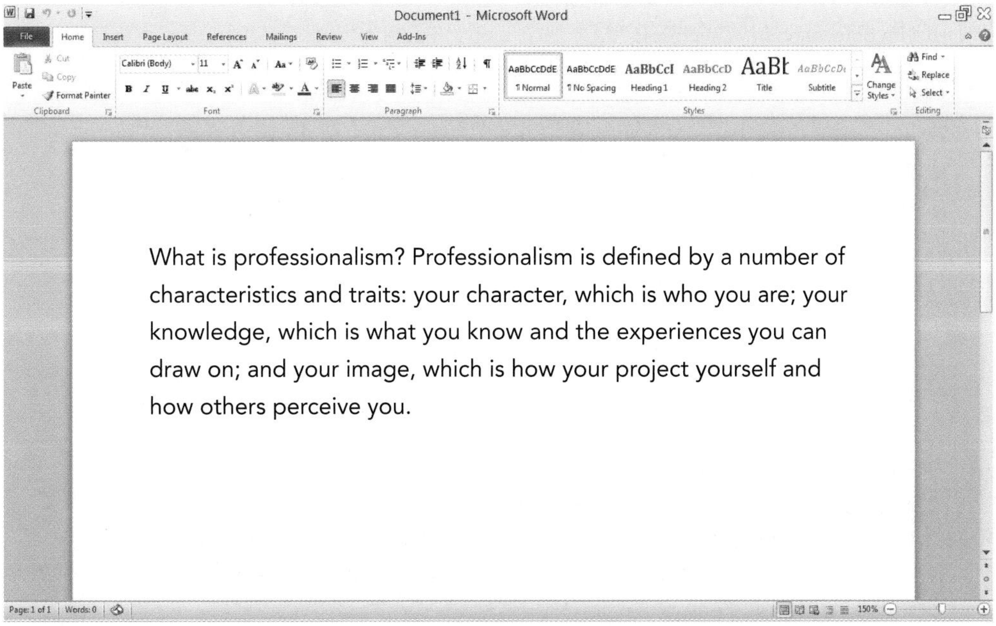
Document1 - Microsoft Word
File
Home
Insert
Page Layout
References
Mailings
Review
View
Add-Ins
Paste
Cut
Copy
Format Painter
Clipboard
Calibri (Body)
Font
Paragraph
Normal
No Spacing
Heading 1
Heading 2
Title
Subtitle
Change Styles
Styles
Find
Replace
Select
Editing
What is professionalism? Professionalism is defined by a number of characteristics and traits: your character, which is who you are; your knowledge, which is what you know and the experiences you can draw on; and your image, which is how your project yourself and how others perceive you.
Page: 1 of 1
Words: 0
150%

Used with permission from Microsoft.

The three main things you need to be able to do with **Word** are:

- Set up and produce documents, letters, and memos
- Import pictures, graphs, and other items from the Internet
- Back up and transport your work by downloading documents to a flash drive

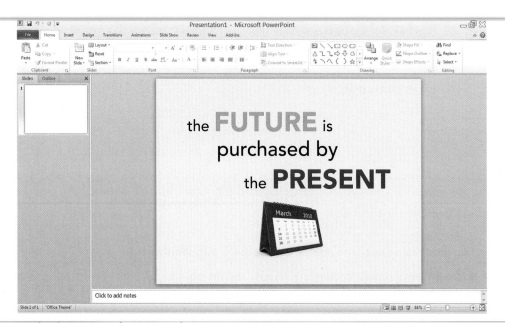

Used with permission from Microsoft.

The three main things you need to be able to do with **Excel** are:

- Understand the parts of a spreadsheet and what you can do with them
- Set up a spreadsheet
- Store values and make calculations

Used with permission from Microsoft.

The three main things you should be able to do with **PowerPoint** are:

- Understand the basics in making slideshows appealing and interesting
- Use the program to design and build a presentation
- Design slides that include animation and imported art and pictures

Used with permission from Microsoft.

The three main things you should be able to do with **Outlook** are:

- Send and receive e-mail
- Manage your calendar and share it with colleagues
- Manage your to do list

Used with permission from Microsoft.

The three main things you should be able to do with **OneNote** are:

- Organize your work into various levels of folders, sections, and pages
- Use note flags to denote importance and action to be taken
- Organize your current responsibilities and be able to find everything in one place

Used with permission from Microsoft.

The three main things you should be able to do with **Publisher** are:

- Design a brochure
- Design a newsletter
- Access and use Microsoft clip art

THE SOCIAL NETWORK GENERATION

What Is the S-Decade?

You might think of the past decade as the e-decade, where the focal points were e-learning, e-books, e-commerce, and the like. The current decade might be labeled the s-decade because of the way cultures and businesses worldwide have embraced social media, social learning, and social networking. Today's students are being challenged to use social media in ways other than communicating with their friends; businesses are scrambling to implement social media strategies for marketing, tracking their customers, and communicating with their customers; and rapidly increasing numbers of people are using social media such as Facebook, Twitter, YouTube, and Second Life. Businesses and universities are using social media to recruit employees and students. Contributors are uploading 13 hours of video every minute of the day, and the number of lurkers (people who follow blogs, discussions, and message boards but do not contribute) is growing at a rapid pace. Many companies are now searching resumés for evidence that candidates are Facebook and Twitter savvy. There is little doubt that social media is becoming the primary method of recruiting and retaining employees from the digital generation.

In the report "Global Faces and Networked Places," Nielsen Online reported that social networks and blogs have now surpassed e-mail as the most popular form of communication. According to the Nielsen report (2009), "Facebook started out as a service for university students, but now almost one third of its global audience is aged 35–49 years of age and almost one quarter is over 50 years."

> *Fifty seven percent of active online users (those people who are online regularly) have joined a social network.*
>
> —Marta Z. Kagan, *social media evangelist*

SO YOU NEED TO LEARN SOCIAL MEDIA

Where Do You Start?

Many businesses and institutions are using social networking sites in numerous ways to interact with customers, send messages, deliver positive advertising, and even connect with internal customers. We highly recommend that you familiarize yourself with all of them, become an expert on at least one of them by practicing and reading everything you can find, and list your expertise on your resumé. Regardless of what field you enter today, most employers will be looking for social media experts to help them develop, expand, and connect with their customer base. Information regarding a few of the most popular and widely used social media are discussed below.

> *Social media is only going to become more pervasive, and as such, become a critical factor in the success or failure of any business.*
>
> *—Brian Solis, social media expert*

Facebook is one of the most widely used and rapidly growing social media in existence. It is used to connect and communicate across social and business lines. Companies are using Facebook to promote their products, announce new products, interact with customers, track their customers' buying habits, and recruit and retain employees. "The fastest growing demographic of Facebook users is those twenty-five years and older" (Kabani, 2010). According to Kabani, Facebook is like a coffee shop; it is a great place to strike up a conversation. Research shows that many people use Facebook to share their personal information and identity. Google has introduced a new social media site called Google+. Google Circles are groups of friends you organize by topic: Friends, Family, College Buddies, Roommates, and so on. Both Facebook and Google+ have changed the way we live and work in the world. You can access Facebook and start your own page at www.facebook.com, and Google+ at https://plus.google.com.

LinkedIn is considered the professionals' site and is described by Kabani (2010) as a "buttoned-down office-networking event. If Facebook is happy hour, LinkedIn is all business,

Linked in.

suit and tie." This is a site that should be treated as strictly business, and is certainly not the place to post unflattering pictures or information that might be damaging to you if a potential or current employer happened to see it. This site usually attracts well-educated people who tend to be more affluent. LinkedIn is a great place to post your resumé because other members might be searching for good employees. You can post recommendations from references (with their permission, of course) or glowing letters of appreciation from customers. If someone posts a recommendation for you, you will get a message giving you an opportunity to accept or reject the recommendation's posting.

You will be provided a space to post a summary of your background and accomplishments. You should give careful thought to this and you should update and improve it often. Consider using keywords that are related to the industry in which you are interested; human resource personnel often search LinkedIn for outstanding employees by using keywords from job descriptions. Discuss your specialties, education, and accomplishments, being sure to use spell check. Since this is a business site, the participants are likely to be much more picky than those who frequent Twitter or Facebook. You can access LinkedIn at www.linkedin.com.

Twitter falls in the category of microblog. A microblog is a brief message (no more than 140 characters long) that typically uses abbreviations or Internet acronyms such as OMG (oh my God or gosh) or LOL (laugh out loud) in order to pack more information in a message. Some people are constantly sending "tweets," telling their friends every move they make. As a professional, you need to leave this behavior to teenage girls and learn how to use Twitter to deliver time-sensitive information to clients or to inform your group about a special event or a big sale. Twitter is an excellent way to grab online visibility and to attract traffic for your company because it allows you to establish a dialogue with your customers and your community of friends.

Your Twitter home page will randomly display a number of messages sent to you by people you are following. If someone sends you an @ reply, the message will show up on your home page and it will also be filed under your replies tab. You need to know that replies are public. Everyone can see them! If you choose to do so, you can send direct messages to people that are not visible to everyone, but these messages are still out there if someone decides to share them.

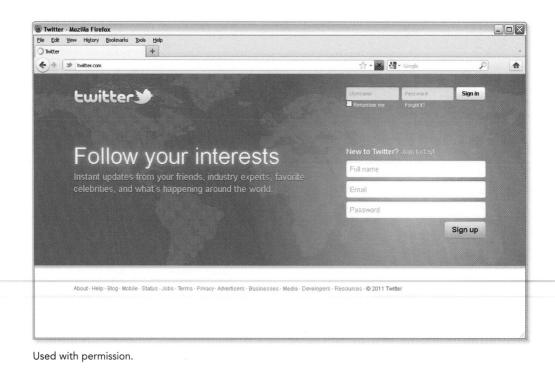

Used with permission.

Collaborative Communication Programs

Today many employees work in virtual teams (teams that work together but are not physically located in the same place) and they find collaborative communication programs to be very helpful and effective. While there are several available, we are going to discuss three of the most popular.

WIKIS.   A wiki is a webpage that can be viewed and modified by anybody with a web browser and access to the Internet—it might be called a webpage with an edit button. This means that any visitor to the wiki can change its content if he or she desires, enabling people to collaborate with others online easily. While the potential for mischief exists because access to is open to anyone, wikis can be surprisingly robust and open-ended. They can be password protected if desired. One good way to use wikis is to post an agenda prior to a meeting, add notes during the meeting, and then save them to a public archive where everyone involved can access the notes and minutes. Teams can also use wikis to work collaboratively on documents.

Always be willing to learn new things, especially technology and software. If training is offered, be the first to sign up, because technology may be the key to your next promotion. Certainly, it will help you perform any job much more competently.

GOOGLE DOCS.   Google Docs is a great tool for virtual teams because it is absolutely free and it enables you to create documents, spreadsheets, presentations, forms, and drawings from anywhere around the world simply by accessing the Internet. Some people refer to it as an online alternative to Microsoft Office, which, of course, is not free. You can share documents with anyone you want from within Google Docs itself without manually finding a file and attaching it as an e-mail. It is also easy to download documents to your hard drive if you want to save them on your computer.

Used with permission.

SKYPE.   Skype is another collaborative program for working, communicating, and celebrating together, although users may be miles apart. This program can be used between two or more people and is a great way to hold a conference when numerous people need to participate. You can hold meetings, have a work session with fellow employees, or just visit with friends. The great thing about Skype is that the basic program is free and can be downloaded to your computer from the Internet. For a small fee, you can communicate internationally with friends and virtual team members. Skype allows you to connect with customers, colleagues, friends, and family, and is a great way to complete business tasks when people need to meet but work miles apart.

Presentation Software

PowerPoint continues to be the most popular presentation software, but **Prezi** has introduced an exciting package as well. You absolutely need to know PowerPoint, but you are also highly encouraged to review the up-and-coming Prezi presentation package at http://prezi.com.

Almost everyone has had to develop a slide presentation while in school, and all of us have tried to stay awake during a long, boring, tedious computerized presentation. This is an area of technology and communications that you need to be able to do well. While entire books have been written on making effective slideshows, we are going to share a few major points with you here:

- You might want to begin your presentation by building a storyboard or using index cards to lay out your program and your slides. Your first slide sets the stage, so be sure it gets attention in a positive way and includes your name, your company, and the title of your presentation.
- Use real pictures instead of clip art—they are more interesting. If you can use photos that fill the complete slide, the visual is more appealing.
- Avoid wordiness! Never put every word you are going to say on a slide and then proceed to read to your audience. This is deadly! Nothing is worse than one slide after another filled with text in a 12-point font that no one can see. Words in the body should be at least 14 points or larger. Titles and headings should be at least four points larger than the body.
- Light text on a dark background is harder to read than dark text on a light background.
- Present no more than one concept per slide.
- Try not to use more than three or four bullet points per slide.
- Number your points to show order and use bullets to emphasize certain points.
- Use no more than one or two fonts and avoid the fancy, hard-to-read styles.
- Use simple, clear graphs and charts that complement your remarks. Photos, graphs, and diagrams can often be used to explain a concept better than words.
- Your slideshow should use one screen design throughout.
- End with a summary slide that reviews your main points.
- Never read your slides word for word. They should be used to complement what you are saying.
- If you've made a handout for the audience, distribute it at the end of the presentation; otherwise people will be focused on reading the handout instead of your slideshow.

Figure 13.3 illustrates a slide that is boring and has too much information. Contrast this with Figure 13.4, which shows an interesting, appealing slide.

Online Videos

YouTube is the most popular video-sharing website. Participants have posted over 100,000,000 videos on YouTube since its inception. Using YouTube, participants can upload, share, and view videos produced by people all over the world. You can find videos on almost any subject. Some are professionally produced and others are rather amateurish. In order to play YouTube videos, you must install the Adobe Flash Player plug-in in your browser. You can access YouTube at www.youtube.com and input keywords to search for videos.

> There has been a fundamental shift in the way we communicate—world famous singers are discovered through a video post on YouTube (the second largest search engine in the world), brands build their names through Tweeting, and debates and conversations form over Facebook groups.
> —MWEB, South Africa's leading Internet service provider

> There have been 100,000,000 videos posted on YouTube.
> —Marta Z. Kagan, social media expert

Figure 13.3 Slide with Too Much Information

MAKE STUDENTS FEEL IMPORTANT

Remember that every student wants to be somebody. Ask them what they want to be. Help them research what it takes to become this person they dream about.

Remember the power of the gold star.

Pay attention to students' strengths and weaknesses.

Create activities that cause interaction.

Be expressive—smile.

Bring high fives to your classroom!

Figure 13.4 Visually Appealing Slide.

the **FUTURE** is
purchased by
the **PRESENT**

EVALUATING YOUR TECHNOLOGY SKILLS

How Will I Ever Learn All These New Programs?

One of the most wonderful things about the world of technology is that if you have never heard of a program or don't know how to use a certain application, there is immediate, useful help online at sites such as www.butterscotch.com and www.youtube.com. If you don't know how to create a movie using Camtasia, all you have to do is go to YouTube and you'll find a tutorial to assist you. This is the beauty of technology. The curse? It seems to change every day. Learning to keep up with the latest technologies and how to apply them at work is imperative. Learning the programs, applications, and terminology is also important.

Figure 13.5 details some of the major programs and applications used in today's workplace. You may not be required to use them all, but it will be helpful to familiarize yourself with some

Figure 13.5 Types of Technology

Description	Program	Website
Software Programs		
Used for word processing and creating presentations, charts, and graphs on PCs and Macs	Microsoft Office (Word, Excel, PowerPoint) PreziPages for Mac	www.office.microsoft.com www.prezi.com www.apple.com/iwork/pages
Group Communication Tools		
Used to communicate in groups and share information on your computer screen with others around the world	Twitter VoiceThread GoToMeeting WebEx	www.twitter.com www.voicethread.com www.gotomeeting.com www.webex.com
Social Networking/Sharing Sites		
Used to network with businesspeople who might help you get a job, chat, make friends, keep in touch, and post the latest news and photos	Facebook Twitter LinkedIn	www.facebook.com www.twitter.com www.linkedin.com
Photo/Video Building and Viewing		
Used to create and/or view videos and share them with friends or colleagues	Jing YouTube Hulu Flickr Camtasia	www.jingproject.com www.youtube.com www.hulu.com www.flickr.com www.techsmith.com
Search/Research Engines		
Used to research topics for work projects; it is wise to use a variety of these sites instead of relying on just one	Google Dogpile Yahoo Ask Lycos Wikipedia Bing Alta Vista	www.google.com www.dogpile.com www.yahoo.com www.ask.com www.lycos.com www.wikipedia.com www.bing.com www.altavista.com
Tools to Help You Learn to Use New Technology		
Offer easy-to-use video tutorials to help you use some of the technologies that may be required in your workplace	YouTube eHow Butterscotch	www.youtube.com www.ehow.com www.butterscotch.com
Document-Sharing Tools		
Used to share your word processing documents with colleagues onsite or at sites around the world	PBWorks Google Docs WorkZone WorkShare	www.pbworks.com www.docs.google.com www.workzone.com www.workshare.com
Digital Note-Taking Systems		
Used to take notes online	MyNoteIt Yahoo! Notes Notefish Ubernote Springnote	www.mynoteit.com www.widgets.yahoo.com/widgets/notes www.notefish.com www.ubernote.com www.springnote.com

different applications and their websites so you can at least speak with some knowledge of each application.

LEARNING THE LANGUAGE OF TECHNOLOGY

What Is a Worm and Why Is It in My Computer?

As you begin to familiarize yourself with the many aspects of computer literacy, there may be terms that pop up that you have not heard before. You will hear many of these terms in the workplace, so it is best to familiarize yourself with them now. The list of terms defined in Figure 13.6 will help you as you discover more about the world of technology and computer literacy.

> *Technology makes it possible for people to gain control over everything, except over technology.*
> —John Tutor

PRIVACY AND SECURITY ISSUES

Did You Know You're a Published Author?

Congratulations! You're an author—that is, if you have ever sent a tweet. As of 2010, the Library of Congress has archived *every tweet ever sent* since Twitter's inception in 2006. If you have ever sent a tweet—good or bad, nice or naughty, serious or silly—you are a part of the Library of Congress collection. This is just one of the many examples of lack of privacy on the web. Privacy issues can be monumental obstacles to you now and later in your life. Therefore, it is important that you guard your privacy and watch your online activities. What you post online now in a silly or romantic moment can come back later to cost you that dream job. Complaints about your boss, colleagues, or company are also short-sighted comments when posted in any public venue. Be careful what you post online—nothing on the Internet is private. In a world of WikiLeaks, hackers, and savvy researchers, your words and photos are public words and photos.

To protect yourself and your online information as much as possible, consider the following tips and suggestions:

- Create a strong, uncommon password for your accounts. Try to use a combination of at least eight letters, numbers, and symbols, such as RO#99@SH.
- Do not share your passwords with anyone, not even your best friends. Friendships change, and you may later regret sharing this information.
- Do not use common events such as your birthday, anniversary, or child's birthday as your password.
- Be careful where you post your photo. Even if you post your photo on your personal Facebook page, it can be found by a simple web search.
- Use only secure websites for any type of financial transaction. Look for security seals such as Verisign, Comodo, and GeoTrust. Do *not* use your debit card online. If you must purchase from an online site, use a credit card or consider getting a PayPal account to protect your credit information.
- Learn how to use online security features and privacy settings. These are offered for your safety and for the protection of your information.
- Don't tell your Facebook or online friends that you will not be home. This invites break-ins and burglary at your home.
- Install and run your security and spyware protections at least twice per week.
- Turn off or delete cookies from other sites and retailers.

Figure 13.6   The Techno-Pedia

Bookmarks	These allow you to tag popular sites so you can easily access them again—usually with one click.
Cookie	This term refers to data that is sent to your computer by a company's computer to monitor your actions while on their site. Cookies remember your log-in and password information and track what you viewed or purchased the last time you visited that site.
Dot com	.com is the most common ending for Internet addresses. However, there are many others. The following will help you direct your Internet searches: .com: Used to search commercial, for-profit businesses .edu: Used to search educational institutions, colleges, and universities .net: Used by Internet service providers .gov: Used to search documents within the U.S. government .org: Used to search non-profit organizations .mil: Used to search information from the U.S. military .us: Used to search any organization in specific countries such as United States (.us), United Kingdom (.uk), France (.fr), Sweden (.se), or Germany (.de)
Hacker	A modern-day bank robber. This is a person who electronically breaks into your computer and steals your private and sensitive information—often to use for illegal purposes.
HDTV/HDV	High-definition television or high-definition video. They are high-quality, crisp, visually appealing TV or video recordings.
Phishing	A scheme by hackers to acquire your private information such as passwords, log-in codes, and credit card information by using real companies' logos in their correspondence. They trick you into updating your information for a company or site you trust, when in actuality, you are directly providing the hacker your information.
PDF	The portable document format was created by Adobe as a document-sharing format that is independent of software programs and applications such as Word and PowerPoint.
Podcast	Combines the terms *iPod* and *broadcast* into a single word. It is a video or audio file you can access on your iPhone.
Malware	Meaning "malicious software," malware are programs that are placed on your computer without your knowledge to cause technological harm. Common types of malware (viruses) are trojan horses, worms, and spyware, which delete files or directory information and cause your computer to function improperly. To avoid them, do not open files from unknown sites or people and keep your spyware and virus programs up to date.
Right click	Refers to clicking the right button of your mouse to reveal additional menus and pop-ups. A mouse is automatically set to the left click for common tasks.
RTF	Rich text format (RTF) was developed by Microsoft as a document file format to make files easier to open in most formats and programs on most computers.
URL	Standing for universal retrieval language, the URL is the Internet address that you type into your search bar, such as www.yahoo.com, www.youtube.com, or www.pearsonhighered.com.
Web 2.0	Web 2.0 is the new age of the Internet. Web 1.0 was created as a one-sided, "you search it; we define it" tool, whereas Web 2.0 is more interactive and includes social media (Facebook, Twitter, etc.), blogs, document sharing, videos, and interactive searches.

- Be very wary of anyone asking for personal information to "update company records." It is probably a phishing scheme. This tactic may be initiated by phone or computer. Reputable companies will not ask for your personal information.
- Teach your children not to provide private information or to go onto unknown sites and rooms.

THE ART OF USING NETIQUETTE TO MAKE A POSITIVE IMPRESSION

Who Cares If I Use Proper Manners in E-Mail?

Netiquette, or Internet etiquette, refers to courteous practices that have evolved over the years since almost everyone started using the Internet. Netiquette, as etiquette, is always related to courtesy or good manners. This term simply means to use your manners when communicating with someone on the Internet. Your messages on the Internet are just as much a part of your image as your other written communications. Study the rules of netiquette in Figure 13.7 carefully to avoid offending internal and external customers.

Figure 13.7 Understanding the Rules of Netiquette

- Never, ever send an e-mail, IM, tweet or any other type of e-communication that you would not want anyone else to read. E-communication is not private, especially when done from a company/work computer. Information is available on the web for a long, long time.

- Not everyone is ethical and some will share your information with others. There is no such thing as privacy online!

- Remember that e-mail messages may be seen by anyone. Never write anything that you might find embarrassing if it were shared with others.

- Remember that e-mail is not anonymous and can be traced back to you.

- Be brief and use lots of white space so the message does not appear foreboding. People are too busy for long e-mails.

- Be sure you complete the subject line and that you are descriptive in the words you use.

- Copy only the people who need to receive the message.

- Be careful not to omit someone from the message list who might be offended if he or she does not receive the e-mail.

- Avoid flaming or using all capital letters, which is an indication that you are angry.

- If you receive a message in which the other person is obviously angry, try to talk to the person face-to-face so you can read his or her body language. Do not respond in a similar manner!

- When responding to a piece of correspondence, use the 24-hour rule if you are angry or if you have to make a very important decision. Do not respond in anger or fear. Once the "send" button has been pressed, you can't take it back. Use restraint, reread the correspondence, and once you have cooled off and thought it through, make your decision.

- If you receive a message in which the other person has gone out of his or her way to be rude, ignore it and do not respond.

- Remember that you do not have your nonverbal communication abilities when sending e-mails. Well-intentioned humor and satire can easily be misunderstood and can cause hard feelings.

- If you are going to disagree with someone, be very gentle and careful in phrasing your words. You might want to point out the good points that the person made and then offer the points with which you disagree.

(continued)

Figure 13.7 Understanding the Rules of Netiquette (*continued*)

- Never forward e-mails that were meant to be confidential to you. If you want to share an e-mail, ask for permission from the writer.

- Be careful not to forward attachments without carefully reading them—you may be highly embarrassed once you know the content.

- Text language (LOL, OMG, BFF, :-(, BTW, FYI) is fine when texting or IMing with your friends, but not for e-mails at work.

- Don't forward e-mail hoaxes, urban legends, or chain letters. Many people find it annoying and viruses are often passed along this way. Anything promising 10 million dollars from an overseas account is a scam, and Bill Gates is not going to give you any money for e-mailing your friends—even if your friend's lawyer checked it out!

- Don't forward chain letters, junk mail, spam, or jokes at work. In fact, don't do this anywhere, because most people find it very annoying.

- If you are constantly sending out blanket e-mails of spam, jokes, stories, and chain letters, people all over the company know you are not working. You are documenting this fact for them. People have been fired for spending their time on this kind of activity when they are supposed to be working.

- If you use someone else's work, document your source or sources correctly.

- Never send inappropriate e-mails to anyone at work—for example, sexually explicit jokes or stories. Actually, you should never send this kind of message to anyone because you have no idea where it will end up.

- Refrain from passing along ethnic or religious or obscene jokes and/or stories. Many people will find them offensive, and you may hurt someone's feelings.

- Assume that Internet mail is not secure. If you wouldn't write something on a postcard, don't write it in e-mail.

- Since we have a diverse workforce today, remember that recipients are human beings who may have a culture, sense of humor, religion, language, and customs that are very different from yours.

- Online e-communications, especially e-mails, should contain proper opening and closing salutations if a person does not know you well or if the e-mail is to an external person.

By adhering to these suggestions, you will soon find that your online correspondence is more effective.

Reflections: PUTTING IT ALL TOGETHER

The world of technology changes rapidly. Because of constant innovations and new inventions, it is sometimes difficult to keep up. However, if you can master the right technologies that are in demand by employers and use them to solve problems, generate creative ideas, and work collaboratively with virtual colleagues, you can leapfrog over many others who may not be as informed. There is no doubt that you will use technology in any job you accept today, and the more you learn, the more valuable you will become. Do yourself a big favor—make up your mind to keep learning and growing and mastering all the appropriate technology you can in your field.

DIGITAL BRIEFCASE

USING TECHNOLOGY EFFECTIVELY

Learn to use Facebook, LinkedIn, or Twitter by going online and setting up an account. After you have spent some time familiarizing yourself with the program you selected, design a Power-Point or Prezi slideshow with no more than five slides that explains how to access this program and how to use some features. Follow the guidelines in this chapter for designing interesting and appealing slides.

REFERENCES

Aducci, R., Bilderbeek, P., Brown, H., Dowling, S., Freedman, N., Gantz, J., Germanow, A., Manabe, T., Manfridez, D., & Verma, R. (2008). The hyperconnected: Here they come. IDC White Paper.

IBM. (2009). Using technology to work smarter. Retrieved May 24, 2011, from www-01 .ibm.com/software/success/cssdb.nsf/CS/CHUY7YKMJA?OpenDocument&Site= default&cty=enus.

Kabani, S. H. (2010). *The zen of social media*. Dallas, TX: BenBella Books.

Manyika, J., Sprague, K., and Yee, L. (2009). Using technology to improve workforce collaboration. Retrieved May 24, 2011, from http://whatmatters.mckinseydigital.com/internet /using-technology-to-improve-workforce-collaboration.

Meister, J. C., & Willyerd, K. (2010). *The 2020 workplace: How innovative companies attract, develop, and keep tomorrow's employees today*. New York: HarperCollins Publishers.

Nielsen Report. (2009). Global faces and networked places. A Nielsen Report on Social Networking's New Global Footprint.

chapter fourteen

PLAN

CREATING A DYNAMIC EMPLOYMENT PACKAGE AND JOB SEARCH PLAN

PART FOUR: MANAGING CAREER

No one can tell you what your life's work is, but it is important that you find it. There is a part of you that already knows; affirm that part.
—Willis W. Harman

Why read this chapter?

Because you'll learn...

- How to write a career objective
- About cover letters and resumés
- How to use action verbs to sell your skills and talents

Because you'll be able to...

- Use the D.O.C.T.O.R. system to write a powerful cover letter and resumé
- Effectively complete an online application
- Design attractive personal business cards

PROFESSIONALS from the Field

Name: Mark Jones

Business: Senior Customer Service Trainer
SCANA Corporation

My advice would be to tailor your cover letter and resumé to the position for which you are applying. Never send a generic cover letter or resumé. Make sure your resumé is typed and can be scanned or sent electronically. Carefully read the company's job advertisement and then use keywords from their advertisement in your cover letter and resumé. Be specific about your skills. Do not state that you are fluent in Microsoft Office Suite; rather state that you know how to use PowerPoint, Word, Excel, and Outlook. This makes your resumé and cover letter stand out from the others, and keywords can be picked up by scanning software.

MyStudentSuccessLab

MyStudentSuccessLab (www.mystudentsuccesslab.com) is an online solution designed to help you "Start strong, Finish stronger" by building skills for ongoing personal and professional development.

PLANNING FOR THE FUTURE

What Am I Going to Do for the Rest of My Life?

"What am I going to do for the rest of my life?" is an overwhelming question for anyone, especially in a dramatically changing, global, technologically driven environment. What was true last year—and sometimes even last week—is no longer true. While many things that worked for your parents and grandparents are still important and relevant today—like ethics, integrity, hard work, education, honesty, teamwork—many practices that were true in their time are no longer valid. Your grandfather may have gone to work for a company and stayed there all his life. Employers were loyal to employees, and employees were loyal to the company. Work stayed pretty much the same one year to the next. All that has changed. You will have many different jobs during your lifetime—you will most likely have at least three or four different careers, and what constitutes your work will be constantly changing.

iStockPhoto

What changes do you foresee coming in your chosen career field in the next five years?

Getting a job, the *right job*, is hard work. Many people in the career development field would say that finding the right job is a full-time job. We agree. One thing that you should have in mind as you begin your job search is that this process is not easy and it is totally yours. No one can complete your job search plan, application packet, and interview but you. Sure, people from your institution's career planning office will help you, but ultimately, you are on your own.

You will need to use every tool in your toolbox to find the job for which you've prepared. You will need to call on the career services office at your institution, scour the Internet for job postings—including corporate websites—use all of your personal and social networking contacts, quiz your instructors about possible leads, read the want-ads, post your resumé with an online job bank or a site such as Monster or LinkedIn, attend job fairs, and possibly even contact an employment or "headhunter" agency. In today's crazy, upside-down job market, you'll need to do everything you can to get your foot in the door. This chapter will help you create an outstanding impression through your cover letter, resumé, reference choices, and business cards so that you can do just that.

> *The four great questions: Why are you here? Where have you been? Where are you going? What difference will you make?*
> —Hal Simon

Your Positive Attitude and the Job Search

Today is the day that I am going to find my dream job. Today is the day that I am going to put my talents, knowledge, and experience to use. Today is the day that I will get to show people just what I can do. Today is the day that I am going to start my professional career.

Today is just another horrible day without a job, and it ain't never going to get any better. Today is another report about high unemployment. Today is the day when more jobs are being shipped abroad. Today is the day I stay home, watch *I Love Lucy*, and just try to forget that I paid all this money for a degree I can't use.

Do you see the difference between these two people? Granted, a positive attitude is not the only thing that you need as you begin your job search, but it is certainly important. Will you hit walls during your search? Yes. Will you meet with rejection? Yes. Will you be frustrated? Yes. These things happen in the best of times. They most certainly are happening now. However, when you have a positive attitude about your search and what you have to offer, this comes across to the people who will be hiring you. Conversely, your negative attitude will also show. You may not notice it, but your attitude affects your actions, speech, interview responses, and nonverbal communication. Choose to be positive.

Career Objective

As you begin your job search both mentally and in writing, the place to begin is with a career objective. A career objective is an introductory statement written for your resumé. It is the only place on your resumé where you can use the words *I, me,* or *my.* This is a personal statement that briefly (usually one sentence) describes your desires, talents, skills, and interest in a specific position. Your career objective will not only make your resumé stronger, it also forces you to prepare mentally for what you really have to offer and what you want in a career.

Think of your career objective as *"an elevator speech."* Pretend you are on an elevator with your dream employer. You have the time span of two floors to tell Mr. Jamison about yourself, your skills, and what you want. Period. Wham! Two floors. What would you say? You need to be able to answer this question before you begin searching for a position, writing a cover letter, or preparing your resumé.

Two career objectives are shown below:

Weak Objective
I want to work as a marketing manager with a major corporation.

Strong Objective
Seeking a marketing position that will utilize my organization talents, oral communication skills, and expertise with Word, Excel, PowerPoint, Prezi, and Facebook in a competitive, engaging, and high-energy environment.

WORKIN' 9 TO 5—OR TRYING TO

Is It Really Possible to Sell Yourself Through a Cover Letter and Resumé?

You've got it all together—education, experience, and a strong sense of self. A positive attitude. What do you do now? How do you pull all of this together? How do you find the job of your dreams? The job for which you have prepared?

Know this! Getting a job—the *right job*—is hard work! Regardless of your status in school, now is the time to begin your job search. If you are in the last months of your program, your job search should be a top priority. If you are just beginning your educational plan, it is never too early to begin assembling a dynamic employment package.

Selling Yourself

Remember the old saying, "You are what you eat"? When searching for a professional position, you could change that to read, "You are what you write." Most likely, the people conducting the job search have never met you and know nothing about you except what you provide to them. A carefully crafted resumé communicates your past history (skills and experience) that makes you the ideal candidate for their position. Your resumé is the first marketing piece and in many cases must stand alone when a recruiter is determining whether to interview you. Just as a well-designed and well-written resumé can be a wonderful first step, a poorly designed and written resumé can doom you before you ever leave your house. A good thing to remember is this: A resumé gets you the interview; the interview gets you the job. Although there is no single way to develop your career resumé and formats may vary from discipline to discipline, this chapter will outline the key components of resumés and discuss how to develop a resumé that will represent your best efforts.

Your second "advertising tool" is your cover letter. A cover letter is basically an expansion of your resumé. A cover letter gives you the chance to link your resumé, skills, and experience together with your interest in a specific company's position. You will need to write many cover letters to make this link work properly; in other words, you most likely need to write a cover letter designed for each job for which you apply. Your cover letter will often be the stepping stone to get an employer to even look at your resumé. Consider it "a teaser," if you will, to all of your talents and experience. Just as you would never send someone a greeting card and not sign it, you would never send a resumé and not tell the person or committee why you sent it. Your cover letter tells why.

What is your elevator speech?

WRITE A POWERFUL AND CONCISE COVER LETTER

How Do You Get Your Foot in the Door?

Careful preparation must be done *prior to starting* the interview process. Two key elements of this preparation are your cover letter and resumé. Both are key components in your career search.

Whenever you send your resumé to a company, whether it is in response to a posted advertisement or was requested by someone, you must send a cover letter with it. Cover letters are extremely important; in fact, most recruiters say that they read four times as many cover letters as they do resumés because if the cover letter does not "strike a chord," then they never look past it to the resumé.

Career development expert, author, and speaker Carol Robins (2006) states, "During my 25 plus years that I've been involved in career development, I have found that of all the paperwork associated with job searching, cover letters give job searchers the most difficulty." The information presented here will help you overcome any anxiety associated with writing your cover letter or resumé.

As you the process of building your cover letter and resumé, consider the general tips in Figure 14.1.

Simply put, the cover letter's purpose is to get the interviewer to read your resumé. It sets the tone for who you are, what you have to offer, and what you want. "It screams—ever so politely—that you have the intelligence, experience, and soft skills to be the answer to an employer's staffing problem" (Britton-Whitcomb, 2003). The cover letter should say to the reader, "You have an opening and a detailed description of what you need, and I can fill your opening and be the person who gets the job done—and done well."

Figure 14.1 Tips You Can't Skip to Build an Effective Resumé

- Both your resumé and cover letter *must be typed*. There are no exceptions to this rule. Ever!

- Your cover letter and resumé must be printed on the same type and color of fine-quality paper. Cheap paper sends the message that you don't care. This is not the place or time to pinch pennies; buy excellent quality, 100 percent cotton stock, resumé-quality paper.

- Check your printer and be sure that the print quality is impeccable. Never send a cover letter or resumé with smudges, ink smears, or poor print quality.

- When you print your cover letter and resumé, be certain that the watermark on the paper is turned in the correct direction. Hold it up to the light and you will see the watermark embedded in the paper. This may sound silly and picky, but people notice attention to detail.

- Do not fold your cover letter or resumé. Purchase a packet of 9" × 13" envelopes in which to send your materials.

- Do not handwrite the address on the envelope. Use a label or type the address directly on the envelope. Remember, first impressions are important.

- Never send a generic photocopy of a cover letter or resumé, even on the finest paper.

- Layout, design, font, spacing, and color must be considered in the building of your cover letter and resumé.

- Unless you are specifically asked to do so, never discuss money or salary history in either your cover letter or resumé. This could work against you. When asked for a salary history, use ranges.

- Your resumé and cover letter must be free of errors. That's right, not one single error is acceptable, including grammar, spelling, punctuation, layout/spacing, dates, or content.

- Each cover letter must be signed, preferably in black ink.

Consider the following **four steps to success** when writing your cover letter:

1. An effective cover letter will be *personally addressed and job specific.* If at all possible (and yes, it is possible with just a little research), address your letter to a specific person. Avoid at all costs the dreaded "Dear Sir or Madam" or "To Whom It May Concern." In most cases, a phone call to the company will provide the name of the person along with his or her title and address. Always verify spelling, even with common names. This single step can set you apart from lazy job-seekers. Also, make sure you spell the company's name correctly.

2. Once your letter is correctly addressed, your first paragraph should be an "attention grabber" and it should answer the question "Why am I writing?" Susan Britton-Whitcomb, author of *Resumé Magic* (2003), calls this "the carrot." This simply means that your first paragraph should have an interesting fact, an appeal, or maybe even a quote—something that makes the reader (hopefully, your future employer) read further. Your first paragraph should also have a transition statement that makes the reader want to read on. For example, your last statement might read, "With a degree in medical assisting and four years of experience at Desert Medical Center, I know that I can make a valued contribution to Grace Care Center."

3. Your second (and maybe third) paragraph(s) should clearly state why you are qualified for the position you are seeking. Use your cover letter to highlight those areas of your experience that specifically qualify you for the job. Your cover letter is not the time to list all of your qualifications, but to indicate the two or three components that most qualify you for the position and closely match the position announcement. You may also include specific attributes that may not be on your resumé. The emphasis here is your value. Relate your education, experience, and talents to the company's need. Mention facts and statistics of how you've been successful in the past. Remember, "Employers are not interested in you for your sake, but rather because of what you can bring to the organization. This might sound harsh, but businesspeople have an obligation to improve the success of their organization. If you consistently show how you can help them do this . . . they will be much more motivated to talk to you" (Farr and Kursmark, 2005).

4. Your final paragraph should address the question of "Where do we go from here?" Do not be ambiguous by saying something trite like "I hope to hear from you in the near future," or "If you have any questions please do not hesitate to call me." Remember, your job search is none of the company's business, nor is it their responsibility. Be proactive by stating that you will be following up with a phone call to discuss your resumé and experience(s) in more detail. Make sure that once you have said that you are going to call that you actually do call. Your final paragraph should also continue to express what you can do for the company. You should end your letter with a statement about your qualities and the company's needs, such as "Mr. Thompson, I will call you on Monday, January 24th at 11:30 a.m. to discuss how my past experiences can help streamline operations and continue superior patient care at Grace Care Center."

Don't forget to **sign your letter**. Figure 14.2 provides a sample cover letter and indicates the correct format and spacing to the left of the letter's content.

POSITIVE HABITS *at Work*

After you have found the position for which you have prepared, you need to think into the future and begin planning for your next job search. "What?" you might be saying. "My next job?" Yes! After you begin your new position, you need to create an e-file where you will save information about your successes, acquired skills, and accomplishments so that you can add them to your next resumé. Your resumé is a living document and must be updated extensively each time you apply for a new position. The best way to keep this information organized is to keep an e-file that lists what you have learned from this job. If you learned how to create an Excel spreadsheet, add that to your file. If you sat on a hiring committee, add that to your file. If you were asked to lead a team, add that to your file. Then, when it comes time to update your resumé, you have all of your successes and updated skills in one place.

UNDERSTAND THE DO'S AND DON'TS OF MEMORABLE RESUMÉS

How Do You Sell Yourself?

Eight seconds. That is all you have to gain the attention of your potential employer, according to author and consultant Susan Ireland (2003). "In eight seconds, an employer scans your resumé and decides whether she will invest more time to consider you as a job *candidate.* The secret to passing the eight-second test is to make your resumé look inviting and quick to read" (p. 14).

A resumé is the blueprint that details what you have accomplished with regards to education, experience, skills acquisition, workplace successes, and progressive responsibility and/or leadership. It is a painting (that you are able to "paint") of how your professional life looks. It is the ultimate advertisement of you! Your resumé must create interest and hopefully a *desire* to find out more about you!

As you begin to develop your resumé, make sure to allow plenty of time to develop it. Plan to enlist several qualified proofreaders to check your work. We cannot stress strongly enough the need for your resumé to be perfect. A simple typo or misuse of grammar can disqualify you from the job of your dreams. Don't allow a lack of attention to detail to stand between you and your future career.

Figure 14.2 Sample Cover Letter with Formatting

Your name and address. Your name should be larger and/or in a different font to call attention. ⟶

The date (then double space) ⟶

The specific person, title, and address to whom you are writing (then double space) ⟶

The formal salutation followed by a colon (then double space) ⟶

Paragraph 1 (then double space) ⟶

Paragraph 2 (then double space) ⟶

Paragraph 3 (then double space) ⟶

Final paragraph or closing (then double space) ⟶

The complimentary close (then four spaces) ⟶

Your handwritten signature in black or blue ink within the four spaces ⟶

Your typed name ⟶

Enclosure contents ⟶

BENJAMIN SHAW

1234 Lake Shadow Drive
Maple City, PA 12345

(123) 555-1234
ben.shaw@online.com

January 3, 2011

Mr. James Pixler, RN, CAN
Director of Placement and Advancement
Grace Care Center
123 Sizemore Street, Suite 444
Philadelphia, PA 12345

Dear Mr. Pixler:

Seven years ago, my mother was under the treatment of two incredible nurses at Grace Care Center in Philadelphia. My family and I agree that the care she was given was extraordinary. When I saw your ad in today's *Philadelphia Carrier*, I was extremely pleased to know that I now have the qualifications to be a part of the Grace Care Team as a Medical Assistant.

Next month, I will graduate with an Occupational Associate's Degree from Victory College of Health and Technology as a certified Medical Assistant. As my resumé indicates, I was fortunate to do my internship at Mercy Family Care Practice in Harrisburg. During this time, I was directly involved in patient care, records documentation, and family outreach.

As a part of my degree from Victory, I received a 4.0 in the following classes:

- Management Communications
- Microsoft Office (Word, Excel, Outlook, PowerPoint)
- Business Communications I, II, III
- Anatomy and Physiology I, II, III
- Medical Coding I, II
- Principles of Pharmacology
- Immunology I, II, III, IV
- Urinalysis and Body Fluids
- Clinical Practicum I, II, III

This, along with my past certificate in Medical Transcription and my immense respect for Grace Care Center, makes me the perfect candidate for your position.

I have detailed all of my experience on the enclosed resumé. I will call you on Monday, January 24, at 11:30 a.m. to discuss how my education and experiences can help streamline operations and continue superior patient care at Grace. In the meantime, please feel free to contact me at the number above.

Sincerely,

Benjamin Shaw
BENJAMIN SHAW

Enclosure: Resumé

GRADUATE *Quote*

Derwin Wallace
Graduate: Devry University and Keller Graduate
School of Management
Career: Director of Corporate Investor Relations
National Association of Investor Corps

In my position, my main responsibility is to put companies that trade in the stock market in front of investors in hopes they may purchase that company's stock. Just as my education gave me limitless opportunities, yours will too. Corporate America is a battlefield and you must get your armor ready. Your education is your preparation for battle—it is your boot camp for the real world.

When you land your new position, live below your means. Doing this gives you freedom. If you buy that BMW, the designer clothes, and the mansion on a hill and all of your money goes to pay the bills, you have lost your freedom and flexibility—you're a slave to a paycheck. The major stressor in life is to be tied to a job that you hate and can't leave because without it you will lose all your material possessions.

Further, your resumé must be 100 percent accurate and truthful. Do not fabricate information or fudge dates to make yourself look better. It will only come back to haunt you in the long run. Dennis Reina, organizational psychologist and author of *Trust and Betrayal in the Workplace,* states, "I think that what you put in a resumé absolutely has to be rock-solid, concrete, and verifiable. If there are any questions, it will immediately throw both your application and your credibility into question" (Dresang, 2007). People have been fired from positions after they were hired because they misrepresented themselves on their resumés, cover letters, or applications.

As you begin to build your resumé, remember to "call in the **D.O.C.T.O.R.**"

D: Design

Visual **design** and format are imperative to a successful resumé. You need to think about the font that you plan to use; whether color is appropriate (usually, it is not); the use of bullets, lines, or shading; and where you are going to put information. You also need to pay attention to the text balance on the page (centered left/right, top/bottom). The visual aspect of your resumé will be the first impression. "Make it pretty" (Britton-Whitcomb, 2003).

O: Objective

Writing a clear and specific **objective** can help get your foot in the door. The reader, usually your potential employer, needs to be able to scan your resumé and gather as much detail as possible as quickly as possible. A job-specific objective can help. Consider the following two objectives:

- **Vague objective:** To get a job as an elementary school teacher in the Dallas Area School District.
- **Specific objective:** To secure an elementary teaching position that will enable me to use my 14 years of creative teaching experience, curriculum development abilities, supervisory skills, and commitment to superior instruction in a team environment.

C: Clarity

Clarity is of paramount importance, especially when including your past responsibilities, education, and job responsibilities. Be certain that you let the reader know exactly what you have done, what specific education you have gained, and what progress you have made. Being vague and unclear can cost you an interview.

T: Truth

When writing your resumé, you may be tempted to fudge a little bit here and there to make yourself look better. Perhaps you were out of work for a few months and you think it looks bad to have this gap in your chronological history. Avoid the urge to fudge. Telling the absolute **truth** on a resumé is essential. A lie, even a small one, can (and usually will) come back to haunt you.

O: Organization

Before you begin your resumé, think about the **organization** of your data. We will provide a model resumé; however, there are several other formats you might select. It is most important that you present your information in an attractive, easy-to-read, comprehensive format.

R: Review

Reviewing your resumé and cover letter is important, but having someone else review them for clarity, accuracy, spelling, grammar, formatting, and overall content can be one of the best things you can do for your job search.

The basic tips in Figure 14.3 will help you as you begin building a dynamic resumé. Some other basic tips include the following:

- Do not date stamp or record the preparation date of your resumé in any place.
- Limit your resumé (and cover letter) to one page each (a two-page resumé is appropriate if you have more than 10 years of experience).
- Use standard resumé paper colors, such as white, cream, gray, or beige.
- Use bullets (such as these) to help profile lists.
- Avoid fancy or hard-to-read fonts.
- Use a standard font size between 10 and 14 points.
- Do not staple anything to your resumé (or cover letter).
- Try to avoid the use of *I, me,* or *my* in your resumé (if you must use them, do so sparingly).
- Avoid contractions such as *don't,* and do not use abbreviations.

Figure 14.3   General Inclusion Tips

Contact information (name, complete mailing address, phone and cell numbers, fax number, e-mail address, webpage URL)	MUST include
Education, degrees, certificates, advanced training (to include dates and names of degrees)	MUST include
Current and past work history, experience and responsibilities	MUST include
Past accomplishments (this is *not* the same as work history or responsibilities)	MUST include
Specific licensures	MUST include
Specific career objective (different for each position for which you apply)	SHOULD include
Summary or list of qualifications, strengths, specializations	SHOULD include
Special skills (including special technical skills or multiple language skills)	SHOULD include
Volunteer work, public service, and/or community involvement	SHOULD include
Internships, externships, and/or extracurricular activities	SHOULD include
Awards, honors, certificates of achievement, special recognitions (at work or in the community)	SHOULD include
Military experience	CONSIDER including
Professional/preprofessional memberships, affiliations, and/or associations	CONSIDER including
Publications and presentations	CONSIDER including
Current business phone number and/or address (where you are working at the moment)	DO NOT include
Availability (date/time to begin work)	DO NOT include
Geographic limitations	DO NOT include
Personal hobbies or interests	DO NOT include
Personal information such as age, sex, health status, marital status, parental status, ethnicity, or religious affiliation	DO NOT include
Photos	DO NOT include
Salary requirements or money issues	DO NOT include (unless specifically asked to provide a salary history)
References	DO NOT include unless specifically asked but have the information ready on a separate sheet of paper that matches your resumé

Figure 14.4 Chronological Resumé

BENJAMIN SHAW

1234 Lake Shadow Drive, Maple City, PA 12345   (123) 555-1234   ben@online.com

OBJECTIVE: To work as a medical assistant in a professional atmosphere that uses my organizational skills, compassion for people, desire to make a difference, and impeccable work ethic.

PROFESSIONAL EXPERIENCE:

January 2007–Present   Medical Assistant Intern
                                    Mercy Family Care Practice, Harrisburg, PA

- Responsible for completing patient charts
- Took patients' vitals
- Assisted with medical coding

February 2003–December 2006   Medical Transcriptionist
                                    The Office of Brenda Wilson, MD, Lancaster, PA

- Interpreted and typed medical reports
- Worked with insurance documentation
- Assisted with medical coding
- Served as Office Manager (1/05–12/06)

March 1998–February 2003   Ward Orderly
                                    Wallace Hospital, Lancaster, PA

- Assisted nurses with patient care
- Cleaned patient rooms
- Served patient meals

August 1995–March 1998   Administrative Assistant
                                    Ellen Abbot Nursing Care Facility

- Typed office reports
- Organized patient files

EDUCATION:

Occupational Associate's Degree—Medical Assistant
Victory Health Institute, Harrisburg, PA
May 2008 (with honors)

Certificate of Completion—Medical Transcription
Philadelphia Technical Institute
December 2002

Vocational High School Diploma—Health Sciences
Philadelphia Vocational High School
August 1995

- Use action verbs such as *designed, managed, created, recruited, simplified,* and *built.*
- Avoid the use of full sentences; fragments are fine on a resumé, but not in a cover letter.
- Use the correct verb tense. You will use past tense (such as *recruited*), except when referring to your current job.
- Do not include irrelevant information that does not pertain to this particular job search.
- Choose a format that puts your "best foot" or greatest assets forward.

Remember that the job market is highly competitive. Your job is to write a resumé that is solid, appealing, comprehensive, and brief. The idea is to get someone to read it and make him or her want to know more about you.

BUILDING YOUR RESUMÉ

What Are the Major Differences?

There are different types of resumés, but primarily they can be classified as chronological resumés, functional resumés, accomplishment resumés, or a combination of the three. Your job package may also contain a portfolio. You might consider submitting a video resumé or a resumé that can be easily scanned and sent electronically. Each is described below.

- A **chronological resumé** (Figure 14.4) organizes education and work experience in reverse chronological order (your last or present job is listed first).
- A **functional resumé** (Figure 14.5) organizes your work and experience around specific skills and duties.
- An **accomplishment resumé** (Figure 14.6) allows you to place your past accomplishments into categories that are not necessarily associated with an employer, but shows your track record of "getting the job done." This type of resumé is usually reserved for those with previous work experience.
- A **video resumé** is a resumé that showcases your experiences and talent through a brief (three- to five-minute) video recording. A video resumé is often used to supplement a traditional resumé and shows your creative and technological skills. Some employers will not accept video resumés because they can lead to claims of bias.
- A **scannable resumé** (Figure 14.7) is a resumé with very little formatting and a clear font such as Courier, Arial, or Times New Roman. These resumés may appear to be less visually appealing, but they are easier to read once scanned. You may be asked to send your resumé as a PDF. A PDF file basically takes a snapshot of your document exactly as it was prepared and ensures that your electronic resumé remains just as you designed it.
- An **electronic (or plain text) resumé** (Figure 14.8) is one that can be easily sent online and scanned electronically for *keywords and skills* based on the company's needs and job advertisement. It is saved in American Standard Code for Information Interchange (ASCII) format. When designing your electronic resumé, consider the spacing, formatting, and fonts. Avoid italics, bullets (use asterisks instead), and columns. Align the text on the left. Do not indent with tabs or use parentheses or brackets. To save your current or future resumé as an electronic or plain text resumé, simply click "Save as" and in the "Save as type" box, select "Plain Text." Then re-open your file and make adjustments, corrections, and additions.
- A *portfolio* is a binder, website, CD-ROM, flash drive, or cloud file that showcases your very best work. It details your projects, awards, certificates, certifications, degrees, transcripts, military experience, and major accomplishments. Your portfolio should always be specific to the position for which you are applying.

Figure 14.5 Functional Resumé

BENJAMIN SHAW

1234 Lake Shadow Drive, Maple City, PA 12345   (123) 555-1234   ben@online.com

OBJECTIVE: To work as a medical assistant in an atmosphere that uses my organization abilities, people skills, compassion for patients, desire to make a difference, and impeccable work ethic.

SKILLS: Bilingual (English/Spanish)   Data Protection
              Claims Reimbursement   Client Relations
              Highly Organized   Problem-Solving Skills
              Motivated, Self-starter   Team Player
              Priority Management Skills   Delegating Ability
              Strategic Planning   Budget Management

PROFESSIONAL PREPARATION:

Occupational Associate's Degree—Medical Assistant
Victory Health Institute, Harrisburg, PA
May 2008 (with honors)

Certificate of Completion—Medical Transcription
Philadelphia Technical Institute
December 2002

Vocational High School Diploma—Health Sciences
Philadelphia Vocational High School
August 1995

PROFESSIONAL EXPERIENCE:

January 2007–Present   Medical Assistant Intern
                                Mercy Family Care Practice, Harrisburg, PA

February 2003–December 2006   Medical Transcriptionist
                                The Office of Brenda Wilson, MD, Lancaster, PA

March 1998–February 2003   Ward Orderly
                                Wallace Hospital, Lancaster, PA

August 1995–March 1998   Administrative Assistant
                                Ellen Abbot Nursing Care Facility

REFERENCES: Provided upon request

Figure 14.6 Accomplishment Resumé

BENJAMIN SHAW

1234 Lake Shadow Drive
Maple City, PA 12345
(123) 555-1234

ben@online.com
www.bjs@netconnect.com

Career Target:

MEDICAL ASSISTANT

A highly qualified medical professional with eight years' experience
in patient care, client relations, and
medical coding seeking a challenging
career that uses my strong problem-
solving skills, deep compassion for the
people, and medical training.

PROFESSIONAL ACCOMPLISHMENTS

Mercy Family Care Practice

✓ Revised and updated medical coding procedures
✓ Increased insurance payments by 11%
✓ Revised and streamlined new patient intake process
✓ Assisted Lead MA with ethics plan revision
✓ Revamped treatment procedure guidelines

Office of Brenda Wilson, MD

✓ Developed new medication administration checklist
✓ Implemented new guidelines for lab specimen collection
✓ Assisted with compliance of OSHA regulations

SKILLS / STRENGTHS

✓ Highly organized
✓ Team player
✓ Impeccable work ethic
✓ Bilingual (English and Spanish)
✓ Budget minded
✓ Motivated, self-starter
✓ Excellent client relations
✓ Superior time management skills

PROFESSIONAL PREPARATION

Occupational Associate's Degree—Medical Assistant
Victory Health Institute, Harrisburg, PA
May 2008 (with high honors)

Certificate of Completion—Medical Transcription
Philadelphia Technical Institute
December 2002 (with honors)

Vocational High School Diploma—Health Sciences
Philadelphia Vocational High School
August 1995

PROFESSIONAL EXPERIENCE

January 2007–Present	Medical Assistant Intern
	Mercy Family Care Practice
February 2003–December 2006	Medical Transcriptionist
	The Office of Brenda Wilson, MD
March 1998–February 2003	Ward Orderly
	Wallace Hospital
August 1995–March 1998	Administrative Assistant
	Ellen Abbot Nursing Care Facility

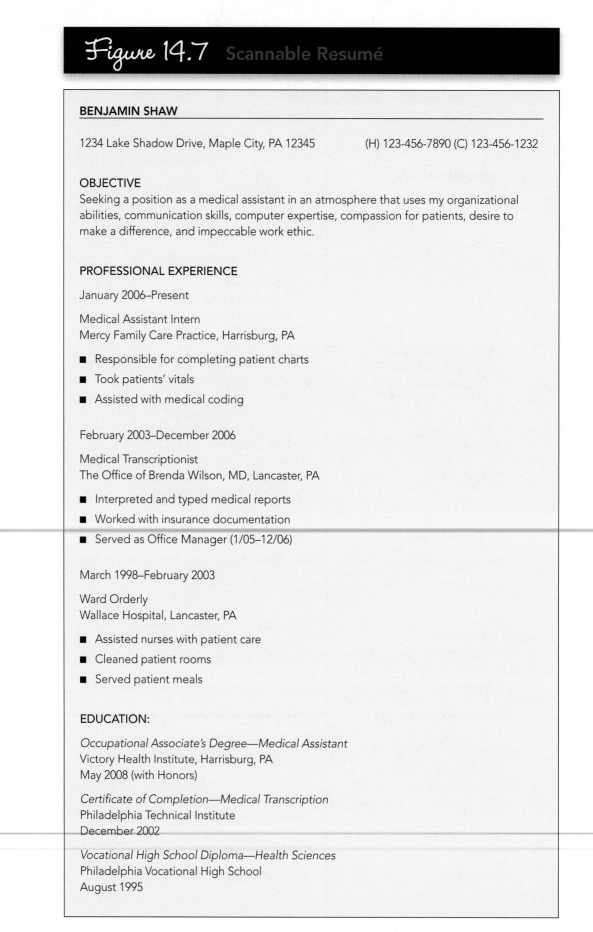

Figure 14.7 Scannable Resumé

BENJAMIN SHAW

1234 Lake Shadow Drive, Maple City, PA 12345   (H) 123-456-7890 (C) 123-456-1232

OBJECTIVE
Seeking a position as a medical assistant in an atmosphere that uses my organizational abilities, communication skills, computer expertise, compassion for patients, desire to make a difference, and impeccable work ethic.

PROFESSIONAL EXPERIENCE

January 2006–Present

Medical Assistant Intern
Mercy Family Care Practice, Harrisburg, PA

- Responsible for completing patient charts
- Took patients' vitals
- Assisted with medical coding

February 2003–December 2006

Medical Transcriptionist
The Office of Brenda Wilson, MD, Lancaster, PA

- Interpreted and typed medical reports
- Worked with insurance documentation
- Served as Office Manager (1/05–12/06)

March 1998–February 2003

Ward Orderly
Wallace Hospital, Lancaster, PA

- Assisted nurses with patient care
- Cleaned patient rooms
- Served patient meals

EDUCATION:

Occupational Associate's Degree—Medical Assistant
Victory Health Institute, Harrisburg, PA
May 2008 (with Honors)

Certificate of Completion—Medical Transcription
Philadelphia Technical Institute
December 2002

Vocational High School Diploma—Health Sciences
Philadelphia Vocational High School
August 1995

Figure 14.8 Electronic (or Plain Text) Resumé

BENJAMIN SHAW

Box F-123   Pittsburgh, PA 12345   Phone: 555-123-4567   E-mail: ben@online.com

----

OBJECTIVE
Seeking a position as a medical assistant in an atmosphere that uses my organizational
abilities, communication skills, computer expertise, compassion for patients, desire to
make a difference, and impeccable work ethic.

QUALIFICATIONS SUMMARY
Health management, client relations, order processing, data protection, interpersonal
skills, accounting, marketing, health policy, claims reimbursement, problem solving,
leadership, responsible, management skills

COMPUTER SKILLS
Word, PowerPoint, Excel, Outlook, Publisher, Prezi, HTML/Web publishing, Facebook,
and Twitter

PROFESSIONAL EXPERIENCE
January 2006-Present
Medical Assistant Intern
Mercy Family Care Practice, Harrisburg, PA
*Responsible for completing patient charts
*Took patients' vitals
*Assisted with medical coding and billing

February 2003-December 2006
Medical Transcriptionist
The Office of Brenda Wilson, MD, Lancaster, PA
*Interpreted and typed medical reports
*Worked with insurance documentation
*Assisted with medical coding
*Served as Office Manager (1/05-12/06)

EDUCATION
Occupational Associate's Degree, Medical Assistant
Victory Health Institute, Harrisburg, PA
May 2008 (with Honors)

Certificate of Completion, Medical Transcription
Philadelphia Technical Institute
December, 2002

RELEVANT COURSES and SKILLS
Human Anatomy & Physiology I, II, III
Public Health Policy
Organizational Health Care
Human Resource Management
Bilingual (English and Spanish)
Excellent Client Relations
Treatment Procedure Guidelines

CHOOSE YOUR WORDS CAREFULLY

Why Are "Power Words" Important to Use?

When constructing your resumé, you will be writing powerful, succinct statements that demonstrate your talents and accomplishments. The best way to do this is to use **action verbs**. When writing your accomplishments, consider the following two examples. As you can see, the active statement is stronger and more concise.

Passive Statements

I was responsible for controlling costs at the front desk

I learned how to train employees on the RoomKey System

Active Statements

Controlled costs at the front desk

Trained front desk employees to use the RoomKey Reservation System

Some action verbs for your resumé include the following. To find more, type "action verbs for resumés" into your search engine.

accomplished	achieved	adopted	applied
assisted	attained	built	charted
conducted	constructed	controlled	contributed
delegated	devised	earned	employed
enforced	exceeded	formed	fulfilled
helped	invested	managed	mastered
organized	oversaw	participated	planned
programmed	regulated	restored	secured
sponsored	undertook	used	verified

CHOOSE APPROPRIATE REFERENCES

Who Can Speak Positively about My Talents and Skills?

If an employer is interested in you, he or she will most likely ask that you provide three to five references: people who can attest to your professional skills, work ethic, and workplace knowledge. There are five steps for successfully soliciting letters of reference.

1. Select three to five people with whom you have had professional contact. As you determine the best ones to select, choose people who are very familiar with your work ability. Current and former employers with whom you have experienced a good working relationship are excellent sources of references. Your instructors are also excellent sources. If you do not have anyone who falls into these two categories, consider asking friends of your family who are respected members of the community. As you consider possible reference sources, be sure to choose individuals who are responsible and timely in their reply to your request. Typically, you should not use your minister, rabbi, or other religious figures as references. References are a reflection of you, and if the reference sources do not respond in the appropriate manner, they will cast a shadow on your credibility. Your references should have excellent written communication skills. A poorly written recommendation letter reflects badly on you.

2. Request permission from your reference sources. Always ask someone before you list them as a reference on an application or resumé. During your conversation with the individual, discuss your career goals and aspirations. Give him or her a copy of your resumé and cover letter. Ask for a critique and make any necessary changes. You should also ask the person to put your letter on his or her company letterhead and send your potential employer an original copy, not a photocopy.

3. Obtain all necessary contact information from them. You should know each reference's professional name, job title, business address, e-mail address, phone number, and fax number so that your potential employer can contact him or her with ease.

4. Send thank you letters to those who agree to serve as references for you. Stay in contact with them throughout your job search. Give them updates and a periodic thank you in the form of a card, an e-mail, or a phone call. At the end of your job search, a small token of your appreciation may be appropriate, but a thank you note is essential.

5. Develop a typed list of all references—including contact information—and take it with you to all interviews. It is now customary that you do not include the names of references on your resumé. You simply state: "References available upon request" or do not mention references at all. Employers will ask if they need them.

In the space provided in Figure 14.9, list three people you could ask to serve as references (or write you a reference letter). Once you have identified these three people, list the skills that each person could speak to on your behalf. Think about this carefully, as it is important to choose references who can speak to your many qualifications, not just one or two. Choose people who know you in different areas of success.

Figure 14.9 Selecting References

Person	Qualifications He or She Can Write About
JoAnna Thompson	My oral communication skills My attention to detail My ability to get along with others
Beau DeTiberious	My ability to form a team My ability to motivate team members My ability to meet deadlines
Person 1	Qualifications he or she can write about
Person 2	Qualifications he or she can write about
Person 3	Qualifications he or she can write about

ONLINE APPLICATIONS

How Can I Make a Strong Impression Electronically?

Often, employers will ask you to complete an *online application* instead of sending a resumé and cover letter. Some will require all three. Employers have found that online applications are easier to disseminate to the right people at the right time. The following tips will help you complete a successful online application and made a strong, lasting impression.

- Verify the existence and authenticity of the company before you complete an online application.
- Complete an online job application package with online sites such as Monster.com, Careerbuilder.com, or LinkedIn.com before you begin filling out company-specific online applications, as the company may ask for a link to your material.
- Read the instructions. Mistakes on an online application are as bad as mistakes on a hard-copy resumé or cover letter.
- Download the application as a hard copy and fill it out in writing before you complete the application online. This gives you the opportunity to polish your wording and check the accuracy of your dates, names, and numbers.
- Use keywords found in the company's job announcement so the computer will select your application.
- If possible, examine sample online applications from the company before completing your application.
- Complete all fields (boxes) of the online application.
- Do not provide any personal information such as mother's maiden name, bank account, or credit card numbers. No reputable company will ask for these in an online application.
- As with your resumé, strive for truth and accuracy in dates, names, locations, skills, and accomplishments. Your online application should match your resumé.
- As with a resumé, tailor your online application to the specific job for which you are applying.
- Send references only if requested.
- Keep a file (hard copy or electronic) of all online applications, materials sent, dates on which they were sent, attachments, and the actual job announcements.
- Reread your application for spelling and grammar. If possible, have someone read the application with you before you send it.
- If at all possible, follow up your online application with a personal e-mail or phone call to the employer.

BIGGEST INTERVIEW *Blunders*

Terrell received the call from Omni Environmental Controls. He had applied for a position as an HVAC industrial specialist. He was certain that the training he received in industrial heating, air conditioning, and ventilation at Century Technical College would give him the upper hand over applicants who had no degree and over those who had not had an internship with one of the major HVAC companies in town. The morning of the interview, Terrell dressed in a t-shirt, jeans, and a baseball cap. Everything was cleaned and pressed. He knew that technicians in his field did not wear suits, ties, and fancy clothes. During the interview, he was able to answer all of the questions that were asked of him with confidence and knowledge. He touted his internship experience. He was pleased. However, toward the end of the interview, Mr. Jamison, the owner of the company, looked at Terrell and said, "Son, if I hire you and send you out to bid on a job, do you have anything else to wear?" Terrell was shocked but answered, "Yes, sir, I do." "Good," stated Mr. Jamison, "You'll need them. We like to present ourselves as professionals to our clients."

LESSON: Always present your best self to any potential employer—in dress, attitude, knowledge, and poise. Even if you think you are being too formal, being overdressed and overpolished is always better than being underdressed and underpolished.

DESIGN AND DISTRIBUTE ATTRACTIVE PERSONAL BUSINESS CARDS

Does a Small Card Really Help?

Setting yourself apart from other job seekers is important, and designing and distributing attractive personal business cards can help with this endeavor. Business cards give you a professional edge, provide your potential employer another contact source, and help contacts stay in touch with you.

Business cards should be the standard size of 2" × 3.5" and should, if possible, be professionally designed and printed. If this is not possible, there are many computer programs and graphic packages to assist you in making your own. You can also purchase sheets of blank business cards for your home printer. You simply design, print, and separate them.

While including a simple graphic is fine (and can be very helpful), avoid flashy, unprofessional colors or "cutesy" graphics. Be certain to include your vital information such as:

Full name
Full address with zip code
Phone numbers (residence, business, cellular, and fax)
E-mail address
Website

Study the examples of appropriate and inappropriate personal business cards in Figure 14.10.

Figure 14.10   Sample Business Cards

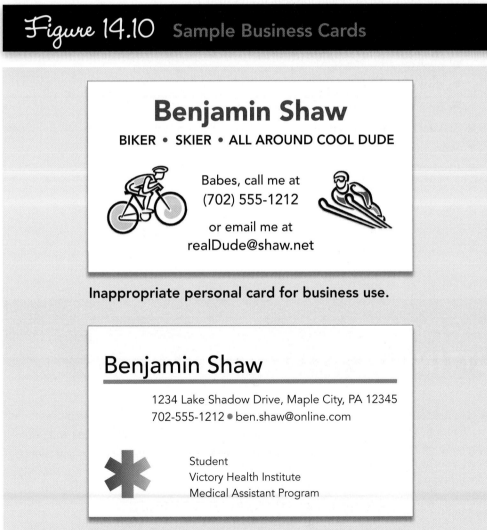

Inappropriate personal card for business use.

More appropriate personal card for business use.

NETWORKING

How Do I Form a Circle of Peers in the World of Work?

It will be important for you to develop a network among the people you know who may work for a company in which you have an interest. People on the inside have an advantage in helping you get your foot in the door. What about your dad's coworker? Your wife's friend? What about a friend who knows your work style and works for a company in which you have an interest? Use every legal, moral, and ethical method you have to get the interview. Some important networking opportunities include:

- Attending events and conferences on and off campus
- Joining professional organizations in your field of study
- Shadowing professionals in your field
- Volunteering within your community
- Working in externships or internships in your field
- Contacting family and friends about opportunities
- Logging onto websites and job search sites such as:
    - www.monster.com
    - www.career.com
    - www.careerbuilder.com
    - www.indeed.com
    - www.craigslist.com
- Talking to your instructors
- Working with headhunters or recruiters
- Contacting a temp agency in the city in which you hope to work
- Working with your school's counselors and career officers
- Interviewing and connecting with guest speakers who came to your class

Reflections: PUTTING IT ALL TOGETHER

This is your one lifetime! You need to prepare to do something you love. No matter how much money you make, you won't be happy unless you are doing something that matters to you, something that allows you to keep learning and becoming, something that provides you opportunities to give back—perhaps the best gift of all.

As you reflect on this chapter, keep the following pointers in mind:

- Learn how to make yourself a desirable employee.
- Set yourself apart with a dynamic cover letter and resumé.
- Select references who can speak to your many talents and skills.
- Learn to promote and sell yourself in an interview.
- Send thank you notes after your interview.
- Present yourself in a professional, educated manner.

DIGITAL BRIEFCASE

YOUR RESUMÉ WORKSHEET

Now, it is your turn. After reviewing the information for resumé writing and the examples of several resumés, begin compiling information to build your own resumé using the template below.

After you have completed this template, go online and find a free resumé building tool such as www.resumebuildertemplate.com.

You can go to any search engine and type in "free resumé template builder." If your school is using MyProfessionalismKit, you can use the resumé builder tool included with this program.

RESUMÉ INFORMATION

Personal Information

Name _____

Address _____

Phone number(s) _____

E-mail address _____   Website _____

Work Experience (Employment History)

1. (most recent)

   Company name _____

   Your position _____

   Your duties _____

2. (next most recent)

   Company name _____

   Your position _____

   Your duties _____

3. (next most recent)

   Company name _____

   Your position _____

   Your duties _____

Education and Training

1. (latest degree)

   Name of institution _____

   Name and date of degree _____

   Honors/Recognition _____

2. (degree)

   Name of institution _____

   Name and date of degree _____

   Honors/Recognition _____

Additional Training

Name of institution _____

Name and date of certificate or training program _____

Name of institution _____

Name and date of certificate or training program _____

Special Skills and Qualifications

List any skills and qualifications that you possess that may be of interest to an employer.

_____

_____

_____

College or Community Service (optional)

List any relevant service that you have performed that the potential employer might need to know.

_____

_____

_____

Personal References

List the names, addresses, and phone numbers of at least three people you could call on to serve as references for you if needed.

1. _____

2. _____

3. _____

Locate a position for which you would like to apply. Practice writing a job-specific objective.

_____

_____

_____

REFERENCES

Britton-Whitcomb, S. (2003). *Resume magic: Trade secrets of a professional resume writer.* Indianapolis, IN: JIST Works Publishing, Inc.

Dresang, J. (2007, April 23). "Liar! Liar! Won't Get Hired. In age of easy information, resume fibs can sabotage hunts for work." *The Las Vegas Review Journal,* reprinted from *The Milwaukee Journal Sentinel.*

Farr, M., & Kursmark, L. (2005). *15 minute cover letter: Write an effective cover letter right now.* Indianapolis, IN: JIST Works Publishing, Inc.

Ireland, S. (2003). *The complete idiot's guide to the perfect resume.* Indianapolis, IN: Alpha Publishing Company.

Robbins, C. (2006). *The job searcher's handbook* (3rd ed.). Upper Saddle River, NJ: Prentice Hall.

chapter fifteen

INTERVIEW

INTERVIEWING LIKE A PRO

The best career advice to give anyone is this: "Find out what you like doing best and get someone to pay you for doing it."
—Katherine Whitehorn

Why read this chapter?

Because you'll learn...

- The value of preparing for an interview
- Important tips for having a dynamic interview
- How to handle inappropriate or illegal interview questions

Because you'll be able to...

- Dress for success for your interview
- Use the R.E.W.A.R.D.S. system to prepare for an interview
- Write a compelling thank you note

PROFESSIONALS from the Field

Name: Brian Epps

Business: Key Account Executive, Maintex, Inc.

In this tough economy, it is imperative that you know how to sell yourself during an interview. The first thing you need to do is become knowledgeable about the company for which you are interviewing and pay close attention to their needs. They are interviewing you because they think you can meet their needs. Be confident, give eye contact, and state with certainty what you can do for the company. Paint yourself as someone who can bring a positive attitude, unique skills, and a strong work ethic to the company. If you don't "sell yourself" during the interview, you won't have the chance to do it later.

MyStudentSuccessLab

MyStudentSuccessLab (www.mystudentsuccesslab.com) is an online solution designed to help you "Start strong, Finish stronger" by building skills for ongoing personal and professional development.

THE BIG DAY IS HERE

How Do You Make the Impression of a Lifetime?

Remember the *eight-second rule* for making an impression. Consider this: During the interview process, you have even less. A judgment is made immediately about you: your dress, your grooming, your stance, your handshake, and your overall visual impression. Right or wrong, the interviewer will form an immediate first opinion of you—just as you will form an immediate first impression of your interviewer.

There are several ways your potential employer might choose to conduct the interview. In today's globally connected world, the standard face-to-face interview may not be the first choice of an employer—especially if the company has to pay to have you visit the office. Your interview may be conducted in one of the following ways:

- **In Person.** This type of interview takes place face-to-face with one person or with a group of people. The interview usually happens at the place of business.
- **Electronic.** With so many electronic ways to communicate, some employers are using the Internet to interview potential employees through Skype, GoToMeeting, WebEx, or other networking sites.
- **Social**. You may have an interview where you are asked to join the members of the interview team at a restaurant or outside the business location.
- **Phone.** Because of the high cost of bringing in someone to an interview, many employers will conduct the first interview over the phone. If you do well and the company is impressed, you will be brought in for an in-person interview.

As you begin to prepare for your interview, consider the following mnemonic. If you confidently carry R.E.W.A.R.D.S. with you to an interview, you will most likely get rewards after the interview, such as a job offer, benefits, and a career in which you can grow and prosper.

R: Rapport

Rapport is basically your "relationship" (intended or unintended) with another person—the emotional alliance you establish with someone. Consider how you come across to others. Rapport involves your verbal and nonverbal communication efforts. You should strive to establish a positive relationship with potential employers and future colleagues.

E: Education and Training

Be confident about what you know, and eloquently promote your abilities, skills, and talents to the interviewer. Remember, if you don't promote yourself, it is unlikely that anyone else will.

W: Willingness

Project a sense of willingness to learn new things, to become a team member, to assist the company with growth and new projects, and to keep up with advancements and changes in the modern world of work. Potential employers enjoy seeing an attitude of willingness and engagement.

Would you be more comfortable with a face-to-face, electronic, social, or phone interview? Why?

Shutterstock

A: Appearance

Dress for success. Pay close attention to your grooming, your hygiene, your hair, your clothing, and yes, even your shoes and socks (or hosiery). It all matters—and it is all noticed. Never make the mistake of thinking that appearance is not important. You will also want to consider dressing for a specific type of job. Careers in health studies may require a different type of interview dress than careers in aviation maintenance, engineering, or business.

R: Response

Project positivity and optimism in your responses to the questions asked in the interview. Even if you have to talk about your weaknesses or past experiences of conflict and turmoil, put a positive spin on them. Let the interviewer know that you have learned from adversity.

D: Demeanor

Cast a quality of confidence (not cockiness), intelligence, professionalism, and positivity. Carrying yourself with confidence during the interview will not go unnoticed. Pay attention to your handshake, eye contact, posture, mannerisms, and facial expressions.

S: Sincerity

No one likes phony people, especially a potential employer. Be yourself and strive to be sincere in your answers, your emotions, and your passion.

PREPARING FOR THE INTERVIEW

What Steps Can I Take to Ensure Success?

Just as you prepared for exams, you will need to prepare for the interview. Please do not make the common mistake of thinking that your degree or past work experience will get you the job. It may, but more often than you would believe, it is the interview and the relationship that you establish that day that gets you the offer. Your experience and credentials are important, but nothing is more important than how well you are prepared for this day and how well you represent yourself. As you prepare for your interview, consider the following sound advice.

Days Before the Interview

- Prepare extra copies of your resumé to take to the interview. Though one person typically conducts interviews, some employers designate several people to sit in on the interview process.
- Place your extra resumés, references, and other job search information in a professional portfolio (leather binder) or nice folder. Avoid carrying loose papers and never carry a backpack to an interview.

- Prepare a typed reference sheet and take several copies to the interview.

- If achievement portfolios are required, update your portfolio with any last-minute, applicable information.

- Using the research that you have done on the company, make a list of questions that you want to ask the interviewer. Never attend an interview without asking questions yourself. You are interviewing them just as they are interviewing you. Interviewers are much more impressed if they think you have researched the company and have questions to ask.

> Nothing splendid has ever been achieved except by those who dared believe that something inside them was superior to circumstance.
>
> —Bruce Barton

- Have a friend or colleague sit with you and ask questions that you might anticipate. Have this person throw a few "surprise questions" your way, too.

- Ask someone whose opinion you trust to look at your interview outfit and give you advice and suggestions for improvement.

- Make sure you know how to get to the interview site. Make a dry run if you have to. Being late for your interview will be the "kiss of death" for that job.

- Check the night before to make certain that you have transportation and that all of your personal needs are met, such as child care.

- Be sure you have enough gas to reach your destination if you are driving yourself. What is the availability for parking? Will you need to allow time for finding a parking place?

The Day of the Interview

- Get up early and spend some time alone reviewing the job announcement, your resumé, your portfolio, the company's profile, and other important information.

- Bring a pen, paper, and calendar with you to the interview. These can be kept in your portfolio, too.

- Know where your items are located so that you do not have to search for them during an interview. Fumbling around makes you look disorganized and unprepared.

- Prepare for the unknown: Take an umbrella, even if it is sunny; leave your home early, even though the interview site is only a few miles away; and so on.

- Be certain that your clothes are clean and pressed.

- Be certain that your shoes are spotless and shined.

- Be certain that you are groomed and that your breath is fresh. Breath mints or sprays go a long way.

- Arrive at the interview at least 15 minutes early.

- If you are a smoker, *do not* smoke in the car on the way to the interview and try to avoid smoking in your interview clothes. Often, the smell of cigarette smoke lingers for hours and clings to your clothing. For many, this is an immediate turn-off. Some employers will find a way not to hire a smoker because of increased insurance premiums paid for smokers.

- Do not carry any type of food or drink into the interview with you.

- Do not chew gum during the interview.

- Before you enter the building, turn off your cell phone, pager, Blackberry, iPod, tablet, or any other electronic device except your hearing aid, pacemaker, or other life-assisting device. *Turn them off.* Period! There is no excuse for your cell phone to ring during an interview. No one, including you, is that important.

- Do not take anyone with you to the interview unless the person remains in the car. Under no circumstances should you take anyone with you into the building!

During the Interview

■ Establish eye contact.

■ Work to develop an immediate rapport.

■ Offer a firm handshake to everyone in the room.

■ Pay close attention to your posture (straight shoulders, positive stride, etc.).

■ Speak with clarity and enunciate your words.

■ Ask where to sit if you are not told.

■ Enter with a positive and upbeat attitude.

■ Jot down the names of everyone in the room as they are introduced to you. You may even draw an impromptu seating chart to remind you of who's who in the room.

■ Refer to people by their names if you address them during the interview.

■ Take notes during the interview.

■ Answer every question asked, as long as the question is legal.

■ You don't have to be deadly serious or stodgy, but it is advisable to avoid jokes or off-color humor during the interview process.

■ Consider your grammar and strive to use correct speech.

■ If you need clarification on a question, ask for it before you begin your answer.

■ Never degrade or talk badly about a past job or employer. This will only come back to haunt you.

■ If at all possible, do not discuss any aspect of your personal life such as children, marriage, or family.

■ During the interview, jot down any questions that may arise that you did not already consider.

■ If you are offered anything to eat or drink, accept only water, just in case your mouth becomes dry during the interview.

■ Never ask about money or company benefits during an interview, especially during the first interview, unless the interviewer approaches the topic. Let him or her lead this discussion. If you are asked about salary requirements, respond with this question: "What is the range for this job?" In negotiations of any kind, you want the other person to offer information first. If you think you are highly qualified, respond with a salary amount close to the top of the range by saying, "Based on my qualifications and experience, I would consider a salary of $_____."

■ Strive to never appear desperate or "begging" for the job. There is a difference between excitement and desperation.

After the Interview

■ Shake hands with everyone in the room and thank them for the opportunity to meet with them. Let them know that you were honored to have the opportunity. Humility goes a long way.

■ Politely let them know that you enjoyed the interview and that you are very interested in the position.

■ Ask each person in the room for a business card. This provides you with their correct name spelling, address, and e-mail address for use in future correspondence.

■ Don't linger around the site unless you are told to wait. This makes you look desperate.

■ Always follow up with a personalized thank you note.

What preparations do you need to make to arrive at the interview on time?

Shutterstock

General Tips

- Remember the cardinal rule of interviewing: Interviewers are not interested in what the company can do for you; they are interested in what you can do for the company. Therefore, you must present your case on why you want to work for the company and the contributions you are prepared to make.

- Be truthful in every aspect of the job search: the application, your resumé, your cover letter, your portfolio, your references, your question responses, your salary history, and yes, your interest in the position.

- Be nice and gracious to everyone you meet. You never know which person will be the one to interview you.

DRESSING FOR SUCCESS

What Do I Wear to My Interview?

This is tricky because there is no general, "one size fits all" answer. A person interviewing for a position at a bank or hospital might dress differently than a person who is applying at maintenance shop or small computer business. Even if you know that the workplace to which you are applying has a casual dress policy, dress up for your interview. Dressing well suggests that you take the interview seriously and that you planned in advance. One overriding rule is when you are in doubt about how to dress, always be more conservative than trendy and always be clean and neat. Any business will appreciate this. And remember, your appearance speaks as loudly as you do and projects a lasting, visual image. Figure 15.1 outlines a few general guidelines for interview attire.

> *If you follow your bliss, doors will open for you that wouldn't have opened for anyone else.*
>
> —Joseph Campbell

ANTICIPATING THE INTERVIEWER'S QUESTIONS

Can You Answer Hard Questions with a Positive Attitude?

Richard Nelson Bolles, author of *What Color Is Your Parachute?* (2011), the most widely published job-hunting book in history with over 10 million copies in print, makes an astounding assertion. He states, "You don't have to spend hours memorizing a lot of 'good answers' to potential questions from the employer. There are only five questions that matter." Wow. Five questions!

With this statement, do not think that you will only be asked five questions. Rather, Mr. Bolles is suggesting that with every question asked of you, the interviewer is trying to get to the heart of the matter—the five basic questions are:

1. Why are you here?
2. What can you do for us?
3. What kind of person are you?
4. What distinguishes you from the 19 other people who can do the same tasks that you can?
5. Can I afford you?

So, how do interviewers get to "the heart of the matter"? How do they pull the answers to these five questions from you? Ironically, they do it by asking many, many other questions. This section will offer you insight into some common and not-so-common questions asked by today's employers.

Figure 15.1　General Tips for Successful Interview Attire

Item	Women	Men
Hair	Always clean and dry; pulled away from the face	Always clean and dry; pulled in a ponytail if you have long hair and trimmed neatly
Nails	Well manicured; clear polish is best; do not use wild colors or decorative designs	Clean and clipped
Tattoos	Cover them for the interview	Cover them for the interview
Teeth/Dentures	Always clean; use mouthwash; take a breath mint	Always clean; use mouthwash; take a breath mint
Perfume/Cologne/ Aftershave/Smells	Wear sparingly or none at all; never smoke before an interview	Wear sparingly or none at all; never smoke before an interview
Makeup	Wear sparingly and in good taste; don't overdo it	N/A
Clothes	Clean, pressed, conservative, coordinated, and traditionally a dark color; no jeans; no tight-fitting, body-hugging outfits; a dark, conservative suit is always appropriate	Clean, pressed, conservative; white long-sleeved shirts with collar; khakis or dress slacks with a belt matching your shoes; no jeans; dry-cleaned navy blue, grey, or black suit (with tie and belt) if appropriate
Shoes	Appropriate for your outfit but always clean and polished; avoid stiletto heels and open-toed shoes; always wear neutral hosiery	Appropriate for your outfit, but always clean and polished; black shoes are preferred; avoid tennis shoes; wear socks that match your shoes, not your pants
Jewelry	Avoid excessive jewelry; choose classic over trendy; remove any jewelry-adorned piercings except stud earrings; no hoop or 6" drop earrings; no dangling bracelets; experts say no jewelry is better than "cheap" jewelry; preferably gold or silver	Avoid excessive jewelry; no gold chains; remove any jewelry-adorned piercings
Accessories	Handbag (plain leather is preferable); nice portfolio; no visible cell phone (make sure it is off)	Nice portfolio; no visible cell phone (make sure it is off)

It is usually customary that the interviewer will make "small talk" for a few minutes to give you time to relax and get comfortable. You should avoid answering questions with a simple yes or no. Briefly elaborate on your answers without talking too much. For example, if the interviewer says, "I hope you had no trouble finding our building," you should not just answer "No." You might say something like, "Not at all. I live near here so I was familiar with the location," or "Actually, I had a part-time job when I was a sophomore and I brought materials to one of your managers from my department manager."

Interviewers will often say to you, "Tell me about yourself." They are not looking for your life history as much as they are gathering background information on you and observing how well you can present information. Provide highlights of your education, experience, and accomplishments. If you are just yourself and enjoy the process, this will show.

The interviewer might then ask you, "What do you know about our company?" This is a good opportunity for you to show how prepared you are. You could open your portfolio and tell

G R A D U A T E *Quote*

Brayton Williams
Graduate!
The University of Nevada, Las Vegas
Career: Hotel Management

The most important thing that I learned about interviewing is to begin preparing for your professional interview years before it occurs. It is very important to take advantage of internships, volunteer, join clubs, and participate in professional organizations. I learned that it was important to do more than the minimum. Stacking your resumé with activities that were not "required" will be looked on favorably by any employer.

the interviewer, "When I was researching the company, I found some interesting facts on your website. I know that you are an international company based in New York and that you have over 4000 employees. I learned that you have several divisions including food processing and distribution, restaurants, and contract food sales. In fact, this information is the reason I applied for a job with you through our Career Center. My minor in college is restaurant management, and I think this company will be a great place to put my knowledge and the skills to great use."

You will, of course, have to adapt your answer to your own situation. There is no way to be completely prepared for the questions an interviewer may ask. The key is to have anticipated the interviewer's questions and to be so comfortable with the message you want to convey about yourself that you sound confident and decisive. As you talk, remember to look at the interviewer and to lean forward slightly which indicates that you are listening intently.

After a brief "let's-get-to-know-each-other" session, you can anticipate more direct and important questions. Some of the more common questions that you might expect include:

- Why should we hire you?
- Why are you interested in this company and in the position?
- When did you decide on a career in _____?
- Tell me about your extracurricular activities.
- What are your strengths?
- What are your weaknesses?
- Why did you leave your last job?
- Do you have a geographic preference? Why?
- Are you willing to relocate?
- Are you willing to travel?
- Do you have job experience in _____?
- What can you do for the company?
- What other companies are you interviewing with?
- Tell me about a difficult problem you had and how you solved it.
- Tell me about a time when you worked under stress.
- What kind of accomplishment gives you the greatest satisfaction?
- What are your long- and short-range goals?

Never wear a backward baseball cap to an interview unless you are interviewing for the job of umpire.

—Dan Zevin

- Where do you see yourself in five years?
- What one word best describes you?
- How do you deal with difficult people?
- Describe one goal you set over the past six months and how you went about accomplishing it.
- What is the biggest mistake you ever made? What did you learn from it?
- What subject in school gave you the most challenges? Why?
- What past experiences or courses have prepared you for this position?
- Would you prefer to work alone or with a group of people? Why?

Some more in-depth and less common questions might be:

- What type of manager would bring out the best in you? Why?
- What is the most important thing to you in a job? Why?
- Who has been the most influential person in your life? Why?
- If I called your past supervisor, how would he or she describe you?
- In what area do you lack the most confidence?
- In what area of this position do you lack the most experience? How do you plan to accommodate for this?
- If you could design your own job evaluation form with only five qualities to be evaluated, what five qualities would you list? Why?
- Tell us about a time when you put your best forward and the end result was still unfavorable. Why do you think this happened? What did you do about it? What did you learn from the situation?
- What is the biggest change to which you have ever had to adapt? What strategies did you employ to adjust to this change?
- How do you effectively deal with interpersonal conflicts?
- How do you effectively deal with miscommunication?
- How do you effectively deal with gossip?
- Of what are you most proud in your professional life? Why?
- If you could not be involved in this job or profession any longer, what would you do for a vocation? Why? Why are you not doing that now?

Regardless of the question asked, your primary responsibility in the interview is to be straightforward and honest and to answer the question to the very best of your ability.

Look over the position advertisement, the company's website, and your own application materials and think about questions that may be asked of you. Write down five questions that you might anticipate that are not listed above.

1. _____

2. _____

3. _____

4. _____

5. _____

ASK INFORMED QUESTIONS

Am I Allowed to Interview the Interviewer?

You should feel free to ask the interviewer questions during the interview, but the interviewer should lead the majority of the first part of the interview. At the close of the interview, you may be asked if you have any questions. If this opportunity is not offered, you should say, "I have a few questions, if you don't mind." Asking questions of the interviewer is impressive and indicates that you are interviewing them as well. Some typical questions follow:

- How would you describe a typical day in this position?
- What kind of training can I anticipate?
- What is the probationary period of employment?
- What are the opportunities for personal growth and professional development?
- To whom would I report?
- Will I have an opportunity to meet some of my coworkers?
- Would you describe the training program?
- When will my first job performance evaluation take place?
- Why do you enjoy working for this company?
- How would you describe the most successful person working at this company? Why?
- What objectives do you expect to be met by your new employee in the first six months?
- Can you tell me about an assignment I might be asked to do?
- What happened to the person who most recently held this position?
- What do you see as the major challenges facing this organization? Why?
- How would you describe the culture of the workplace in this organization?
- What does this company value?

ROUGH, TOUGH, HARD QUESTIONS

How Do You Effectively Manage Inappropriate or Illegal Questions?

Sadly, you may encounter questions that are inappropriate or even illegal. Remember, federal and state laws may prohibit many questions that deal with your personal life, and federal laws such as the Civil Rights Act of 1964 and the Americans with Disabilities Act of 1990 do regulate certain questions that can be asked during an interview, but some employers may still ask inappropriate and illegal questions.

BIGGEST INTERVIEW *Blunders*

Margaret's interview outfit was flawless. Her suit was immaculate, her blouse was beautiful and well-coordinated, her shoes were polished, and her hair and makeup were salon-quality. She had prepared for the interview days in advance and even got a friend of hers to quiz her on many different interview questions. Margaret made two huge errors, however. She arrived a few minutes late. And even though she was dressed to the nines, to calm her nerves, she smoked two cigarettes in the car on the way to the interview. Mrs. Compton, the interviewer, immediately noticed the smell, and this began the interview on a negative note. However, the worst was yet to come. Upon being seated in Mrs. Compton's office, Margaret reached into her purse and pulled out a Red Bull. "I'm running late this morning," she said. "I need to have a shot of energy."

Margaret answered the questions well and did not stumble on any responses. She had the education for which they were looking and she was polite and confident. However, the two strikes at the beginning of the interview were hard to overcome. At the end of the interview, Margaret's cell phone rang and she answered it. *Strike three.*

LESSON: A part of interviewing is respecting the person who is conducting the interview by showing up on time and giving him or her your undivided attention. Regardless of what you did or did not eat for breakfast, you would never pull out food or beverage during an interview. Leave your cell phone in the car or at home. You've worked too hard to have a ringing phone cost you your dream job—and it will.

How do you plan to handle questions that may be illegal to ask?

Shutterstock

If illegal or inappropriate questions are asked in person or on an application, it can be challenging to manage them and still retain your composure and decorum. It is up to you how much you want to tell a potential employer about your personal life or lifestyle, and they cannot demand an answer unless the question is in direct relationship to the job for which you applied, such as certain jobs in aviation and service industry jobs where alcohol is served.

First, review the list of questions that many experts consider illegal, or at best inappropriate, and later in this section, we will discuss how to respond if you are asked an illegal or unethical question.

With some exceptions, such as religious organizations, employers should not ask you about:

■ **Your age.** You should generally not be asked this question. However, some professions are age-restricted (such as airline pilots and bartending) and this question is perfectly legal.

■ **Your marital status, your parental status, or your living situation (who lives with you or why).** If you are asked this question, the employer is really trying to find out if you will be at work on a regular basis or if you can travel. It is legal to ask, "Does your personal schedule permit extensive travel?" but it is not legal to ask, "Would you get into trouble with your wife or children if you were asked to travel a lot?" It is illegal to ask if you are planning a family, if you are pregnant, or if you have ever had an abortion.

■ **Your race or national origin.** You should not be asked about either of these categories, nor should you ever be asked to provide a photo of yourself. However, every employer can, on employment, ask that you provide legal documentation that you are eligible and clear to work in the United States. At this point, an employer can also ask for a photograph for security and identification purposes.

■ **Your sexual orientation.** This is tricky, but generally it is still legal (albeit unethical) for a potential employer to ask about your sexual orientation. It is up to you if you choose to answer this question. Some interviewers try to get at this answer by asking about your marital status, which is illegal to ask.

■ **Your religious affiliation.** This question is illegal and should never be asked. However, if you are asked this question, the interviewer is probably trying to determine if your religion might prevent you from working on weekends, Sundays, or certain holidays. It is legal to ask, "Would you be willing to work on Sunday?" or "Would you be willing to work on Christmas?"

■ **Your political affiliation.** It is legal to ask this question; however, "Some states ban discrimination on this basis and political affiliation may not be used for discriminatory purposes in federal-government employment" (Smith, 2007).

■ **Your physical, mental, or emotional limitations.** You cannot be asked a question such as, "Have you ever been treated for depression or any mental illness?" but you can be asked a question such as, "This position requires that you deal with many stressful situations and many situations in which you will encounter conflict. Do you feel that you have any limitations that might prevent you from managing these situations effectively?" It is never legal to ask about your HIV status, your disabilities, or any prescription drugs that you may take.

- **Your physical attributes.** You cannot be asked questions about your height or weight unless this is directly tied to job performance due to specific, predetermined limitations.

- **Your financial status.** An employer cannot ask you if have a checking or savings account, how much money you save each month, or any question about your credit rating. However, many states do allow potential employers to run credit checks on applicants and potential employees.

- **Your personal habits.** Generally, employers can ask if you smoke at home, but this question has led to some lawsuits. "Currently, 31 states ban policies prohibiting off-duty smoking" (Smith, 2007).

- **Your arrest status.** Your arrest status is completely different from your conviction status. It *is* legal to ask if you have ever been convicted of a crime. A few states do allow an employer to ask if you have been arrested if it is job related.

- **Your affiliations.** It is not legal to ask you to which organizations you belong, except for certain professional organizations (such as The National Association of Architects if you are applying for a position in the architectural field). An employer, cannot, however, ask if you belong to the Shriners, Freemasons, or any union.

- **Your military status.** You may not be asked what type of discharge you had from the military. You should not be asked if you ever belonged to the military unless it is job related.

- **Your school and/or college records.** School and college records may be sought only with your consent. Usually, you have to order the official transcript and have it sent directly to your employer.

Anderson Ross/Picture Arts/BrandX/Jupiter

In the past, what preparations have served you best in getting ready for an interview?

Basically it comes down to money. It is very expensive to hire, train, and retain an employee in today's workforce. An employer wants to know as much about you as possible—basically, they want to know if you are qualified, if you will get along with others, and if you will be at work when you say you will be there.

So, how do you handle questions that may be illegal or inappropriate? This can be tricky at best and "the kiss of death" at worst. Consider this: Can an employer ask you if you are married? No, they cannot. However, if this type of question arises, you can always view it as a positive moment. You might respond: "Yes, I am married and my spouse and I fully support each other's careers and advancement possibilities."

Can an employer ask, "Are you gay?" Generally, yes, but again, you have to decide how you would answer this question (whether the answer is yes or no). If you are uncomfortable with this question, you may respond, "Before I answer that question, can you discuss how this is related to this particular position?" or "I choose not to answer that question based on my personal beliefs."

Sometimes, you will have to do an evaluation of the employer. You may need to ask yourself, "Do I really want to work for a company that would ask an illegal or inappropriate question?" Ultimately, the choice is yours.

As an exercise, choose one area above and pretend that you were asked a question that was illegal, inappropriate, or taboo. State the question; then give your response to this question.

POSITIVE HABITS
at Work

Work hard every day to become a true professional. Regardless of your profession, professionalism is a hallmark that employers seek in any employee. Professionalism includes things like helping without being asked, nurturing others who need assistance, representing your company with a positive attitude, avoiding gossip and hearsay, maintaining a strong ethical and moral base, managing the company's money well, using your time wisely, following company policy, and being a team player. If you learn how to do these things now, your current supervisor will not forget this when it comes time to write a letter of recommendation for you in the future.

Question:

_____

_____

My response:

_____

_____

_____

WIN, LOSE, OR DRAW, ALWAYS SAY THANK YOU IN WRITING

Do I Have to Say Thank You Even If I Don't Get the Job?

Indeed, it is safe to say that sending a thank you note is "the most overlooked step in the entire job search process" (Bolles, 2011). Yes, this is a mandatory step for every interview, and you

---

Figure 15.2   **Thank You Note: After the Interview**

CARSON SCOTT
1234 Lake Shadow Drive
Maple City, PA 12345
Scott@bl.com

January 20, 2013

Mr. James Pixler, RN
Director of Placement
Grace Care Center
123 Sizemore Street
Philadelphia, PA 12345

Dear Mr. Pixler,

Thank you for the wonderful opportunity to meet with you and the team at Grace Care Center on Monday. Your facilities are amazing, and the new wing is going to be a remarkable addition to your center.

I enjoyed learning more about the new position in Medical Assisting, and I think that my qualifications and experiences have prepared me for this challenging opportunity. I would consider it an honor to answer any further questions that you might have or to meet with you again if you consider it necessary.

I look forward to hearing from you at your convenience. If you need any additional information, you can reach me at 123-555-3454.

Thank you,

Carson Scott
CARSON SCOTT

must send one to every person who interviewed you. Period. In today's world of high-tech and run, run, run, this one act will set you apart from the thousands who interview on a daily basis. And yes, you must send a thank you letter even if you do not get the job. "When do I send the thank you note?" you might ask. ***Immediately after the interview***.

Sending a simple thank you note does many things. It lets the employer know that you have good manners, that you respect other people's time and efforts, that you are considerate, that you really do care about the position, and that you have positive people and communication skills. Yes, all of that from a card and stamp that can cost less than $2.00.

Figures 15.2 and 15.3 show examples of two thank you notes. Review them and consider using them as templates to build your own notes.

Figure 15.3 Thank You Note: After a Position Rejection

CARSON SCOTT
1234 Lake Shadow Drive
Maple City, PA 12345
Scott@bl.com

January 20, 2013

Mr. James Pixler, RN
Director of Placement
Grace Care Center
123 Sizemore Street
Philadelphia, PA 12345

Dear Mr. Pixler,

Thank you for the opportunity to meet with you and the team at Grace Care Center on Monday. I enjoyed learning more about your center and the planned addition.

While I was not offered the position, I did want to let you know that I appreciate your time, and I would like for you to contact me if you have any future openings where you feel my qualifications and experiences would match your needs. Grace is an incredible facility, and I would consider it an honor to hold a position there.

If you need to contact me in the future, you can reach me at 123-555-3454.

Thank you for your time and assistance, and good luck to you and your colleagues.

Sincerely,

Carson Scott
CARSON SCOTT

Reflections:
PUTTING IT ALL TOGETHER

Your chance to shine comes in many forms, such as your resumé and cover letter, but nothing speaks so loudly as **you** during an interview. Do not take this opportunity lightly. Just because the company is interested in you does not mean that you can glide through. Remember, there are countless people out there who are just as qualified and ready as you are. YOU have to sell you, and the interview is the perfect place to close the sell.

As you reflect on this chapter, keep the following pointers in mind:

- Go to the interview prepared.
- Practice interview questions with your friends or family.
- Anticipate illegal or probing questions.
- Ask informed questions of your interviewers.
- Dress for the interview like you want the job.
- Promote yourself. If you don't, no one will.

Job security is gone. The driving force must now come from the individual.

—Homa Bahrami

DIGITAL BRIEFCASE

SEARCHING FOR A POSITION

Search the Internet, newspaper, or corporate website and find a position for which you are (or soon will be) qualified. Send the ad to five friends on your social network and have them look at the company's website. Then have them formulate two questions each that may be asked by the interviewer from this company. Return your responses to the people who asked the question, and ask for feedback

REFERENCES

Bolles, R. (2011) *What color is your parachute? A practical manual for job hunters and career changers.* Berkeley, CA: Ten Speed Press.

Smith, R. (2007, August 14) Don't ask—maybe. Retrieved January 11, 2012, from www.forbes.com.

chapter sixteen

·

CHANGE

DIRECTING YOUR LIFE THROUGH CONTINUOUS POSITIVE CHANGE

We cannot become what we are capable
of being by remaining who we are.
—Unknown

PART FOUR: MANAGING CAREER

Why read this chapter?

Because you'll learn...

- To accept change as a natural part of life
- To distinguish between drivers, skaters, and defeatists
- To practice "carpe mañana"

Because you'll be able to...

- Understand the skills employers are looking for in employees
- Develop your own career plan

PROFESSIONALS from the *Field*

Name: Sheriff James Metts

Business: Sheriff of Lexington County, Lexington, SC

As a professional in the criminal justice system, I am continuously learning new life skills, adjusting to change, and reinventing myself. One of the biggest life skill changes I ever made was to earn my Ph.D. from the University of South Carolina, and today I am the only sheriff in the country who has a doctorate. I believe in education and encourage you to always continue learning. One of my jobs as the sheriff of a large county in South Carolina is to lead people in my department in developing themselves by providing training and educational programs. Our team is always learning about illegal drug trafficking, handling domestic violence, dealing with traffic violators, and many other areas of law enforcement—we can never learn too much and neither can you. To be successful in any position,

(continued)

MyStudentSuccessLab

MyStudentSuccessLab (www.mystudentsuccesslab.com) is an online solution designed to help you "Start strong, Finish stronger" by building skills for ongoing personal and professional development.

you have to become an entrepreneur of your own life, so I encourage people to have a plan for their lives with goals and directions and action plans. I encourage my team to go back to school, to become involved in the community where they can gain positive recognition, and to accept change because it is constant.

YOU ARE ON YOUR WAY

How Do You Plan to G4I (Go for It)?

Once you get a position and begin to prove yourself in this new job, you need to think about long-range plans, thriving in your career, and making a name for yourself as a hard-working, creative team player. There are many ways to do this. Of course, the most important thing you need to do is to excel at the entry-level job you accept in the beginning. You may not like some of the menial tasks assigned to you, and in your heart, you may know that you can do bigger and better things. The fact remains, however, that if you don't do this first job well, there won't be any promotions. So you need to start strong and never let up. Start strong and finish stronger! You should do everything possible to be a good colleague who gets along well with everyone. But this doesn't mean you can't simultaneously plan and strategize to move up the ladder, get a position with more authority and higher pay, and gain recognition for your accomplishments. The best way to make this happen is to plan for it. As you have already learned, you need short-term and long-term goals, you need to brand yourself, and you also need a career plan.

> Your time is limited, so don't waste it living someone else's life.
> —Steve Jobs,
> CEO of Apple Computers

As you mature and gain confidence, your priorities and interests will change. When you begin working in your first job, you may be willing to go anywhere and explore the world. At certain times in your career, you may welcome change, and at others, you may just want things to hold steady. "At some stages, there are likely to be significant pressures on your career due to family commitments" (Eby, Casper, Lockwood, Bordeaux, and Brinley, 2005). For now, you need to focus first on the job at hand while looking down the road at where you want your career to go. So what do you need to do besides doing a good job right out of the gate? In this chapter, we will provide many ways you can make a name for yourself, find rewards inside and outside of work, build your personal brand, continue learning and growing—and most importantly, continue changing.

You will learn soon enough that you are responsible for you. Even if you have an excellent mentor and supportive network, you are still in charge of your life, and it's basically up to you to make things happen. You may encounter many people who are willing to help you, but no one is going to make things happen in your career but you. While doing a good job is imperative, working hard by itself may not get you ahead. Haven't you known people who worked hard all their lives and never really got ahead? We will show you how to work hard and smart and to embrace change as a natural part of your life.

> Change is the essence of life. Be willing to exchange what you are for what you can become.
> —Unknown

Previously, we asked you to set goals and to know what you want. This chapter is about doing the extras, taking the next step, going out of your way, giving back to others, and finding many ways to grow and expand your potential so you can accomplish your goals and dreams. It is designed to help you focus more attention on your own personal brand and to learn to gain positive visibility that can help you earn promotions and respect. And most

> *It is not the strongest of the species that survive, nor the most intelligent, but the one most responsive to change.*
> —Charles Darwin

of all, it is about embracing change, taking risks, and never looking back. It's about getting ready to G4I!

ACCEPTING CHANGE AS A NATURAL PART OF LIFE

How Can I Learn to Embrace Change When It Scares Me to Death?

Change is the one constant that you can expect when you go to work. It is a myth that change will go away! Most people are afraid of change, even good change, because they are leaving their comfort zone. It is much less frightening to us if we just keep going on the way we are. The good news is that you can learn strategies for accepting change and making positive things happen. Choose to be a navigator of change rather than a victim.

You will probably hear the term *paradigm* used in the workplace. A paradigm is simply a way of doing things—it's a pattern and a system of how things are working right now. A *paradigm shift* is a rapid change from doing things one way to a totally new way—it's a transformation or a revolution. Paradigm shifts don't just happen; they are usually driven by a leader or a management team that shakes things up. When people are heavily invested in an old paradigm and have worked hard to get to this position, they are very likely to resist the new paradigm. You can't afford to be one of these people. When a company makes a paradigm shift, there is usually a good reason: The competition is getting keener; the global economy is putting pressure on production; or the old ways are simply not working anymore. If the leader of the company or your division wants to change, you need to help make his or her ideas work. If you embrace change, you will become a navigator of change; if you reject it, you will become a victim. Change is coming! How you deal with it is up to you.

> *Choose to be happy!*
> —Michael J. Fox

DRIVERS, DODGERS, AND DEFEATISTS

Which Will You Become?

When we are faced with rapid change or a dramatic loss of some kind, people become **drivers, dodgers,** or **defeatists.** Drivers make up their minds to embrace the change that has come their way and take control by driving their own lives and decisions. Others, dodgers, dodge the change and just let life happen to them; still others, the defeatists, let hard times and rapid change defeat them.

How you deal with change is in your hands. You can choose to be a driver or you can choose to be a defeatist. A great deal of how you become a driver rather than a dodger or defeatist will depend on your attitude. Study Figure 16.1 for traits that explain each category.

STRATEGIES FOR DEALING WITH CHANGE

How Can I Practice Carpe Mañana?

You might ask, "What in the world is **carpe mañana?**" You have probably heard of carpe diem, which means "seize the day." Carpe mañana means "seize tomorrow." That term probably describes better than anything what we want you to be prepared to do after reading and studying

Figure 16.1   Drivers, Dodgers, or Defeatists

Drivers	Dodgers	Defeatists
Realize that change is coming and they can't stop it. They know that to reduce their personal anxiety, they have to go to work and embrace the changes.	Try to pretend that they are accepting change but secretly work against it; they may feel entitled to having things stay the same because they have been there a long time.	Are frequently scared and uneasy and afraid of what is coming; will say things like "We are doing fine. Why do we need to change?" or "We've never done this before." Uncertainty breeds fear.
Are genuinely excited about the changes that are happening and the new opportunities it presents for their career.	Are only focused on themselves and no one else or the company; worry about their job changing; wonder if they will have to do more work or a job they don't like.	Think the world is against them and their boss is out to get them; fear losing control over their work or personal situation; worry about losing status that they have gained in the past.
Try to learn everything they can about where the organization is headed so they can participate in leading change; anticipate change.	Complain a lot and try to undercut the boss without being open about it while secretly hoping things will stay the same.	Usually openly resist change and try to stop it by sabotaging ideas; pull back; undercut the boss with negative remarks and actions.
Think about ways change can enhance their personal career; attack the future instead of protecting the past.	Are passive-aggressive in many ways; make no efforts to embrace change or to lead.	Many times leave their job voluntarily or are among the first to be downsized because they have shown they cannot or will not change.

this chapter. We want you to learn to work hard and smart today as you prepare for more success tomorrow. In the world we live in, you cannot afford to be focused only on today.

Life seems to just serve up change, ready or not. It is simply a part of life. Change happens, and with it comes some level of discomfort, but what change does to you is really up to you. We tend to pay more attention to bad or disastrous change than we do to things that actually bring

GRADUATE *Quote*

Zack Karper
Honor Graduate!
The Art Institute of Philadelphia
Career: Head of Video Production
    buggleproductions.com, Dream Camp Foundation

The biggest lesson that I learned in college was to treat every project, whether a paper, a speech, or a film, as if it was your baby. Nurture it. Care for it. Feed it. Make it great and never raise it halfway. Give your baby your all. Today, as head of video production at Buggle Productions, I live my dream of working in film and I get to help troubled kids who were in the same shoes I was in. I get to make a difference. If you work hard and put 100 percent into your projects, you will get to help people, too.

Figure 16.2 How to Practice Carpe Mañana When Dealing with Change

- Focus on carpe mañana, which means "seize tomorrow." Don't allow yourself to get comfortable with what is happening today. Be prepared for what is coming by making yourself better. *Prepare* is a keyword for being able to deal with change of any kind. Anticipate!

- Practice *kaizen*, a Japanese term that means "continuous improvement," by doing little things better and by setting and achieving increasingly higher standards.

- Face change by embracing it—good or bad—and look for the new opportunities that change brings. View change as growth. You cannot get better unless you change.

- Deal with change by understanding its phases:
  - Denial (includes focusing on the past, apathy, withdrawal)
  - Resistance (includes blame, anxiety, depression)
  - Adaptation (includes loss of energy, confusion, frustration, and beginning to adjust)
  - Commitment (includes clearer focus, new ideas, working better with others)

- When dealing with change, we encourage you to move up to the next level—create. In other words, make things happen; don't just accept things as they are. Turn the challenge of change into a positive. What new opportunities does change bring for you?

- If change puts everyone back at zero, seize the opportunity! You now have a level playing field with other employees who have been there a long time. Make the most of it!

- Associate with people who are embracing change, not resisting it. You want to be seen as a navigator, not a victim. Avoid those who are negative and pulling back. They will be among the first to go.

- Look for the signs of change so you are not shocked when they happen. Try to spot trends. Don't bury your head in the sand and keep doing the same things you have always done. Is the company changing leadership? Is the stock doing well? Are factories moving

- overseas? In the old days of chariot warfare, a dust storm was an indication of an approaching enemy. Do you see the dust storms before they engulf you?

- Think differently—obviously, things are changing in your company, or they should be. In what ways is your company changing and how do you fit in better? Help create value by making yourself useful and available to try new things.

- Revise your personal budget and save more money so you can survive a loss of job or any other bad event; increase your cash reserves; and reduce your debt.

- Reach out to friends and your support system for help during difficult changes, such as loss of job, death of a family member, or a painful divorce, but do not overburden them by focusing on your problems all the time. Seek professional counseling if you are severely depressed.

- Avoid negative coping mechanisms such as alcohol, denial, overeating, blaming, passiveness, and revenge. All of these just make a bad situation worse.

- Begin today to look down the road and try to figure out what is happening next. How can you learn strategies that help you "leapfrog" over people who are sitting still and pulling back and refusing to change?

- Ask yourself these questions on a regular basis: "How do I span the distance between what I am today and what I want to become? How do I continue to make the right changes that promote growth and success?"

- Keep moving! Exercise to remove stress from your body. Do not lie on the couch and watch endless television. Convert fear into energy! Get out of the ditch of depression and up on the road, where you are in the driver's seat. If you want milk, go find a cow instead of waiting for the cow to find you.

- Balance yourself. Find ways to bring joy into your life. Simplify your life. Take care of yourself and those whom you love.

us joy and happiness. In addition to being prepared for difficult change, we need to prepare for joyful change, and we need to set ourselves up to have joy and happiness in our lives. Abraham Lincoln said, "We are just about as happy as we make up our minds to be." We need to make up our minds to be happy and joyful and to deal with what comes our way.

No matter how optimistic and prepared we are, however, some bad things are going to happen to us. This kind of change may take more time to work through, but there are special ways of coping with difficult changes. Since you know change will always be coming, you can always be prepared, to some extent, to deal with it. To prepare for change, you have to have a good attitude, you must be flexible, and you have to be optimistic that you can handle it. Having a positive self-worth is very important to being able to deal with change. Figure 16.2 provides some ways for handling change effectively.

SKILLS AND ABILITIES VALUED BY EMPLOYERS

Do You Have the Right Stuff?

As you begin to map out your career plan, you need to give careful attention to certain skills that employers value highly. Although some positions require very specific job skills and knowledge, almost all jobs today require a set of universally sought-after skills. These skills can be developed if you are missing some, but it is important to be able to showcase all of them on your resumé. Figure 16.3 is a list of the top 10 skills most valued by employers (ASVAB, 2009).

As you can see, all these skills can be developed. You have to be honest with yourself and identify the ones you need to work on most. So exactly what do employers want in each of these categories?

Shutterstock

Have you ever used negative coping mechanisms? If so, what did you learn?

What Employers Are Saying

According to the report *College Learning for the New Global Century* (Association of American Colleges and Universities, 2007), "Employers want college graduates to acquire versatile knowledge and skills. Fully sixty-three percent of employers believe that too many recent college graduates do not have the skills they need to succeed in the global economy and a majority of

---

Figure 16.3   Skills Highly Valued by Employers

Review the list. Then rank the skills from 1–10 by each skill according to which ones you think are most highly valued.

Analytical skills	_____	Interpersonal skills	_____
Communication skills	_____	Problem-solving skills	_____
Computer skills	_____	Strong work ethic	_____
Flexibility/Adaptability	_____	Teamwork skills	_____
Initiative	_____	Technical skills	_____

Once you have ranked the skills, check them against the answers that were most selected by participants in the survey, which are provided below.

Skills Rank

1. Communication skills
2. Strong work ethic
3. Teamwork skills
4. Initiative
5. Analytical skills
6. Computer skills
7. Flexibility/Adaptability
8. Interpersonal skills
9. Problem-solving skills
10. Technical skills

> *Life is about change, and about movement and about being something other than what you are at this very moment.*
>
> —Oprah Winfrey

employers believe that only half or fewer recent graduates have the skills or knowledge needed to advance or to be promoted in their companies."

Whether we like it or not, a massive transformation is going on all around us in this country, as well as all over the world. Thriving in the coming years is going to be more difficult than in the past and will require certain new and different abilities and attitudes to be successful. You will need to learn the skills that will make you competitive, give you an edge, and help you master a life filled with changes and challenges.

Many of these skills are outlined in the following section. These skills will be needed for your success, personal independence, and growth in the new economy. Study them carefully, as each one will help you create a positive transition to the world of work.

CORNERSTONES FOR SUCCESS IN A CHANGING WORLD

What Major Skills Do I Need to Be Successful on the Job?

SEEK EXCELLENCE AS A COMMUNICATOR. Writing, speaking, and listening skills are constantly listed by employers as mandatory for success in any profession. Few people actually possess these qualities—especially all three. If you want to put yourself ahead of the competition, enroll in classes, attend seminars, join Toastmasters—anything that will help you learn more effective writing, speaking, and listening skills.

BECOME A SOUGHT-AFTER EMPLOYEE. A strong work ethic is another valuable quality that sets you apart from the other job seekers. A work ethic can include a variety of characteristics, including your pride, passion, professionalism, ability to work on a team, and ability to adapt, grow, and change. Your work ethic is how you perform at work without a job description, constant supervision, or someone threatening you. Your work ethic is not tied to what you do to get a raise or a promotion, but rather what you do because it is the right thing to do. In today's work environment, employers want to make sure that you are dedicated to your job, your company, and your colleagues.

Shutterstock

Are your communication skills an asset or a liability?

PRACTICE LOYALTY AND TRUSTWORTHINESS. Loyalty to your employer is a highly valued trait. However, one's loyalty cannot be measured by a resumé or determined by a simple interview. Proving that you have the characteristics of loyalty and trustworthiness comes over time. It may take years to establish loyalty and trustworthiness with your company and within your industry, but with hard work, dedication, and honesty, it can and will be achieved. Be forewarned, however. While it takes years to build trust, it only takes seconds to destroy it.

ACT WITH CONFIDENCE AND MAKE BOLD DECISIONS. Appropriate confidence and boldness are important to employers. There is a difference between having confidence in yourself, your work, and your decision-making ability and being "cocky." Confidence comes from experience, calculated risk taking, and previous successes. Employers are looking for confident people who are not afraid to make hard decisions. They are also seeking individuals who have confidence through experience. There is a difference between bragging about doing something and actually doing it. There is a difference between being hard and making hard decisions.

USE CRITICAL-THINKING SKILLS. The ability to think your way through problems and challenges is highly valued by employers. Employers are looking for people who can distinguish fact from opinion; identify fallacies; analyze, synthesize, and determine the value of a piece of information; think beyond the obvious; see things from varying angles; and arrive at sound solutions. They also want people who possess the emotional intelligence to critically and creatively work to resolve challenges.

MANAGE YOUR PRIORITIES WELL. Setting priorities and managing time are essential to success in today's stressful workplace. Today, maybe more than any other time in mankind's history, we are faced with more and more to do and what seems like less and less time in which to do it. Your success depends on how well you manage your priorities, both personally and professionally. Priority management not only involves getting today's work accomplished, it also involves the ability to plan for your personal and professional future. Use your time wisely at work, at home, and in leisure.

MULTIPLY BY MULTITASKING. The ability to multitask, or accomplish several things at once, will serve you well in the workplace and at home. A recent newspaper cartoon suggested that you are too busy if you are multitasking in the shower. This may be true, but in keeping pace with today's workforce, this is another essential task—the ability to do more than one thing at a time, and the ability to do them all very well. If you have not had much experience in multitasking, we suggest that you begin slowly. Don't take on too many things at one time. As you understand more about working on and completing several tasks at a time, you can expand your abilities in this arena. An example of multitasking at home is to have a casserole baking while clothes are washing at the same time you are researching a project on the Internet. To be successful in today's fast-paced world, you must be able to manage several tasks at once—without burning dinner.
Shutterstock

STAY CURRENT AND BUILD TRANSFERABLE SKILLS. Keeping your skills and knowledge current is essential to your success. Building skills that can be transferred from one position to another is essential in today's workplace. Fine-tuning your computer skills

> *The future belongs to those who see possibilities before they become obvious. When you see the bandwagon coming down the road, it is too late.*
>
> —Unknown

Shutterstock

Can you multitask without getting too distracted and accomplishing nothing?

Are you sure you are not posting photos that can come back to haunt you?

Shutterstock

can set you apart from many of today's applicants. Your skills should include the ability to work with word-processing programs, spreadsheets, databases, and Power-Point. Some careers will require knowledge and expertise of industry software, and you will need to be an expert if this is true in your field. Learn to develop webpages, and create your own website that reflects a professional, career-oriented person. Learn to use social media for more than socializing.

CONTINUE TO GET EXPERIENCE AND EDUCATION. Never stop learning! You may not want to hear it, but your education will never end. Your formal schooling will eventually come to an end, but as long as you are working in today's global economy, you will need to keep abreast of the changes in your field. Seek out opportunities to expand your knowledge base. Get certified in areas that will make you more marketable. Take a continuing education course to brush up on changing workplace skills. Earn an advanced degree. Make yourself the best, most knowledgeable, well-rounded applicant in the field.

AVOID INTERNET AND SOCIAL MEDIA BLUNDERS. Don't let social media mistakes come back to haunt you and cause you to miss out on your dream job! You may think that posting that photo of yourself half-naked with a bottle of bourbon in one hand and a stuffed poodle in the other is cute and that your friends will love it. They may. Your current or future employer may not. Whether you like it or not, employers don't want people who do not represent them well. What you post online today may very well come back to haunt you in the future—even if you remove it, it can still be accessed. You may not lose your current position over a crazy, spur-of-the-moment posting, but it could cost you a future position. You may tell yourself that your Facebook, LinkedIn, or webpage is private and no one's business, but remember, nothing is private online, and everything is someone's business in the world of business.

Would your credit rating help or hurt your career? What can you do to improve it?

Shutterstock

WATCH YOUR CREDIT RATING. Building a good credit rating is one of the most important jobs you have. "Really?" you may think. "My credit rating? What in the world does my credit score have to do with my employment?" The answer: A great deal. More and more, employers are accessing your credit history and score as a part of the hiring procedure. Why? Because some employers believe that your credit history paints a clear picture of your working future. Bad credit history means a bad employee. Missed payments mean missed work. Low score means low morale. Careless errors mean a careless job performance. This is just one of the many ways that your credit history and score can follow you for years.

> *You want to be the most educated, the most brilliant, the most exciting, the most versatile, the most creative individual in the world because then, you can give it away. The only reason you have anything is to give it away.*
> —Leo Buscaglia, Ph.D.

REMAIN OPEN-MINDED. The ability to accept, appreciate, and interact with a highly diverse workplace and the inherent differences and cultures that will be commonplace is important. You will need to develop the ability to listen to others with whom you disagree or with whom you may have little in common and learn from them and their experiences. The ability to learn a new language (even if your mastery is only at a primitive, broken, conversational level) and the ability to conduct yourself in a respectable and professional style will set you apart from other employees.

PRACTICE ACCOUNTABILITY. The ability to accept responsibility and be accountable for all aspects of your future—including your psychological and spiritual well being, your relationships, your health, your finances, and your overall survival skills—is vitally important. Basically, you must develop a plan for the future that states, "If this fails, I'll do this," or "If this job is phased out, I'll do this," or "If this resource is gone, I'll use this," or "If this person won't help me, this one will."

POLISH YOUR HUMAN RELATIONS SKILLS. Polish your people skills and learn to get along with people from all walks of life. We saved this one for last, certainly not because it is least important, but because this quality is an overriding characteristic of everything listed previously. Employers are looking for individuals who have "people skills." This concept goes so much further than being a team player; it goes to the heart of many workplaces. It touches on your most basic nature, and it draws from your most inner self. The ability to get along with grouchy, cranky, mean, disagreeable, burned-out coworkers is, indeed, a rare quality. But don't be mistaken: There are those who do this, and do it well. Peak performers, or those at the "top of their game," have learned that this world is made up of many types of people, and there is never going to be a time when one of those cranky, grumpy people is not in our midst. Smile. Be nice. Remain positive.

Take some time now and work through the exercise in Figure 16.4. You will find several skills and traits for which employers are looking in the left-hand column. In the right-hand column, create two tips that outline ways *you* can impress an employer.

MOVING UP THE LADDER

How Do I Get Promoted?

When you start to work, you should make every effort to do an outstanding job in your current position, but you should also start thinking about how you are going to get promoted to your next position. You might even need to make a lateral move that better positions you to move up, so don't rule out such an offer before thinking about it carefully. Does a lateral move better position you in a track that will allow you to move up faster? In addition to the items previously listed, you need to pay attention to these hints:

- Give your employer an honest day's work for an honest day's pay. Don't slack off even if everyone else does. Get to work on time; don't take an extra long lunch; don't take sick leave unless you are sick; don't waste time chatting and gossiping when you should be working; and don't play games and send unprofessional e-mail at work.

- Plan every day in detail. Don't go to work and wander around in the desert. Hit the ground running. Do the big, important jobs that will get you noticed first.

- Be nice to your coworkers. Write thoughtful notes; send birthday cards; bring snacks; and use your manners.

- Try to get a mentor who can provide guidance for you. Mentors can spread good news about you and help you get noticed for your accomplishments. People above you on the career ladder often know information that will be helpful to you. If someone mentors you, you need to be prepared to return the favor by helping him or her.

- Support your boss! Make the boss look good, and he or she will not forget! Make your boss look bad, and he or she won't forget this either. When you

Do you know several ways to move up the ladder?

Shutterstock

Figure 16.4 Skills for Gainful Employment

Skill/Trait Employers Seek	Two Tips To Impress
Priority/Time management	1.
	2.
Attitude	1.
	2.
Written communication	1.
	2.
Interpersonal communication/Relationships	1.
	2.
Ethics	1.
	2.
Dress/Personal grooming	1.
	2.
Computer/Technology skills	1.
	2.
Decision-making / Problem-solving skills	1.
	2.
Confidence	1.
	2.
Advanced training/Certifications	1.
	2.

POSITIVE HABITS at Work

Plan to be successful by developing a career plan. Work on your plan every day by observing what successful people are doing. Adjust your plan when you find a better way of doing things. Pay the price to be successful by going back to school, taking in-house seminars, or learning a language. Build good relationships with internal and external customers. Include in your plan the ability to survive and thrive if you are outsourced.

have a formal evaluation, let your boss know that you want to move up and seek his or her advice as to what you need to do to be successful.

- **Sell yourself.** Send reports to your boss detailing your accomplishments. Do this in a modest way, but be sure your boss knows what you are doing. There is an old saying that is very true: "He who tooteth not his own horn, the same shall not be tooted."

- **Build a network inside and outside the company.** The more people you know, the better. Take advantage of any opportunity to make good connections. Join professional organizations, volunteer for jobs, and go to lunch with different people in a variety of positions and companies. The next promotion you get may be in an entirely different company.

- **Stand out from the pack.** Come early; stay late. Go the extra mile. Dress sharp, regardless of what everyone else is doing. Help other people when they are swamped, as long as you have done your work. Never say, "That's not in my job description." Have something worthwhile to say in meetings—do your homework!

- Take solutions to your boss. Bosses get problems reported to them and dumped on their desks every day. It's fine to tell your boss there's a problem. It's great to be able to say, "Here's how to solve it."

- Be willing to move! Some people are willing to go anywhere. They'll jump at the chance to go work in India or China, whereas others don't want to leave their hometown. If you are willing to move—at least for the first few years—your chances of moving up faster are increased.

CREATING MULTIPLE REVENUE STREAMS

How Can I Earn and Save Money in Addition to My Salary?

Smart people learn early the value of multiple sources of income. There are many reasons to earn extra money: First, you can save it or invest it; second, you can develop new skills that might lead to your own business; and third, this income can tide you over if you lose your main source of income. Because of today's volatile job market, we highly encourage you to develop at least one alternate source of income. "How do I do this?" you might ask. Be creative. What are your talents and skills? Who can you partner with to start a part-time business? Some suggestions follow (though this is by no means a complete list):

- Are you musically talented? Can you play in a band? Can you perform children's music at parties? Can you be a disk jockey? Can you be a pianist for a small church that needs a part-time musician?

- Can you paint houses on the weekends?

- Can you have a booth at craft shows and sell materials?

- Can you make jewelry and sell it on the Internet?

- Can you buy and sell things on eBay?

- Can you design websites or perform other computing services for small companies?

- Are you good with accounting? Could you keep books and file reports for small companies?

- Are you good with children? Can you babysit on the weekends? Can you start a service using reliable friends?

- Are you good with landscaping? Could you and a friend start a part-time landscaping business?

- Are you especially talented in an academic subject? Can you provide tutoring for a high school or middle school student? Can you start a service business? Can you work for an established tutoring service?

The list of creative ideas is endless. The point is: Get started now! If and when you really need this money to survive, you will have saved enough to pay your bills, and you will still have income. If the worst-case scenario never happens, you can take a great vacation to China or Africa or buy a house or work on a master's degree. Use your talents to build security and confidence.

Shutterstock

What skills do you have that you could turn into additional revenue streams?

DOWNSIZING, RIGHTSIZING, RIFS, TERMINATIONS, OUTSOURCING, LAYOFFS

How Would I Survive Losing My Job?

Today it is quite common for employees to get the dreaded "pink slip" (letter telling an employee that they have been let go from their job) when they have done nothing to deserve it. If this happens to you, you should know that it is normal to be scared, disoriented, and depressed, but it is not the end of the world. You can overcome it and perhaps even do better.

> *Barn's burnt down . . .*
> *now I can see the moon.*
> *—Masahide, Japanese philosopher*
> *(1657–1723)*

In a tight economy, many companies find that they have too many employees to support relative to the income they are producing, so they have to reduce their workforce. If this happens to you, you need to be prepared. There are lots of qualified people looking for work, so you have to be focused and strategic when finding your next employment. Hopefully, you have initiated another source of income and can survive a few months while you search for the right job. You should always keep your resumé updated and ready to use at a minute's notice.

Try not to become adrift and depressed; instead, look at this event as an opportunity to do something totally new that might be a better fit for you. Sometimes it takes something like losing a job to force us out of our comfort zone and help us realize our potential. This may be the perfect time to reinvent yourself as the person you always wished you could be.

Being prepared for loss of job includes the following steps:

- Sign up for unemployment benefits the same day you lose your job. There is a period of about three weeks before you will start receiving benefits.
- Before you leave your job, copy all e-mail addresses, phone numbers, and contacts.
- If you have a company cell phone, copy the information to your own phone.
- Get your own personal e-mail address if you don't have one so employers can reach you and so you can file resumés online.
- Protect your credit rating. Try to make your minimum payments, but let your creditors know if you are having problems.
- Put your resumé on LinkedIn, Monster.com, Careerbuilder, and TheLadders.
- Look up the term "resumé blasting" and follow the directions for this process.
- Don't burn any bridges with the employer who laid you off. Your next job may be a recall from that company.
- Mobilize yourself. Quit moping about your bad luck, get off the couch, and mix and mingle with people who might have leads for jobs. Let your friends and colleagues know that you are looking for a job, and provide them with your resumé.
- If you have joined professional organizations, let the people you know in these groups that you are searching for a job.
- Attend career fairs and employment agencies that might be able to help you find work.
- Go to the gym. Exercise will produce chemicals that are a natural high, and it takes stress out of your body. If you feel better, you are likely to "sell" better to people looking for employees. Protect your health during this stressful time.
- Consider temporary employment that can help you pay the bills.

- If you have children, keep them at home temporarily instead of using expensive day care.
- Cut your grocery bills by eating less expensively.
- Rent movies instead of going to the theater.

As you can see, there are strategies to follow to avoid outsourcing or to survive it and thrive when it happens to you. You might want to consider this tip: "Go where the puck is going!" Sound crazy? The great hockey champ Wayne Gretzky made the comment that this one step had been his key to success. What does it mean? He said that when he was playing hockey, he did not skate to where the puck was at the moment—he skated to where the puck was going. He anticipated the direction of where the puck was going to be hit, and when it came his way, he was already there—ready to play.

Think of your career in this light. Go to companies that will be bright in the future, not necessarily where it is bright at this moment. Look ahead and try to determine what is going to be "hot" in the coming years, not what is hot right now. Plan ahead. Look at trends. Read. Ask questions. Stay prepared. Try to work in *sunrise industries* (those businesses that are new and emerging, such as solar energy), not *sunset industries* (textile factories). Think in the future tense, not the present.

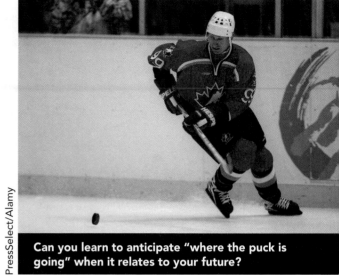

PressSelect/Alamy

Can you learn to anticipate "where the puck is going" when it relates to your future?

DESIGNING A CAREER PLAN

What Steps Do I Need to Take to Chart My Course?

This is not an easy, one-hour assignment. It takes time to think through your entire career and to design a plan that will take you where you aspire to go. You should know that this plan will change as you move up the ladder and as your confidence, skills, and knowledge grow. There is no doubt, however, that you will be far better off with a plan than you are just drifting along hoping someone will notice you and give you a promotion. A career plan will focus your efforts on doing all the right things to be successful. Simply looking at the next job down the road is not designing a career plan!

Before you chart your career path, you need to take an introspective look by considering the questions in Figure 16.5. You need to know what brings you happiness before you move toward the wrong career. After you have studied Figure 16.5, begin developing your own career plan. Don't be concerned if you can't complete the plan right now; the important thing is to start and continue.

Now you are ready to begin charting your path. Remember, this may take months, even years, because it will change as you move forward. The important thing is to always have a career plan. The great majority of people will not have a career plan; this plan puts you way ahead of the competition because you know what you want and have determined what you must do to get it. Study the sample career plan in Figure 16.6.

Rings and gems are not gifts. They are only imitations of gifts. The only true gift one can give is himself.

—Unknown

Figure 16.5 A Career Plan

1. What kind of work do you want to do? _____

   _____

2. What are you passionate about? _____

   _____

3. Are you a people person? Why or why not? _____

   _____

4. Do you want to live in a large city? _____

   _____

5. Are you willing to move around? Would you like a job that leads to an international position? _____

   _____

6. What are your strongest values? Does the company you are interested in match your values? _____

   _____

7. What kind of organization best fits your needs? Do you need to work for a large company or a small company, or do you

   need to start your own business? _____

   _____

8. Can you deal with the stress of a high-powered career, or would you be happier in a more laid-back type of work?

   _____

   _____

9. Are your career aspirations really yours, or are you trying to please someone else? _____

   _____

10. Are you driven by money or a feeling of satisfaction in doing a good job and in doing what you always wanted to do?

    _____

    _____

Now, answer two more questions before you begin designing your career plan.

What does "happiness" mean to you? (What would it look like? How would it feel? What would you be doing? What would you have? Who would you be with? How do you spend your leisure time? Do you have a family?)

What is "success" for you? (What does it look like? What are you doing? Who are you working for or with? How much money are you making? How does it feel? What are the rewards of success?)

Figure 16.6 Model Career Plan

What I Want to Achieve:

Having majored in business, I want to find an entry-level position that offers upward mobility according to how hard I work and how I use my education and abilities. I would like to begin my career as a consultant with a major consulting firm that will expose me to a variety of aspects of business and provide an entry into a company that matches my goals and aspirations. From that position, I would like to move into management, begin my MBA in international business, learn to speak Mandarin, and move to my dream company, XYZ, where I hope to attain a management position that will lead me to an executive management position.

Job 1: Business consultant

Skills required: Degree in business administration; in-house training with company, working with a team to learn the consulting area; excellent soft skills; specific technology and software skills; report-writing skills.

Skills assessment: I have degree, excellent soft skills, need more training on software, need to improve report-writing skills.

Duties and responsibilities: I will be working with a team to recommend IT practices, accounting systems, and interviewing skills.

Plan to get this job: Take a course in report writing, teach myself accounting software, send resumés to top 10 companies for business consulting, network with people I know who are doing this kind of work.

[After getting his first consulting position, Josh should then begin preparing to become a manager. He needs to pay attention to other managers, as well as his own. He needs to let HR and his supervisor know that he would like to move toward a supervisor position and would like to take advantage of any special training.]

Job 2: Supervisor of business consultants

Skills required: Ability to lead and manage other people, ability to delegate, ability to shape a vision for a group; skills in evaluation, excellent soft skills, sales ability.

Skills assessment: I need to take seminars in leading and managing and salesmanship; need to study visionary planning, how to evaluate people.

Duties and responsibilities: I will be leading a team of consultants and evaluating their performance; I will have

to sell our team to businesses as consultants; I will have to be able to delegate and make decisions.

Plan to get this job: Do an excellent job as a consultant; let management know I want to be a supervisor, take advantage of any in-house training available; take courses at the community college; build excellent relationships with people internally and externally; begin working on MBA in international business at night and on weekends; taking a course in Mandarin at community college; spend vacation in China.

[Assume Josh has done well in the first two jobs and he is now ready to seek employment in management with another company. You cannot plan to stay with the same company for your entire career; that rarely happens today. Remember, "go where the puck is going." XYZ is an international company that can ultimately offer Josh the opportunity to work in China, which is one of his top career goals. Do you see how Josh's plan is building on each previous position and how he will ultimately reach his top goal?]

Job #3: Sales position in XYZ Company

Skills required: Degree in business administration; Mandarin is an asset; international travel is considered a plus; sales and management experience required; ability to build relationships with clients; ability to learn XYZ software and technology.

Skills assessment: Have degree and working on MBA; learning Mandarin; have been to China; have sales and management experience; have built excellent relationships with external clients and could get recommendations from them; have ability to learn the software and technology based on past experience.

Duties and responsibilities: I will be a member of a team that sells XYZ software to international companies; some international travel required; ability to interact with international customers; must demonstrate software and technology and be able to make excellent presentations.

Plan to get this job: Send resumé with recommendations from several external clients; ask Mr. Robinson, who works at XYZ, to put in a good word for me; have my Mandarin professor write a letter about how well I am doing in this class; emphasize my international travel experience and desire to travel internationally; emphasize that I have almost completed MBA in international business.

[Notice how Josh is anticipating what is required for his next career move. He is not "letting things happen"; he

(continued)

Figure 16.6 Model Career Plan (continued)

is making things happen. He has prepared to be successful by anticipating what skills and knowledge are required and gradually accumulating all of them. Success does not just happen. Success is planned!]

Job 4: Manager of international sales team in XYZ Company

Skills required: Master's degree in business administration; experience in a variety of business areas including accounting and IT; knowledge of software and technology; ability to shape a vision for a department; ability to lead a team and to build external relationships with customers; fluent Mandarin or Spanish skills; excellent salesmanship abilities.

Skills assessment: Lack one course in MBA program; program included Advanced Salesmanship and Advanced Communications and Presentation Skills; have experience in leading others and shaping a vision for a team; have excellent relationships with external businesses; need to learn company-specific software for XYZ; learning Mandarin.

Duties and responsibilities: I lead a team that will sell XYZ's exclusive software to international companies; must be able to set priorities for team; shape a vision; interact with international clients; be able to travel internationally; must speak Mandarin; must have excellent communication and presentation skills.

Plan to get this job: Let the management team making the selection know I want this job and tell them what I have been doing to prepare for it; share my portfolio that includes travel to China, Mandarin course, communications and presentation skills, and examples of presentations I have made; try to get my manager to recommend me.

[If Josh gets this job and continues to prepare as he has been doing, he will most likely reach his goal of being a member of the Executive Team at XYZ. His career opportunities and desires may change along the way, but regardless, he has set himself up to be successful because he had a plan, he worked hard and smart, and he went where the puck was going.]

Reflections: PUTTING IT ALL TOGETHER

After reading this chapter, you have realized that change will be an important part of your life and career, and how you deal with it will no doubt have a big impact on your success. We encourage you to embrace change, anticipate changes that are coming down the road, and plan for change. It is very important for you to develop a career plan that will guide you and help you realize your ambitions much faster. We hope you will also prepare for a potential loss of employment at some time during your career by using multiple sources of revenue to cushion the blow, as well as provide more income for investments, savings, and entertainment.

DIGITAL BRIEFCASE

CONNECTING WITH BUSINESS COLLEAGUES THROUGH LINKEDIN

LinkedIn is a professional network designed to help businesspeople interact. Think of it as Facebook for business. It is a great tool for increasing visibility and can assist you in showcasing your expertise. When beginning your job search, a great place to start is by creating a profile on

LinkedIn and then making connections with people you know. You can use LinkedIn to connect with current and former colleagues, supervisors, and clients.

Use the following tips to get started in creating and using your LinkedIn profile.

- Before you begin, think about what your want to accomplish with your LinkedIn profile. Do you want to expand your network, are you looking for a job, or are you looking to reconnect with colleagues from former jobs who may be able to recommend you?

- First, follow the steps to register on the LinkedIn.com site.

- Click on the "Profile" link.

- Click on "Edit Contact Settings" and choose the types of people with whom you want to connect.

- Click "Save Changes."

- Next, select an attractive, professional headshot.

- Post a profile summary that is honest and discusses results of things you have accomplished that might interest an employer. Keep it simple and straightforward and not too long. You can list your education, honors, and awards in other sections of your profile, but your summary should be brief and to the point.

- For *each company you have worked for*, fill in the job title and describe your duties. You can click on the link right below the position field, which can provide you assistance in describing your duties.

- When you have finished listing your positions, you can enter information about your education into your profile. You will see that LinkedIn provides a pull-down menu that allows you to search for your institution. You can add information about your degree, your major, the date your attended the school, and other information about your educational experience.

- Work experience and education are the two main parts of your profile, but if you scroll down, you will see places where you can add information such as your website, interests, awards, and other items.

- Once you have completed your profile, read it one more time to check for errors and to be sure that it represents you in an exemplary manner. You can always go back and change or add things later.

- Click the tab "View My Profile" at the top of the profile screen to see how others will see your profile.

- Finally, look over to the right and locate a link that says "Edit Public Profile Settings" and select "Full View." Then you can choose the features that you want to be visible to anyone who accesses your profile.

- Finally, if you are happy with your profile, click "Save Changes" down at the bottom of the screen.

REFERENCES

Association of American Colleges and Universities. (2007). *College learning for the new global century.* Retrieved June 28, 2011, from www.aacu.org/leap/documents/GlobalCentury_final.pdf.

ASVAB. (2009). Career exploration program. Retrieved June 23, 2011, from www.asvab program.com/downloads/ASVABIdeaSkillsMostValued.pdf.

Eby, L. T., Casper, W. J., Lockwood, A., Bordeaux, C., & Brinley, A. (2005). *Work interference with life domains.* Retrieved July 29, 2011, from www.shrm.org/about/foundation /research/Documents/Ryan%20Final%20Report%20610.pdf

Accountability, personal, 316–317
Adams, John Quincy, 211
Age diversity, 200, 202, 203–205
Albrecht, Karl, 158
Alcohol use, 122, 124–126
American Express Global Customer Service
    Barometer, 156–157
Amygdala, 229, 230
Angelou, Maya, 18
Anxiety
    and depression, 113–114
    and stress, 112–113
Ash, Mary Kay, 141
Attitude
    about change, 312–313
    definition of, 20
    influences on, 20–21, 22
    about job loss/unemployment, 320–321
    and job search, 269–270
    and performance/success, 19–21, 22–23
    about personal strengths, 8–9
Attire. See Dress
Auto title loans, 57–59

Bahrami, Homa, 306
Baldridge, Letitia, 117
Ball, Lucille, 40
Barton, Bruce, 295
Beatles, The, 40
Beliefs, 18–19. See also Values
Benefits, job, 141–145
    and accepting/choosing a position, 49, 144
    cost to employers, 141, 142
    knowledge about, 140, 142–143
    laws about, 142
    selection of, 143–145
    types of, 49, 141, 142–143
    value of, 141
Bennis, Warren, 218, 235
Binge drinking, 126. See also Alcohol use
Bixler, Susan, 168
Blogs/blogging, 180, 181, 182
Board of directors, of company, 149–150
Bolles, Richard Nelson, 297
Borges, Leo G., 166
Borrowing money. See Loans
Bosses. See Supervisors
Brain, and emotions, 229, 230
Branding, personal, 19, 25–27
Brannon, Steve, 214
Briggs, Katharine, 11
Briggs-Myers, Isabel, 11
Budgets/budgeting, 48–51. See also Money
    management
    definition of, 49
    development of, 66–69
    elements of, 50–51
Buscaglia, Leo, 316
Bush, Jim, 156
Business cards, and job search, 286–287
Business casual, 131–132

Business documents. See also Written
    communication
    e-mail, 179–180, 181
    letters/envelopes, 176, 177, 178
    memos, 179, 180

Cade, Valerie, 121
Cafeteria benefits plan, 143. See also Benefits,
    job
Cain, Lawrence, 249
Calendars, 106, 108. See also Schedules/
    scheduling
Campbell, Joseph, 297
Car, purchase of, 64–65
Career objective, 270, 275–276
Career planning
    and high-growth fields, 3
    and job search, 270. See also Job search
    ongoing nature of, 309
    and personality type, 13
    self-assessment for, 3, 15–16, 321, 322–324
    and technology, 247
Carpe mañana, 310–313
CEO, of company, 149–150
Change, 309–325
    attitude toward, 312–313
    and employment/workplace, 313–314
    and goal setting, 73, 84–86, 309–310.
        See also Goals
    inevitability of, 310, 311–312
    responses to, 310, 311
    strategies for dealing with, 310–313
Character, 31–43
    damage to/loss of, 31–32, 38–39
    definition of, 32, 34
    development of, 31, 34–37. See also Ethics
    elements of, 31–33, 35, 37–38, 39–41
    and self-esteem, 38
    in workplace, 34–37
CHARACTER COUNTS! Coalition, 35
Cheating, among students, 32
Check cashing centers, 58, 59
Chinese proverb, 232
Churchill, Winston, 21, 160
Clinton, Bill, 247
Clothes/clothing. See Dress
Collaboration communication, technology for,
    257, 260
Colleagues, relationships with, 198–199.
        See also Workplace relationships
Collins, Jim, 223, 227
Collins, Mike, 210
Comfort zone, and goal setting, 73, 74
Commitments, honoring of, 40–41
Communication, 167–186
    channels/forms of. See Nonverbal
        communication; Verbal communication;
        Written communication
    and conflict, 231
    elements of, 167–168
    and first impressions, 168–170

formal vs. informal, 170–172
    guidelines for, 171
    nature of, 167
    process of, 167–168
    and technology, 249–250
    value of skills in, 3, 167, 168, 183,
        313, 314
Company, organizational structure of,
    148–151. See also Work/workplace
Computer software, knowledge of, 250–254,
    259–261
Conflict, 229–244
    causes of, 231–235
    definition of, 229
    harassment as, 237, 239
    inevitability of, 229, 231, 232
    in interpersonal relationships, 231–232,
        234
    management of, 237, 238
    and personality, 240, 241–243
    resolution of, 231, 232–237, 240, 241–243
    responses to, 229–230, 231, 234–235
    in workplace, 229, 231, 232–237, 239,
        240, 240, 241–243
Conflict Management Assessment, 237, 238
Connectivity, and technology, 248–250
Constantine, Rodger, 80
Contaminated people, 23. See also Difficult
    people/situations
"Contribution ethic," 36–37
Core values statement, of company, 147
Cosby, Bill, 82
Cover letters, 271–273
    example of, 274
    guidelines for, 272–273
    purpose of, 271
Coworkers, relationships with, 198–199, 317.
        See also Workplace relationships
Credit cards, 54–57
Credit counseling, 57
Credit rating/score, 52, 57, 58, 59–62, 316
Credit reporting agencies, 59, 60
Critical thinking, value of skills in, 315
Crucible, The (Miller), 33
Culture
    of United States, 174, 196
    of workplace, 192–195
Customer service, 155–163
    customers' views of, 156–157, 160
    in difficult situations, 160–161
    definition of, 158
    and e-commerce, 162–163
    elements of, 155, 156
    and service economy, 155
    strategies for providing, 157–159, 160–161

Daily time sheet/calendar, 101–104, 108
Dante, 38
Darwin, Charles, 310
Daskaloff, Alexander, 56
Dauten, Dale, 36–37